Ideologies and Attitudes: Modern Political Culture

WILLIAM T. BLUHM
The University of Rochester

Prentice-Hall, Inc., Englewood Cliffs, New Jersey

Library of Congress Cataloging in Publication Data

BLUHM, WILLIAM THEODORE.
   Ideologies and attitudes.
   Bibliography: p.
   1. Right and left (Political science) 2. Collec-
tivism. 3. Liberalism. 4. Ideology. I. Title.
JC348.B55   320.5   73-16236
ISBN 0-13-449553-5
ISBN 0-13-449520-9 (pbk.)

© 1974 by

Prentice-Hall, Inc., Englewood Cliffs, N.J. 07632

10 9 8 7 6 5 4 3 2 1

Prentice-Hall International, Inc., London
Prentice-Hall of Australia, Pty. Ltd., Sydney
Prentice-Hall of Canada, Ltd., Toronto
Prentice-Hall of India Private Limited, New Delhi
Prentice-Hall of Japan, Inc., Tokyo

Acknowledgements

The author gratefully acknowledges permission to quote the following material: In Chapter 1, excerpts reprinted from *The Political Culture of the United States,* by Donald J. Devine, by permission of Little, Brown and Company, Publishers, copyright © 1972 by Little, Brown and Company; and from *Ideology and Utopia,* by Karl Mannheim, by permission of Harcourt Brace Jovanovich, Inc. and of Routledge & Kegan Paul Ltd., copyright © 1936 and 1954 by Harcourt Brace Jovanovich, Inc. and by Routledge & Kegan Paul Ltd.

In Chapter 2, excerpts reprinted from *Medieval Political Ideas,* Volume 1, edited by Ewart Lewis, by permission of Alfred A. Knopf, Inc., published 1954 by Alfred A. Knopf, Inc.; and from *The Operational Code of the Politburo,* by Nathan Leites, by permission of McGraw-Hill Book Company and The Rand Corporation, copyright © 1951 by The Rand Corporation.

In Chapter 3, excerpts reprinted from *Democracy in America,* by Alexis de Tocqueville, translated by H. Reeve, revised by F. Bowen and P. Bradley, Volumes 1 and 2, by permission of Alfred A. Knopf, Inc., copyright © 1945 by Alfred A. Knopf, Inc.; from *Ideology and Utopia,* as above; from *Political Ideology: Why the American Common Man Believes What He Does,* by Robert E. Lane, by permission of Macmillan Publishing Company, Inc., copyright © 1962 by The Free Press of Glencoe; and from *The Political Culture of the United States,* as above.

In Chapter 4, excerpts reprinted from *The Conscience of a Conservative,* by Barry Goldwater, by permission of Barry Goldwater, copyright © 1960 by Victor Publishing Company.

In Chapter 5, excerpts reprinted from *The American Right Wing,* edited by Robert Schoenberger, by permission of Holt, Rinehart and Winston, Inc., Publishers, copyright © 1969 by Holt, Rinehart and Winston, Inc.

In Chapter 6, excerpts reprinted from *The New Left,* by Massimo Teodori, by permission of the Bobbs-Merrill Company, Inc., copyright © 1969 by Massimo Teodori; from *DO IT! Scenarios of the Revolution,* by Jerry Rubin, by permission of Simon and Schuster and Jonathan Cape, copyright © 1970 by Social Education Foundation.

In Chapter 7, excerpts reprinted from *Childhood and Society,* Second Edition, Revised, by Erik H. Erikson, by permission of W. W. Norton

& Company, Inc., and Chatto and Windus Ltd., copyright 1950, ©
1963 by W. W. Norton & Company, Inc. and Chatto and Windus Ltd.;
from *Hitler's Weltanschauung: A Blueprint for Power,* by Eberhard Jäckel,
(Herbert Arnold, translator), by permission of Wesleyan University Press,
copyright © 1972 by Wesleyan University; from *The Voice of Destruction,* by Hermann Rauschning, by permission of G. P. Putnam's Sons,
Publishers, copyright © 1940 by G. P. Putnam's Sons; from *Inside the
Third Reich,* by Albert Speer (R. and C. Winston, translators), with
permission of Macmillan Publishing Company, Inc., and of Weidenfeld
& Nicolson Ltd., Publishers, copyright © 1970 by Macmillan Publishing
Company, Inc.; from *Nazi Culture,* by George L. Mosse, by permission
of Grosset & Dunlap, Inc., Publishers, copyright © 1966 by George L.
Mosse; from "Feudal Aspects of National Socialism," by Robert Koehl,
by permission of the *American Political Science Review,* copyright ©
1960 by the *American Political Science Review;* from *Anatomy of the
SS State,* by Helmut Krausnick, *et al.,* chapter by Hans Buchheim (Rich-
ard Barry, *et al.,* translators), by permission of Collins Publishers and
Walter-Verlag AG Olten, copyright © 1968 by William Collins Sons &
Company Ltd.; from *The Politics of Cultural Despair: A Study in the
Rise of the Germanic Ideology,* by Fritz Stern, originally published by
the University of California Press; reprinted by permission of The Regents
of the University of California, copyright © 1961 by The Regents of the
University of California; and from *Childhood and Society,* as above.

In Chapter 8, excerpts reprinted from *The Operational Code of the
Politburo,* as above; from *Marxist Ideology in the Contemporary World:
Its Appeals and Paradoxes,* by Milorad M. Drachkovitch, editor, with the
permission of the publishers, Hoover Institution Press, copyright © 1966
by the Board of Trustees of the Leland Stanford Junior University; and
from *Soviet Russian Nationalism,* by Frederick C. Barghoorn, by permission of Oxford University Press, Inc., Publishers, copyright © 1956 by
Oxford University Press.

In Chapter 9, excerpts reprinted from *Ideology and Organization in
Communist China,* by Franz Schurmann, originally published by the
University of California Press; reprinted by permission of The Regents
of the University of California, copyright © 1966 by The Regents of the
University of California; and from *Party Leadership and Revolutionary
Power in China,* by John W. Lewis, editor, by permission of Cambridge
University Press, Inc., Publishers, copyright © 1970 by Cambridge Uni-
versity Press, Inc.

Additionally, in Chapter 3, excerpts reprinted from "Fundamental
Principles of Democracy: Bases of Agreement and Disagreement," by
James W. Prothro and Charles M. Grigg, *The Journal of Politics,* 22,
No. 2, by permission of *The Journal of Politics,* copyright © 1960 by
The Journal of Politics.

For Cathy, Susanna, and Andy,
my three ideological
pragmatists

Contents

Preface

We are accustomed to describing political conflict by using expressions such as "democracy versus communism," "the struggle for freedom," "liberalism versus conservatism," "the fight for equal rights." We are aware that the behavioral reality identified in each case is the rivalry of individuals and groups for power and control over public policy. Yet to make that rivalry intelligible and to distinguish one conflict from another we talk about politics as a warfare of ideas. The "ins" and the "outs" are never simply "ins" and "outs." We identify them by the ideological labels they wear and that others pin on them. This is a book about those ideological labels and about the complexes of ideas and attitudes for which they are shorthand expressions.

I intend to write about what A. D. Lindsay has called "operative ideals," concepts that are actually found in use in the world of observable political behavior. (See A. D. Lindsay, *The Modern Democratic State*, New York: Oxford University Press, 1962.) This means that the focus of my attention will not be on the elaborate systems of logically connected abstractions that we call political philosophy, but on the much cruder and often illogical sets of ideas that are employed in daily political discussion. I shall concentrate as well on the subideological attitudes and feelings that accompany political ideas and that furnish the motor power of behavior. Naturally, in order to understand Russian or Chinese Communism we shall have to know something about the writings of Karl

Marx, just as a grasp of what American Liberalism is all about implies a knowledge of John Locke. But to suppose an identity between the "great books" and the "operative ideals" of the political marketplace would be erroneous. Unfortunately, most texts and most extant collections of readings on ideology, composed of selections from such writers as John Locke, John Stuart Mill, Edmund Burke, and Karl Marx, foster the notion that such an identity, or close approximation to one, exists. Political philosophies and the ideologies of the political arena are related but still very distinct and separate realities, and they must be treated so by scholars. The "great books" are the sources of certain symbols of crucial importance in the arena, but often they are not more than this.

The focus of my study, in short, will be upon political culture. This is a phrase that in recent years has been developed by political scientists to express in precise fashion what A. D. Lindsay was attempting to get at with the notion of "operative ideals." Lindsay's starting point was the traditional one—the writings of philosophers—but he labored to select out those ideas that could be shown to underlie behavior. The student of political culture, by contrast, starts with the data of behavior and from them seeks to elicit an ideological system, using ideological writings only as a guide to research.

In an article of 1956, Gabriel Almond, building upon conceptions of culture created by such sociologists and psychoanthropologists as Clyde Kluckhohn, Ralph Linton, and Talcott Parsons, defined a specifically political area of culture that, in collaboration with Sidney Verba, he proceeded to study empirically in five democracies. The findings were published in 1963 in *The Civic Culture* (Princeton, N.J.: Princeton University Press, 1963). A few years earlier, working independently of Almond, Samuel Beer and Adam Ulam presented a somewhat different definition of the concept in a comparative government text of 1958 (*Patterns of Government*, New York: Random House, 1958). Since then a number of scholars have sought to refine the idea and use it in detailed political explorations. Thus in 1972 Donald Devine, working in the area of American politics, published a book entitled *The Political Culture of the United States*, in which he combined Almond's idea of political culture with an Eastonian conception of the political system. (See Donald J. Devine, *The Political Culture of the United States*, Boston: Little, Brown & Co., 1972.) Also of note in this area are the conference deliberations of a group whose field of interest is comparative communist studies. Under the chairmanship of Robert C. Tucker, these students of comparative communism held a conference on the application of the political culture concept to their area of concern in 1971 but have not yet completed any studies using the new tool. My analysis will combine ideas of my own with elements of the frames of reference of Almond and of Beer and Ulam.

I understand the various political cultures described in this book not as discrete entities but as aspects of a single political reality, the revolution of modernity. This is a dynamic reality with a long history, and it is precisely its dynamic quality that accounts for the salient characteristics of ideological activity in the modern world, for what is peculiar to modern political culture. The beginnings of that history are, of course, foreclosed to empirical analysis using the tools of modern social science. Nevertheless, to make its contemporary phases intelligible we must give some description and explanation of the revolution's early years, using the materials that are at hand.

The book is devoted to the description of two basic kinds of modern political culture—Liberal and Collectivist. In each case the specific form of modernity is explained in relation to particular historical givens. Several chapters on the United States highlight the elements of Liberal stability and crisis in a postindustrial state where Liberal evolution has been unhampered by either aristocratic or proletarian *ressentiment*. Here also the strains of industrialization were not experienced until after the roots of a Liberal political culture formed from age-old principles of Western constitutionalism had been put down. A chapter on Nazi Germany describes the shape of modernity in a culture where traditional politics dominated society well down into the period of economic modernization and were supplanted by Liberal institutions in a time of military and economic collapse. Thus I contrast the best with the worst conditions for establishing a Liberal culture and describe the totalitarian results of a failed Liberalism. Chapters on Russian and Chinese communist culture trace the Collectivist pattern of modernity that results from the late revolution of a nonwestern traditional culture of an absolutist and patriarchal sort.

This is a descriptive and not a philosophical study. My purpose is to describe what ideas political men employ in understanding and in acting, what the factors are that give rise to one rather than another set of ideas in a given political context, and how those ideas are related to political behavior. No systematic attempt is made to evaluate particular ideologies in terms of their moral goodness, metaphysical truth, clarity of articulation, or logical consistency. It is clear, nevertheless, that the frame of reference, especially the criteria of significance I employ in the selection and analysis of ideological phenomena, embodies a philosophical commitment of my own. This includes principles of moral judgment that will be evident to the reader. The framework is, however, both eclectic and tentative. And my intention in the book is to give a report of empirical reality, not to recommend a metaphysic or teach a moral lesson. It is rather my hope that this report contains descriptions that may be of use in furthering the philosophical enterprise by helping to delineate the area of our freedom to choose values and structures.

Among my teachers I owe a special debt to Daniel J. Boorstin who taught me to think about ideology in psychological and sociological terms, rather than as the equivalent of political philosophy. His own work on American political culture, especially *The Genius of American Politics,* was a special inspiration to me. I am also grateful to my colleagues at the University of Rochester for stimulating discussion of political theory that helped me to become clear on a variety of epistemological problems connected with the study of ideologies. To William H. Riker, Alvin Rabushka, and Winthrop Hudson I am particularly indebted in this regard. I should also like to thank Theodore Anagnoson, Michael Coveyou, and James Noble, graduate students in political science at the University of Rochester, for help with the manuscript. Discussions of Chinese political culture with Mr. Noble were helpful in writing Chapter 9. I am also grateful to him for a digest of important literature on this subject. Messrs. Anagnoson and Coveyou provided trenchant critiques of the draft of Chapter 3, and Mr. Anagnoson also supplied me with some useful data for that chapter. Papers by two undergraduates, Susan Lauscher and Neil Rimsky, provided some material for the "national purpose" section of the same chapter.

The University of Rochester granted me a semester's leave of absence during which the foundations of the book were laid. I am also grateful to my patient and skilled secretaries, Peg Gross and Janice Brown, for long hours of typing the various drafts of the manuscript. The love, good counsel, and companionship of my wife Elly were indispensable helps in the accomplishment of this work.

W. T. B.
Rochester, N.Y.

1

Ideology and Political Culture

This book is about ideology and about those complexes of ideas, attitudes, and feelings we call political culture. The disagreement about the definition of the first of these concepts constitutes a historical controversy of long standing. Moreover, our second concept contains ambiguities because it is new and has not yet been widely applied. Our first task, therefore, must be to define our key terms as precisely as we can and to show how we intend to use them in this book. We begin with "ideology."

1. Historical Origins

In its beginnings the concept of "ideology" was a product of the French Enlightenment. It stood for a science of ideas with which Enlightenment thinkers hoped to reduce the concepts of commonsense discourse to their simplest elements and then reconstruct them into precise instruments of scientific understanding and control. This was to be done by the rigorous application of strict logical and empirical formulas. In the realm of politics the philosophers' governing assumption was that discord and misery were the product of the prejudices and inexact reasoning of common sense. This meant that ideology, as the science of politics, could produce a sure plan for political well-being, a design for the just and happy polity.[1]

In its earliest meaning, then, "ideology" stood for a body of revolutionary thought aimed at the destruction of traditional beliefs and the structures associated with them. Its characteristic marks were logical system and a claim of insight into laws of empirical causality on the one hand and an apocalyptic utopian social and ethical vision on the other. The various forms of Liberalism and Socialism, both Marxist and non-Marxist, which have developed since the eighteenth century have all had these characteristics to one degree or another. So have various more recent social scientific theories of "political development."

The first meaning of "ideology," set by its proponents, thus had positive connotations much like those which attach to the word "science" in our own day. Its application to political practice, however, soon begot a reaction which produced pejorative meanings that today are more commonly associated with the concept than are the positive ones, making it no longer possible for the word to be viewed as equivalent to "science." The change was the work of conservatives who were appalled at the political surgery both planned and accomplished by the "*idéologues*" during the French Revolution. In the mouths of men like Antoine Rivarol, the word "ideology" came to stand for a naïve logical construct notable for its abstract neatness but lacking a genuine understanding of the complex givens of human nature and of historical reality. It meant also a dangerous and destructive doctrine, inimical to good political and social order. "They [the *idéologues*] have aspired to nothing less than the reconstruction of everything, by means of a revolt against everything," wrote Rivarol. "And without remembering that they themselves are in the world, they have torn down the pillars that support the world." Ideology "had an appearance of boldness and loftiness that enchanted youth and conquered mature men, a readiness and a simplicity that obtained everyone's approval and eliminated all resistance. Indeed, instruments of destruction are so very simple!"[2]

2. Modern Meanings of "Ideology"

When inveighing against doctrines with which they disagree, Liberals as well as Conservatives today commonly use the word "ideology" in a pejorative sense much like that of Rivarol. Who the particular enemy is

[1] For a detailed exposition and illustration of the original meanings of "ideology," see Richard H. Cox, ed., *Ideology, Politics and Political Theory* (Belmont, Calif.: Wadsworth Publishing Co., Inc., 1969), Chap. I.

[2] Antoine Rivarol, *De la philosophie moderne*, 2ième édition (Paris, 1802); reprinted in Cox, *op. cit.*, pp. 28, 29.

makes little difference. Ideological Liberals may use the term to criticize Fascists, Communists, or socialists of various persuasions. "End of ideology" Liberals use it to castigate their erstwhile cohorts, both Liberal and Socialist, for failing to see that the good society has been established and that the use of abstract ideology as a guide to further change can work only harm. Conservatives use the word to critize the ideals and projects of Liberals and Socialists.

Normative Definitions. On the Marxist side, and among certain schools of non-Marxist social science as well, "ideology" figures as a different sort of bad word. Rather than the product of rationalist naïveté, it is seen as the conscious or unconscious rationalization of class interests, a weapon with which to dupe the unwilling into supporting those interests and to give a color of legitimacy to what are basically politically imposed values. The Marxist usage shares with the usage of Liberals and Conservatives the connotation of distortion and partial truth. Universally, then, in the political arena the term "ideology" has achieved a meaning precisely the opposite of that intended by the philosophers who coined it. Instead of standing for creative truth it has come to represent destructive falsehood.

Not in every context, however, is the word used with negative connotations. It may also have a purely neutral descriptive significance and refer to a system of political ideas pure and simple. Political leaders when not engaged in heated controversy have used the term in this way.[3] And so have scholars as well. It is my intention to employ the word in just such a neutral and descriptive sense, which seems best suited to the enterprise at hand.

The political sociologist Robert MacIver, in the introduction to a volume devoted to the subject of European ideological systems, offers the following definition:

> A political and social ideology . . . is a system of political, economic, and social values and ideas from which objectives are derived. These objectives form the nucleus of a political program.
>
> Political ideologies . . . are more or less consistent. . . . Some are only outlined, such as peasant ideologies of Eastern Europe. . . . Others such as Socialism, Communism, and Anarchism are thoroughly elaborated down to the most subtle details. Often they form a complete, harmonious, and consistent system of explanation of the purpose of society and of the surrounding social, economic, and political phenomena. Setting forth dynamic and practical objectives to influence future social and political developments, they try—with a most ambitious design—to decide mankind's destiny.[4]

[3] See Cox, *op. cit.*, p. 4.
[4] Robert M. MacIver, "Introduction" to Feliks Gross, ed., *European Ideologies* (New York: Philosophical Library, 1948), p. 5.

MacIver's definition highlights three characteristics of ideologies: their normative character, their inspirational function. and their logical order. They present total schemes of social, political, and economic values—a complete theory of the good life for man in society. They inspire both specific political goals and comprehensive projects; they aim at shaping mankind's entire future way of life. They are often tight and highly detailed logical packages, though sometimes they are only more or less consistent outlines or sketches. With the exception of the last statement about incomplete logical system in some cases, these are all characteristics of "ideology" in its original meaning, with the value judgment as to whether they in fact redound to the good or evil of mankind left out. We shall focus on each of them as we survey the particular ideologies which have dominated the political life of our time and attempt to understand how they are related to political behavior.

Descriptive Definitions.   So far we have stressed the normative role of ideologies. MacIver's definition, which we are using as our point of departure, omits an important descriptive dimension which other writers have stressed. Walt Rostow, for example, sees one important aspect of ideology as "a particular conceptual vocabulary," "a set of concepts and terms by which men interpret the world around them." [5] Ideologies tell us not only what is good and what we ought to do, but also explain the way things are and why they are that way. They establish a framework of cause-and-effect relationships. They constitute, in short, an entire *Weltanschauung.* The early Liberal idea, for example, that faulty reasoning is responsible for civil conflict and suffering is just such a causal concept. The Marxian idea of the "dialectic"—that political history moves from poverty to abundance by a determinate law which is characterized by the generation of social and economic states from their opposites (e.g., monopoly out of free competition) and the final synthesis (socialism) of the leading characteristics of the opposed—is another. That politicians typically make shady deals in smoke-filled rooms when supposedly tending honestly to the public business is still another, not readily identifiable with any classical ideological statement yet very much an operative idea in American democratic political culture.

⸰ How universally can the word "ideology" be used to designate ideas that are politically active? In recent years an entire literature has grown up around the question of whether ideology has not come to an end, and Daniel Bell, the well-known sociologist, has even written a book entitled *The End of Ideology.*[6] Rebuttals have come in from all

[5] Walt W. Rostow, "A Note on the Diffusion of Ideologies," *Confluence,* 2(1), March 1953, 32, 33.
[6] Daniel Bell, *The End of Ideology: On the Exhaustion of Political Ideas in the Fifties,* rev. ed. (New York: The Free Press, 1962).

sides, and at the end of the sixties two collections of writings on both sides of the debate appeared.[7]

The basic reason for the controversy may be the way the word "ideology" was originally used in the eighteenth century—both in its positive and negative meanings. It grew up as a label for political thought related to change and revolution. Liberalism was in the first instance a critique of the *ancien régime* and a program for the creation of a new political and social order. Conservatism arose from the need of a systematic intellectual defense of the old regime. Since then the great *isms* of our time have all been aimed at some sort of revolution or defense of the status quo—socialism in all its forms, Nazism, Fascism, and a plethora of nationalisms, including the modernizing forms operative in the developing areas.

Characteristic of ideology in this context is its self-consciousness, its conceptual articulateness, and its tendency toward ideational elaboration. In its most developed form an ideology constitutes an explanation of the nature of man in the universe, a critique of existing society from the standpoint thus established, and a description and justification of the good or legitimate political and social order. In revolutionary ideologies the critique of the status quo and the vision of the new society are separate enterprises. In conservative ones they constitute a single descriptive-evaluative statement.

Now when the winds of revolution have died down and society returns to relative quiet and stability, the stridency of ideological pronouncement declines and the volume of ideological output also tends to diminish. At least this has been the case in the Western Liberal world. Political thought ceases in such times to be juxtaposed to political life and tends to disappear from the scene. It is absorbed into political habit. We are at "the end of ideology" as self-conscious, abstracting, reflective intellectual behavior. Does this mean, however, that ideas are no longer politically important, that they have ceased to affect behavior in the political system? Or have they merely gone underground?

3. Political Culture

By broadening the concept of ideology into that of political culture we are able to resolve the problem. I have found especially useful the elaboration given that concept in a comparative government text edited by Professor Samuel Beer. His interest in the expression arose out of a need for a concept to designate the conscious psychological patterns of a

[7] See M. Rejai, ed., *Decline of Ideology?* (Chicago: Aldine-Atherton, 1971); and Chaim I. Waxman, *The End of Ideology Debate* (New York: Funk and Wagnalls, 1968).

culture as one causal or conditioning factor in the explanation of political behavior. "Certain aspects of the general culture of a society," Beer writes, "are especially concerned with *how* government ought to be conducted and *what* it should try to do. This sector of culture we call political culture." [8] We are reminded of the normative elements in the definition of "ideology" developed above. Descriptive features are also present, for Professor Beer goes on to write that "the principal components of the political culture are *values, beliefs,* and *emotional attitudes.*" [9] The term "beliefs" embraces here what Rostow calls a "set of concepts by which men interpret the world." Notable also about the statement is the inclusion of emotional attitudes along with values and beliefs as components of political culture. Here we are at a subideational level of psychic behavior, still in the mind but below the level of self-conscious thought.

In this fashion the concept of political culture allows us to take account of ideals and beliefs embedded in structures of habit and life style, manifesting themselves in behavioral displays of attitudes. We shall see later that, for the purpose of analysis, social scientists can raise attitudes to the ideational level, making subjects self-conscious. We also shall see that this is a delicate process, subject to all sorts of distortion at the researcher's hands, but nevertheless an important procedure of research.

A Model of Political Culture.   Professor Beer and his co-authors present a detailed outline of the structure of political culture. They divide the normative segment of political culture into procedural and goal values. Procedural values, which they call "conceptions of authority," refer to how the political system ought to be structured in order to carry out its purposes. Modern liberal democracy insists upon representation and direct election as appropriate procedures for designating political officials, whereas medieval men thought of their kings as rulers by divine right who derived their authority from God as well as from the political community. In modern Communist states an elite Party rules the polity as the "vanguard of the proletariat," enacting the decrees of history. Legitimacy is the key concept in every case—that which is morally right, fitting, proper. Beer points out that although authoritarian and totalitarian systems may employ overt force to a greater degree than liberal democracies to obtain compliance, they also rest on some principle of rightful or legitimate authority.

Conceptions of purpose, the other aspect of normative political culture, refer to what government is expected to do. The idea of "constitu-

---

[8] Samuel H. Beer *et al., Patterns of Government* (New York: Random House, 1958), p. 12.
[9] *Ibid.*

tional government" implies that the polity is not omnicompetent but should be restricted to specific social functions. The classical form of liberal polity limited these to the preservation of order and property at home and the maintenance of defense against aggression from abroad. Emphasis was laid on the economic freedom of the individual as well as on religious liberty and freedom of speech as limitations of the legitimate scope as well as methods of political government. Modern liberalism, in adding the broad concept of "welfare" to the proper province of government, diminishes the legitimate area of unrestricted individual action. Professor Beer notes that conceptions of purpose affect conceptions of authority. If, for example, swift industrialization is an overriding social goal, to be realized primarily by government policy, authoritarian procedural norms permitting a great measure of compulsion will be adopted rather than democratic and liberal ones.

The term "beliefs" refers to the images which people carry around in their heads about the way the political world is actually structured and operated in relation to the world in general. In contrast to conceptions of authority and of purpose, which, as "values," refer to what "ought" to be, "beliefs" designate what "is"—or rather, what people *take* to be the reality which surrounds them. Aristocracy rests on the assumption that some people have qualities which give them a superior right to govern. Democrats believe that people are enough alike so that all should have a share in the making of public policy. "Beliefs" thus often form the ground for the adoption of one or another system of "values." More general cultural beliefs than these are relevant for political culture. The medieval theocentric conception of the world as ordered by indwelling divine purpose to an end beyond itself and beyond time, and with its structures and roles given by divine mandate, is associated with a graded and static political, economic, and social order aimed at transcendent salvation. The modern secular view of the world as incessant change ordered by mechanical historical processes and by goals which are entirely human creations is associated with an open and dynamic socioeconomic order aimed at material terrrestrial well-being and individual self-realization.

Emotional attitudes are the great underwater segment of the iceberg of political culture. In the followership world, as we shall see, they often constitute virtually the whole of political culture and are tied in with very primitive and often mutually inconsistent conceptions of purpose, conceptions of authority, and beliefs. We are dealing here with expressive feelings as they are tied in with political symbols. For example, the restrained "House of Commons manner," Professor Beer points out, expresses a whole range of emotional feelings about the values and beliefs which underpin the British system of government. (By contrast one could point to the often riotous mood of the Austrian parliament in the last years of the Habsburg Empire as expressing a very different set of attitudes and feelings toward the values and structures of the decaying imperial system.) As the authors of *Patterns of Government* note, attitudinal patterns may correspond not to an existing system but to an earlier political order, in which case they will serve to inhibit the effective working of the new system. Authoritarian attitudes carried over from the German past into the Weimar Republic are a case in point.

The Attitudinal Dimension: An Illustration.   Perhaps a more extended illustration of the attitudinal level of political culture and its relationship to the ideational levels would be useful. Our example also will reveal differences between leader and follower culture. A few years ago a referendum was held in Cambridge, Massachusetts, on the question of whether sodium fluoride ought to be added to the Cambridge water supply as a public health measure to arrest dental decay. The election was preceded by a rather vigorous campaign in which the virtues and vices of fluoridating water were canvassed in detail. A social scientist studying the fluoridation debate investigated the question of whether the dialogue in fact implied an ideological conflict among voters, for opposition leaders pitched their argument at this level.[10]

On election day the social scientist made a survey of attitudes toward fluoridation in one precinct. The probability sample consisted of 190 registered voters of whom 141 (74 percent) were actually interviewed. The social profile of the sample was lower middle and working class. Half of them had less than a high school education. Most were of Irish or Italian descent and were second- or third-generation Americans. Seventy-one percent of the sample were Catholics. The researcher focused his study on the hypothesis that opposition to fluoridation was being viewed by its opponents as an attack on individual rights, and that the debate therefore had an ideological foundation. Using Beer's scheme, one would say that the researcher wished to test the theory that the conflict was one between different conceptions of authority.

The results of the survey invalidated the hypothesis at the self-conscious ideational level. Virtually none of the opponents of fluoridation interviewed among the followership employed ideological statements in explaining his opposition to the surveyors. That is, they did not bring up the subject of the sanctity of individual rights on which leaders had harangued them. A secondary hypothesis that at the attitudinal level opponents of fluoridation were more sensitive to violation of individual rights than proponents also proved false. When queried on their attitudes toward other civil rights issues, differences between proponents and opponents were shown to be negligible.

[10] William A. Gamson, "The Fluoridation Dialogue: Is It an Ideological Conflict?" *Public Opinion Quarterly*, 25(4), Winter 1961, 526–37.

An explanation of opposition to fluoridation was discovered in a high correlation between opposition and alienation. Alienation was defined for the purpose of the test as "powerlessness and meaninglessness," feelings of being in the clutches of powerful persons who act in ways deemed to be unmeaningful. The respondents were asked to agree or disagree that:

1. "Public officials don't really care about what people like me think."
2. "Sometimes politics and government seem so complicated that a person like me can't really understand what's going on."
3. "Human nature being what it is, there will always be war and conflict."

Sixty-two percent of the opponents of fluoridation registered alienation by responding affirmatively to these statements, but only 32 percent of the proponents did so. The survey report concluded with the statement that "the hypothesis that opponents will have greater feelings of helplessness and a lower sense of political efficacy than proponents is fairly well supported by the data given here." [11] Alienation was discovered to be the root cause of opposition to fluoridation and thus the ground of explanation of that opposition.

In the surveyors' conceptual scheme the fluoridation debate turned out *not* to be explicable by reference to ideological differences. In the conceptual scheme that we have adapted from the work of Professor Beer and his colleagues, however, it would be.   This is because Beer's scheme would classify the attitudinal concept of "alienation" as a sub-ideational element of the ideology—or overall world view—of the respondents in question. If the three "alienated" statements had not merely evoked an emotional response when voiced by the surveyors, but had actually been voiced by the respondents themselves, we would have had to place them at the ideational level and classify them as "beliefs" about the political world which conditioned the respondents' value judgments about fluoridated water. Such beliefs are not derivable from the standardized versions of "liberalism" and "communism" from which we have drawn many of the examples we have used in earlier paragraphs. They are part and parcel of the political mental set of the survey sample of fluoridation opponents we have been discussing, however, and are properly designated aspects of the "ideologies" or political culture of these people. Throughout the book we shall thus be using the word "ideology" in this broad sense, and not merely as a label for the classical "isms,"

[11] *Ibid.*, p. 536.

which are only one type of the various ideational and psychological phenomena which constitute the subject matter of this study.

4. Forensic and Latent Ideology

Our explanation of psychic political phenomena with the concept of political culture allows us to accept the notion of the "end of ideology" without limiting the use of "ideology" to revolutionary debate. We can now distinguish in political culture two kinds of ideological behavior, which can usefully be called "forensic" and "latent" ideology.[12] Forensic is a word which refers to debate, and "forensic ideologies" are the elaborate, self-conscious word systems, formulated at a rather abstract level, which constitute the language of political discussion in times of severe political stress and strain. "Latent ideologies" are the implicit sets of political words which are expressed in attitude and behavior during more settled times, but which can be "excavated"—that is, raised to the forensic level—by social scientific research. Throughout this book we shall maintain the distinction between forensic and latent ideology. We shall attempt to show the conditions under which each kind flourishes, and the conditions under which each is converted into the opposite kind of political culture. We shall describe the methodological tools for grasping and analyzing each kind, and shall try especially to point out the pitfalls the social scientist must seek to avoid as he conducts his scholarly work. To highlight these important technical concerns we shall sometimes dwell on "horrid examples" as well as on excellent research. In some cases the horrid examples have enjoyed the reputation of fine scholarship.

5. Political Culture: Single or Plural

In its young life the concept of "political culture," like the concept of "ideology," has fallen prey to certain distortions or overemphases which we shall seek to avoid in this study. Developed as a concept in order to explain what men have in common, it has been employed by some writers in such fashion as to imply that a given political culture is a homogeneous or monolithic whole. Donald Devine, for example, uses the idea of political culture to demonstrate that "generalized support from the ordinary member of the political system is an important way of explaining how some polities are able to maintain themselves in the face of severe stress," and that in the United States in particular such support

---

[12] See Robert Lane, *Political Ideology: Why the American Common Man Believes What He Does* (New York: Free Press of Glencoe, 1962).

is forthcoming. "The scientific perspective of culture," he writes, "focusses upon basic values which are widely, that is consensually shared." He cites one social psychologist, Goodwin Watson, who calls culture "the total way of life characteristic of a somewhat homogeneous society of human beings." And he himself goes on to write that culture can be viewed as a "value system which expresses the unique attitudes that a people passes from generation to generation." He defines political culture as "a historical system of widespread, fundamental, behavioral, political values actually held by system members," and he elsewhere calls it "the repository of the supportive attitudinal values actually held by members as they relate to the regime and community." [13]

In one place Devine qualifies the conservative implications of these definitions by writing that political culture may be composed of attitudes that "may or may not be congruent with politically sanctioned values," thus allowing for deviant, and even revolutionary, ideology. But he goes on to write in the very same paragraph that "to be considered cultural these values must also be transmitted, learned and widely shared over a substantial period of time." [14]

We shall not in this book limit the concept of political culture in this conservative fashion. We see no reason not to refer to newly learned ideas and attitudes—those of the "New Left" in the United States, for example, barely a decade old, or the emerging patterns of thought and habit in the USSR and China—as political culture. Indeed, the understanding of revolutionary political culture involves precisely an awareness of how new ideas and attitudes are inculcated and old ones modified. It may well be that many revolutions carry forward very old ideas and attitudes. For this reason we shall attempt to demonstrate the importance of such continuity as we go along. Yet despite all this, no one would dream of *simply* identifying Soviet with Czarist culture nor the culture of Mao Tse-tung's cultural revolution with Confucianism.

We also make no assumption in this book that political culture is a homogeneous whole or seamless garment. A political culture may be a complex entity of discontinuous parts, and in a time of change this is usually the case. We shall devote one chapter to a description of "Established Liberal" culture in the United States which deals with the ideological phenomena of the American Center, with which Professor Devine equates the whole of the American political cultural scene. Chapters on the New Left and on Conservatism and the Radical Right show that the consensual pattern on which Devine dwells is much overdrawn.

Even within a given ideological community, as we shall show,

---

[13] Donald J. Devine, *The Political Culture of the United States* (Boston: Little, Brown & Co., 1972), pp. 2, 3, 5, 17, and 29.

[14] *Ibid.*, p. 6.

political culture is composed of diverse parts. Especially in totalitarian politics it is clear that leaders operate with one set of ideas, attitudes, and expectations and followers with another. In democracies the differences are less marked but are still discernible. I do not subscribe to the proposition that the concept of ideology can properly be applied only to the thought of elites, and that the thoughts of up to 90 percent of a population reveal no "ideological constraints." [15] It has been demonstrated that the political world of the average man is not formless but does have ideological structure. This may be more latent than overt and capable of being elicited only by lengthy and elaborate procedures. But it is there and constitutes an important political reality which should be studied and comprehended. The concept of political culture, along with the tools that have been developed to study it, gives us access to this latent ideational world. Hence, where materials are available, we shall separately analyze leadership and followership (or elite and mass) ideological systems.

6. The Functions of Ideology

To this point we have taken ideas and attitudes as givens. We must also ask how and whence they emerge if we are to give a full explanation of ideology and political culture. Are they irreducible root causes of political choice? Or can they be referred back to another kind of reality as cause? The roots of ideology have been a matter of major debate among philosophers over the years. The great debate between Idealists and Materialists—Hegelians and Marxists, for example—as to whether ideas are causes or effects never will be settled by empirical social science, because it turns on the nature of ultimate reality rather than on observable events. Moreover, the stream of empirical events can be adequately and exhaustively explained from either standpoint, although the standpoints themselves are not confirmable by observation. In neither view is the individual observer an autonomous reality capable either of independent understanding or action, but only a pawn of vast, impersonal forces, variously "ideal" and "material," which move him at will as they work out their purposes in the world.

The Interest Theory.   Theories of ideology which are based on psychological rather than metaphysical assumptions—assumptions which are therefore to some degree capable of being confirmed or infirmed

---

[15] Philip E. Converse, "The Nature of Belief Systems in Mass Publics," in David E. Apter, ed., *Ideology and Discontent* (New York: Free Press of Glencoe, 1964), pp. 206–62.

by observation—may be of more use for our purposes. One of these, which has been variously articulated, we may call the "interest theory." It resembles the Marxian rather than the Hegelian point of view in that ideas are seen as results rather than causes of another reality. The basic cause, however, is the psyche of the individual person rather than impersonal historical forces. In this theory human nature is understood as a bundle of subrational drives for status, income, and power of which reason is a mere helpmate, not a governor. In the seventeenth century Thomas Hobbes gave the idea classical expression when he wrote of our ideas and thoughts as "Scouts, and Spies, to range abroad, and find the way to the things Desired." [16] With this goes the idea that abundant value accrues to the man of capacity and ingenuity, the man of superior calculating reason and vigor who can manipulate social as well as physical reality and make it work for him. In this view ideology is merely a rationalization of nonrational interest, necessary to have because men are unable to live comfortably with the crass demands of nature which command the "rule of the fittest," unless that rule is clothed over and disguised by a myth of dispassionate justice.

The political sociologist Gaetano Mosca has ably formulated this view in the following terms:

> No political class, however constituted, will say outright that it rules because . . . its members are the ones most fit to rule. Instead, that class will always try to justify its power on the ground of an abstraction which we shall call the political formula. To say that all officials derive their authority from the official sovereign, who, in turn, derives it from God, is to make use of a political formula; another version is expressed in the phrase that all power resides in the people.

Mosca says that the universal use of political formulas is grounded in the need of human nature "to believe that it is easier to submit to an abstract principle than to another man, who rules him because he knows how to rule." [17]

The Truth Theory.   The social philosopher Hannah Arendt has criticized the Marxian view of ideology in terms which apply also to the "interest" theory of Mosca. Modern social science, she claims, agrees with Marx, who did not take seriously "what people say," but only "the real active human being" whose thoughts are "ideological reflexes and

16 Thomas Hobbes, *Leviathan* (New York: E. P. Dutton & Co., Inc. [Everyman's Library], 1950), p. 59. For a modern view, see Max Lerner, *Ideas Are Weapons: The History and Uses of Ideas* (New York: Viking Press, 1943).

17 Gaetano Mosca, *Teorica dei Governi e Governo Parlamentare* (rev. ed., Turin, 1925), Chap. 1, quoted in James H. Meisel, *The Myth of the Ruling Class* (Ann Arbor: University of Michigan Press, 1958), p. 55.

echoes of his life process." [18] "Marx's theory of ideological superstructure," she writes, "based on the distinction 'between what somebody pretends to be and what he really is,' . . . is entirely based on [the] identification of political action with violence. For violence is indeed the only kind of human action which is mute by definition. . . . In all other kinds of action . . . we act in speech and our speech is action." [19] Thus if we regard ideology as only a weapon in the battle for material interest we are in effect saying that our social life is meaningless violence, *mere* conflict—a conclusion which Arendt finds abhorrent. The view of Marx, which she also attributes to social science in general, disregards "the truth-revealing quality of speech," she tells us.[20] Other speech we regard as an instrument for communicating about reality, for seeking and stating the truth about things, and political speech also must be so regarded if we are not to reduce the political world to the mere play of passionate force. In this view ideas appear to be an independent cause, grounded not in social or material status or nonrational necessity but in the rational desire to know the truth. Presumably truth, when realized, can serve as a cause of social and political change aimed at conforming external reality to itself. In Arendt's theory we appear to have a psychological rationalism (or Idealism) which, like Hobbes' and Mosca's psychological irrationalism (or Materialism), brings us down out of an empirically unverifiable metaphysical world into one of observational verification. What is not yet clear, however, is what set of observations will tell us whether rationalist or irrationalist psychology contains the more valid empirical judgment.

The Social Strain Theory.   Though we have labeled one of them "irrationalist" and the other "rationalist," the two theories of ideology which we have just described both see ideology as the product of self-conscious motivation. On the one hand, ideology derives from the conscious pursuit of interest, on the other from the conscious pursuit of truth. Other writers have found its origins in the unconscious. "Ideology is a patterned reaction to the patterned strains of a social role," says one such definition.[21] In this view ideology is a symptom of, and to some degree a remedy for, emotional ills produced by the role-demands of modern society. Nail-chewing, alcoholism, and psychosomatic disorders are among the alternatives to it.[22] The remedial function of developing or embracing an ideology may be any one of four kinds. Conspiracy theories which make

---

[18] Hannah Arendt, citing *The German Ideology*, in "Religion and Politics," *Confluence*, 2 (3), September 1953.

[19] *Ibid.*, p. 116.

[20] *Ibid.*

[21] F. X. Sutton *et al.*, *The American Business Creed* (Cambridge: Harvard University Press, 1956), pp. 307–8.

[22] *Ibid.*

"The Jews," "The Reds," or "Big Business" responsible for everything that goes wrong in society perform a cathartic function; by allowing the person who is oppressed by his social role to let off steam, they provide an escape valve. Ideologies which emotionally reaffirm the rationale for the existing system (e.g., the struggling small businessman's enthusiastic praise of the American system of free enterprise) perform a morale function by denying the pain-giving strain or legitimating it in terms of high principle. Threatened groups or groups which are pressing for radical change develop ideologies which serve a "solidarity function" by giving the group the cohesion it needs if it is to win. White supremacy ideology in the American South is a case in point. Ideologies also perform an "advocatory function" by which attention is called to pressing ills which society can ignore only at the peril of radical upheaval. Black Nationalism is an example of ideology performing an advocatory function.[23]

The Cultural Strain Theory.   Critics of these theories of ideology argue that they do not demonstrate how or why ideologies transform sentiment into significance. Lacking an adequate analytical framework, sociologists have been reduced to "viewing ideologies as elaborate cries of pain." One of these critics favors another sort of theory which he designates a theory of "cultural strain," which addresses itself to the problem of the connection between sentiment and meaning. He proposes that ideology results from social dislocations which not only cause psychological strain but which destroy old meanings, old orientations to action. The development of our modern differentiated polity "brings with it conceptual confusion, as the established images of political order fade into irrelevance or are driven into disrepute."[24] Ideology appears as a means of putting meaning back into the world and of setting forth a plan for rebuilding the polity both in its authority structure and in its purposes. Like religious, philosophical, aesthetic, and scientific systems, ideology is a "program," a culture pattern which provides a "template or blueprint for the organization of social and psychological processes."[25]

> The function of ideology is to make an autonomous politics possible by providing the authoritative concepts that render it meaningful, the suasive images by means of which it can be sensibly grasped. . . . The search for a new symbolic framework in terms of which to formulate, think about and react to political problems, whether in the form of nationalism, Marxism, liberalism, populism, racism, Caesarism, ecclesiasticism, or some variety of reconstructed traditionalism . . . is . . . tremendously intense.[26]

[23] All of these functions are critically reviewed—and found wanting—in Clifford Geertz, "Ideology as a Cultural System," in Apter, ed., *op. cit.*, pp. 52–55.

[24] *Ibid.*, p. 64.

[25] *Ibid.*, p. 62.

[26] *Ibid.*, pp. 63, 65. The last statement was made by Mr. Geertz with special reference to ideology in the developing areas of the world.

The "cultural strain" theory of ideology combines some elements of Arendt's rationalist "truth-seeking" theory with elements of all those irrationalist theories (both the "conscious" and "unconscious" kinds) which view ideology as a response to pain and stress which derive from the social situation. It defines the end of ideology as "truth-seeking" so that meaningful action is possible, but it explains the *origins* of ideology in terms of the psychological stress produced by social dislocation. As we move through the rest of the book it will be well to keep all these theories in mind—the "interest theory," the "truth-seeking" theory, and the theories of social and cultural "strain." We shall ask ourselves from time to time whether the data with which we are dealing are best illuminated by one of these theories or another, or perhaps by some combination of them.

7. Ideology and Political Culture in Relation to the Political System

We have so far presented a variety of definitions of ideology and political culture and indicated which ones we intend to use for the purposes of this study. We also have reviewed a variety of theories about the functions of ideology in the political system, to which we shall recur from time to time as explanatory instruments. The student also needs a frame of reference which will enable him to relate what he learns about ideological behavior to his other work in political science which focuses on the organizational and institutional aspects of politics—courses in electoral behavior, the party process, the legislative process, the judicial process, and so forth. To provide this, we should "place" the phenomena of ideology and political culture somewhere in a conceptual scheme which is well known among political scientists and widely used in political science courses.

One of the best-known general conceptual frameworks in modern American political science today is the model developed by David Easton in his book, *A Systems Analysis of Political Life*.[27] Defining the function of politics as "the authoritative allocation of values," Professor Easton describes the polity as a system in which allocational demands are processed into authoritative decisions. The decisions in turn feed back into the system as part of the material which generates new demands. Inputs to the system are demands and supports. Outputs are the authoritative allocations.

[27] David Easton, *A Systems Analysis of Political Life* (New York: John Wiley & Sons, Inc., 1965).

Where do ideology and political culture fit in this conceptual schema? I suggest that they can best be understood as elements in the "environment" of the political system, a concept which Professor Easton employs in his framework but does not fully elaborate. They are not demands, supports, issues, or outputs of the system but rather psychological entities which influence the form and workings of all these things.[28] A political culture characterized by liberal democratic procedural norms and a belief in the sanctity of private property will not give rise to demands for the expropriation of capital by the state. Nor will its majority coalitions punish opponents with show trials and summary mass executions. Communist political culture, by contrast, has not given rise to a system of demand-processing by opposed parties competing publicly for electoral support in the context of election campaigns characterized by mutual criticism and recrimination.

We shall also hypothesize that political culture not only influences but can be influenced again by outputs of the system, and, as it alters, can alter in turn subsequent inputs of demand and support. As an output of the American political system, for example, the long duration and high cost both in blood and money of the Vietnam War obviously influenced the progress of alienation from the old norms of political culture, especially among the youth, and reduced support for the regime as well as for the government of the day. Anarchist and direct-democracy norms increasingly were articulated by certain sections of the young intelligentsia. Correlatively, protest behavior on the streets, in political conventions, and in the courtroom indicated a demand not only to change the "war output" to one of "peace" but also to alter the processing procedures of the system itself. We shall thus treat ideology and political culture as a complex of ideas and attitudes which are closely correlated with the *kinds* of demands and supports and the *kinds* of outputs characteristic of a given political system. They supply the vocabulary and conceptual framework with which demands, supports, and decisions are articulated. They appear to influence demands and supports and to be influenced in turn by outputs. A more precise analysis of their interaction with the decision-making behaviors which constitute the political system will be attempted in the body of the book as we study in detail the working of particular ideologies in particular polities.[29]

---

[28] *Ibid.* See pp. 23, 43–45. Cf. Devine (*op. cit.*, p. 24), who calls political culture "an input subsystem structure near the boundary between the environment and the system. It acts as a *screen* on wants and is affected by them."

[29] Cf. the conservative view of the "screening" function of political culture employed by Donald Devine, who conceives it as "a major structural component of diffuse support." *Op. cit.*, p. 29.

8. The Problem of an Autonomous Social Science

We have been considering the proposition that political ideas in the marketplace may serve as weapons of interest and escape valves for psychological malaise rather than as vehicles for the pursuit and expression of truth. At the least, they will be subject to all those limiting and distorting factors which constitute the special world view of an historical period. All this, of course, raises a question about the possibility of objective knowledge of politics. Even though a conscious effort be made by students of society and politics to view their data as though they were "men from Mars," from a standpoint beyond the pressure of the day's interests and issues, is such objectivity and neutrality possible? If there is evidence that everyone else is a captive of his interests, passions, neuroses, and historical position, how does the social scientist escape such conditioning (and implicit warping) of his conceptual framework? Is social science possible? Or is it condemned inevitably to be just one (partial) ideology among others?

Some of our best minds who have pondered the question believe there is no escaping the dilemma of ideological relativism. Alfred North Whitehead, for example, applies the theory of historical distortion to the writing of history: "In our estimate of [the agencies of historical change] everything depends upon our standpoint of criticism. . . . Our history of ideas is derivative from our ideas of history, that is to say, upon [sic] our own intellectual standpoint." [30] From Gibbons' *Decline and Fall of the Roman Empire,* Whitehead maintains, we can learn as much about the eighteenth century and its typical ideas as we can about the ideas of the ancients.

Reinhold Niebuhr, a well-known contemporary theologian and political philosopher, applies the interest theory to the study of politics.

> The opinions which men and groups hold of each other and the judgments which they pass upon their common problems are notoriously interested and unobjective. The judgments of the market place and the political arena are biased, not only because they are made in the heat of controversy without a careful weighing of evidence, but also because there is no strong inclination to bring all relevant facts into view. While the ideological taint upon all social judgments is most apparent in the practical conflicts of politics, it is equally discernible, upon close scrutiny, in even the most scientific observations of social scientists. The latter may be free of conscious bias or polemic interest. Yet every observer of the human scene is distinguished from the scientific observer of the sequences

[30] Alfred North Whitehead, *Adventures of Ideas* (New York: The Macmillan Company, 1933), p. 8.

of nature by the fact that he is, in some sense, an agent in, as well as an observer of the drama which he records.[31]

Problem of the Scientist's Values.   William E. Connolly, a political scientist, has recently given us a rather striking illustration of what Niebuhr had in mind. He does this in a comparison of the approaches employed by C. Wright Mills and by Robert Dahl to the study of the distribution and exercise of political power in the United States.[32] Mills, he notes, looked at American society in elitist terms. He assumed that power was monopolized by a relatively confined "power elite" set over a dominated public and he then proceeded to identify and describe its membership and their characteristics. Professor Dahl, by contrast, assumed a broad and decentralized distribution of power and described the American polity in pluralist terms. Both agree that America is a consensual society, but for Mills the consensus has been manufactured by the elite; that is, "The consensual framework is wrapped in a rhetoric to which the mass is responsive and which consoles and deadens them." [33] Thus the operative framework of decision is hidden and works to preserve the status, wealth, and power of the elite. For Dahl the consensual rhetoric is a genuine representation of things: he sees it as "a collective product of society; it pushes up from below and surrounds the political process." [34] Both writers agree that there are some inequalities in the system and that not all potential issues are processed or even formulated by the polity. But Dahl sees these things as a marginal deviation from the normal pluralist condition of things whereas Mills treats the suppression of potential groups and potential issues as a major factor which preserves the political freedom and superiority of the power elite.

Connolly argues that the different assumptions with which Dahl and Mills begin their work affect the entire conceptualization and strategy of their research. Dahl focuses on formal decision-making procedures because he believes that it is there that the basic power relationships of American society can be observed. Mills focuses on the *"non-decision process"* and tries to discover who it is that suppresses potential issues and why it is that certain "troubles" do not get formulated as issues. Their different starting points affect their definitions of the central concept of "power." For Dahl, power is the ability to obtain *intended* results, whereas Mills sees both *intended* and *unintended* results of an action as exercises of power. Connolly concludes that the analyses of American

[31] Reinhold Niebuhr, *Christian Realism and Political Problems* (New York: Charles Scribner's Sons, 1953), pp. 75–76.
[32] William E. Connolly, *Political Science and Ideology* (New York: Atherton Press, 1967).
[33] *Ibid.*, p. 28.
[34] *Ibid.*

society which result from the application of these very different frames of reference "are in large part self-fulfilling. In each case the focal points of analysis . . . and the conceptual decisions made seem to foster the interpretation rather than to provide a test of it." Thus the procedures of empirical verification employed in each case are largely illusory. "Neither position is empirically established. . . . It is clear that the theory of the power elite and the theory of pluralism are, at root, *both* ideological interpretations of American politics." [35]

Hopes for an Objective Science.   Other writers have argued to the possibility of an objective and neutral science of politics. One of the most subtle and elaborate arguments to this effect was made by a German scholar, Karl Mannheim, who is known as the father of the "sociology of knowledge." Mannheim tells us that down to the present all political thinking has been "relational"—that is, closely tied in with the interests and situation of the thinker. Ideology is characteristically an incomplete picture of reality. One sees only those aspects of a political situation which suit one's intention and interest. Only a man who has a different and opposed position in society will be able to point out the distortions in any given ideological view.[36]

Mannheim distinguishes two chief kinds of ideological thinking. One, which he calls "Utopian," is the thought of the reformer who is unhappy with the existing state of things and wishes to tear it apart and build new institutions and values:

> Certain oppressed groups are intellectually so strongly interested in the destruction and transformation of a given condition of society that they unwillingly see only those elements in the situation which tend to negate it. Their thinking is incapable of correctly diagnosing an existing condition of society. They are not at all concerned with what really exists: rather in their thinking they already seek to change the situation that exists. Their thought is never a diagnosis of the situation; it can be used only as a direction for action.[37]

Despite the fact that they are the product of selective perception, however, not all the elements in a "utopia" are ideological—that is, doomed to unreality—according to Mannheim, for to the extent that they can succeed in achieving change they become consistent with reality. Thus arguments in favor of the democratic franchise and the abolition of slavery were not ideological elements in reforming Liberalism, even

[35] *Ibid.*, pp. 29, 30, 48.
[36] Karl Mannheim, *Ideology and Utopia*, trans. L. Wirth and E. Shils (New York: Harcourt Brace Jovanovich, and London: Routledge & Kegan Paul, Ltd., 1936). The quotations are with permission of the publishers.
[37] *Ibid.*, p. 36.

though the Old Guard at the time tried to condemn them as unrealistic by calling them "utopian." The goal of the perfectly free market, or "perfect competition," by contrast, *was* an ideological element in early Liberalism, inasmuch as it has never been achieved.

"Ideology" in a more restricted sense signifies for Mannheim doctrines which defend a *status quo* which is under attack. It emerges when "ruling groups can in their thinking become so intensively interest-bound to a situation that they are simply no longer able to see certain facts which would undermine their sense of domination." [38] By definition such an "ideology" is wholly out of keeping with the realities of the situation.

In Mannheim's view, however, not all conservative positions are doomed to beget ideologies. Sometimes a condition of equilibrum emerges in a society in which stress is so diminished that ideological and utopian thinking disappear from view:

> Conservative mentality as such has no predisposition toward theorizing. This is in accord with the fact that human beings do not theorize about the actual situations in which they live as long as they are well adjusted to them. They tend, under such conditions of existence, to regard the environment as part of a natural world-order which, consequently, presents no problems. Conservative mentality as such has no utopia. Ideally it is in its very structure completely in harmony with the reality which, for the time being, it has mastered. . . . The conservative type of knowledge originally is the sort of knowledge giving practical control. It consists of habitual and often also of reflective orientations towards those factors which are immanent in the situation.[39]

This appears to describe the condition of society which eventuates in what we have recently been calling in the United States "the end of ideology," a condition in which forensic doctrines disappear from the field and the student of political culture must probe for significant ideological phenomena at the level of half-conscious attitudes.

But let us return to the question of the possibility of an objective and neutral social science. The father of the "sociology of knowledge" closes his major work with an expression of belief that the modern intellectual is becoming capable of scientific objectivity in the study of society, a capability which he attributes to what he sees as the class-free status of the intellectual today. In modern "open" liberal society the intelligentsia have become "free-floating" (*"freischwebend"*). They are no longer attached to a class and no longer lead the assault on the established order in the name of one "utopia" or another, but are rather detached from the world of political conflict. Mannheim's implication is that society today has so far solved the problems of class conflict that change from here on

[38] *Ibid.*
[39] *Ibid.*, pp. 229–30.

out can occur in a purely peaceful and orderly way according to the objective norms of scientific development.

This view has been restated much more recently by another well-known practitioner of political sociology, Professor David Apter. "Social science," writes Professor Apter, "has become the ultimate ideology and science the ultimate talisman against cynicism. It defines its own purposes through the logic of enquiry." [40] The practitioners of science in all its branches, Apter finds, constitute in developed countries today a "meritocracy," a new ruling class different from all those in the past in that it rests on knowledge rather than on interest or power. And social scientists, by virtue of what *they* know, share this new status of authority and "are accorded an increasing monitor role in political life. . . . By gaining a superior insight into the conduct of their fellows . . . they create a new role and an ideology that follows from it, a hierarchy of power and prestige based on intellectual ability." [41]

Conclusion.   If Professor Apter is right, the dream of the eighteenth-century "idéologues" will have been realized in our time. And ideology will have been restored to its original meaning by being converted into science. When the control of social science has been fully established, books like this one will trace out the mirror image of the scientists' thought as reflected in the minds and actions of the men of "silver" and of "brass" over whom they rule. Another possibility, of course, is that Professor Apter is wrong, and that books about ideology will simply be distorted representations of other distortions. My own aspiration is for a half-way house in which the patterns, causes, and effects of ideology will be understood as what they are—important aspects of political reality. Since I have not solved the problem of the true philosophy of politics, I shall try to avoid describing these interesting realities as distortions of anything, while recognizing that their origins may well be in the sub-rational factors we have been discussing. It is to be hoped that the material so garnered will not constitute a rationale for a preexisting ideology of my own but will rather provide a basis for philosophizing, and for further scientific inquiry.

Bibliography

APTER, DAVID E., ed., *Ideology and Discontent.* London: The Free Press of Glencoe, 1964.

ARENDT, HANNAH, "Religion and Politics," *Confluence*, 2(3), September 1953: 105–26.

[40] Apter, *op. cit.*, p. 39.
[41] *Ibid.*, p. 40.

ARON, RAYMOND, "The Diffusion of Ideologies," *Confluence*, 2(1), March 1953: 3–12.

BERGMANN, GUSTAV, "Ideology," *Ethics*, April 1951.

CONNOLLY, WILLIAM E., *Political Science and Ideology*. New York: Atherton, 1967.

COX, RICHARD H., ed., *Ideology, Politics and Political Theory*. Belmont, Calif.: Wadsworth, 1969.

JANSSON, J. M., "The Role of Political Ideologies in Politics," *International Relations*, 1(11), April 1959: 529–42.

LERNER, MAX, *Ideas are Weapons: The History and Uses of Ideas*. New York: Viking Press, 1943.

LICHTHEIM, GEORGE, *The Concept of Ideology and Other Essays*. New York: Random House, 1967.

LOWENSTEIN, KARL, "The Role of Ideologies in Political Change," *International Social Science Bulletin*, 5(1), January 1953: 51–74.

MACINTYRE, ALASDAIR, *Against the Self-Images of the Age: Essays on Ideology and Philosophy*. New York: Schocken Books, 1971.

MACRAE, DONALD G., *Ideology and Society*. New York: The Free Press of Glencoe, 1962.

MADGE, CHARLES, *Society in the Mind: Elements of Social Eidos*. New York: The Free Press of Glencoe, 1964.

MANNHEIM, KARL, *Ideology and Utopia: An Introduction to the Sociology of Knowledge*, trans. L. Wirth and E. Shils. New York: Harcourt Brace Jovanovich, 1936.

NAESS, ARNE, et al., *Democracy, Ideology and Objectivity: Studies in the Semantics and Cognitive Analysis of Ideological Controversy*. Oxford: Basil Blackwell, 1956.

PYE, LUCIAN W., and SIDNEY VERBA, eds., *Political Culture and Political Development*, Studies in Political Development, 5. Princeton: Princeton University Press, 1965.

——————, "Personal Identity and Political Ideology," *Behavioral Science*, 6(3), July 1961: 205–21.

SARTORI, GIOVANNI, "Politics, Ideology and Belief Systems," *American Political Science Review*, 63(2), June 1969: 398–411.

SCHULZE, R., "Some Social-Psychological and Political Functions of Ideology," *Social Quarterly* 10(1), 1969: 72–83.

TOCH, H., "Crisis Situations and Ideological Revaluation," *Public Opinion Quarterly* 19(1), Spring 1955: 53–67.

PART ONE

LIBERAL CULTURE: REVOLUTIONARY AND ESTABLISHED

Modern man loves change, new things and experiences. And he views the future as something to be created, not inherited from the past. He stands free of tradition and taboo and assumes a calculating attitude toward a manipulable and open future. He is, therefore, rational and goal-oriented. He measures success by his achievements, not by the purity of his faith. His test of value is pragmatic: "Does it work?" Most importantly, modern man is empathic, he can relate to others and put himself in their shoes. He is participant, he reads newspapers, listens to the radio, exchanges values in the market, has opinions on public issues. And his society operates not according to divine mandates hieratically mediated, but through public consensus constantly renewed through comparison and accommodation of personal decisions on public issues. All this implies that modern man is also flexible, adaptive, "ready to incorporate new roles and to identify personal values with public issues." He possesses "psychic mobility."

This is Daniel Lerner's portrait of modern man, whom Lerner, in his study of political and social change in the Middle East, contrasts with "traditional" and "transitional" man.[1] *The portrait is normative, for it embodies the chief traits of the good Liberal personality who "fits with" and is capable of operating efficiently the institutions of a specifically*

---

[1] Daniel Lerner, *The Passing of Traditional Society* (New York: The Free Press, 1958), pp. 47ff.

Liberal Democratic modern society. The Liberal is independent and self-reliant. He sees government as a utility for the service of individual values and as a mechanism for coordinating the interests of autonomous individuals like himself. He, the individual, is in command. Citizens of Fascist and Communist political culture display different traits, different aspects of modernity, though there is an area of shared characteristics throughout modern political culture.

In Lerner's description of the modern mobile and empathic personality we have a good example of the way in which political culture as a behavior pattern can reveal ideology.[2] For the things that Lerner describes as manner and attitude can be reduced to ideological propositions: to conceptions of authority and of purpose; to considerations of liberty, equality, fraternity, and to their associated "beliefs," such as the idea of progress. They reveal much of what we call "Liberalism."

Before we turn to a detailed study of Liberal Democratic culture today, we will first give an account of how the modern Liberal way developed and acquired the authority it presently enjoys. To permit the most fruitful comparisons of Liberal with Collectivist forms of modern culture, we must in the process also describe the most general characteristics of modernity as such, which set off all the "isms" and their corresponding cultures from the ideologies and cultures of the past. After this rather abstract and compacted overview we will concentrate our attention on the political culture of a contemporary society in which Liberalism is established as an authoritative and, until recently, unchallenged way of political life, the United States of America. This will allow us to see Liberalism in its purest form, unalloyed with the vestiges of traditional order with which it is associated in its European embodiments. It also will allow us to point up the salient differences between a modern political culture rooted as established habit (a gradually evolutionary culture) and the revolutionary versions of modernity. Next we shall look at challenges to established Liberalism on the left and the right that emerge from the stresses to which the post-industrial Liberal society is subject, and also make an effort to measure the present stability of Liberal culture in the United States.

---

[2] Cf. the picture of the bearer of the "civic culture" drawn by Gabriel Almond and Sidney Verba in *The Civic Culture* (Princeton: Princeton University Press, 1963).

2

The Revolution
of Democratic Liberalism

1. Ideology as Secular Religion

Modern forensic ideologies have been described as political religions. More precisely, they play the role of surrogates for religion in the establishment of modern political culture. In traditional Western European political culture, Christianity formed the backdrop for politics and established the meaning and significance of political institutions and values. Its theology justified the established order of things. When in the course · of time that order came under attack, the religious categories in which it had been understood and justified were not so much abolished as transmuted into new realities, secular versions of their former selves. Because change, the building of something new, was the business of the day, it was natural that those religious doctrines which related to change and fulfillment were the ones that were retained and transformed. Thus the categories of Christian eschatology—the doctrine of the last things, of the culmination of human history—formed the matrix out of which the language grew in which the new politics in its various versions expressed its ultimate goals and ideal forms. Examples are the Liberal ideas of "progress" and of a "perpetual peace," the Communist "classless society," and the Nazi "thousand-year Reich." Ideology thus substitutes for religion as a set of ideas that give meaning to human experience as a secular political experience. It arises to cope with what Clifford Geertz calls "cultural strain," and asserts itself as the specific form of modern political culture.[1]

During the Middle Ages, "meaning" was monopolized by the roles, structures, and rituals of the Church, all of which pointed to fulfillment beyond the temporal—i.e., beyond time. Political (i.e., civil) authority was treated as ephemeral and unimportant. Gradually, however, during the medieval period itself, the dual representation of society began to break down. The beginnings of change are seen in the writings of Joachim von Flora, a thirteenth-century monk who used the symbol of the Trinity to interpret the course of history:

> The first period of the world was the age of the Father; with the appearance of Christ began the age of the Son . . . ; it will be followed by a third age of the Spirit. The three ages were characterized by intelligible increases of spiritual fulfillment. The first age unfolded the life of the layman; the second age brought the active contemplative life of the priest; the third age would bring the perfect spiritual life of the monk.[2]

For each age, according to Joachim, there was a charismatic leader. Abraham was the leader of the first age, Jesus of the second. And for the third Joachim predicted there would come by the year 1260 a *Dux e Babylone*, a captain to lead the people out of Babylon.

From the time of the Reformation, which destroyed the unity of the Western Church, the incorporation of the transcendent in the temporal has proceeded by leaps and bounds. All the political ideologies of our time are instances of the process. Each is characterized by a spiritual, mystical, religious component by means of which the holy, the absolute good, the absolutely just is represented in political life. In each case the *form* of doctrine is a secularization of the Christian idea of perfection in a Heavenly Kingdom.

We also need to ask *why* the modern age should be apocalyptic in its political outlook, and why that apocalypse should have a primarily material and historical rather than a spiritual and transcendent character. One writer asserts that the utopian hopes for secular fulfillment in the context of material abundance, which are characteristic of all modern ideologies, are both a cause and an effect of the industrial revolution in its various phases. The beginnings of the industrial revolution were in part produced by Liberal ideology. And the accomplishments of the revolution in the late nineteenth and early twentieth centuries—an era of expanding productivity and abundance such as the

---

[1] See Eric Voegelin, *The New Science of Politics* (Chicago: University of Chicago Press, 1952).
[2] *Ibid.*, p. 111.

world has never known—have made plausible the vast hopes for material
well-being which are found in all the later "isms." [3]

Apocalyptic Politics: The Revolution of Modernity.　All the characteristic features of modern ideologies can thus be explained by this
special relationship to the industrial revolution. For example, of the
militantly revolutionary aspect of modern ideologies Frederick Watkins
writes, "The characteristic function of modern ideologies has been to
persuade men that it was both possible and right for them to further
the progress of the Industrial Revolution by launching a revolutionary
attack against the established political order." [4] In each case the traditional legitimation of authority by reference to transcendent divinity is
replaced by legitimation through immanent divinity—some version or
other of "popular sovereignty." Modern ideologies are therefore all
democratic; their mandates are carried out in the name of the "people"
and their appeal is to mass movements. Paired with this in most cases,
however, is elite leadership by a vigorous and talented minority—the
Leninist idea of the Party as vanguard, the Fascist elite party of supermen. Goals are unrealistically optimistic—the capitalist "free market,"
the Marxist "classless society." And the adherents of each of the doctrines
is imbued with a sense of righteousness about his own values and goals.

Another writer in a recent definitional essay has emphasized the
self-consciousness of modern ideology and its special view of history as
a unilinear field of human endeavor tending toward the perfection of
the social world. Willard Mullins, citing Barnard and Porter, writes:

> Ideology incorporates a type of "historical consciousness" characteristic
> of the modern age, in which a high degree of social change is recognized,
> where 'change' [means] the coming into being of new and specifically
> *different* constellations and not merely the replacement of one set of
> conditions by a new set of the same specific type. . . ." [5]

He believes this is why ideologies are spreading from the West to the
Third World of "developing nations" as a solvent of traditional ideas
and ways. In the process of change, ideology, as Mullins sees it, serves
as an active instrument and is not merely a reflex of the process of
social transformation. Traditional consciousness takes the world as given,
whereas the historical conciousness of ideological thinking "implies the
possibility of imagining qualitatively new social arrangements, of em-

---

[3] Frederick Watkins, *The Age of Ideology* (Englewood Cliffs, N.J.: Prentice-
Hall, Inc., 1964), Chap. 1.
[4] *Ibid.*, p. 4.
[5] Willard A. Mullins, "On the Concept of Ideology in Political Science,"
American Political Science Review, 66(2), June 1972, 504.

pathetically placing oneself in them, and of conceptualizing the extent to which individuals, including oneself, might be causally effective in bringing new arrangements about." [6] Mullins is here using a conception of "ideology" equivalent to what we have called "forensic ideology."

These, then, are some of the characteristic features of modern political culture, the things that make it specifically modern. Let us now take a closer look at the matrix of medieval culture from which it grew, for the character of this matrix had much to do with the special forms modern ideology has developed, both as outgrowth and as reaction.

2. Medieval Political Culture

A Theocentric Conception of Authority.   Daniel Lerner's "traditional" man is a bearer today of ideas of authority and value that predate the modern era. They are medieval in origin. The leading characteristic of medieval political culture, which radically distinguishes it from that of our own time, was its theocentrism. God was seen as the author of all things in the world, both animate and inanimate, and His will and reason were therefore authority in all matters. Disputes about truth, about causality, about the legitimacy of political authority were always referred in the last analysis to God. The chief medieval conception of authority was therefore the sovereignty of God. It can be rendered by the normative exhortation, "Obey the authority appointed by God," or by the declarative statement, "The authority which God appoints is legitimate." Probably no statement about politics was more often quoted and interpreted during the Middle Ages than the words of St. Paul in the thirteenth chapter of Romans:

> Let every soul be in subjection to the higher powers: for there is no power but of God, and the powers that be are ordained of God. Therefore he that resisteth the power withstandeth the ordinance of God: and they that withstand shall receive to themselves judgment. And wouldst thou have no fear of the power? do that which is good, and thou shalt have praise from the same: for he is a minister of God to thee for good. But if thou do that which is evil, be afraid; for he beareth not the sword in vain: for he is a minister of God, an avenger for wrath to him that doeth evil.[7]

Associated with this conception of authority were a variety of contradictory "beliefs" (in the Beer and Ulam sense) about the way in which God exercises his supreme authority. One of these was to the effect that *every* ruler is appointed by God, be he just king or tyrant— a doctrine which gave rise to the subordinate conception of authority

[6] *Ibid.*
[7] Romans 13:1–5.

which maintains that all constituted power is to be obeyed. Augustine explained tyranny as a divine trial of the just: "For to the just all the evils imposed on them by unjust rulers are not the punishment of crime but the test of virtue." [8] Corollary to these notions of passive obedience were various adaptations of Roman law maxims dealing with the manner in which the king's administrative power (the sphere of power designated as "gubernaculum," or "government") is exercised. Thus the thirteenth-century lawyer Bracton writes: "Neither justices nor private persons ought or can dispute concerning royal charters and royal acts," and "No one can pass judgment of a charter or an act of the king, so as to make void the king's act." These ideas are summed up in the maxim *"Rex non sub homine sed sub Deo ac Lege"*—"The king is not subject to men but to God and to the law." [9]

Constitutionalism and Participation.   In one respect, therefore, European political culture in the Middle Ages was a profoundly subject culture, like the typical traditional society of the nonwestern world today.[10] The ordinary man's chief political role was to be ruled, to obey the divinely constituted political authority set over him. But this was only part of the picture, for juxtaposed to these "beliefs" were others which pointed in a very different direction. A strong constitutionalist strain in medieval culture stressed the essentially legal character of the ruler's will. And the ultimate test of its legality was the conformity of the king's will to "natural law," sometimes conceived as "what natural reason has established among all men" (a formulation of the second-century Roman lawyer Gaius) and sometimes identified with divine law as expressed in Scriptures (Gratian).[11]

Combined with these ideas was the notion that the law which limits the will of the king includes the unchanging custom of the realm. The king's function included *jurisdictio* (saying what the law is), but not *legislatio* (making the law). And in declaring the law—that is, fundamental legal relationships regarding rights and obligations, especially those governing the ownership and use of property—the king was expected to act in conjunction with the council of elders and magnates (later the parliament of the realm) because law was held to be a possession of the whole society.[12] Only in his administrative acts could the

---

[8] *City of God*, trans. Marcus Dodds (New York: Modern Library, 1950), p. 112.

[9] See Charles Howard McIlwain, *Constitutionalism, Ancient and Modern*, rev. ed. (Ithaca: Cornell University Press, 1947), p. 72.

[10] See Gabriel Almond and Sidney Verba, *The Civic Culture* (Princeton: Princeton University Press, 1963), and Daniel Lerner, *The Passing of Traditional Society* (New York: Free Press of Glencoe, 1958).

[11] See Ewart Lewis, ed., *Medieval Political Ideas* (New York: Alfred A. Knopf, Inc., 1954), I, 7, 8, 9. With permission of the publisher.

[12] *Ibid.*, I, 2–5.

king act autonomously. It was commonly understood that on receiving his crown the medieval king, by his coronation oath, swore to uphold the customary law of the realm.[13] Thus Bracton, interpreting a maxim of Justinian on the relationship between imperial and popular authority, transmutes a principle of absolutism into one of constitutional or limited authority. Justinian had written: "What pleases the prince has the force of law, because the people by a royal act have conferred on him all their Imperium and Potestas." Bracton makes the Latin expression "*quid cum lege regia*" read "when in accordance with a royal law" instead of "because by a royal law." The "royal law" is here understood as the king's coronation oath.[14]

Deriving from these beliefs, then, there were in medieval political culture a number of subordinate conceptions of authority of a constitutionalist and limitedly participant character. If the king failed to stay under the law—either natural, divine, or customary—*somebody* had to act to bring him back under its control. This might be a bishop or the Pope, the chief keepers of the divine law, employing spiritual sanctions such as excommunication or even political sanctions extending to deposition. Or it might be the organized community—the parliament, the assembled baronage of the realm, resisting the king to the extent of making war on him, as the English barons assembled at Runnymede were prepared to do in the case of King John. Thus in the early medieval law book the *Sachsenspiegel* we read that "a man must resist his king and his judge, if he does wrong, and must hinder him in every way, even if he be his relative or feudal lord. And he does not thereby break his fealty." [15] Sometimes the metaphor of the compact or contract, which was to figure so prominently much later in Liberal thought, was used to express the conditional obligation of the subject to his king. Thus we find in the writings of an eleventh-century publicist, Manegold of Lautenbach, the following formulation:

> When he who has been chosen for the coercion of the wicked and the defence of the upright has begun to foster evil against them, to destroy the good, and himself to exercise most cruelly against his subjects the tyranny which he ought to repel, is it not clear that he deservedly falls from the dignity entrusted to him and that the people stand free of his lordship and subjection, when he has been evidently the first to break the compact for whose sake he was appointed? [16]

Some writers were even ready to justify tyrannicide by a private person as an instrument of divine retribution against a wicked king.

[13] See Fritz Kern, *Kingship and Law in the Middle Ages* (Oxford: Basil Blackwell, 1939), pp. 76–79.
[14] See McIlwain, *op. cit.*, pp. 70, 71.
[15] Kern, *op. cit.*, p. 84.
[16] Cited in Lewis, *op. cit.*, I, 165. With permission of the publisher.

Thus John of Salisbury writes: "To kill a tyrant is not only licit but fair and just. For he who has taken up the sword deserves to die by the sword." [17] Others, however, including Thomas Aquinas, thought such license "would be dangerous to the multitude and to its rulers. . . . Such presumption would be more likely to result in the loss to the multitude of a good king than in the beneficial abolition of a tyrant." [18] Aquinas found preferable action by authorized representatives of the community.

Another conception of community control related to the selection of the ruler. Divine designation and heredity were two sources of authority, but the Germanic idea of monarchy also contained an elective element. Thus, although the eldest son had a presumptive right to the throne, he could be passed over in favor of a younger brother with markedly superior physical, intellectual, or moral qualifications. The range of community choice was, indeed, limited to members of the royal family, and it could be exercised only by the baronage, but at least the *notion* of election was there.

The principle of consent was also present in the medieval conception of authority. Not all rights and obligations were established by status in the realm. The feudal contract conferred specific rights and privileges on the vassal who accepted them in return for service of various kinds which the vassal obligated himself to render to his liege. Most important, the contract was phrased in specific and concrete terms.

Thus in competition with the idea of authority as directly constituted by God there was in medieval culture a vaguely defined notion of the political community, the "people" as a source of authority as well, which operated in the choice of rulers, the designation of their powers and rights, and in the active limitation of their activity to a specified lawful range. These were ideas which later were to develop into central concepts of Liberal and Democratic thought—a principle of community participation in government and of legal restraint on arbitrary power.[19]

Conceptions of Purpose and Associated "Beliefs": Organicism.   Theocentrism also underpinned the ideas of medieval men about individual and social purpose. It was not up to the individual as in our modern liberal democracies to decide what he was to do with his life. This was settled by the determination of God. The whole world was seen as a stratified order of statuses decreed by the Almighty. And for the most part birth determined the particular status that each individual was destined to occupy. The world of human society was a divinely ordained moral organism, each part of which had a special role to play in pro-

---

[17] *Ibid.*, p. 276.
[18] *Ibid.*, p. 286.
[19] See Almond and Verba, *op. cit.*, for a description of the "civic culture," which supports the institutions of Liberal democracy, as characteristically participant.

ducing the health and happiness of the whole. A most graphic picture of this organism is given us by the twelfth-century writer John of Salisbury in a work entitled the *Policraticus*, a medieval handbook on good government:

> Now a commonwealth is a certain body which is given life by benefit of divine favor and is made by the highest equity and is ruled by a certain moderating reason. And those things that establish the rites of religion in us and teach us the worship of God . . . take the place of the soul in the body of the commonwealth. Those men who preside over the rites of religion should be honoured or revered as the soul of the body. . . . The prince takes the place of the head, subject to God alone and to those who act as His representatives on earth. The senate corresponds to the heart, from which proceed the beginnings of good and evil deeds. The offices of eyes, ears, and tongue are claimed by the judges and the governors of the provinces. Officials and soldiers correspond to the legs. Those who are always about the prince are likened to the sides. Treasurers and warders . . . are like the belly and intestines, which if they become congested with excessive greed and too tenaciously keep what they collect, generate innumerable incurable diseases, so that ruin threatens the whole body. . . . Tillers of the soil correspond to the feet. . . .[20]

The perusal of such a statement might well lead one to cry, with the editor of *New Yorker*, "Block that Metaphor!" For it is indeed an elaborate and comprehensive one. The individual is reduced to his social role. But it also should be pointed out that the implications of the statement are not totalitarian in the modern sense, for medieval men never forgot that organicist conceptions of this kind *were* metaphors. All medieval philosophers agreed with Aristotle that existential reality belonged only to individuals, which they described as "primary substances." These substances might be organized for various purposes in organic universal forms. But it still remained true that "nothing is prior to the individual." The feudal contractarianism which we have already described also mitigated the force of organicist conceptions of society.[21]

Purpose, therefore, in all its dimensions, was seen as something generated not by men, either individually or collectively, but by a ruling deity, and social purpose was expressed by the deity in terms of a hierarchy of organically related roles and functions. The overall purpose of the entire organism was dual—to produce happiness for mankind, both temporal and eternal. The realization of temporal values was given into the hands of civil authority, and of eternal life to an ecclesiastical authority, the Church.

Because spiritual values—everything that goes beyond physical comfort—all relate to the development of the soul whose end is heaven,

---

[20] Lewis, *op. cit.*, I, 225.
[21] See *ibid.*, pp. 199, 194.

the temporal happiness over which the civil authority was given charge consisted only of external things, such as the provision of security, adequate shelter, clothing, and the regulation of external relationships such as trade. Civil government also was called in as a helpmate to the spiritualty, which exercised no coercive authority itself, where coercive actions were deemed necessary for the salvation of the soul—e.g., the punishment of heretics. But even here it was only the external, physical man which was reached by the sword of the state.

The direction of the internal man belonged entirely to the Church, with its elaborate all-European hierarchical order ranging from Pope down to parish priest and lay parishioner. The divine ordering of all values and purposes was therefore communicated to the individual chiefly through this system, though conscience also played a role and could be invoked in a limited way against the public authority of the Church. The presumption, however, was that the dictate of Church authority was supreme.

In principle the Church spoke with more authority than the civil ruler, for its task was the weightier and superior one. As Pope Gelasius, writing at the end of the fifth century, put the matter:

> There are two authorities by which principally this world is ruled, the sacred authority of the bishops, and the royal power, and the obligation of the bishops is the heavier of these two in proportion as they shall render account to God for the kings of men themselves.[22]

In some things its jurisdiction extended even to temporal objects, as a security of autonomy in the execution of these weighty purposes. They included absolute control of Church property, wherever it might be, and the exemption of that property from temporal regulation and taxation. Members of the clergy in their persons were also subject only to ecclesiastical authority, and their offenses could be tried only in Church courts. Ecclesiastical courts also had jurisdiction over all persons when matters of Church law (canon law) were involved, as in marriages and testaments. In addition, because the Church was guardian of morals as well as faith, any civil act governing external moral behavior had to be in accordance with divine and natural law as interpreted by the Church if it was to be considered valid.

Throughout the Middle Ages the existence of two parallel systems of authority gave rise to jurisdictional conflict. From the beginning it was clear that in dignity and responsibility the spiritual sword was the senior partner. But in the event of a disagreement as to where the boundary line lay between the two authorities, there was no rule as to

---

[22] Quoted in Charles H. McIlwain, *The Growth of Political Thought in the West* (New York: The Macmillan Company, 1932), p. 165.

how it might be arbitrated. The result was that at various times each of the two powers asserted a "plenitude of power," or what we would today call sovereignty, to settle the question. Popes resorted to excommunication, deposition, and the absolution of subjects from their oaths of allegiance as sanctions against defiant monarchs. And kings and Holy Roman emperors in turn sought to depose popes through the authority of councils called by themselves. The upshot was that the principle of limited government was strongly affirmed and the position of the community as a source of lawful power was enhanced, structural principles of great importance which we have already treated in our discussion of medieval conceptions of authority.

Respublica Christiana. Theocentrism, in supplying a medieval conception of purpose, also supplied a principle and focus of community. Europeans were united as a single great religious commonwealth. Their first allegiance was to Christ, through the Church, whose rules and ordinances were enforced by the secular powers—the kingdoms, principalities, and baronies which made up the curious mosaic of medieval political life. These latter were simply parochical administrative adjuncts of the Universal Church. The Holy Empire was a rallying point for some, and in men like Dante it had its dedicated ideologists. But it was difficult to build loyalty around two universal jurisdictions, and the Papacy was more firmly grounded and more centrally structured than the Empire. The dynastic principle was not to gain ascendance as a focus of political community until the Reformation had broken the power of the Church, and the day of the nation was still far off.

Medieval political culture, in its theocentric orientation, thus contained a mixture of conflicting principles. Unlike most theocentric and hieratically dominated societies, it was only partly an absolutist and subject culture. A constitutionalist tradition was also strongly developed, as we have seen, which limited the exercise of authority at every level of both priestly and civil power. In the opposition and balance of spiritual and temporal jurisdictions we can find an important root in tradition for modern Liberal culture. But this is true only of Western Europe in the Middle Ages. Traditional culture in Eastern Europe and elsewhere was uniformly absolutist and subject. Its legacy, as we shall see, has greatly affected the way in which these areas have been modernized.

3. Collapse of the Medieval Consensus

The first herald of the breakup of medieval consensus was the claim put forward by King Philip the Fair of France, in the fourteenth century, that he was an emperor in his own kingdom. This amounted to an assertion of a right to exercise in France the kind of absolute and unlimited power that the emperors had enjoyed in ancient Rome. It contained the principle of secular sovereignty and drew territorial boundaries around the dynastic state. Philip was trying to serve notice on the clergy that their days of exterritorial immunity and privilege, which hobbled the independence of civil power, were numbered.

As is usual with ideological change, the new principle was asserted in a changing social situation. The growth of a commercial economy was already establishing new sets of basic relationships between man and man and therewith loosening old ties and old ideas of authority and community. In laying claim to territorial sovereignty, a medieval king like Philip found conditions developing which made that claim appealing to a growing class of potentially powerful persons. Rich burghers, interested in the security of property and trade rather than in military glory and chivalric honor, groped their way toward an alliance with vigorous dynasties of state-builders at the pivotal centers of European life.

The new territorial state developed more readily as fact than as ideal for more than one hundred years. Ideological change was held back by the continued dominance of the Catholic Church as an all-European government. In the face of the continued authority of this universal institution, parochial and secular ideas could not easily gain a foothold. The fragmentation of the Church as a result of the Reformation controversies of the sixteenth century, however, opened the way for vast changes in the ideological order, both within the religious frame of reference and running counter to it. The Reformation was not a religious revolution solely, but also a most profound social and political upheaval, which called sharply in question traditional concepts of authority and purpose and gave rise to a variety of new ways of looking at the world—new secular "beliefs." Change was gradual, however. It took more than 250 years for a fully secular *Weltanschauung* to become generally authoritative as the underpinning for a variety of new secular political ideologies, both authoritarian and democratic in character—our modern "isms."

New Conceptions of Authority: Their Situational Determination. It cannot be demonstrated that the strictly religious beliefs of the warring Catholic and Protestant sects implied any particular political theory. Political theories in the first instance were ad hoc byproducts of the conflict, constructed to fit new political circumstances, new power relationships, rather than deductions from theological premises. In those parts of Germany where Lutheranism triumphed there developed a conception of authority which was remarkably like the Gallican theory that gained a dominant position in Catholic France. In both cases medieval constitutionalism gave way to Caesaro-Papist royal absolutism. Gone were the restraints of feudalism and gone also the brakes on royal authority deriving from the existence of an independent and competing parallel hierarchy. In both the German Lutheran and Gallican Catholic systems the Church became simply an arm of civil authority, whose function was to teach and preach the official religion of the realm of which the prince had become the high priest and chief caretaker. Church and state were still both conceived as one community, but religious consensus served less and less the purpose of salvation and more and more the end of political order and stability. The new political salience of religion was given frank expression in a Machiavellian principle of international law—*Cuius regio, eius religio,* "You must adopt the religion of the prince in whose kingdom you reside."

A late expression of the absolutist theory which derived from the new religious situation is found in the political writings of the English King James I (1604):

> Kings are justly called Gods, for that they exercise a manner or resemblance of Divine power upon earth: For if you will consider the Attributes to God, you shall see how they agree in the person of a King. . . . they make and unmake their subjects: they have power of raising and casting downe: of life, and of death: Judges over all their subjects, and in all causes, and yet accomptable to none but God onely. They have power to exalt low things, and abase high things, and make of their subjects like men at the Chesse; A power to take a Bishop or a Knight, and to cry up, or downe any of their subjects, as they do their money.[23]

French Huguenots, espousing a conception of authority which inverted the relationship of civil and ecclesiastical, were constitutionalists when out of power. And Catholics, where they were unable to make sure of the Crown, were attracted to a Jesuit theory which vested ultimate power in the people rather than in the ruler and called for constitutional restrictions on the exercise of civil power and the right of revolution against a tyrant.

4. The Passing of Traditional Society: Foundations of Modern Ideology

The state-church and church-state theories developed to fit the special circumstances of the new territorial politics were hardly more than

---

[23] James I, Speech to Parliament, March 21, 1609, in *Political Works* (Cambridge: Harvard University Press, 1918), pp. 306–7.

variations on the positions taken by popes and emperors in the centuries-long ideological battle about the relationship of the spiritual and temporal swords of the *Respublica Christiana*. They were stated in the old language with the well-worn concepts of the medieval world view: theocentrism, organicism, and hierarchy. The first real break with the medieval paradigm of political culture is an outgrowth of the seventeenth-century English civil wars, which also produced the beginnings of a recognizably modern parliamentary system of government. The most articulate formulator of the new way of looking at the world is the Whig philosopher-publicist John Locke (1632–1704).

Locke set out deliberately to restructure European man's view of the world by reworking prevailing conceptions of knowledge. His purpose in writing *An Essay Concerning Human Understanding* was to "inquire into the original, certainty, and extent of human knowledge, together with the grounds and degrees of Belief, Opinion, and Assent." [24] A "new way of ideas," a new understanding of what constitutes knowledge, was to turn the medieval world upside down and produce a wholly new set of beliefs and values.

As a new view of reality, the writings of Locke had no great currency in his own time, especially in England. His role was rather to herald an ideological system which over the years was to take hold of the European and American mind, and finally spread out to the ends of the earth. Locke's ideas would be reworked in a thousand different variations and extensions, especially by the rationalist *philosophes* of the eighteenth-century French Enlightenment and by Jean-Jacques Rousseau, the father of democratic Romanticism, as well. They would gradually come to represent the leading assumptions of the modern mind in society at large.

We are not saying that Locke *created* modern political culture or that he directly influenced the form of its development. The sociology of knowledge can make no definite pronouncement on so complex a causal order. We are simply saying that Locke was one of the first to articulate a set of ideas—a conception of authority, of purpose, and an accompanying "belief" system—which gave coherence to and made sense of the emerging institutional order. In Geertz's terms, it furnished a template which could render intelligible the new reality. To what degree it also inspired and channeled that new reality is indeterminate. All we know is that in a special way the two "fit" one another. The "fit" is especially good in the case of the Liberal Democratic version of the new society. But some of Locke's concepts are the common currency of all modern ideologies.

---

[24] John Locke, *An Essay Concerning Human Understanding*, ed. A. S. Pringle-Pattison (Oxford: Clarendon Press, 1924), Book I, Chap. 1, Sec. 1, p. 9.

The Purpose of a Commonwealth.   In his *Letter Concerning Tolera-tion* Locke writes:

> The commonwealth seems to me to be a society of men constituted only for the processing, preserving, and advancing their own civil interests . . . life, liberty, health . . . and the possession of outward things, such as money, lands, house, furniture, and the like.

And of the church he says: "A church . . . I take to be a voluntary society of men, joining themselves together of their own accord in order to the public worshipping of God . . . a free and voluntary society." [25] Both thoughts were revolutionary. From the time of Constantine ecclesiastical and civil order were seen as simply two facets of the life of a single community. And before the Christianizing of the Empire this had been the characteristic assumption of pagan societies. Each city-state and kingdom had had its own gods, so that citizenry and subjects were at the same time partners in a religious fellowship. All through the Middle Ages it was assumed that the relationship was a necessary one, that religion had to be the bond of civil society. Thus the persecution of heretics by the temporal authorities was for the purpose of maintaining civil order, not to save the souls of the heretics. But years of bloody conflict over the nature of true religion, stemming from the final success of a heresy on a large scale, had begun to show that a new view had to be adopted. With the Church shattered in a hundred pieces, how could one hope to build viable political order on religious uniformity without constant and excessive repression? Locke's solution was to urge that the civil and ecclesiastical spheres be seen as two separate communities.

It was Locke's view of the Church that was the most radical aspect of his theory. The commonwealth remained a public, compulsory, and coercive society. One might leave a commonwealth one disliked, he suggested, but property could not be taken along. This made such defection a difficult affair. But churches were reduced to purely private and voluntary associations, whose membership would be entirely a matter of individual preference.

The Privatization of Religion.   Notice that in the passage quoted above Locke uses the expression "*a* church" rather than "*the* church." A world of new meaning is encompassed by the simple substitution of the indefinite for the definite article. "*The* church" implied a public order— that is, an order publicly known to be divinely mandated. To speak of "*the* church" implied a public criterion of divine truth, accessible to all, incontrovertible, certain. To persecute a heretic within such a context

    [25] John Locke, *A Letter Concerning Toleration*, Little Library of Liberal Arts, No. 22 (New York: Liberal Arts Press, 1950), pp. 17, 18.

did not seem cruelty, because the heretic by rejecting "*the* church" was rejecting public truth. Heretical behavior could only be that of a fool or a knave, to use the language of John Calvin. The definitive success of a variety of heresies, however, acknowledged in the Treaty of Westphalia of 1638, which wrote an end to the international phase of the religious wars, raised a strong presumption against the idea of a self-evident criterion of religious truth. Locke's formula signifies that religion must be a private matter because in fact no public criterion exists. The highest things had become a matter of private and various opinion, about which there could be no certainty. Only in the practical order of the commonwealth did agreement remain on the need for a public authority to safeguard property, life, and limb, incontestably universal values, based on the certainty of desire rather than of knowledge.

A New Weltanschauung.   It is significant that the philosophical as well as theological truth of the Middle Ages was undermined by the fragmentation of the Christian Church. The evidence is abundantly clear in the epistemologies of writers like Locke and Thomas Hobbes, and after them men like Bishop Berkeley and David Hume. From Aquinas back to Plato and Aristotle it had been assumed that the mind could directly intuit behind the images of the empirical world a substantial reality of forms and essences, which in the established theology were easily interpreted as the ideas of God. Their interconnections constituted a natural law, which was also a reflection of the divine and the eternal law. But beginning in the seventeenth century men were no longer sure that such a world of substantial reality-in-itself was available to the human mind. For Hobbes it was possible to go no further than an observation of appearances in motion as the only accessible reality, which would have to be made the basis of a reconstruction of the world of nature and of society. For Locke reality was vested in the order of our minds, which were capable of organizing the appearances of our experience for practical purposes, but which yielded no substantial truth of an ultimate kind. Ideas produced by sensation are for him "in the mind no more the likeness of something existing without us than the names that stand for them be the likeness of our ideas." [26]

The new skepticism about the power of the human mind to know an ultimate reality was to be a powerful solvent of the entire medieval structure of reality, which was based on the scholastic epistemology of intelligible essences. The entire system of hierarchical and organically related roles and functions which was the medieval view of society would be swept away as unverifiable nonsense, and an entirely new beginning

---

[26] John Locke, *An Essay Concerning Human Understanding*, Book II, Chap. 8, Sec. 7, p. 66.

would have to be made. All authority in medieval life derived from God. This is what we mean by a theocentric order. But if God cannot be publicly and certainly known, His word cannot be the basis of public order. Citizens as private men may have their private revelations and associate together for the private practice of their beliefs, but the general and public order must have another foundation. The ultimate political consequence of the new privatization or subjectivication of religious inspiration are graphically revealed in the political debates carried on in the Puritan Army. One agitator spoke of the role of his own religious revelations for his sense of political obligation: "Whatsoever hopes or obligations I should be bound unto, if afterward God should reveal himself, I would break it speedily, if it were an hundred a day." [27]

The new foundation of public authority would nevertheless have to be the individual. In the afterglow of religious order, he would continue to be considered a child of God by all the contending sects and by secular-minded Deists as well—a fact which explains the widespread belief in "the dignity of the individual," a leading conception of modern political culture in its Liberal form. But among Protestants and Deists the individual was seen as an independent and self-reliant being, naked and alone before God, rather than as a member of some divinely decreed social or ecclesiastical order. As the new view of reality gave rise to a new conception of knowledge—science, as the knowledge of the motions of phenomena—man also was to be seen simply as a point of matter in space. The basic social reality was simply an aggregate of such individual points, each experiencing his own existence and the attraction and repulsion of other bodies as the product of blind desire. All else is conscious invention and artificial creation, the product of self-subsistent individuals fashioning the social world to meet their needs as one would ingeniously construct a machine. From divinely inspired organism the world had been converted into a meaningless mechanism. When with Rousseau the organic metaphor received new currency it would be legitimated solely by myth, a human invention.

In politics all traditional authorities were made illegitimate by the new *Weltanschauung*. The individual had suddenly become the source of all authority. And the way from individual to public order could only be by the consent, either tacit or expressed, of individual men contracting together to establish the institutions of the commonwealth. This new set of ideas contained a most profound principle of political and social revolution.

Daniel Lerner, in a study of *The Passing of Traditional Society*, writes:

[27] Buffcoat, quoted in A. D. Lindsay, *The Modern Democratic State* (New York: Oxford University Press, 1962), p. 85.

Western men need only reflect on the titanic struggles whereby, over the course of centuries, medieval lifeways were supplanted by modernity. Hindsight now summarizes these struggles as The Age of Exploration, The Renaissance, The Reformation, The Counter-Reformation, The Industrial Revolution. But well we know that this historical sequence worked itself out through millions of individual lives; that many suffered, others prospered, while their world was being reshaped in the modern image. In the end—and the end is not yet—all men of the West had acquired a new style of life.[28]

The revolutions going on today in Asia, Africa, and Latin America, and the more orderly processes of change which we call "political modernization" or "economic and political development" represent the contemporary working out in traditional nonwestern societies of the revolutionary view of reality which had its inception in Europe in the time of Locke. We must examine now the characteristic conceptions of purpose and authority and the associated beliefs which are the political corollaries of that view of reality.

Our purpose here is to present in the abstract those concepts and sentiments which emerged first in this process of change to form the fundamental characteristics of modern political culture. Some of them became specific to Liberalism, the first form of the modern system of ideas fully to develop. Others became the common currency of the entire contrapuntal scheme of modern thought, Liberal, Conservative, Fascist, and Communist.

5. New Conceptions of Purpose

With the world of divine purposes suspended, a new hierarchy of human aims had to be evolved. In the realm of truth the end of public religion meant a new emphasis on individual freedom. Instead of protecting an official truth, the role of government would be to enhance the freedom of the individual mind and to protect and regulate the free market in ideas. From the free sharing of private opinions, tentative agreements could be worked out at the level of social utility. Freedom of religion and freedom of expression thus emerged as two leading negative conceptions of purpose, mandating a significant contraction of the area of public authority. John Milton's essay *Areopagitica*, a resounding defense of freedom of the press, is an eloquent early statement of the new idea. This particular value, however, is one which became specific to a particular variety of modernity—Liberal political culture. We must leave it to another place to explain why this occurred.

[28] Lerner, *op. cit.*, p. 43.

Freedom was also the newly authoritative principle for the use of private property and the general conduct of economy. Here, too, public purpose was required to withdraw in favor of private purposes. Medieval political culture had minimized the importance of economic goods; although rules existed to restrict the civil power from arbitrary confiscations of property, it remained the business of government to see that not too much value was laid on heaping up the things of this world. Aquinas, for example, in his *Essay on Kingship*, calls for limitations on the spread of commercial pursuits as a corrupting influence on morals. The city, he writes, ought not "to superabound in delightful things" which make men "dissolute through pleasures . . . neglecting necessary matters and all the pursuits that duty lays upon them." [29] After all, the primary business was salvation. What was to become a central institution of modern capitalist economy—lending money at interest—was then prohibited as immoral usury. Prices were also extensively regulated by municipal authorities and by monopolistic guilds, according to the doctrine of the "just price." Entry into the various trades and professions was similarly controlled for the sake of the common good.

Here, too, however, as in the world of religion and opinion, the way was paved for new principles by the prior appearance of new practices. By the time of the sixteenth-century Reformation, the agrarian order had retired before a vigorously expanding commercialism, eagerly fostered by a growing class of people living in towns. The old restrictions on trade were gradually falling into abeyance as the immoral practice of usury turned into the respectable business of banking. Rulers of the new centralizing states of France, England, and Spain saw their chief work to be the increase of national wealth, which they pursued with a variety of regulatory devices which we commonly refer to as the system of mercantilism. A new attitude was developing toward the things of this world.

Again, in the writings of Locke we find the first systematic formulation of a new principle of economic purpose focusing on the concepts of wealth and property framed within the new world view of self-reliant individuals. One of the chief themes of Locke's *Second Treatise of Civil Government* is the human battle to overcome scarcity. It is God's intention, writes Locke, that the potential abundance of nature be realized by the labor of men, mixing their labor with the raw materials given to them in common. This is not only something that we *may* do, but that we are *enjoined* to do. "Land that is left wholly to Nature . . . is called,

[29] St. Thomas Aquinas, *Essay on Kingship*, trans. Gerald B. Phelan (Toronto: Pontifical Institute, 1949), II, 8 (148, 147), pp. 80, 79.

as indeed it is, *wast."* [30] And waste was then, as now, a bad word. By the mingling of one's labor with the common store, one appropriates property out of the natural condition and makes it one's own. And it is through the individual effort so stimulated, by the possibility of private appropriation, that the total sum of goods is increased:

> He who appropriates land to himself by his labour, does not lessen but increase the common stock of mankind. For the provisions serving to the support of humane life, produced by one acre of inclosed and cultivated land, are . . . ten times more, than those which are yeilded by an acre of Land, of an equal richnesse lyeing wast in common. And therefor he, that incloses Land and has a greater plenty of the conveniencys of life from ten acres, than he could have from an hundred left to Nature, may truly be said, to give ninety acres to Mankind.[31]

Because we are enjoined by God to make the earth fruitful, and because the great instrument of increase is private property, this institution suddenly achieves paramount importance. Locke goes so far as to assimilate property to personality, saying that the foundation of property is the property one has in one's person, to which no one else has a right. The chief business of government, therefore, becomes the protection of life and of property. And here we have the justification of Locke's definition of the commonwealth in the *Letter on Toleration:*

> The commonwealth seems to me to be a society of men constituted only for the procuring, preserving and advancing their own civil interests . . . life, liberty, health . . . and the possession of outward things, such as money, lands, houses, furniture and the like.[32]

In the writings of Locke we also find in rudimentary form the central principle of the capitalist economy which was to develop inside emerging Liberal society—the idea of price as a free function of supply and demand. Instead of public authority proclaiming what is just and equitable in the light of known standards of fairness, the impersonal and blind forces of the market, the product of the interplay of many individual egos, mechanically produce the price of a commodity:

> He that will justly estimate the value of any thing must consider its quantity in proportion to its vent, for this alone regulates the price. The value of any thing is greater, as its quantity is less in proportion to its vent

30 John Locke, *Second Treatise,* paragraph 42 in John Locke, *Two Treatises of Government,* Peter Laslett, ed. (Cambridge: Cambridge University Press, 1967), p. 315.

31 *Ibid.,* p. 312 (paragraph 37).

32 *Letter on Toleration,* p. 17.

[demand]. . . . For if you alter the quantity, or vent, on either side, you presently alter the price, but no other way in the world.[33]

The full development of the doctrines of Capitalism had to wait another century for the work of Adam Smith, who attempted to demonstrate in a comprehensive way that it was not the mercantilist system of government regulation which best contributed to the wealth of nations, but rather free, unhampered trade, the free competition of rationally acquisitive individuals:

> Every individual is continually exerting himself to find out the most advantageous employment for whatever capital he can command. It is his own advantage, indeed, and not that of society which he has in view. But the study of his own advantage naturally, or rather necessarily leads him to prefer that employment which is most advantageous to the society.[34]

6. New "Beliefs": The Work Ethic and Political Activism

Directed no longer by external authority to the performance of one's divinely ordained function, what would now furnish motivation to the autonomous individual to work hard to accomplish the new end of economic increase, which had become a growing preoccupation? Traditional society was lazy, or at least easygoing, and it did not stress the values of acquisition and accumulation. But middle-class man was industrious, hard-working. One explanation was that while man is by nature passive (a body at rest), he is motivated to work by the promise of pleasure that the products of work hold and the fear of pain of deprivation that idleness entails. This means that society should guarantee an individual the fruit of his labor and allow him to follow the occupation he chooses. Involuntary servitude makes for indolence. Correlatively, society must stand ready to allow the individual to be deprived if he does not work, in order to ensure his industry. The social welfare function as a prime role of government is consequently diminished in favor of the "nightwatchman state" which maintains the rules of the competitive game. Thus Arthur Young, writing in 1771 as the capitalist system of freedom was taking full form, says that "Everyone but an idiot knows that the lower classes must be kept poor or they will never be industrious." [35]

---

[33] John Locke, "Some Considerations of the Consequences of the Lowering of Interest and Raising the Value of Money," in *Works*, 12th ed. (London, 1824), IV, 40–41, in Ruben A. Goldwin, "John Locke," in Leo Strauss and Joseph Cropsey, eds., *History of Political Philosophy* (Chicago: Rand McNally & Co., 1963), p. 445.

[34] Adam Smith, *An Inquiry into the Nature and Causes of the Wealth of Nations*, ed. Edwin Cannan (London: Methuen & Co., Ltd., 1961), I, 475.

[35] Quoted in Harry K. Girvetz, *From Wealth to Welfare, The Evolution of Liberalism* (Stanford: Stanford University Press, 1950), p. 39.

Similarly, Albert Dicey, writing at the height of the period of Classical Liberalism in English political culture, says of the Poor Law of 1834 that it was passed "to save the property of hard-working men from destruction by putting an end to the monstrous system under which laggards who would not toil for their own support lived at the expense of their industrious neighbors." [36] The idea is still prevalent in today's liberal society, in which the traditional concept of social obligation to care for the poor has been restored. One respondent in the Lynds' study of "Middletown" said: "Men won't work if they don't have to. Work isn't fun. None of us would do a lick of work if he didn't have to." [37]

At the outset of the new system, however, before the world view of European man had become completely secularized, another ideology of work which Max Weber has termed the "Protestant Ethic," was widespread. The early capitalist, Weber argues, was a religious man who looked at his temporal work as a divine calling in life. The Protestant view of the life acceptable to God was not one of monastic asceticism, but rather a fulfilling of the obligations imposed by one's position in the world. At a time when more and more people found their calling in trade and manufacture, this implied a religious motive for industry and money making. According to Weber, this motive was markedly enhanced by the peculiar Calvinist doctrine of election. Gone were the comforting sacraments of the medieval Church, which was ready to detail the mind and will of a reasonable God and promise salvation to all who had faith. The new religion, as a halfway-house to the mechanical atomism of Hobbes, left man alone as an individual with a God whose will was mysterious, obscure, and apparently arbitrary. He knew that from birth he had been foreordained either to Heaven or to Hell. But the large question was which. To resolve the dilemma it became a duty to consider oneself chosen and to combat doubts about election as temptations. Lack of self-confidence was simply the result "of insufficient faith, hence of imperfect grace." [38] Intense activity in one's calling, it was found, could be an enormous support for such confidence. "It and it alone disperse[d] religious doubts and [gave] the certainty of grace." [39] In this way, material success, combined with a modest, disciplined, "respectable" mode of life, relieved the tensions of Calvinist determinism and furnished the spirit of that capitalism which grew up with early or Classical Liberalism.

[36] Albert V. Dicey, *Law and Public Opinion in England*, 2nd ed. (London: Macmillan & Company, Ltd., 1926), p. 203 quoted in Harry Girvetz, *The Evolution of Liberalism*, 2nd ed. (New York: Collier Books, 1963), p. 39.

[37] Robert S. and Helen M. Lynd, *Middletown, A Study in Contemporary American Culture* (New York: Harcourt, Brace & Co., 1929), quoted in *ibid*.

[38] Max Weber, *The Protestant Ethic and the Spirit of Capitalism*, trans. Talcott Parsons (New York: Charles Scribner's Sons, 1958), p. 111.

[39] *Ibid.*, p. 112.

When the fully modern secular culture had developed, the "Protestant Ethic"—or, as it is also called, the "work ethic"—had become self-sustaining. It was to remain unchallenged as a basic "belief" or, rather, ingrained habit down to the present, when ideologues of the "New Left" called it sharply in question, along with the institutions of which it is the informing spirit.

An important aspect of the "work ethic" is its spirit of rational calculation. To the medieval Catholic, good works were indeed an evidence of faith. But he was not wholly reliant on them, because the confession of sin, of evil works, could always restore him to the friendship of his God. But the Calvinist found himself wholly reliant on his good works as a demonstration of his election. They could not therefore be planless and occasional, as before. They had to be an entire system, rationally worked out, the product of careful reflection and planning. "Only a life guided by constant thought could achieve conquest over the state of nature." [40] It also required fullest use of one's time. For "not leisure and enjoyment, but only activity serves to increase the glory of God. . ." [41] Waste of time thus becomes the first and deadliest of sins, and rational labor in one's calling the highest virtue. The total result was the way of life of the solid middle-class home on the one hand, and the efficiency-oriented scheme of rationalized production we call the mature industrial economy on the other. [42]

A key motivating factor of Liberal Capitalist society, the work ethic, or an adequate substitute for it, has been acknowledged by Communists as necessary in the construction of an industrial economy, for all modern ideologies share with Liberalism a preoccupation with material well-being. In 1924 Stalin reflected on the virtues of "American practicality . . . that spirit . . . that simply must go through with a job, once it has been tackled, even if it be of minor importance." [43] He thought it important for Russians to study this kind of behavior in order to combat the Slavic trait of lack of perseverance. Indeed, throughout the entire underdeveloped world today modernizers are busy searching for means to motivate their people to industrious activity. This is an important aspect of the politics of mass mobilization everywhere in the traditional world. Marxist Communism and other ideologies may furnish a political culture capable of creating and maintaining a modern industrial state, but to do this they will have to incorporate something like

[40] *Ibid.*, p. 118.
[41] *Ibid.*, p. 157.
[42] For an incisive critique of the Weberian theory of the Protestant Ethic, see H. M. Robertson, *Aspects of the Rise of Economic Individualism: A Criticism of Max Weber and His School* (Cambridge: Cambridge University Press, 1933).
[43] Quoted in Nathan Leites, *The Operational Code of the Politburo*, Rand Series (New York: McGraw-Hill, 1951), p. 30.

the Protestant Ethic, which grew up in the context of Liberal emergence.

Accompanying the Protestant Ethic as a characteristic attitude of the modern mind, and arising like it out of the revolution of religion in England, was the spirit of the political activist and reformer whose chief representatives in our own time are the dedicated Red cadres of the Chinese Communist revolution.

According to Michael Walzer, the Harvard political theorist, the new spirit made itself first felt in Puritanism, which he describes as a "response to disorder and fear, a way of organizing men to overcome the acute sense of chaos." It "gave meaning to the experience of disorder and provided a way out, a return to certainty." [44] Walzer defines the spirit as "a kind of military and political work-ethic, directly analogous to the 'worldly asceticism' which Max Weber has described in economic life, but oriented not toward acquisition so much as toward contention, struggle, destruction, and rebuilding. Calvinist conscience gave to war and to politics . . . a new sense of method and purpose." [45]

Walzer notes that Puritanism was peculiarly appealing to newcomers to London, which experienced a great influx of population at the end of the sixteenth century. It served the purpose of helping these men make the transition from their lost roots in the countryside to a new life in the city. Central to the religion was a great emphasis on discipline to fit one for fearful struggle against an all-encompassing wickedness. It provided a means for conquering the overpowering feelings of anxiety notable in the Puritan mind, a sense of security eventuating in self-righteousness and fanaticism. The external instrument for imposing discipline was the congregation, with its regimented order analogous to that of the modern Communist party cell.

The Puritan, Walzer argues, was not an economic man—he disliked and despised "projectors"—but rather a political activist.[46] And his political imagery was drawn not from Catholic and Anglican organicism but from the world of coercion and sovereignty. His concern was primarily with control rather than with harmony. His object was to overcome "social instability and all its moral and intellectual concomitants."[47] The rational organization of power is the central theme of Puritanism, as it was of the writings of Machiavelli, the fifteenth-century theorist of "reason of state" and the creator of the modern name for political society, "*lo stato*." Walzer gives as other exemplars the "Jacobin man of

---

[44] Michael Walzer, "Puritanism as a Revolutionary Ideology," in Judith Shklar, ed., *Political Theory and Ideology* (New York: Macmillan, 1966), pp. 51, 58. For a more extended development of this thesis, see Michael Walzer, *The Revolution of the Saints* (New York: Atheneum, 1969).

[45] Walzer, *Revolution of the Saints,* p. 13.

[46] Walzer, "Puritanism as a Revolutionary Ideology," p. 59.

[47] *Ibid.,* pp. 60–61.

virtue become an *active citizen,* and the hardened . . . Bolshevik, first a *professional* revolutionary and then, in Lenin's words, a 'leader,' 'manager,' and 'controller.' " [48] In all these cases, as in the more recent experience of the Chinese Cultural Revolution, we find self-conscious organization supplanting the unconscious spontaneity of a traditional organic society which has fallen into ruin. "Organization," writes Franz Schurmann in the prologue to his study of *Ideology and Organization in Communist China,* "in contrast to a social system, needs conscious efforts to survive. . . . Ideology provides the moral cement that not only arouses commitment but creates the cohesive forces which prevent struggle from turning into disintegration. Cohesion through conflict [for the Chinese Communists] . . . has been a life and death matter." [49] This passage could as well be an excerpt from Walzer's book about the English Puritans. We are dealing here with a leading characteristic of modern political belief systems.

7. The Idea of Progress

Another "belief" characteristic of modern political culture is the idea that constant change is good because it makes for the improvement of mankind. The ancient and medieval ideal had been fundamentally static, and the Renaissance looked back to antiquity as the time of greatness. Change for these traditional societies had meant decay. In Liberal culture, however, the cult of improving change has taken the form of the idea of progress, which envisions a peaceful evolutionary process at a variety of levels—technological, educational, social, economic, and political—eventually culminating in an earthly paradise of peace, freedom, social well-being, and material abundance. All the old enemies of man— war, poverty, disease, even death itself—are eventually conquered by "progress." Here is an early statement of the idea by the Marquis de Condorcet, who died on the guillotine of the French Revolution, but remained optimistic to the end:

> No bounds have been fixed to the improvement of the human faculties; . . . the perfectibility of man is absolutely indefinite; . . . the progress of this perfectibility, henceforth above the control of every power that would impede it, has no other limit than the duration of the globe upon which nature has placed us. . . .
> [We may eventually arrive at] the moment in which the sun will observe in its course free nations only, acknowledging no other master

[48] *Ibid.,* p. 61.

[49] Franz Schurmann, *Ideology and Organization in Communist China* (Berkeley: University of California Press, 1966).

than their reason; in which tyrants and slaves, priests and their . . . instruments, will no longer exist but in history and upon the stage. . . .

A period must one day arrive when death will be nothing more than the effect either of extraordinary accidents, or of the slow and gradual decay of the vital powers; and that the duration of the middle space, of the interval between the birth of man and his decay, will itself have no assignable limit.[50]

Sometimes the idea of progress is expressed in the crass form of advertising slogans, like "Progress is our most important product." It is measured by annual changes in car design, dress lengths, and hair styles. It is also measured by government economists when they announce the annual growth rate. And the element of faith in it is seen in the assumption that economies are capable of expansion into an indefinite future. (Only very lately has it been suggested that to solve the problems of pollution we may have to cut down on "progress," to expand less rapidly or even to regress. To live at all, we may have to live more poorly. This may indicate the onset of a major crisis of modernity. For the challenge to "progress" has been accompanied by similar challenges to the work ethic.)

The loftier side of the idea of progress appears in the Liberal dream of gradual moral improvement, the victory of John Stuart Mill's "higher pleasures" over purely appetitive delights. With this goes the hope for a society in which every group and every individual has been raised to a dignified level of material life and to a status of equal respect and freedom. Sharp inequalities will have been done away and the world will be at peace. Like the ill-fated League of Nations, the United Nations with its Universal Declaration of the Rights of Man and of the Citizen is an institution which carries the Liberal dream of a happy world order.

While it appears in some ways to be a secularized version of the Christian Kingdom of Heaven, the Liberal dream of Progress does not envisage a final static condition of achieved perfection. It sees rather a perpetual process of change and improvement which remains forever open-ended. The search for new values through "experiments in living," as recommended by John Stuart Mill, continues indefinitely.

It is the idea of progress that expresses the dominant optimistic attitudes of Liberal culture. These were measured recently in an experiment with school children sponsored by UNESCO. The researchers told an unfinished story about a sum of money lost in a classroom. The ex-

---

[50] Marquis de Condorcet, *Outline of an Historical View of the Progress of the Human Mind* (1795), in John Hallowell, *Main Currents in Modern Political Thought* (New York: Holt, Rinehart & Winston, 1950), pp. 132–34. See also J. B. Bury, *The Idea of Progress* (New York: Dover Publications, 1932).

periment was conducted among ten thousand fifth graders in eleven different countries. The children were asked to supply their own ending to a story about money collected for the purchase of art paper which disappeared from the drawer of a teacher's desk during a mathematics exercise. The sample of American children, 1,700 strong, reported that the money had not been stolen, but only lost. It would be found and the children in the class would deal truthfully with the teacher. The teacher would believe the children and no one would be punished. The children from Europe—where Liberalism has had a more spotty and sporadic acceptance than in America, where it has formed the national culture from the beginning—supplied a very different ending to the story. They maintained that the money had been stolen and would not be returned, that the children would lie, that their teacher would not believe them, and that assuredly someone would be punished.[51]

In Communist political culture the counterpart of the Liberal idea of progress is the doctrine of dialectical development. It does not, like Liberalism, envisage peaceful and harmonious change, but rather contradictions and sharp conflict, with much pain and suffering instead of increasing happiness up to a final revolutionary break with the capitalist form of social and economic order. After that the picture of utopia is almost exactly like the Liberal—the harmonious development of all their talents by autonomous individuals in a context of material abundance and peace. Change and development continue indefinitely, as in the Liberal dream. Fascism too enshrines change as the order of the day, though for the fascist it is a process of ceaseless struggle and conflict from which supermen emerge as ruthless exploiters of the weaker types. Inequality is the central value, and the doctrine has no place for equality or for a generalized freedom. Only the conqueror is free.

8. Contract, Constitutionalism, and Control: Liberal Concepts of Authority

Modern political culture in the West has emphasized contract and constitutionalism as principles of rational political control, a pluralist model of power. These have seemed the most fitting instruments for the accomplishment of the new purposes of society, which emphasize spiritual, intellectual, and, above all, economic freedom and abundance.

Having reduced the functions of government to the enforcement of contracts and to the protection of life and property, Liberalism sought

---

[51] This experiment was reported by Karl Deutsch in a symposium, "A Design for Political Science," *Annals of the American Academy of Political and Social Science,* Monograph 6 (December 1966), p. 226.

to keep government within these confines by a number of legal limitations on the exercise of sovereign power. Primary has been the myth that government originates in a limited contract of a free citizenry to establish a public authority for specific purposes. The authority so established stands in the relationship of an agent to his principal, whose power is a trust which can be revoked by the principal for cause. Authority is no longer dual, but resides solely in the community of contracting individuals.

A number of legal devices are created for empowering, staffing, and recalling the governmental trustee. Popular election and limited terms of office became typical Liberal institutions to accomplish these purposes. Special practices developed to suit local circumstances. In England, where centralized authority resided in a parliament controlled by the middle classes, the solution was to make the parliament supreme over the traditional monarch and vest its direction in a responsible cabinet of ministers. In the United States, the influence of the new mechanistic world view can be seen in the elaborate system of separated and divided, checked and balanced powers of the federal system and the tripartite organization of authority in the national government, with numerous access points for grass-roots interest organizations. The system of constitutional limitation was in each instance reinforced by the medieval memory of limited government, based as it was on a different conception of the source of authority and incorporated in quite a different institutional complex.

To give substance and vigor to the formal institutions of community control, Liberal political culture also developed an elaborate theory of individual right to freedom and equality, based on the concept of a state of nature prior to the establishment of the social contract and the delegation of political authority. This might be stated concretely as a Bill of Rights promulgated by Act of Parliament, like the British Bill of 1689. Or it might be conceived as an appendix to the original contract of government, as in the first ten amendments to the Federal Constitution of the United States of America. Or, as in the practice of the French, it might take the form of a philosophical Declaration of the Rights of Man and of the Citizen. In each case the normative statement drew its force from the new world view we described on an earlier page—the picture of ultimate reality as a cluster of individual and interchangeable (equal) points of matter in motion.

The first crisis of the Liberal order came when a class different from the self-reliant bourgeoisie who instituted it became numerous, self-conscious, and disenchanted with the system of economic freedom the middle class had created, and with their arbitrary limitation of the franchise to men of property. This problem was in a sense built into the Liberal order, for the normative principles of this order were essentially not class principles, but universal standards applicable to man as man. Even Locke had seen the basis of property not in some external holding, but in the body of the individual. Manipulated for class interest, the demand arose that these principles be given their logical extension. The property-less workers could effect a revolution of the middle-class order, there-fore, within the established principles, not against them, and particularly the extension of the franchise to embrace new social groups. This was at least a possibility in places where those principles had already put down strong roots. But under some circumstances important modifica-tions of the original doctrine, away from individualist assumptions to-ward group control, would occur. They would imply new conceptions of purpose as well.

9. The Other Side of the Coin: Populist Conceptions of Authority and Purpose

We saw earlier that in medieval political culture there was not a single, clear governing principle of authority but rather a duality of principles—royal absolutism and constitutionalism—which were to a large degree an-tagonistic. The duality has carried over into modern political culture as well. For over against the individualist concepts of contract and limited government that we have been describing there is set the idea of popu-lar sovereignty, which implies the supremacy of the group and its un-limited authority. Psychologically and historically we can see in populist conceptions of authority a successor to the medieval idea of the sover-eignty of God. When for whatever reasons the authority of the contracting individual is weakened in modern political culture, those who have come to mistrust him (and themselves as individuals) set up the rival authority of "the People." Often done in an attitude of mystical fervor, this repre-sents the emotional and romantic side of modern politics whereas indi-vidualist contractualism represents its rational aspects. Sometimes the cultures are fused, as in Jeffersonianism, but more often they are pitted against one another. When the opposition occurs it is sharply drawn—pure, unthinking emotionalism against a purely calculating and self-cen-tered rationalism.

The populist or communitarian theme in modern ideology may also be seen as a revival of aspects of the organicism which was a defining feature of traditional political culture. Sometimes it has a pluralist or corporative character, as in British political culture, where the legitimacy of traditional organicism has persisted into modern times. The version of populism which we associate with Jean-Jacques Rousseau is more specifically modern in its monism and egalitarianism.

Populist conceptions of authority are found both in Liberal Democratic and in Collectivist political culture. In Liberal societies they are often in competition with rational individualism, whereas in Collectivist societies they are in absolute ideological control. This is not to say that individualist behavior does not exist in Collectivist states; it simply has no legitimacy there. Policy is made in the name of the *"Volk"* or of the class, and the individual is required at every point to give way to the authority of the group—that is, to those who speak in its name. In the Communist version of totalitarian democracy (for we are talking about democracy in the broadest sense) a promise is held out of a future utopia in which the sovereignty of the class and of all groups will give way to the purest individualism. But this is a far-off time which plays a role analogous to that of the concept of the Heavenly Kingdom in Christian theology.

It should be evident that populist conceptions of authority imply populist conceptions of purpose quite different from those individual-oriented purposes we have discussed above. When the authority of the "People" is invoked, it is usually in the name of some kind of egalitarianism, which involves using the authority of the group to reorganize relationships among individuals, either their political power or their property, or both. The values of the group as group, rather than of the individual, become the focus of attention in populist regimes. Policy is framed with reference to the good of the nation or of the authoritative class—the proletariat in Communist ideology. We shall come back to this theme in our discussion of nationalism.

The beginnings of modern egalitarian populism may be seen in the English Leveller, or more especially the True Leveller Movement of the seventeenth-century civil war, which expressed the world view of the poorest strata of English political activism. Both groups, however, were Rationalist rather than Romantic in their outlook, and remained firmly wedded to values of individual liberty, especially of conscience, and to the principle of consent. Voluntarist and authoritarian populism emerges full-blown for the first time only more than a century later during the Jacobin phase of the French Revolution. Its articulate prophet and oracle was Jean-Jacques Rousseau, whose writings predate the revolution itself.[52]

---

[52] For a desription of these movements see Christopher Hill, *Puritanism and Revolution* (New York: Schocken Books, 1964) and *The World Turned Upside Down* (New York: Viking Press, 1972), and Joseph Frank, *The Levellers* (Cambridge, Mass.: Harvard University Press, 1955).

Although Rousseau grounded the origin of society in contract, like Locke, he vested it, once it was in being, with omnipotence. Thus he writes of "the complete alienation by each associate member to the community of *all his rights*," and he tells us that "whosoever refuses to obey the general will shall be constrained to do so by the whole body." [53] A variety of political inferences have been drawn from this way of viewing things, ranging all the way from majoritarian populism in America to "folkish" fascism in Germany and proletarian Communism in Russia, China, and elsewhere. Rousseau says that the social coercion and molding involved in being constrained to obey the general will "is no more than to say that it may be necessary to compel a man to be free—freedom being that condition which, by giving each citizen to his country, guarantees him from all personal dependence and is the foundation upon which the whole political machine rests, and supplies the power which works it." [54] We are reminded of totalitarian procedures of brainwashing and "self-criticism" to fashion the perfectly socialized patriot.

Populism is not the only concomitant of the new atomism that has totalitarian implications. Along with the idea of reality as meaningless points of matter goes the idea of the scientist as the observer who understands the natural laws of their motion and as the manipulator who uses those laws to control these motions. "Scientific" nature is manipulable, so that the correlate of scientific undersanding is power. Because the world is now conceived in purely naturalistic categories, no inherent principles of right furnish parameters to the machinations of the man in power. There arises from the mechanical hypothesis applied to society "the distinction between the creative power of the planner and the mass of atomistic individuals to be planned. Hitler's distinction between the master minds and the servile masses is only the logical conclusion of this fundamental attitude." [55] In the private (elite) doctrine of both Nazism and Communism we shall find the principle of scientific manipulation written very large. The spirit is to be found in Liberal capitalism as well, where the entrepreneur in applying scientific method to industry "thought of his workpeople as 'factors of production' to be coordinated efficiently and scientifically along with the other material factors of production." [56] In both Communist totalitarian and Liberal capitalist culture the elitist manipulatory theme would quickly evoke a democratic and humanistic response.

[53] Jean-Jacques Rousseau, *The Social Contract,* trans. Gerald Hopkins, Book I, Chaps. 6 and 7, in Ernest Barker, ed., *Social Contract,* (London: Oxford University Press, 1947), pp. 256, 261.
[54] *Ibid.*, pp. 261–62.
[55] Lindsay, *op. cit.*, p. 80.
[56] *Ibid.*

10. A New Focus of Political Unity: The Nation

What constitutes a nation has been much debated by students of the subject—whether it is common language, a common history, common ideals, or something else. Hans Kohn has reduced the forming element to a single criterion—"a living and active corporate will. Nationality is formed by the decision to form a nationality." [57] The specifically modern character of this idea, which fits all cases of the phenomenon, is evident. With God withdrawn from the scene, and with the disappearance along with Him of a divine plan for all things, the world has to be built up again from the autonomous individual. Only the will of the individual, in conjunction with those of his fellows, can be authoritative for forming political units or anything else in the social world.

An Early Liberal Formulation of "Nation."   The idea of the "nation" did not spring immediately into being with the decay of the universal order of Christian Europe. For a while it was the dynasty, imposing its rule by war and marriage and cementing it with uniform religious practices, that was the determinant of political unity. But with the decline of Divine Right, which brought forward the community itself as the source of authority, a new way had to be found to identify that community. This need produced "the nation." An early statement of the national ideal is found in the work of Henry St. John, Viscount Bolingbroke, a Tory leader in the Age of Queen Anne, a period of consolidation following the domestic upheavals of the seventeenth century. His book, *The Idea of a Patriot King* (1738), abandons the old Tory ideal of Divine Right and represents the king as the leader of a self-conscious nation. A skeptic rather than a believing Christian, Bolingbroke retains some of the old religious symbolism, but it is deistic rather than theistic in character.

God, wrote Bolingbroke, has created the various nationalities of mankind and marked them off from one another by difference of geography, climate, language, character, and government. For their direction He has legislated two great natural laws, the "Universal Law of Reason" and a particular law for each state in keeping with its special and unique characteristics. The one safeguards the rights of humanity, the other those of nationality. The two are compatible with one another, and both are revealed to man by his reason. Every government is required by nature to further primarily national (rather than dynastic or class) in-

[57] Hans Kohn, *The Idea of Nationalism; A Study in Its Origins and Background* (New York: Macmillan, 1961), p. 15.

terests, but the true national interest requires a foreign policy of peace and respect for the rights of others.

Every nationality, according to Bolingbroke, has its special genius. The British genius lies in its constitutional order, with its limited monarchy, national church, and privileged nobility. Its leader is a patriot king who aids the moneyed classes with encouragement to trade and commerce and who stimulates in the people a spirit of national patriotism which will make them spurn all factions and place national honor first as the highest of values.[58]

The nationalist ideal of Bolingbroke's book had no revolutionary impact, for the British nation he described had already come into being. The glory of the nation had replaced the glory of a charismatic king as its unifying value.

Nationalism and Revolution. In France, where dynasticism lasted a hundred years longer, the nation came suddenly into its own with the revolution that swept away the dynasty and the social order associated with it. Its first symbolic recognition was by the leaders of the Third Estate, assembled by the King to attend the Estates General at Versailles. Refusing to accept any longer the old royal system of representation by estates, a class order based on the distinction between the clergy, the nobility, and the commons of the realm, they called for one National Assembly, representative of the whole community of culture, language, and customs—of Frenchmen as equal members of a national community.

In the slogans of the French Revolution, alongside "Liberty" and "Equality" to designate the conceptions of authority of the new society, was placed "Fraternity"—the symbol of national brotherhood as the new principle of unity. The Declaration of the Rights of Man issued by the revolutionary National Assembly announced that "the source of all sovereignty is essentially in the nation; no body, no individual can exercise authority that does not proceed from it in plain terms." In November 1789 a newly created National Guard took an oath to defend the Fatherland, and in it Frenchmen were called brothers. During the Feast of Federation of July 14, 1790, an oath of national brotherhood was sworn by all participants on altars raised in towns and cities to the Fatherland, bearing inscriptions of the Declaration of the Rights of Man.

The doctrine of national self-determination emerged from the deliberations of the revolutionary government and was first applied by the people of Avignon (a Papal enclave within France), who declared for union with France in a plebiscite of 1791 in the face of unavailing

[58] Carleton J. H. Hayes, *The Historical Evolution of Modern Nationalism* (New York: Richard R. Smith, Inc., 1931), pp. 17–22.

Papal protests. The act was a marvelously succinct symbol of the transformation of political culture—the passing of theocratic universalism and the birth of secular nationalism.[59]

When the revolutionary government became embroiled with the royal states surrounding it in Europe, French nationalism in rallying the people to its defense rapidly became a Collectivist ideology—the first example of a kind of political culture which has become one typical form of modernism. Writing of the Jacobin phase of the revolution, when Robespierre and the Committee of Public Safety governed France with authoritarian terror, Carleton Hayes says:

> "The people" has become "the nation", a mystical entity, an absolute sovereign, a Moloch not only of classes but of individuals. It catechizes its own citizens, and by force it seeks to catechize the citizens of other nations. It conscripts youth for war or for schools and abrogates the historic rights of the father and the family. It can seize everything and destroy anything, for above it is no law. The will of the nation is God. It feels itself immense and irresistible. It has horrors of divisions, schisms, minorities. It labors for unity, uniformity, concentration. It proudly proclaims personal liberty and boldly abridges particular liberties which appear to be at variance with national interests. Its vaunted liberty . . . is for the national state. . . . The nation may do whatever it will; the individual may do only what the national state determines.[60]

Hayes might as well have been writing about Nazi Germany in the 1930s or about the Chinese Cultural Revolution carried out under the banner of militant Communism in the 1960s.

In contrast with the peaceful nationalism of the established nation invoked by Bolingbroke, the nation being forged by revolution became the champion of an imperialist foreign policy. From a defensive war to save the revolution emerged the Jacobin and Napoleonic crusade to spread the ideals of the revolution by conquest abroad. "Every people," read a declaration of 1792, "who, refusing liberty and equality or renouncing them, may wish to maintain, recall, treat with the prince and privileged classes" was to be deemed an enemy. The forging of the German and Italian nations would in a similar but even more destructive way disrupt the peace and order of Europe in the twentieth century.

It was to be primarily as a national ideal that the Liberal concepts of the French Revolution were carried from Western to Central, Eastern, and Southern Europe, and thence into the Middle and Far East. During the last part of the nineteenth century it was nationalism building on the principle of language and ethnic unity that undermined the dynastic Empire of the Habsburgs in Central and Southern Europe,

[59] See *ibid.*, pp. 35–38.
[60] *Ibid.*, p. 69.

giving birth finally in 1918 to Poland, Czechoslovakia, Hungary, and Yugoslavia. Spreading to the Ottoman Empire, it spawned there another cluster of new nations and transformed the Imperial center itself into the nation-state of Turkey. From here the "nation" moved south and east across the globe. In China the Communist nationalism of Mao Tse-tung is a successor of the Liberal Nationalism of Sun Yat-sen and Chiang Kai-shek, who were the inheritors, even in an organizational sense, of the Liberal Nationalism of Giuseppi Mazzini, an ideological father of modern Italy. In the Third World we study the progress of the "nation" today under the rubrics of nation-building and political development.

·Thus, whether the sense of unity is related to similarity in language, common territory, a common history, ethnic community, common religion, or cultural community of some other sort, the "nation" has become the principle of political unity of the modern age, the mortal god of secular culture. As Boyd Shafer has put it, nationalism

> is that sentiment unifying a group of people who have a real or imagined common historical experience and a common aspiration to live together as a separate group in the future. This unifying sentiment expresses itself in loyalty to the nation-state whatever the government, in love of native land however little known, in pride in common culture and economic and social institutions though these may not be understood, in preference for fellow nationals in contrast to disregard for members of other groups, and in zeal not only for group security but for glory and expansion.[61]

Whether a political culture is Liberal, Conservative, Fascist, or Communist, it is always national. Though a parochial sentiment, nationalism is the most universally shared aspect of modern political culture. We have seen that the form of nationalism and its intensity vary greatly, depending on a variety of circumstances. We shall trace out the variety further as we proceed with our discussion of particular political cultures.

11. Liberalism and Liberal Political Culture Today

In describing the modern revolution in its Western Europeon beginnings, we have described many of the central ideas and ideals of Liberal political culture in its early or Classical phase. These concepts were among the first distinctively modern principles of political order to develop from the medieval matrix, and we who inhabit a Liberal culture today consider them constitutive of modernity in its healthy or normal form.

While referring to these ideas—freedom of religion, freedom of ex-

---

[61] Boyd Shafer, *Nationalism: Myth and Reality* (New York: Harcourt, Brace & Co., 1955), p. 10.

pression, private property, constitutional limitations on the exercise of power—as "Liberal," we have refrained from speaking of them as constituting the doctrine of Liberalism, except prospectively. For they did not appear all at once as a full-blown and compact doctrine called "Liberalism," but rather over a long period of time as individual ideals which only much later were understood as aspects of a single cultural development.[62] Moreover, its development has been singularly dynamic and multiform. As a consequence, histories of "Liberalism" use varying emphases in describing its characteristic marks, and after reading three or four different accounts of the phenomenon one is tempted to ask, "Will the real Liberalism please stand up?" Harry K. Girvetz, in a leading study, describes Classical Liberalism as a weapon of the rising capitalist class which in the seventeenth to nineteenth centuries transformed an agrarian and handicrafts culture into an urban and mechanized one. Alternatively, he tells us that the doctrine can be read as a "set of generalizations about man and society for which universal validity is claimed." [63] Under the latter rubric Girvetz emphasizes the individualist, mechanist, and secular "beliefs" which we have stressed in the present account. He also finds economic values central in the Liberal way of thought, as we have, but he describes the constitutionalist political creed as subservient to economic goals in a more radical way than we have.

A very different view of the matter is found in J. Salwyn Schapiro's *Liberalism and the Challenge of Fascism*. While noting that the expression "Liberalism" came into use only in the nineteenth century, Schapiro tells us that the attitude of mind underlying it is as old as Socrates—"a belief in the power of reason to regulate the conduct of life . . . critical views of dogmatic beliefs, . . . an experimental attitude towards problems in government and society." [64] His stress is thus on the universality of its ideals. The characteristic form of the ideals of "Liberalism" he sees as the product of certain social conditions—emerging capitalism, the sovereign state, and secular culture. All of these things had in them "the germinating principle of liberalism." [65] Unlike Girvetz, Schapiro does not refer to the doctrine as a class weapon, though he does take note of its

[62] The term "Liberal" originated as the name of a Spanish political party, the *Liberales,* nineteenth-century advocates of constitutional government. "Later 'liberal' was taken over in other countries to designate a government, a party, a policy, or opinion that favored freedom as opposed to authoritarianism." J. Salwyn Schapiro, *Liberalism: Its Meaning and History* (Princeton: D. Van Nostrand Co., Inc., 1958), p. 9.

[63] Girvetz, *op. cit.,* p. 23.

[64] J. Salwyn Schapiro, *Liberalism and the Challenge of Fascism* (New York: McGraw-Hill, 1949), p. 1. Girvetz describes the early Liberal mind as favoring deductive argument and as very dogmatic in its attitudes.

[65] *Ibid.,* p. 2.

bourgeois origins. And he does not, like Girvetz, make economic concepts central.

Girvetz drew his materials largely from English intellectual development, where Schapiro's sources are largely French—the ideas of the *philosophes* of the eighteenth-century Enlightenment. From their writings he distills a doctrine which highlights the fundamental goodness of man (his sociability?), faith in the good will of the average man as long as he is secure, the idea that evil is a product of inept social order rather than of human nature, belief in secularism, and confidence in the power of reason to solve all problems standing in the way of realizing "the rights of the citizen or of the people." [66] Girvetz's emphasis, by contrast, was on egoism and on the recalcitrance of natural man, the need to compel him by institutional constraint and to trade on enlightened interest rather than natural sociability to make society work. The idea of progress, which we have underlined in our own account, is not mentioned by Girvetz but is given a prominent place in the creed by Schapiro. Neither author mentions nationalism, and Schapiro's way of describing the Liberal conception of individual dignity hardly leaves room for the national ideal. "The autonomous individual," he writes, "would be free to roam from one occupation to another, from one opinion to another, from one faith to another, from one country to another, from one allegiance to another, in his search to find full scope for his talents and for his ambitions." [67] Cosmopolitanism of this kind was, indeed, a part of the creed of *philosophes* like Voltaire, but it had little general appeal and no impact on the shape of the Liberal revolution as it unfolded in France and elsewhere.

In describing the dynamic development of Liberalism, Schapiro calls it an expanding principle, which has grown out from a conception of purely legal right to political and economic freedoms of a comprehensive character. "The bourgeois liberals," he writes, "aimed to advance chiefly the interests of the middle class. Yet in the process of doing so, they unwittingly and inevitably created political machinery that served wider interests." They "proclaimed a political and social philosophy which in the end was to be turned against the very class whose interests they championed." [68] Liberalism, he concludes, has today been identified with "working-class interests, with state intervention, . . . with an emerging socialist economy." [69]

Girvetz's account of the transformation of Liberalism describes it as a less continuous—that is, in terms of the continuity of ideas—and as a

[66] *Ibid.*, p. 5.
[67] *Ibid.*, p. 9.
[68] *Ibid.*, p. 397.
[69] *Ibid.*, pp. 402–3.

more conflict-ridden process. He finds the ideas and attitudes which underly the present version of Liberalism (Welfarism) to be more amorphous and less coherent than those of the Classical form, and also less vigorous. Correspondingly, he finds modern Liberals less self-assured, less sure of what it is they are about. In striking contrast with the optimistic language of culmination and fulfillment used by Schapiro to describe the present state of Liberalism, Girvetz calls revised Liberalism a fluid and elusive doctrine, lacking towering ideologues like Locke and Adam Smith, who are regarded with suspicion by the Right and with contempt by the Left. He comes close to describing modern Liberals as an "Establishment" in crisis, a theme we shall develop later.[70]

The description of contemporary Liberalism poses fewer problems than the description of its classical antecedent because it is closer at hand and more homogeneous in its features, wherever it is found. The contemporary Liberal who presides over the welfare state has a world view, a set of "beliefs" considerably different from those of the Classical Liberal, though he remains a secularist like his Classical predecessor.[71] He rejects hedonism and egoism and favors the findings of recent psychological and anthropological studies which indicate that man is group-oriented. The restoration of the idea of man as a social animal is actually found much earlier in the literature of democratic culture, and specifically in the work of Rousseau, as we have seen. Neo-Liberalism borrows here from the populist tradition, with which it shares an antipathy to hedonist individualism. Like populism, its stress is on equality and community. But unlike pure populism, it also makes the individual a central concern. It represents a fusion and synthesis of constitutionalism and populism in modern Liberal Democratic political culture.

The modern Liberal, relying on the works of John Dewey and Thorstein Veblen, also rejects the earlier view of human nature as basically passive in favor of a concept of activity as the manifestation of the life process. Again, the starting point can be found in Rousseau, who made Will the central concept of his theory of society.

The contemporary Liberal also repudiates the ultra-rationalism of the Classical doctrine and its accompanying doctrine of the harmony of interests. Free enterprise and the nightwatchman state did not make for the greater happiness of all but rather for the exploitation of the many by the few and for class warfare. The Classical Liberal had given too much attention to rational abstraction and not enough to historical behavior in an institutional context. Classical Liberalism is no longer adequate for the contemporary Liberal because it is incapable of explaining why monopoly and oligopoly rather than free competition devel-

[70] Girvetz, *op. cit.*, (2nd ed.) pp. 153–54.
[71] This section follows Girvetz closely; see *ibid.*, pp. 157ff.

oped from original capitalism. It also overestimated the mobility of labor, and its categories were unable to account for the devastating reality of trade cycles. Neo-classical Liberals (Conservatives) treat these things as exceptional and accidental events, the result of governmental interference with the natural laws of trade to which they would give full sway. But the new Liberal does not believe them; he thinks the assumptions must be revised. He nevertheless refuses to reject the basic institutional pattern of the market economy and prefers to make adjustments within this framework, because of the great productivity the system has evinced. His panacea for the faults of the original system is large-scale government intervention to ensure adequate purchasing power for low-income groups, in the form of compensatory spending and welfare programs of a variety of kinds. It also includes extensive government regulation to ensure that the vast economic power in private hands is used for the general welfare. The basic institution of private property, however, is retained.

The new Liberal put less emphasis on property rights than did the Classical Liberal. He insists that property must justify itself functionally —another restoration of the organicist view characteristic of traditional order. He emphasizes human rights over property rights and supports programs of social security designed to alleviate the economic hazards of illness, accident, and old age. He champions the right of every man to employment commensurate with his abilities and insists on the right to equal education for all.

In his outlook on governmental institutions, the new Liberal puts much less reliance on the formal institutions of government, emphasizing rather the importance of underlying political groups—parties and interest groups, especially labor unions and consumer organizations—as instruments for making government with increased power responsive to popular needs. The new Liberal sees the programs of the positive state as a primary instrument for giving substance to the idea of freedom for the many in a democratic society.

Despite these important revisions in the doctrine, however, what we call Liberalism today still has much in common with the original doctrine. Though differently expressed, both make the individual and his dignity a central concern. Although he restores the older traditional conception of man as a social animal, the new Liberal does not swallow the individual up in society but sees society as existing only for the sake of the individual man. He sees the polarity of individual and group as a false juxtaposition indeed, and he accepts the idea of social intervention for the individual good, within a democratic framework. He views "democracy [as] a fraternity in which *all* men are free. In it there is no room for an economic any more than for a political monopoly of power. In this sense, contemporary liberalism is simply an extension and completion of the historical liberalism of the 18th and 19th centuries, providing for the first time for the majority of humanity the freedom heretofore reserved for the few." [72]

12. From General to Particular

To this point we have described in abstract and generalized terms the emergence of modern political culture from the traditional culture of medieval western Europe. We have emphasized in this description the growth of the Liberal form of modernity, again in generalized form. It is now time to move to a more focused level of discussion, to the description of particular modern political cultures, a level of analysis to which we shall hold from here to the end of the book.

The next several chapters we shall devote to an analysis of the various aspects of liberal political culture in the United States. The emphasis is justified for a variety of reasons. For one thing, this book is written primarily for American students, who have a special need to understand their own political culture. At the theoretical level, we point out that Liberalism in America had the most unimpeded, most "natural" development it has experienced anywhere in the world. For it was built up there in a wilderness, a context as close to the Lockean "state of nature" as we can imagine, and according to typically Lockean rubrics— the rubrics of "contract." No earlier culture had to be accommodated before Liberal development could be undertaken. The Indians were simply brushed aside. The United States furnishes in a very real sense the archetype of the Liberal experience, and reveals the characteristic features, both strong and weak, of that experience in a graphic way.

Bibliography

ALMOND, GABRIEL A., and SIDNEY VERBA, *The Civic Culture: Political Attitudes and Democracy in Five Nations.* Princeton: Princeton University Press, 1963.

BECKER, CARL L., *The Heavenly City of the Eighteenth-Century Philosophers.* New Haven: Yale University Press, 1932.

BULLOCK, ALAN, and MAURICE SHOCK, eds., *The Liberal Tradition: From Fox to Keynes.* New York: New York University Press, 1957.

CHERRY, GEORGE L., *Early English Liberalism: Its Emergence through Parliamentary Action.* New York: Bookman Associates, 1962.

GIRVETZ, HARRY K., *The Evolution of Liberalism*, rev. ed. New York: Collier Books, 1963.

[72] *Ibid.,* p. 387.

GRIMES, ALAN P., "The Pragmatic Course of Liberalism," *Western Political Quarterly*, 9(3), September 1956: 633–40.

LASKI, HAROLD J., *The Rise of Liberalism: The Philosophy of a Business Civilization*. New York: Harper & Row, 1936.

MINOGUE, KENNETH R., *The Liberal Mind*. London: Methuen, 1963.

VON MISES, LUDWIG, *The Free and Prosperous Commonwealth: An Exposition of the Ideas of Classical Liberalism*, trans. Ralph Raico. Princeton: Van Nostrand, 1962.

ORTON, WILLIAM A., *The Liberal Tradition: A Study of the Social and Spiritual Conditions of Freedom*. New Haven: Yale University Press, 1945.

DE RUGGIERO, GUIDO, *The History of European Liberalism*, trans. R. A. Collingwood. Boston: Beacon Press, 1964.

SCHAPIRO, J. SALWYN, *Liberalism and the Challenge of Fascism: Social Forces in England and France, 1815–1870*. New York: McGraw-Hill, 1949.

WATKINS, FREDERICK, *The Political Tradition of the West*. Cambridge, Mass.: Harvard University Press, 1948.

3

Established Liberalism:

Consensual America

The "natural" quality of American modernization was recognized early in the nineteenth century by the French historian Alexis de Tocqueville. He wrote that America had reaped "the fruits of the democratic revolution . . . without having had the revolution itself," and he said that he had chosen to study "the nation . . . in which its development has been the most peaceful and the most complete, in order to discover its natural consequences and to find out, if possible, the means of rendering it profitable to mankind." [1] Tocqueville was working on the assumption that a careful analysis of the purest, undiluted form of democratic culture would reveal all the hidden tendencies and logical potentialities of the new way. This knowledge could be of great use to political leaders everywhere, faced as they were with the need to cope with the problem of modernization in the form of democratization, a process which Tocqueville regarded as inexorable, as a "providential fact. It has all the chief characteristics of such a fact: it is universal, it is lasting,

---

[1] Alexis de Tocqueville, *Democracy in America*, trans. Henry Reeve, (New York: Alfred A. Knopf, 1951), I, 1, 14. For a contrasting view see Michael Kammen, *People of Paradox: An Inquiry Concerning the Origins of American Civilization* (New York: Alfred A. Knopf, 1972), p. 7. Kammen writes: "My own view is that the Colonial period had many medieval characteristics, both figurative and literal, and hence much to be discarded and diffused before emerging into the bright glare of modernity."

it constantly eludes all human interference, and all events as well as all men contribute to its progress." [2]

1. The American Liberal Tradition

A Spirit of Religion and a Spirit of Liberty.   What did Tocqueville see as the leading aspects of the dynamic of democratic modernization as he observed it working in the United States in the 1830s? Two mutually supportive cultural factors were determining: a spirit of religion and a spirit of liberty. The first yields a fixed world of moral principles in which "everything is classified, systematized, foreseen, and decided beforehand." The second yields an uncertain and malleable world in which "everything is agitated, disputed, and uncertain," an innovative spirit.

Given the pluralism of American religion, it is at first glance difficult to see how Tocqueville could describe the spiritual world of the United States as one of fixed and certain principles. But he is here speaking of ethical principles, and there was in this area a great deal of practical agreement, a set of common moral habits, shared by the Protestant sects that dominated the culture. Given the Lockean separation of church and state that prevailed, disagreement on fine points of theological dogma lay beyond the public world of practical action and ethical agreement. With basic moral questions settled in a context of political freedom, experimental change could go forward without provoking the profound cleavages found in clerical-anticlerical Europe. The separation of religion and freedom in this context strengthened each of them. Tocqueville summed the matter up as follows:

> Religion perceives that civil liberty affords a noble exercise to the faculties of man and that the political world is a field prepared by the Creator for the efforts of the mind. Free and powerful in its own sphere, satisfied with the place reserved for it, religion never more surely establishes its empire than when it reigns in the hearts of men unsupported by aught besides its native strength.
>
> Liberty regards religion as its companion in all its battles and its triumphs, as the cradle of its infancy and the divine source of its claims. It considers religion the safeguard of morality, and morality as the best security of law and the surest pledge of the duration of freedom.[3]

In Tocqueville's view, then, it was not the secularizing aspects of democracy that were decisive for the American Liberal experience, but rather the separation of religion from the sphere of secular politics,

[2] *Ibid.*, p. 6.
[3] *Ibid.*, p. 44.

against the background of ethical agreement. Here, in effect, is Tocqueville's explanation of the absence of forensic ideology, of the "end of ideology" and the beginnings of pragmatic politics in the United States. It was also to be a politics of modernization and development—political, economic, social:

> Political principles, laws, and human institutions seem malleable, capable of being shaped and combined at will. As they go forward, the barriers which imprisoned society and behind which they were born are lowered; old opinions, which for centuries had been controlling the world, vanish; a course almost without limits, a field without horizon, is revealed: the human spirit rushes forward and traverses them in every direction. But having reached the limits of the political world, the human spirit stops of itself; in fear it relinquishes the need of exploration, it even abstains from lifting the veil of the sanctuary; it bows with respect before truths which it accepts without discussion.[4]

As a mark of basic agreement, of the nonideological character of American political culture, Tocqueville pointed to the absence of "great parties" committed, in the European style, to ideological programs of abstract principle.[5]

Popular Sovereignty and Utilitarianism.   In addition to describing American culture at the attitudinal level, Tocqueville also provides an account of the values—the conceptions of authority and purpose—that accompanied the attitudes that defined the fundamental configuration of the culture. He found the principle of popular sovereignty to be absolute among Americans. Combined with it he also found a strongly utilitarian spirit. The American, he writes, "acknowledges the utility of an association with his fellow men and he knows that no such association can exist without a regulating force." [6] Established on a basis of equality, popular sovereignty in this utilitarian context produced something very much like Lerner's "empathic" modern man. The individual opened up to society, and in a spirit of enlightened interest identified its weal with his own, and developed a spirit of national patriotism.[7] If the natural tendency of the privatization of religion and the destruction of hierarchical authority was an atomizing individualism, this was offset by the necessities of effective action within a democratc framework. Democratic institutions "remind every citizen in a thousand ways that he lives in society. They every instant impress upon his mind the notion that it is the duty as well as the interest of men to make themselves useful

---

[4] *Ibid.*, p. 43.
[5] *Ibid.*, pp. 175–76.
[6] *Ibid.*, p. 64.
[7] *Ibid.*, I: 243, 244; II: 121–22. See also Daniel Lerner, *The Passing of Traditional Society* (New York: The Free Press, 1958).

to their fellow creatures." [8] The public spirit necessary to a working democracy was the result. The good American was both an individualist and a good citizen.

Tocqueville says little about American conceptions of purpose. Aside from the general principle of equality, which was not interpreted by Americans in a leveling spirit, but rather in a spirit which "incites men to wish all to be powerful and honored," public policy is relegated to the area of pragmatic experimentation, with consequences rather than principle as the test of goodness. Here one presumably would measure in vain for abstract consensus on values to be pursued in the concrete. Perhaps connected with this was the American commitment to majoritarianism as a decision-making rule which Tocqueville found to be very firmly established. "For as the minority may shortly rally the majority to its principles, it is interested in professing that respect for the decrees of the legislator which it may soon have occasion to claim for its own." [9] He also found, however, a certain absolutist quality in American majoritarianism, based on a belief in the superior intelligence of the majority and on a judgment that the interests of the many are to be preferred to those of the few. Here was a bias that could well militate against the individualist and libertarian elements of the culture, that could well provide the seed of a populist tyranny—a danger whose existence Tocqueville readily admitted. We already have noted the logical conflict between Liberal constitutionalism and absolutist populism in our discussion of the development of Liberal culture in Europe, and we compared this conflict with the tension between constitutionalism and absolutism in the medieval world.

Lockean Populism.   In describing the leading aspects of American political culture, Louis Hartz has given similar emphasis to our populism, a characteristic that he identifies with our Lockeanism.[10] He contends in his study of the American Liberal tradition that universal acceptance of Lockeanism in America has produced a stifling and oppressive conformitarianism. "When a liberal community," he writes, "faces military and ideological pressure from without it transforms eccentricity into sin, and the irritating figure of the bourgeois gossip flowers into the frightening figure of an A. Mitchell Palmer or a Senator McCarthy." He equates this with the "tyranny of the majority" described by Tocqueville over a century earlier.[11] Married to this, however, he finds, as did Tocqueville, a

---

[8] Tocqueville, *op. cit.*, II, 105.

[9] *Ibid.*, II, 248.

[10] Hartz, citing George Santayana, uses the expression "Natural Liberalism" to characterize our political culture. Louis Hartz, *The Liberal Tradition in America* (New York: Harcourt, Brace, and World, Inc., 1955), p. 5.

[11] *Ibid.*, p. 56.

strong tradition of individualism and dissent, represented by Brandeis, Roosevelt, and Stevenson. This, too, is a fruit of the Lockean heritage, and it struggles periodically to transcend our conformitarianism.

2. Individualism and Collectivism in American Thought

Ideological Counterpoint.   An overview of American political thought reveals an interesting counterpoint of individualist and populist themes which, variously phrased, have persisted side by side since the beginning of the republic.[12] Individualism appeared first as the individualism of men of property, in good Lockean fashion; this was an individualism which implied in the political realm the denial of all absolute power, no matter where vested—which implied, in short, constitutional government. John Adams was no more ready to trust popular government than to trust royal or aristocratic government. "As to usurping others' rights, they are all three equally guilty when unlimited in power," he wrote. "The majority has eternally and without one exception usurped over the rights of the minority." Both rich and poor would be subject to exploitation in a simple system of democratic government, Adams thought:

> In every society where property exists, there will ever be a struggle between rich and poor. Mixed in one equal assembly, equal laws can never be expected. They will either be made by numbers, to plunder the few who are rich, or by influence, to fleece the many who are poor.[13]

An antidote to the problems of popular government flowing from concentrated power was embodied in the Federalist-written Constitution, with its elaborate mechanisms of balanced powers and mutual checks. Thus James Madison wrote in *The Federalist,* justifying the new instrument of government to the electorate:

> In framing a government which is to be administered by men over men, the great difficulty lies in this: you must first enable the government to control the governed; and in the next place oblige it to control itself. . . .

12 Michael Kammen writes of the "dualistic state of mind" found in the American value system. "We are comfortable believing in both majority rule and minority rights, in both consensus and freedom, federalism and centralization. . . . We have tended to hold contradictory ideas in suspension and ignore the intellectual and behavioral consequences of such 'doublethink.' . . .

"The Congress . . . is a repository of American ambivalence. The founders created a bicameral body so that it would expressly embrace contradictions. The House was dedicated to the proposition of majority rule, and the Senate to the sacredness of minority rights." *Op. cit.,* p. 280. Kammen employs the expression "collective individualism" to epitomize our dualistic political culture, p. 290.

13 John Adams, "A Defense of the American Constitutions," in *The Political Writings of John Adams,* George A. Peek, Jr., ed. (New York: Liberal Arts Press, 1954), 149, 158.

[The] policy of supplying, by opposite and rival interests, the defect of better motives, might be traced through the whole system of human affairs, private as well as public. We see it particularly displayed in all the subordinate distributions of power, where the constant aim is to divide and arrange the several offices in such a manner as that each may be a check on the other—that the private interest of every individual may be a sentinel over the public rights.[14]

One can readily see that a Calvinist pessimism about human motives is an important "belief" underlying the constitutionalist prescription.

Populist absolutism was embodied at the outset of the new regime in the political doctrines of Thomas Jefferson and the policies of the Jeffersonian Republican Party. In 1790 we find Jefferson declaring that "the law of the *majority* is the natural law of every society of men." He had in mind the social majority, for in other places he defines a republic (his word for good government) as "a government by its citizens in mass, controlling directly and personally, according to the rules established by the majority." [15] Every other government he thought more or less republican according to the proportion in it of the "direct action of the citizens." What is more, the right of the majority was to extend to the most fundamental institutions, which the constitutionalists had tried to place as far as possible beyond all popular influence:

We may consider each generation as a distinct nation, with a right, by the will of its majority, to bind themselves, but none to bind the succeeding generations. . . .

The idea that institutions established for the use of the nation cannot be touched nor modified . . . may perhaps be a salutary provision against the abuses of a monarch, but is most absurd against the nation itself.[16]

Here we see the community symbol of the "nation" united with the conception of majority will, providing a conjunction of symbols which in the American experience were to carry the modern version of the old divine absolutism. As Rousseau had said, "The voice of the people is the voice of God." [17]

[14] James Madison, The Federalist (New York: Modern Library, 1937), No. 51, p. 337.

[15] Saul K. Padover, ed., Thomas Jefferson on Democracy (New York: Appleton-Century [Mentor ed.], 1939), p. 15 ("Opinion on location of seat of government," 1790) and p. 40 (letter to J. Taylor, 1816).

[16] Ibid., p. 15 (letter to J. W. Eppes, 1814) and p. 16 (letter to Governor Plumer, 1816).

[17] It is not my intention to deny that Jefferson expressed a regard for minority rights along with his praise of majority rule. (See, e.g., his First Inaugural, 1801, in ibid., p. 34.) My purpose, rather, is to underline certain characteristic emphases. We already have described American political culture as lacking in sharp ideological divisions.

. Behind Jeffersonian majoritarian nationalism we find a more optimistic theory of human nature than that mirrored in the Calvinist mistrust that characterized the Federalists. "I sincerely . . . believe," wrote
Jefferson, "in the general existence of a moral instinct." "I believe . . .
that morality, compassion, generosity, are innate elements of the human
constitution." If these virtues were lacking, he thought it better to supply
them by education than to limit popular powers.[18] Here we have an echo
of Rousseauist optimism, as well as of the opinion of Locke, as understood
by some of his interpreters.

From the time of Adams and Jefferson, the principles of limited
government and popular sovereignty have remained central themes of
the American belief system, variously accented by a variety of different
groups, according to the demands of the situation. At times they have
found a relatively harmonious way of combining with one another, while
at others they have been set in relatively sharp opposition. During the
years in which Jeffersonian Republicanism dominated the political scene,
the Neo-Federalists became rancorous in their condemnation of the common man and of democracy, turning out numerous books filled with dire
prophecies of expropriation and popular tyranny. Events, of course,
eventually proved such fears unfounded, as Jeffersonian democracy
unfolded and gave way to Jacksonianism. Jefferson's Inaugural of 1801,
in which he assured his hearers that "we are all Federalists, we are all
Republicans," had not, however, been adequate assurance. The average
American proved not to be a propertyless proletarian ready to follow the
demagogue, but was himself a man of property (modest though it might
be) intent on improving his lot by laboring diligently with the economic
opportunities presented him by the free market and within the legal
structure provided by the Constitution. He was soon to become, in fact,
Horatio Alger.[19]

Counterpoint Resolved.   As a result of the moderate behavior of the
American democrat, the Whig successors to the traditions of Neo-Federal-
ism abandoned the quasi-ideological battle and embraced the average man
instead of castigating him. They suddenly realized that his aspiration
to become a capitalist made him as likely a supporter of Whig candidates
as the rich man. And if they were to win elections within the emerging
two-party system, the Whigs would have to make an effort to garner
democratic votes. An ideological turning point was the Whigs' employment of democratic ballyhoo, involving log cabins and coonskin caps,

---

[18] *Ibid.,* p. 17 (letter to T. Earle, 1823) and p. 18 (letter to Dupont de
Nemours, 1816).
[19] See Hartz, *op. cit.,* Chaps. III, IV, V, and VIII, and Robert E. Brown,
Charles Beard and the Constitution (Princeton: Princeton University Press, 1956).

in the election of 1840, which brought victory to their presidential standardbearer, William Henry Harrison.

From then until the crisis of the Civil War it was impossible to distinguish Democrat from Whig on first principles, and certainly not in terms of the dichotomy of constitutionalism and popular rule. A testimony to the "end of ideology" in this period is the frequency with which the pragmatic theme of "experimentation," present from the beginning, was employed in the literature of Jacksonianism. In his Farewell Address General Jackson himself described the Constitution as an experiment (as had the authors of *The Federalist*), but he declared that it was "no longer a doubtful experiment." James Fenimore Cooper wrote that "so far, all our experiments have been in favor of democracy," and urged his readers always to take experience as their standard. And Charles Stewart Davies sounded the theme of moderation in reform:

> Be Bold! Be Bold! And everywhere, BE BOLD!
> BE NOT TOO BOLD! [20]

Social Darwinism.   As the struggle over slavery and the nature of the union grew, the national Whig and Democratic parties both disintegrated, and cleavages developed along regional lines. Once again the debate—this time between North and South—involved the principles of absolutism and limited government, with the argument turning on the comparative legal powers of the national and state governments. With the triumph of the North, the problem of principle again settled into the background, with the dominant Republicans sounding the themes of individual right and national authority in an entirely new synthesis. Individualism was now expressed in the Social Darwinist language of Herbert Spencer, an English ideologist who became the darling of American captains of industry, like Andrew Carnegie. But the injunction to compete in the market combined with a eulogy of the nightwatchman state in quasi-biological terms were just as appealing to the little man going west to make his fortune as to the robber barons of eastern business already ensconced in the seats of power. The appeal of the doctrine was heightened by its combination with the collectivist theme, now expressed as "Americanism," an absolutism which turned outward against foreign devils (some of whom, however, were found at home) rather than inward against property and position.[21]

In Social Darwinism the justification of laissez-faire took the form

---

[20] Joseph L. Blau, ed., *Social Theories of Jacksonian Democracy* (New York: Liberal Arts Press, 1954), p. 2 (Farewell Address of Andrew Jackson); p. 59 (James Fenimore Cooper, *Notions of the Americans Picked Up by a Traveling Bachelor*); and p. 52 (Charles Stewart Davies, *An Address*).

[21] Hartz, *op. cit.*, pp. 208–11.

of biological description rather than an invocation of natural laws of personal and property right, as in the original Classical Liberalism. The description concerns the process of natural selection in the social world. Nature, if left to herself (i.e., in the absence of public government), sees to it that the strongest and most fit come to the top. Men are unequal in endowment, and nature wills that the "best"—those of "energy, courage, perseverance, and prudence" predominate.[22]

There is a definite teleological quality to the idea of allowing nature to select her best creatures for rule and status, for the processes of nature are evolutionary, they insure that "progress" occurs when they run untrammeled. They present the able with opportunities to display their capacity. For the Social Darwinists, the definition of liberty was that political condition which permitted unhampered operation of these natural laws. "All institutions are to be tested by the degree to which they guarantee liberty," wrote William Graham Sumner, a Yale Professor who elaborated the Spencerian doctrine.

The principles of Social Darwinism make the proper function of government purely negative: to guarantee the condition of freedom to compete for the good things of life and to enforce contracts. When government extends its role beyond this it is likely to disturb the intention of nature and end up plundering society. Thus individualist values come to be embodied in a program of minimal government. The will of nature that the fittest should survive and that the incompetent perish takes precedence over the intent of any democratic majority to enact social reform or welfare legislation, which would give artificial support to the weak.[23]

It is interesting to note that the metaphysics of Social Darwinism also played a large role in another form of modern ideology, German Nazism. There, however, not the market but more violent forms of struggle furnish the field for the naturally fit to manifest their virtue. The elitist note is much the same, however, as are the emphasis on power and the disregard for suffering and pain. It is perhaps significant that Nazism built on the failure of German liberalism and appealed to the same middling social strata as did the Liberal creed.

A Nationalist Note. The nationalist Americanism which was the collectivist counterpart of Spencerian individualism in some of its formulations also bears a significant resemblance to the nationalist formulas of Nazism. John W. Burgess, a professor of political science at Columbia University, wrote in 1899 about the characteristics of the nation and the

---

[22] William Graham Sumner, *What Social Classes Owe to Each Other*, 1883, cited in David W. Minar, *Ideas and Politics: The American Experience* (Homewood, Ill.: Dorsey Press, 1964), p. 295.

[23] See *ibid.*, pp. 299, 301, 302.

nation-state. Aryan nations he thought to be the most politically talented, and among them "the Teuton really dominates the world by his superior political genius." As such they have a right "to assume the leadership in the establishment and administration of states." [24]

Burgess's theories, however, are an extreme statement and do not represent the norm of American nationalism at the turn of the century. "The Darwinian framework of the nationalist, economic and racist theories of imperialism was not without its receptive base in a land whose development had led it to embrace Herbert Spencer on an unprecedented scale," writes Louis Hartz. "Even the theory of racial supremacy, and this quite apart from Darwinism, found a twisted root in American life." But, he continues:

> The fact remains that all this was basically alien to the national liberal spirit: it had to work within and around it. Mahan believed in competition, but the competition of sublime organic national entities was unfamiliar to the American mind, and moreover it swallowed up the atoms of Horatio Alger's world and jelled them into a solidary whole that they did not like at all. It had been one of Sumner's central passions to assail the Germanic idea of state and nation, to blow up into individualistic bits what Mahan [learning from men like Burgess] wanted to create.
>
> Thus in a liberal community the imperialist drive at the turn of the century was hamstrung by a unique nationalism: national liberalism.[25]

The seeds of hypernationalism were nevertheless there, and the twentieth century would see them sprout up in certain quarters of the American political culture.

Counterpoint Again: Populism.   In the formulations we have been describing, individual freedom lived in problematical combination with a national collectivism. In Populism and Progressivism, however, we have a resurgence of the old opposition of collectivist absolutism (though different indeed from the nationalism we have been discussing) to individualist principles. Populism was a movement of agrarian protest that developed in the 1890s in response to the dynamics of urbanization and industrialization. Its roots are found in Jeffersonian and Jacksonian doctrine. In 1892, the movement achieved organizational form as a political party which developed from a federation of a number of farmer alliances with the Knights of Labor.

In 1896 the spirit and program of Populism were largely absorbed into the Democratic party under the leadership of William Jennings Bryan, though the movement retained a noticeable social influence after it ceased to be a party. It stressed the extension of governmental power

---

[24] *Ibid.*, p. 289, citing John W. Burgess, *Political Science and Comparative Constitutional Law*, 1891.

[25] Hartz, *op. cit.*, pp. 291, 282.

in the interest of the "little man" (e.g., public ownership of railroads and more extensive regulation of utilities) and it was markedly egalitarian. Its theory of political authority placed no limits on the popular will, demanded a monolithic national community, and tended to exalt the demagogic leader. Populists tended to be suspicious men who gravitated naturally toward conspiracy theories of social history. They saw constitutionalism, as embodied in the structures of indirect government and separated powers, as a protection of selfish privilege, "the interests," which were antagonistic to the public good. Populism's appeal was found chiefly in the smaller cities and towns of the south and west.[26]

Progressivism. Progressivism, a more moderate version of Populist doctrine, came to influence policy in both major political parties in the first decades of the twentieth century. Traces of its impact can be found in the "trust-busting" campaign during the administration of Theodore Roosevelt and in such things as the income tax amendment passed during the presidency of Woodrow Wilson. A federal eight-hour law and wages and hours legislation of the states also reveal the Progressive influence. In the realm of political procedure Progressivism called for more direct democracy at the state level—the direct primary, the initiative, referendum, and recall. Like the Populists, Progressive politicians and writers viewed existing political structures as a conspiracy of the privileged against the common man. Writers like Charles Beard and H. Allen Smith were ready to indict the framers of the Constitution as the chief conspirators. At every point, however, their program of reform was gradualist and was to be realized by using the existing rules of the game. Nor were their principles novel, for they were drawn from old democratic tradition.[27]

The New Deal. The opposition of democracy and individualism ebbed once more in the early 1920s, when Classical Liberalism experienced its last great wave of popularity as consensual doctrine. The depression of 1932, however, dealt it a blow from which the pure doctrine of laissez-faire never recovered, though the present authority of the Milton Friedman brand of economic theory is a sign of its resurgent vitality. In the policies of the New Deal we find a new emergence of Populist-Progressivism and a revision of the doctrines of liberalism in a reformist, even organicist direction, with accent on the positive role of government in the establishment of justice and the promotion of the general welfare. This new Progressivism was not propounded, however, as abstract forensic ideology, but as a program of practical amelioration administered in a pragmatic spirit of social experimentation. Its high priest, if it had one, was John Dewey.

[26] Minar, *op. cit.*, pp. 343–49.
[27] See *ibid.*, pp. 349–55.

3. American Political Culture Today

Givenness.   We have described the leading ideals of a political culture marked by broad areas of historical agreement and cloven only by moderate ideological diversity and conflict. An insightful historian, writing in the ideological calm of the 1950s, described its consensual character with the concept of "givenness," a concept that retains significance in the seventies, despite the recent ideological battles of the sixties. " 'Givenness' is the belief that values in America are in some way or other automatically defined," writes Daniel Boorstin. We assume that " 'the American Way of Life' harbors an 'American Way of Thought' which can do us for a political theory, even if we never make it explicit or never are in a position to confront ourselves with it." [28] We do not feel compelled to define and justify principles as did the men who made the English and French Revolutions and founded the institutions of liberal democracy.

Boorstin's concept of "givenness" does not imply the absence of principles so much as their reduction to a latent state. We all believe that we *have* principles. We just do not think and talk a great deal about them. Professor Boorstin tells us that we see our values—our conceptions of purpose and of authority, to use the language of Beer and his colleagues—as "given" in three ways. First, we think of them as a gift from the past, as preformed for us by the Founding Fathers, who did all the theorizing necessary to sustain the polity. Our role is not to invent but continually to test and apply them in the great and continuing "American experiment." The fact that we can point to a clear beginning, a specific moment of founding, when the Pilgrims stepped on to Plymouth Rock in 1620, or when the Constitution was ratified in 1789, makes the preformation idea a realistic one. A classic example of its articulation is Lincoln's Gettysburg Address, which he opens with a confession of faith in what the Fathers established "Four score and seven years ago."

Boorstin notes that even at moments of supreme crisis our sense of "givenness" forestalled the tendency to develop new ideologies. Neither the Civil War nor the depression of the 1930s, two great traumas, produced new theories. The watchword of the New Deal was "Experiment," pragmatism *sans* theory. As Franklin D. Roosevelt said, "The community demands bold, persistent experimentation. It is common sense to take a method and try it: if it fails, admit it frankly and try another." [29]

Second, we think of our values as given by the present, by the "American experience." Our very geography, our landscape, is a bearer

[28] Daniel J. Boorstin, *The Genius of American Politics* (Chicago: University of Chicago Press, 1953), p. 9.
[29] Quoted in *ibid.*, p. 21.

of values. We do not speak about our "true political theory" but about "the *land* of the free," the "American Way of Life." James Stevens describes Paul Bunyan, the giant frontier woodsman, as feeling "amazed beyond words that the simple fact of entering Real America and becoming a Real American could make him feel so exalted, so pure, so noble, so good." [30]

Having experienced no self-conscious ideological revolution, we tend to homogenize the value-giving experience of the present with the values given by the Founders. We stress continuity, even beyond what is actually there. This is the third characteristic aspect of our sense of "givenness." Our present commitment to religious and political liberty we read back into the practice of the Puritans, who were actually quite intolerant people. Our written constitution facilitates this way of thought, for we are constantly discovering meanings in the words of the framers to support quite novel policies and institutions—e.g., our recent reading of the word "equality" in the Fourteenth Amendment. When the Supreme Court overrules its past holdings it quite frequently discovers what it is that the Constitution has meant all along. The American way is not to theorize but to demonstrate the truth of the theory which was given at the beginning as a deposit of faith.

Another writer, the sociologist Daniel Bell, impressed as Boorstin was with the absence of forensic ideology from American life during the 1950s, referred to the phenomenon as "the end of ideology," and wrote a book with that title. Subtitled *On the Exhaustion of Political Ideas in the Fifties*, it implied, however, that this was a special and, indeed, a new reality. Unlike Professor Boorstin, Bell did not read the past as overwhelmingly consensual.[31]

Uncertainty.   Toward the end of the decade, the ideological calm appeared to be over. Storm signals began to appear on the horizon in the form of a growing uncertainty among American leaders about the condition of the national purpose, America's goal values. There was a feeling of loss of direction, an uncertainty about values and purposes, apparently a function of the Cold War with the Soviet Union. Facing an opponent with a ringing doctrine, our leaders began to worry whether we were capable of responding in kind. Could we be similarly articulate and persuasive about what the country stood for and about the direction in which we wished to lead the world?

In a moment of ideological self-consciousness we began to wonder whether all was right with our theory after all. President Eisenhower established a "Commission on National Goals" to work over the problem.

[30] Quoted in *ibid.*, p. 24.
[31] Daniel Bell, *The End of Ideology: On the Exhaustion of Political Ideas in the Fifties*, rev. ed. (New York: The Free Press, 1962).

Its members were selected from among leaders in business, labor, government, philanthropy, the news media, and higher education. The administration of the project was handed over to the American Assembly, a "think tank" affiliated with Columbia University. A number of well-endowed foundations, among them Ford, Rockefeller, Sloan, and U.S. Steel, furnished financial support for the work of the Commission. The mandate given to the Commission was to "set up a series of goals in various areas of national activity." [32] Similar efforts appeared elsewhere in "Establishment" outlets. *Life* sponsored a forum on the value problem to which a variety of "Establishment" intellectuals were invited to contribute, including the poet Archibald MacLeish, Adlai Stevenson, *New York Times* editor James Reston, the journalist Walter Lippmann, evangelist Billy Graham, and others of comparable centrist stripe.

If ideology is, indeed, as Karl Mannheim maintains, a response to threat, an antibody to the virus of revolutionary utopia, these projects were designed to cope with a purely external problem. No revolutionary utopian manifestoes were being declaimed at home, nor were there revolutionary groups afoot at the time. The "New Left" was not yet born, nor was black militancy yet a factor to be reckoned with. The "end of ideology" remained everywhere a fact. There was only a certain spirit of disquiet. "More than anything else," runs the Foreword to a *Life* series on the subject, "the people of America are asking for a clear sense of National Purpose. . . . What now shall America *do* with the greatness of their nation? And is it great enough? And is it great in the right way? . . . What are we trying to do, overall? Where are we trying to get? What is the National Purpose of the U.S.A.?"

Givenness Reaffirmed.   The result of all this soul-searching was the publication of three volumes of vapid prose whose authors responded to their mandate simply by repeating the well-worn maxims expressing "givenness." (The essays commissioned by *Life* were published as a series in *Life* and in the *New York Times*, and together as a volume entitled *The National Purpose*. Later they were made the kernel of a larger volume edited by Oscar Handlin of Harvard University under the title *American Principles and Issues*.[33] To buttress the "givenness" thesis, the larger volume surrounded the original essays with an historical background drawn from public documents, philosophical speculations, poetry, and fiction. This fact and the general character of all the essays constitute a perfect empirical verification of Boorstin's theory.) If ideology were

---

[32] President's Commission on National Goals, *Goals for Americans* (Englewood Cliffs, N.J.: Prentice-Hall, Inc., 1960), p. xi.

[33] *The National Purpose* (New York: Holt, Rinehart & Winston, Inc., 1960), and *American Principles and Issues* (New York: Holt, Rinehart & Winston, Inc., 1961).

needed to arm us morally against Russian Communism, it would remain latent, implicit in our experience. All we needed was to affirm our traditional beliefs.

"The paramount goal of the United States was set long ago," says the Introduction to the report of the President's Commission on National Goals. "It is to guard the rights of the individual, to ensure his development, and to enlarge his opportunity. It is set forth in the Declaration of Independence drafted by Thomas Jefferson and adopted by the Continental Congress on July 4, 1776. The goals we here identify are within the framework of the original plan and are calculated to bring to fruition the dreams of the men who laid the foundation of this country." [34] The essays published by *Life* repeat the same theme over and over—the reaffirmation of the doctrines of the Founders. "The fact is, of course," writes Archibald MacLeish, "that we *have* a national purpose—the most precisely articulated national purpose in recorded history—and that we all know it. It is the purpose put into words by the most lucid mind of that most lucid century, the 18th, and adopted on the Fourth of July, 1776, as a declaration of the existence and national intent of a new nation." [35] "We need to recapture the spirit of '76," writes Billy Graham. James Reston tells us that "the first national purpose is to know who we are and what we stand for; it would be an impertinence to try to improve on the second paragraph of the Declaration of Independence as a guide to the problem." "The ultimate ends are fixed," says Walter Lippmann. "They are lasting and they are not disputed. The nation is dedicated to freedom. It is dedicated to the rights of man and to the consent of the governed." [36]

Through the turbulent sixties and into the seventies, the "Established Liberals" who contributed to *The National Purpose* retained their sense of the "givenness" of America's basic ideological principles, although a more worried note creeps into some of their utterances. They continued to view political and social problems in terms of a discrepancy between theory and practice, rather than as a function of defective principle. Their stress remained on the need for more vigorous action, within the established framework, not on the need for a new framework. Thus James Reston sees a need for more vigorous presidential leadership to bring our energies to "bear on the great purposes of the nation." Echoing his language of the fifties, Albert Wohlstetter calls for "sober thought about the concrete problems of extending democracy inside our own country, of helping the economic and political self-development of other countries." More pessimistic than in the 1950s, Archibald MacLeish began to fear that

[34] President's Commission on National Goals, *op. cit.*, p. 1.
[35] *The National Purpose*, p. 38.
[36] *Ibid.*, pp. 63, 122, 127.

American ideals may be losing their meaning for Americans, many of whom seem to have rejected the national purpose. He calls for America to set an example of free government to the world and to help others achieve "liberation." Walter Lippmann espouses democratic participation and action on the domestic scene, especially at the local level, as does John Gardner. Gardner reaffirms his faith that America remains devoted to her ideals, but he worries about the efficacy of some of our institutions. Quotations from the Declaration of Indejendence continue to abound.[37]

Another recent example of our continued adherence to the myth of "givenness" is found in Lyndon B. Johnson's Inaugural Speech of January 20, 1965, which launched the "Great Society":

> Our destiny in the midst of change will rest on the unchanged character of our people—and on their faith.
> They came here—the exile and the stranger, brave and frightened—to find a place where a man could be his own man. They made a covenant with this land. Conceived in justice, writ in liberty, bound in union, it was meant one day to inspire the hopes of all mankind. It binds us still. And if we keep its terms we shall flourish.

Our values are given both by the Founding Fathers and by the landscape —"They made a covenant with this land."

4. Bringing Latent Ideas to the Surface: The Empirical Study of Political Culture

When asked to articulate "goals for Americans," the intellectuals of the "Establishment" respond with the abstractions of 1776. Do these correspond to the values of the man in the street? What ideas are actually operative in the daily lives of the American people, and how can we discover them? In an unself-conscious political culture characterized by a widespread sense of "givenness," where Fourth of July clichés substitute for forensic ideology, can it be said that ideas are operative at all among the general public? If they are, is there a popular consensus about political values in the United States, and what is its content?

[37] See James Reston in *The New York Times*, February 11, 13, and 16, 1972; Albert Wohlstetter, "Illusions of Distance," *Foreign Affairs*, 46(2), January 1968; Archibald MacLeish, "A View of Oxford, Mississippi," *Atlantic Monthly*, February 1963, and "A Decent Respect," *Saturday Review*, June 3, 1965; Walter Lippmann, "The Great and Good Society," *Newsweek*, November 22, 1965, and "Order and Justice," *Newsweek*, July 1, 1968; John Gardner, "A Nation Is Never Finished," *American Bar Association Journal*, 53, November 1967, "A Task to Test Our Mettle," *Readers Digest*, 94, February 1969, and "Priorities for the Seventies," *New Leader*, 53, January 5, 1970.

The Psychological Interview.   A variety of empirical methods, ranging from depth interviews to survey research, have been developed in the past twenty years to answer these questions. So far we do not have a great quantity of hard data on political culture, but pioneering studies have been done which throw some light on the questions we should like to have answered. The results of one of these are presented in a volume by Robert Lane entitled *Political Ideology: Why the American Common Man Believes What He Does,* published in 1962. They constitute an analysis of the political culture of fifteen men of upper working-class status in New Haven, Connecticut (which Lane calls "East Port"), all of whom are residents of a middle-income public housing development which Lane names "Hilltop." The respondents were mostly Catholic and were native-born persons of Italian, Irish, Polish, Danish, Russian, and Yankee stock. They had attended elementary and high school.

The interviews were conducted as unstructured, often rambling discussions of "what people are thinking these days." "Turning to the large ideological questions that form the core of political theory," Lane writes, "we discussed at some length the meaning of freedom, equality, democracy, the uses and abuses of government." [38] Professor Lane's object was not to elicit simplified versions of the Declaration of Independence and other basic doctrines for comparison with the original, nor to discover consensus or the lack of it on specifications of abstract ideas. No particular theories were used as a point of departure. The aim was rather to find in the self-organized ideological statements of the respondents the private import of those statements for the men making them and to get at latent meanings in them. It was assumed that the discussions of ideology would reveal the basic orientations of the respondents to politics and also yield something on the social implications of these orientations. Because the interviews were biographical in character they revealed how life experiences produce attitudinal patterns and how these are fashioned into political concepts. The book, in short, is an effort to tie personality and social characteristics together with social thought, and to show how these things function in relation to one another. [39]

The discussion of "freedom" as one of our leading value words produced results rather different from the civics book definitions of the word. None of the respondents emphasized freedom from legal restrictions, after the manner of the Declaration of Independence or the Bill of Rights. Perhaps this indicates merely that values which have been

---

[38] Robert E. Lane, *Political Ideology: Why the American Common Man Believes What He Does* (New York: The Free Press of Glencoe, 1962), p. 8. Copyright 1962 by The Free Press of Glencoe. With permission.
[39] *Ibid.,* pp. 9, 10.

safely secured tend to pass out of mind. Freedom of speech was little mentioned, and freedom of religion meant freedom to choose one's religion without *social* stigma. Freedom of movement and to choose one's occupation were highly valued, although the respondents perceived little opportunity for upward mobility. On-the-job restrictions were noted as a source of depression and irritation. Freedom as intellectual independence was greatly admired among leaders, and all of the men saw themselves as intellectually independent rather than as conformists. They were, according to their own reports, men who made up their own minds about things and did not need to be told.

The Burden of Freedom.   One of the most interesting findings about what freedom meant to Lane's respondents has to do with the psychological effects of individual choice and decision. All of them experienced freedom as a burden, a cause of anxiety:

> You're bombarded by so much—ah, pressure in the present day, pressures of business, pressures of actual day-to-day living—cost of living—the pressures of whether you are bringing your children up right, or whether you said the right thing to your child. . . . There are so many things that you are constantly bombarded with—tiny messages the people are trying to get across to you in their effort to sell you.[40]

Although all to one degree or another expressed a longing for a simple life, the significant thing is that most of the men were tolerant of the burden of freedom and did not expect to escape from it. We are reminded of Mannheim's description of the difficult pressures of decision which are part and parcel of Liberal Democratic political culture:

> The merchant, the entrepreneur, the intellectual, each in his own way occupies a position which requires rational decisions concerning the tasks set by everyday life. In arriving at these decisions, it is always necessary for the individual to free his judgments from those of others and to think through certain issues in a rational way from the point of view of his own interests. This is not true for peasants of the older type nor for the recently emerged mass of subordinate white-collar workers who hold positions requiring little initiative, and no foresight of a speculative kind. . . . Men who in their everyday life are not trained by occupations which impel toward individualization always to make their own decisions, to know from their own personal point of view what is wrong and what is right, who from this point on never have occasion to analyse situations into their elements, and who, further, fail to develop a self-consciousness in themselves which will stand firm even when the individual is cut off from the mode of judgment peculiar to his group and must think for himself—such individuals will not be in a position, even in the religious sphere, to bear up under such severe inner crises as scepticism. Life in

[40] *Ibid.*, p. 27.

terms of an inner balance which must be ever won anew is the essentially novel element which modern man, at the level of individualization, must elaborate for himself if he is to live on the basis of the rationality of the Enlightenment.[41]

What Mannheim did not note was that under certain conditions the kind of person he describes *can* bear the burden of choice in ambiguity, which is the price of Liberal society. Lane has indicated that such an individual can imitate the example of the upper middle classes, whom he admires, by acting as a grass-roots opinion leader. It also should be pointed out that acceptance of the burden of freedom implies acceptance of a dualism in truth, the idea that another point of view, different from one's own, is legitimate. These concepts are at the basis of democratic give-and-take and form the foundation of the conception of the loyal opposition, a key Liberal institution. Most of Lane's respondents liked to hear more than one side of an issue.

In the next chapters, in which we examine challenges in American society to the Liberal Democratic order, we shall see that it is precisely those persons, both on the "Right" and on the "Left," who are unable to tolerate the anxieties produced by the confusion of "the many tiny messages" who articulate these challenges in words and who are leading the attacks on our institutions which have been increasing in recent years.

Lane points out that one of the things which gives his respondents some surcease and relief from the anxiety engendered by freedom of choice is the sense that basic values and institutions are settled and beyond debate. He has discovered a valuable social function for the myth of "givenness" which Boorstin has so ably described. None of Lane's respondents felt any problems of choice among the great competing world "isms"—whether Communism, Fascism, or whatever.[42]

The Fear of Equality.   The analysis of "equality" brought even more surprises than the discussion of "freedom." Despite their low status on the American totem pole, and despite their support for specific welfare state measures, Lane's respondents expressed a marked fear of thoroughgoing equality. Inequality had great value for them. This runs contrary to Tocqueville's finding that a spirit of equality was a prime characteristic of American political culture during the Jacksonian period. According to Tocqueville, the spirit of equality was not a leveling spirit, as it tended to be in Europe, but rather one which "incites men to wish all to be powerful and honored"—leveling upward, if you will. He took

[41] Karl Mannheim, *Ideology and Utopia: An Introduction to the Sociology of Knowledge,* trans. L. Wirth and E. Shils (New York: Harcourt Brace Jovanovich, Inc., 1963), pp. 31–32. Copyright 1954 by Harcourt Brace Jovanovich, Inc. and by Routledge & Kegan Paul, Ltd. With permission.

[42] Lane, *op. cit.,* pp. 31–32.

this attitude to be a product of the very great equality of conditions which actually prevailed among the first settlers and which itself had been produced by their middle-class social origins, by the absence of a class with feudal privileges, even in the south, by the democratic impact of the Revolution, and by the conditions of frontier life.[43] Perhaps Lane's very different finding is a testimony to increasing stratification in American society in recent years or to differences in mentality related to the eastern and southern European peasant background of his respondents, in contrast with the British middle-class origins of Tocqueville's Jacksonians.

Lane notes that American society announces that "all men are created equal" but also enjoins its members to compete and become unequal. The fifteen residents of "Eastport" had all gotten the message, which is quite compatible with the main tenets of the political tradition. (The Declaration of Independence speaks of natural rights to life, liberty, and property and James Madison, in *Federalist* No. 10, tells us that governments are instituted to protect unequal property holdings.)

All the "Eastporters" saw America as a land of opportunity, though they discerned differential opportunities for persons of different backgrounds. They viewed the rich as persons who have a right to their wealth because they had earned it. The lower classes also got what they deserve, and Lane's men had little sympathy for persons lower on the social scale than themselves. They neither wanted to be raised to a level above the one which they themselves had achieved nor to have the lower stratum equalized with them by government policy. They were glad to have an elite watching over them and said that absolute equality would destroy this much needed leading echelon. They also feared that equality would destroy incentive and disorganize social functions. They had all internalized the "Protestant Ethic," which we discussed in Chapter 2 as a central code of a working modern society. (This is a theme to which we shall recur frequently in the subsequent chapters of this book.) They had sacrificed hedonistic inclinations in order to achieve middle-class respectability. Many of them held two jobs. And they were opposed to measures which would yield equality for the "loafers" on the bottom rung of the ladder of success.

In discussing conceptions of authority, Lane discovered that "Eastport" men do not see democracy in terms of majority rule and minority rights. They think, rather, in terms of majority rights. Democracy equals "freedom of the nondeviant individual to do what the majority thinks is right." [44] We recall that in the 1830s Tocqueville had found the same unabashed assertion of the majority principle. He wrote that in America

[43] Tocqueville, *op. cit.*, I, 53.
[44] Lane, *op. cit.*, p. 83.

popular sovereignty had "acquired . . . all the practical development that the imagination can conceive. It is unencumbered by those fictions that are thrown over it in other countries, and it appears in every possible form, according to the exigency of the occasion. . . . The people reign in America as the Deity in the universe. They are the cause and the aim of all things; everything comes from them, and everything is absorbed in them." [45] The populist theme was strongly accented in the group Lane examined, the individualist and constitutionalist theme much less so.

All of Lane's respondents believed in the virtues of the democratic suffrage and assented to the Rousseauistic proposition that man is basically good and socially oriented. They viewed democracy as both a strong and a flexible system of government. They disliked the idea of dictatorship even in emergencies. "Oh, definitely, it does [create confusion] because everybody has a chance to voice, and the times it is all thrashed out and everything, definitely, there is a lot of time wasted—but it's good. It's time not wasted because regardless of how small or how big you are, everybody's opinion is heard, and it is balanced out, and I think that is the most important thing, regardless of time." [46]

The "Eastporters" tended to be mistrustful of private power—and as much of union power as of the power of business, despite the fact that these were upper working-class people. But the majority viewed public government without suspicion and saw it as working for them. They also saw everybody as having some power, which they related to freedom of association. Individually weak, little men were capable of exercising control if they joined together. Tocqueville had discovered the same belief in collective strength despite individual weakness a hundred years earlier during his rambles around the America of Jackson's time. [47]

Limitations of Lane's Findings.   Interesting as they are, Lane's findings give us little basis for broad generalization about the latent ideologies of Americans. We have no way of knowing how representative his fifteen men are, even of the upper working-class community in which they live, let alone of American mentality in general. Because they do not constitute a scientific sample, we cannot even be sure that the proportion of undemocrats in the population of "Hilltop" is not quite different from that of Lane's respondents. He has presented us with insightful hypotheses for further investigation, but not with conclusive evidence. Lane's interviews have at least established that in the realm of conceptions of authority, American common men do have latent ideological sets that can be made conscious by probing. Furthermore, his findings have helped us

[45] Tocqueville, *op. cit.*, I, 57, 58.
[46] Lane, *op. cit.*, p. 85.
[47] Tocqueville, *op cit.*, II, 109.

verify and qualify some of the assertions of more impressionistic historical studies. We must now ask what the salient things are that Americans are agreed upon. On what conceptions of authority is there national consensus? Is consensus also to be found at the level of belief? Of emotional attitude? This brings us to the tools of survey research.

A Synthesis of Survey Research.   The large problem we must face in measuring for consensus is to decide what to look for. A priori, what ideas should we *expect* to find agreement on? And what data do we need in order to conduct an adequate inquiry? The most exhaustive study of this kind so far has been carried out by Donald J. Devine of the University of Maryland, in the form of a secondary analysis of a broad range of empirical data on political ideas and attitudes collected over a period of thirty-five years.[48]

The first half of the methodological conundrum (what ideas to measure for), Devine has settled by selecting the ideas of John Locke and James Madison as the content of the presumptive American value consensus. He chose Locke on the grounds that he was the political theorist whose ideas were most influential in the mother country early in the formative colonial period; it was Locke who "provided a rational explanation for the founding and development of the colonies." The republican principles formulated by Locke, Devine tells us, "were reinforced and adapted to American circumstances by Madison and the other 'Founding Fathers' of the Constitution."[49] Moreover, following Hartz and Neal Riemer, Devine assumed that the ideas of Locke and Madison have remained the substantial content of American political culture over the years:

> It is maintained that the values of Locke, Madison, and the other liberals of the seventeenth and eighteenth centuries represent essentially the same values which comprise the American political culture at the present. Although it has changed, the remarkable phenomenon is that American political culture has survived so unchanged under substantial environmental pressure.[50]

Devine answered the second half of the methodological question (what data to examine) by relating "the values of Locke and Madison systematically and directly to the available opinion data."[51] In this

---

[48] See Donald J. Devine, *The Political Culture of the United States* (Boston: Little, Brown & Co., 1972). Copyright 1972 by Little, Brown & Co. Quotations with permission.

[49] *Ibid.,* pp. 46, 47–48.

[50] *Ibid.,* p. 65. See Neal Riemer, "Two Conceptions of the Genius of American Politics," *Journal of Politics,* November 1958. Devine cites Riemer in his study (p. 64), and adds that he will use "the Hartz thesis . . . as a working hypothesis" (p. 65).

[51] *Ibid.,* p. 135.

second aspect of his method Devine has produced an important synthetic study. He selected most of his data from politically oriented national probability samples taken between 1935 and 1970. Three operational criteria were used in selecting poll questions to study: either (1) that the question be related to public reaction (either positive or negative) to an obvious liberal value; or (2) that a question deal with individual assessment of an American political institution or process; or (3) that a question relate to the politically related attitudes noted in the national characteristic literature.[52]

Another important methodological question is the definition of consensus. This has been variously handled in the literature. One scholar has defined consensus as an agreement approaching 90 percent. Another has used the figure of 75 percent—halfway between unanimity and a simple majority, and the degree of agreement required to amend the United States Constitution.[53] Devine used a still less restrictive figure, arguing that 75 percent was too high because of the large number of persons who have no opinion on any question propounded. He chose instead to follow the rule that "there must be (1) at least a *majority for* the value and (2) a *substantial difference* (at least twenty percentage points) between the majority and minority positions." [54]

With these matters settled, we still are not ready to measure for consensus. There remains the important and tricky question of culling Locke and Madison for specific ideas to identify in secondary analysis of the opinion data used. Here, as in all such survey research, a very subjective factor enters in—the personal judgment of the analyst as to relevance and significance. To keep the subjective factor to a minimum, Devine conducted a content analysis of Locke's *Second Treatise* and of Madison, Hamilton, and Jay's *Federalist* to determine the specific values to be measured.

In categorizing value ideas, Devine did not employ the dichotomy of conceptions of purpose and conceptions of authority we have been working with, but rather the categories of "belief system" and "rule system." These two systems are distinguished in part by level of abstraction. A belief system embraces very abstract values such as liberty and equality, whereas a rule system specifies these in terms of legitimate legal procedures, or rules. The rule system thus becomes equivalent to our "conceptions of authority" category, while the belief system embraces both authority and purpose.

[52] *Ibid.*, pp. 67, 68.
[53] See James W. Prothro and Charles M. Grigg, "Fundamental Principles of Democracy," *Journal of Politics*, 22 (2), May 1960, 276–94; Herbert McClosky, "Consensus and Ideology in American Politics," *American Political Science Review*, 58 (2), June 1964, 361–82.
[54] Devine, *op. cit.*, p. 70.

Findings on Consensus. Devine identified as the content of the American belief system four major values—liberty defined as political autonomy (freedom from governmental restrictions), equality, property, and religion—and three subordinate values: education, achievement, and altruism. Substantial majorities registered support for all seven. Of these seven values, liberty was accorded the highest rank in the data examined. In a survey conducted in 1948, eight out of ten respondents rated liberty over economic security, and in a study of 1960, seven of ten placed it above duty to the state. The specific liberty of freedom of the press was valued by about 70 percent in studies done in 1937, 1939, 1943, 1945, and 1948, and over 95 percent of the samples supported free speech in surveys of 1938 and 1940. (A large group, however, saw freedom of speech as a limited liberty; support for unlimited free speech ranged between 49 and 64 percent in six studies done between 1940 and 1953.) Political equality is supported by 75 percent of the population, and 81 percent support private property. Sixty percent support achievement over job security, and more than this number would place no restrictions on achievement. Belief in God is virtually unanimous.[55]

Under the rubric of basic rules that define liberal political culture, Devine singled out popular rule and elections, legislative predominance, federalism, and decentralized parties as salient. Seventy-six percent of the population support popular rule and 91 percent reject dictatorship as an alternative. But there is no consensus as to whether that rule should be unqualified. Thirty-eight percent believe that the "majority of the people in this country are usually correct in their ideas on important questions." Forty-two percent believe they are not usually correct. Americans appear more ready to accord correctness of judgment to their elected representatives than to themselves. In 1939 a plurality thought Congress right more often on broad national issues than they themselves.

More than 75 percent support legislative predominance, with the President and the Supreme Court receiving a lesser degree of support. Federalism is generally valued, and 73 percent think the states more efficient than the central government. The political parties, which are viewed as properly decentralized and loosely disciplined, are supported by 80 percent. Substantial majorities believe the congressman should make up his own mind and do not expect him to follow party leadership.[56]

Devine concludes, after detailing the findings we have summarized

[55] *Ibid.*, Chapter IV, pp. 179–230. A problem with Devine's findings is that they usually are stated generally, as though they were constant for the entire period of approximately thirty-five years. Yet particular statements depend on data limited to specific times within that period, frequently a single year as far back as the late 1930s or 1940s.

[56] *Ibid.*, Chapter IV, pp. 135–79.

above, "that the liberal tradition is the core of the political culture of the United States." [57] How significant is this conclusion, and is it warranted by the data tabulated? The question of significance requires us to focus on problems associated with the use of the word "core." What does this mean in practical terms? Is it possible to predict behavior from beliefs which are the "core" of a culture? Leaving aside the operational meaning of the word "core," how do we know that the ideas listed are indeed core or central? All we know for certain is that Devine looked for assent to these ideas and found substantial consensus around them. How do we know that there are not other ideas which are more the core, more central for the system, which would be accorded more consensual agreement if Devine had thought to look for them? Does the viability of a political system presuppose the vitality of certain "core" ideas and attitudes? Are there crucial areas of *disagreement* which threaten the stability of the system which were not measured for?

These questions point to the large ambiguity of the word "core," and Devine has given us no answer to them. Perhaps we have here laid our finger on some of the problems of survey research as a method of political discovery. An approach like that of Lane, if it could be used on a broader scale, might give us more reliable information about the role and function of political ideas.

Beyond the question of consensus, empirical research in political culture has been concerned with the comparative structure of leader and follower political cultures, and with the congruence of ideological judgments at the abstract and at the concrete levels. Information in both of these important areas is scarce and inconclusive, but a few important studies exist.

Consensus, Abstract and Concrete. In 1960 James W. Prothro, a political scientist, and Charles M. Grigg, a sociologist, did a study of two urban communities that produced evidence in both problem areas. The survey was designed not only to test the hypothesis that a consensus on basic values in American political life can be discovered, but also to determine whether such a consensus has influence on the making of political decisions at the grass-roots level. In order to limit their investigation to manageable scope, Prothro and Grigg decided to confine themselves to basic questions about how political power is won. From the speculative literature on political consensus and from general studies of democracy rather than from one or more of the classics they selected majority rule and minority rights (defined as freedom to dissent) as the basic procedural principles for granting official power in our system. They then proceeded to test for consensus on these norms, which cor-

[57] *Ibid.*, p. 230.

respond to the antithetical individualist (constitutionalist) and collectivist (absolutist) traditions whose historical importance we traced earlier.[58]

Respondents were asked to agree or disagree with a series of statements intended to embody these general principles. Five abstract propositions were presented, followed by ten other propositions applying these principles to specific situations. These are the abstract statements:

PRINCIPLE OF DEMOCRACY ITSELF
Democracy is the best form of government.

PRINCIPLE OF MAJORITY RULE
Public officials should be chosen by majority vote.
Every citizen should have an equal chance to influence government policy.

PRINCIPLE OF MINORITY RIGHTS
The minority should be free to criticize majority decisions.
People in the minority should be free to try to win majority support for their opinions.[59]

The general rules were then applied to specific cases. The principle of majority rule, for example, was particularized in such sentences as the following: "If a Negro were legally elected mayor of this city, the white people should not allow him to take office." "If a Communist were legally elected mayor of this city, the people should not allow him to take office." "A professional organization like the AMA (the American Medical Association) has a right to try to increase the influence of doctors by getting them to vote as a bloc in elections." The minority rights principle was specified with such sentences as: "If an admitted Communist wanted to make a speech in this city favoring Communism, he should be allowed to speak." "If a person wanted to make a speech in this city against churches and religion, he should be allowed to speak." [60] In the view of the researchers, the correct democratic response to the statement about the AMA, the Communist speaker, and the speaker against religion is "Yes," and to the others "No."

The registered voters of Ann Arbor, Michigan, and Tallahassee, Florida, were selected as the population to be sampled. These two communities were chosen in order to afford a regional comparison and to allow a detailed comparison of the views of the highly educated with those of the poorly educated. The survey thus produced a comparison

---

[58] The findings are reported in Prothro and Grigg, *op. cit.* See the consensus literature footnoted in this article, especially Ernest S. Griffith, John Plamenatz, and J. Roland Pennock, "Cultural Prerequisites to a Successfully Functioning Democracy: A Symposium," *The American Political Science Review,* 50 (1), March 1956:101–15.
[59] *Ibid.,* p. 282.
[60] *Ibid.,* pp. 282, 283.

of elite and mass views. Overrepresentation of the highly educated, deriving from the academic character of the communities surveyed, made the second comparison possible. It also biased the results in favor of the hypothesis that consensus exists.

On the abstract principles the survey yielded a high rate of agreement, ranging from 94.7 to 98.0 percent. The "agreement transcended community, educational, economic, age, sex, party, and other common bases of differences in opinion." [61] On the specific statements, however, no consensus was found. For over half the questions responses were "closer to perfect discord than to perfect consensus." [62] More "correct" responses were garnered in the midwestern than in the southern community, and more from persons with high education than from those with low education. Of the two variables, region and education, the latter was judged to be the more important. But even in the group of the highly educated, consensus in a meaningful sense was not found. In the survey of 1956 that we have mentioned above, McClosky also found consensus disappear when he moved from abstract questions about freedom of speech and opinions to specifications of these values. Prothro and Grigg concluded that it cannot be maintained "without qualification that consensus on fundamental principles is a necessary condition for the existence of democracy," inasmuch as the abstract agreement seemed to have no behavioral significance, judging from the answer about concrete situations.[63] A working agreement on specific questions was lacking not only in the population at large but also among the most highly educated members, who should be the carriers of the creed. The researchers ventured the opinion that political apathy was a major factor in preventing disagreement from unstabilizing the system.

Methodological Problems.   More problems of obtaining reliable empirical information about the phenomena of political culture by the method of survey research are revealed by this survey. The authors made a large and perhaps debatable assumption in the rule which they adopted for determining what the "correct," or democratic, responses to the particular questions ought to be. In each case the decision was made by selecting that response which could be derived by logical inference from the general principle. This seems to conform to Professor McIver's view of ideology as a set of abstract ideas from which an entire program of policy objectives can be derived. Is this, however, the only possible way to proceed? And is it, in fact, the way most people go about making up their minds about specific problems?

If principles are to be applied to situations in a perfectly deductive

---

[61] Prothro and Grigg, *op. cit.*, p. 286.
[62] *Ibid.*, Table 1.
[63] *Ibid.*, p. 293.

manner, we must assume that the entire catalog of principles which constitute the ideological system under investigation is perfectly consistent—that the application of one principle in no way hinders the realization of any other value. Yet we know that in fact this is not the case. It is commonly said that "liberty" and "equality" in some of their definitions may be in conflict with one another. Certainly in the area of social policy, the extension of welfare legislation and economic regulation in the name of greater "equality" interferes with the "liberty" of persons to engage in certain forms of economic activity. Consider the historic debate on the application of the principle of "liberty of contract." Another example can be found in the way in which the First Amendment guarantee of freedom of expression has been applied to particular cases. The principle is stated in perfect abstraction in the Constitution. Yet in applying it the Congress and the courts have not employed anything like a deductive method, because in some instances freedom of expression may constitute a threat to the fundamental security of society. Traditionally we have judged that it must be limited when such a threat arises. The decision is a prudential one—weighing competing values against one another and analyzing the circumstances of the case to see what the traffic will bear.

The circumstances, not the principles, furnish the answer. And what that answer should be is often not clear. In the cases before the Supreme Court which have dealt with the concept of freedom of contract and with the concept of freedom of expression, not only have the justices been unable to achieve the level of agreement which Prothro and Grigg call consensus (something approaching 90 percent) but they also have changed their minds from case to case and have reversed their rulings on how the principles are to be applied. Since this is so in a small group like the Supreme Court, it is only to be expected that consensus is not to be found in the population at large. Moreover, it seems clear that what we really are measuring in asking questions about specific circumstances is not consensus on principles but consensus on the prudent mode of combining them or choosing among them in the multiform world of daily decision making.

A glance at the specific questions asked of the respondents also shows that the policy areas involved—the integration of the black man in white American society, the rights and privileges of persons who place themselves beyond the consensus (Communists)—are precisely those areas in which it is commonly acknowledged that there is little agreement. The consensus-building processes of our political and social order have been set in motion to work out an agreement on new definitions and applications of old principles in these areas. In this sense, the survey does not reveal anything more than we supposed to be the case on the basis of less systematically obtained evidence. But perhaps we should arrive at a different conclusion from that of the authors. Instead of concluding that apathy has stabilized the system despite the presence of value conflict, perhaps we should see this systematic evidence of value conflict as a sign of impending instability. In other words, if our institutions do not reconcile the manifest differences in question, particularly the difference involving integration, they probably will collapse. It is not self-evident that our democracy *is* working properly, as the authors assume.

At least in one instance it also could be argued that the authors of the survey were mistaken in the response which they deemed to be the "correct" one—the affirmation of the right of groups like the AMA to engage in bloc voting. Certainly the populist strain in our political culture, which holds that organized special interests are inimical to the working of democracy, yields a negative response to this statement. Although in fact American majorities are frequently coalitions of special interests, the political tradition does not unequivocally legitimize the practice. One would therefore not expect to find consensus on such a way of specifying what is meant by "majority rule." That the authors themselves detect a problem in the deductive method which they have employed is found in a comment which they make on the question about restricting the vote in a referendum on tax-supported undertakings. "As a matter of policy," they write, "perhaps the vote should be restricted—as it often is —under the circumstances indicated. We simply note that such a position is inconsistent with the unqualified major premise." [64] But they do not go further to call in question the appropriateness of purely logical inference as a way of arriving at operative consensus (or the lack of it).[65]

Ideological Differences between Leaders and Followers.   Survey research has produced somewhat more definite and reliable information about the relationship between leader and follower conceptions of authority in the United States. Although they did not find a consensual agreement among elites any more than among followers at the specific level, Prothro and Grigg did find more "correct" responses at the concrete level among the more highly educated respondents than among the less well educated. Herbert McClosky, in a 1956 study whose major object

[64] *Ibid.*, p. 292.

[65] Devine, in commenting on the Prothro-Grigg study, finds difficulties arising from their employment of a "less explanatory mechanical, rather than the biological-system analogy" (Devine, *op. cit.*, p. 294). He also comments, in terms similar to those used by this writer, on the abstract-concrete discrepancy: "Their assumption seems to be that a value should be supported regardless of the intervening circumstances. The system analogy, however, emphasizes the limitations of the one-to-one relationship under all circumstances, and leads one to suspect that intervening circumstances may be crucial" (*Ibid.*, p. 295).

was to compare leaders with followers, found extensive differences between leader and follower opinion.

The questions McClosky used to test support for the "rules of the game" (conceptions of authority embodied in the Constitution) covered minority rights, the right to vote, and respect for nonviolent and legal process. A majority of the electorate proved supportive of the rules but came close to consensus on only two items, rejecting a statement approving "direct action" in certain contingencies rather than waiting for the machinery of government to move and a statement giving the majority the right to abolish minorities. These two statements were rejected by 73.1 and 71.6 percent of the sample respectively. By contrast, the leaders achieved consensus on eight of the twelve items and were near consensus on three of the remaining four. On scales of "faith in direct action," McClosky points out, 26.1 percent of the actives and 42.5 percent of the followers scored high. McClosky sees these results as confirming Prothro and Grigg's findings "that a large proportion of the electorate has failed to grasp certain of the underlying ideas and principles on which the American political system rests." [66] Because his questions avoided the problem of the deductive fallacy and did not concentrate on issues known to be bones of contention in America, McClosky's findings may well be more conclusive than those of the earlier study.

In response to abstract questions about freedom of speech and opinion, both samples registered overwhelming consensus. This appeared significant to McClosky, inasmuch as the statements eliciting the response were not merely familiar clichés but paraphrases of Mill's *Essay on Liberty*. Nevertheless, when the abstractions were brought down to concrete cases, the consensus declined markedly, especially among the electorate. The political actives displayed more consistency in moving from general to particular.

In the area of equalitarian values there was marked dissensus both among influentials and followers in McClosky's findings. (In the way questions were posed, questions about purpose were mixed in with questions about authority.) Nor was there agreement on whether the people have the ability to rule themselves, understand their long-run interests, understand issues, or choose leaders wisely. Interestingly, the elite stratum scored higher on the "popular democracy" questions than did the electorate. The followers, however, proved somewhat more equalitarian in economic matters. Measures to prevent extreme inequalities from developing, such as social security policies, were supported. But so were private enterprise, competition, and the unlimited pursuit of

[66] McClosky, *op. cit.*, p. 365. McClosky here implies that American populism is a standing threat to our constitutionalism.

profit, which foster inequality. Both samples were divided on ethnic equality.

Speculating about the reasons for so marked a dissensus as he found on equality, McClosky suggests several possible explanations. One of these is the historical connection between liberalism, with its equalitarian emphasis, and capitalism, with its elitist implications. Another is the diffuse. character of the concept, which has not only political and economic but also legal and moral meanings (universal suffrage, equality of property and of opportunity, equality before the law, and the right to be treated as an end rather than a means). Also relevant is the ambiguity of such expressions as "All men are created equal," which can be understood either as a factual or as a normative statement.

McClosky's study suggests that it is not the public in general but rather a more homogeneous class of influential actives who "serve as the major repositories of the public conscience and as the carriers of the Creed." Responsibility for keeping the system going, McClosky concludes, falls most heavily upon this active stratum. Conversely, "the findings furnish little comfort for those who wish to believe that a passion for freedom, tolerance, justice and other democratic values springs spontaneously from the lower depths of society, and that the plain, homespun, uninitiated yeoman, worker and farmer are the natural hosts of democratic ideology." [67]

Devine's elaborate study of American political culture gives little attention to elite-mass comparisons. In one place Devine says expressly that the question of "elite support [for the values of the liberal tradition] is beyond the scope of the present study," perhaps because he believes that "little reliable data on American leadership attitudes regarding political culture are available." [68] He notes in passing, however, that the mass-elite study done by Samuel Stouffer showed leaders more committed to some elements of the tradition than the general public. [69] In addition, Devine points out that in another essay he had himself shown that a fairly low-level elite group, which he calls "the attentive public"—people who are tuned into political events more than the average man—appear "to support the liberal tradition values more than those less attuned to politics." [70]

The Civic Culture.   An approach to the analysis of political culture somewhat different from the ones we have been considering has been

---

[67] *Ibid.*, pp. 374, 375.

[68] Devine, *op. cit.*, pp. 286, 284.

[69] Samuel Stouffer, *Communism, Conformity, and Civil Liberties* (New York: John Wiley & Sons, Inc., 1966).

[70] Devine, *op. cit.*, p. 255.

developed by Gabriel Almond and Sidney Verba. Their stress has been on attitudinal and affective elements of culture, rather than on its purely cognitive aspects, where the emphasis usually lies. And they have tried to develop a generalized model of liberal democratic culture rather than one whose elements are tied to a specifically American experience. Their purpose in developing such a model was to enable them to fashion an instrument of analysis for cross-national studies of democratic culture. That it is difficult, if not impossible, to develop such a general model without drawing on a specific national experience is shown by the fact that the Almond-Verba conception of "civic culture" has a peculiarly British cast, as is readily admitted by the authors. "We have concentrated on British experience," they wrote, "because the whole story of the emergence of the civic culture is told in British history." [71]

What are the elements of the civic culture? The authors arrange them for us under three headings: cognitive, affective, and evaluative. Cognitive elements refer to the respondent's perception of what government does and how he is affected by that action. These are generally comparable to at least some of the ideas which in the Beer framework are called "beliefs." Evaluative elements obviously correspond to Beer's "values" ("conceptions of purpose" and "conceptions of authority"), although the stress is on specific normative rules rather than on abstract ideas of what is legitimate. (Indeed, the emphasis throughout Almond and Verba's study is active rather than contemplative.) Finally, affective elements correspond to Beer's "attitudes and emotional feelings" expressed in response to political symbols.

The whole complex of "civic culture" consists of about ten elements. All of them are analyzed as ideas and attitudes which are active mental and psychological states rather than as abstract concepts and propositions. Here we have the specific differences between this study and those by Prothro and Grigg, McClosky, Lane, and Devine, which employed self-conscious value statements drawn from political discourse. Some of the mental states described by Almond and Verba can be reduced to general and abstract formulation comparable to the kind of statement which we find in forensic ideology and in the sorts of simplified propositions we have been examining. The ten are listed below first as psychological states. When an abstract proposition of a more traditional sort can be elicited from the description of the mental state this is given in parentheses. The bearer of "civic culture" possesses the following characteristics:

[71] Gabriel Almond and Sidney Verba, *The Civic Culture* (Princeton: Princeton University Press, 1963), p. 8.

1. Awareness and favorable evaluation of government output for himself.
2. A high level of interest in and information about the workings of public government.
3. Pride in the political institutions of his nation.
4. Expectation of equal and considerate treatment by officials. (Legitimate government provides for equality before the law.)
5. Willingness to communicate about politics with others. (Citizens have an obligation to concern themselves with public as well as private affairs and to participate in the public discussion of the public interest.)
6. Open and moderate partisanship. (Loyal opposition is both legitimate and useful.)
7. Having feelings, especially satisfied feelings, about political events, especially campaigns.
8. A high sense of competence to influence government by political activity in cooperation with one's neighbors and a sense of obligation to exert influence. (Citizens have an obligation to participate in the forging of the "general will" in cooperation with their equal fellow citizens.)
9. A high sense of competence to appeal successfully to general rules of law against arbitrary action. (All good government is according to the equal dictates of impersonal law, not the arbitrary whims of men. The individual has a right to due process of law.)
10. A belief that participatory democracy is a good and desirable system. (Democracy is the best form of government.)

It should be noted that in the cognitive areas the things which constitute the civic culture are entirely procedural and not substantive. What is more, the emphasis throughout is on "Rousseauistic" rather than "Lockean" democracy—that is, on participation and equality rather than on abstract individual right. The only individual rights implied are the rights to equal and due process under general rules, not the "natural rights" of man. In short, the emphasis is much more organic than individualist. It would be difficult to equate this with the populist-individualist contrast we have been examining, for its basis is British traditionalism, not American populism.

Before any measurements are made, one knows that British respondents will score highest on the vital dimensions. Yet what better method for developing a model might be suggested? Perhaps Lane's open-ended approach in depth with a limited number of respondents in several democratic polities might have produced a more genuinely empirical standard for comparison. Instead, Almond and Verba's study eventuates in a description of how four other democracies compare with the British, which is arbitrarily assumed to be the perfect democratic culture. Beyond this, their study does not show the interdependence of the "civic culture" with behavior. It fails to demonstrate that the ideas and attitudes which have been picked out for comparative measurement do in fact condition the polity to operate as it does—a problem we have found with other studies of political culture as well.

In Almond and Verba's study, Americans measured very high on all cognitive questions. In comparison with the citizens of all the other nations surveyed they showed the highest levels of knowledge of governmental output and of favorable evaluation of the impact of government policy. In short, they displayed the highest percentage of allegiant attitudes toward their government, which is what our intuition would lead us to expect if in fact the "silent majority" of the center is still a dominant majority.

A characteristic aspect of American political culture was revealed in the measurement of national pride. In answering this question, 85 percent of the American respondents mentioned some feature of government or of the political tradition in designating objects of national pride —things like "the Constitution, political freedom, democracy." Only 46 percent of the British sample offered political referents of national pride and Germany and Italy only 7 and 3 percent respectively. In the latter two cases the finding may be taken as a measurement of the continued lack of roots for democratic traditions in these countries, but certainly not in the case of Great Britain. The difference between the American and British responses probably is indicative of the contractarian aspects of American polity by contrast with the more organic character of British life, for what most strongly joins Americans together is our consciously chosen experiment in liberal democratic politics rather than the totality of our historical culture. The greater compartmentalization and pluralism of American life may also be revealed here, for these data indicate that we *define* the nation politically; what we all have in common is a system of constitutional rights. Beyond this lies a complex cultural sphere, the vast area of private life. A more organic society like Britain does not make such a separation of the areas of life one from another.

The questions concerning expectations of considerate treatment by the police also reveal important differences between the quality of the "civic culture" in the United States and elsewhere in the democratic world. In response to this question 74 percent of the British respondents expressed an expectation of serious consideration for their point of view. But Americans scored only 56 percent, which was lower than the Germans. This must be set beside the finding that expectation of *equality* of police treatment in Britain and the United States was equally high —89 and 85 percent. The difference on considerateness of treatment again may be referred to the difference between an individualist-populist United States and an organic Britain. Individualist-populist culture generally accents participant norms and gives less stress to subject rules. Almond and Verba "suggest . . . that Americans have not as fully assimilated the role of subject in relation to administrative authorities as have the German and the British." [72]

In response to questions about obligation to participate in the affairs of the local community—not only politically but also in terms of all outgoing activity—Americans scored highest (51 percent). The British were next with a 39 percent response. This may be taken as evidence of the correctness of Tocqueville's judgment a century ago that in a democratic culture like that of the United States, which has never had an aristocratic class to give leadership in public undertakings, the average citizen feels a much greater obligation to get the work of the community done.[73] We shall relate this a little later to the phenomenon of "joinerism" and the importance of the voluntary association to other aspects of democratic culture.

The findings of Almond and Verba on citizen competence (the subjective feeling of capacity to have an influence on public decisions) contained evidence that Lane's respondents were a nationally representative group. A strong sense of civic competence, it will be recalled, was held by a majority of Lane's men. Sixty-seven percent of the American sample in the civic culture survey expressed a sense of subjective citizen competence both at the local and at the national level. The British scored only 57 percent. (Expectations of being able to change an unjust regulation were higher: 77 percent with regard to local regulations and 75 percent with regard to national regulations in the American sample; 78 percent local and 62 percent national in the British.) The marked participatory character of our democracy was revealed in this measurement. In all nations more reliance was laid on informal than formal groups to exert necessary influence, but in the United States, which achieved the highest score on this measure, 56 percent of the respondents saw themselves as competent to create structures to bring government under control and to remedy injustice—further testimony to the continued allegiance of the majority to the system and to the adequate working of American institutions for processing demands into a democratic pattern of policy.

[72] *Ibid.*, p. 107.
[73] See Tocqueville, *op. cit.*, II, 109.

The reader should be clear that in writing of civic or citizen competence, Almond and Verba are measuring subjective feelings of capacity to influence, not actual influence exerted. As a matter of fact, they found relatively low levels of actual political activity in the United States—a fact which they, like Prothro and Grigg, consider a positive rather than a negative sign for the health of our democracy. Very high levels of participation might be a sign of instability rather than stability inasmuch as they might indicate widespread dissatisfaction with outputs. The authors read apathy as contentment with the way in which our representative institutions are operating.

Conclusion.   We have attempted to excavate the latent political ideals of Americans with a variety of empirical research tools. Although we have reviewed virtually all the work that has been done, the evidence required for definitive conclusions is incomplete. And we have pointed out problems of validity that stem from flaws in methods employed to collect the evidence that exists. Nevertheless, we have discovered some interesting things.

From Lane's psychological interviews we have obtained empirical evidence that Boorstin's thesis about the "givenness" of our political values is correct. We also discovered that it has the positive function of relieving anxieties caused by the volume of individual decision in a free society. From the same research we learned, however, that a sense of givenness does not foreclose a person's having specific ideological concepts or being able to articulate them in a detailed way.

Our empirical survey also has shown us something about the unequal relative importance of specific "given" values which appear to be of equal significance in formal statements of the American political "creed." From two sources, McClosky and Lane, we have evidence that elite groups are more sensitive to constitutionalist norms than the average man, for whom populist conceptions have an overwhelming authority. That almost half the population are willing to support popular direct action to achieve their ends may indicate a fundamental weakness in the liberal areas of our liberal democracy. The strength of participatory norms described by Almond and Verba, however, paired with the finding of a widespread sense of civic competence, an ability to control the political system, is evidence of democratic health. We also learned that "liberty," especially freedom to compete for economic and social status, is a much more popular concept than "equality" among the general public—evidence of the continued authority of a central Classical Liberal value. We discovered that although most of our leading political value ideas are found in traditional statements of the liberal democratic creed, some are not—for example, the definition of freedom in terms of social nondiscrimination for certain religious groups.

A most interesting finding reported by two sources is that political consensus varies with the level of abstraction of a concept, with broader agreement at the more abstract level. This calls in question the significance of abstract value consensus for political behavior, for a concrete position seems closer to action than an abstraction. We may have evidence here that the primary function of ideology is that suggested by Geertz—to give meaning to political action or to explain and legitimate an action or a political system, rather than to guide action. In later chapters, however, we shall see that the abstractions do play something of a restrictive role in a liberal democratic culture, or at least that they stand as a sign of important inhibitions in such a culture. We shall also discover that abstractions that do not fit the consensual pattern, at least under certain circumstances, are not as important as institutional habit in the behavior of alienated persons.

5. The Maintenance of Liberal Democratic Culture: Causes and Conditions

Let us now try to give an account of the conditions—historical, psychological, social—that appear to support the ideational and attitudinal pattern we have been describing. This will give us some basis for venturing a prediction about the future stability and continuity of "established liberalism" in America.

Historical Roots of Liberal Culture.   Historical origins are no doubt an important explanatory factor, and here Tocqueville's thesis is of paramount significance. It was the absence of a feudal tradition and a feudal class armed for its defense, he maintained, that allowed democratic liberalism to spread peacefully throughout the land and become quickly absorbed as unconscious reflex and habit rather than as self-conscious ideology. Hence the latency of American political ideas, the absence of forensic debate at an abstract level from the beginning. To this Hartz has added that unchallenged middle-classness at the outset has made for unchallenged middle-classness today. Unchallenged by a feudal aristocracy in the eighteenth century, the American middle class never begot the antibody of a proletariat, but rather a working class that has found the system open to achievement and that has shared the values and beliefs of businessmen and entrepreneurs. Historical traditions will be of major importance for explaining the political cultures of Germany, Russia, and China later in this book. But in no other case will historical factors be the authors of singleness and continuity of such an extensive order.

Character and Political Culture.   In some empirical work on political culture an effort has been made to describe the characterological supports of liberal democratic ideas and attitudes. For a political culture is not only a set of abstract ideas, as we have seen, but an entire way of being. Hence with an ideology we can expect a correlative set of personality traits. The authors of *The Civic Culture* hypothesized that if a political system built on cooperating and working with others implies a high incidence of civic competence, this quality further implied a high valuation of such character traits as generosity and considerateness which seem to go with effective cooperation. The survey showed that British and Americans valued these qualities considerably more than the citizens of the other three polities included in the studies. Sixty-five percent of the British and 59 percent of the Americans put generosity and considerateness at the head of the list of traits they admired. The score for Germans was 2 percent, for Mexicans 36 percent, and for Italians 25 percent. The same pattern was discovered when the respondents were asked to choose among statements indicating their feelings about the safety and responsiveness of their environment. Some of the statements involved fundamental judgments about human nature, a theory of man. More than 80 percent of the British and Americans, for example, responded favorably to the statement: "Human nature is fundamentally cooperative." Mexicans also scored in the eighties on this one, but the score for Germans and Italians was in the fifties. Fifty-five percent of the Americans and 49 percent of the British thought that "most people can be trusted." Mexicans scored 30 percent and Germans and Italians 19 and 7 percent respectively.

Writing in 1962, Lucian Pye also emphasized the importance of "the cooperative attitude of *trust*" as an aspect of the sense of community identity among the members of a society:

> The feeling of basic distrust leaves people unsure of their control over the world and hence fearful that the world is either against them or indifferent to them. Distrusting others, they must distrust their own capacity to influence others, and hence they have feelings of impotence. . . . When basic trust is replaced with cynicism, a people will suspect that behind the screen of political promises their leaders are really "out to get everything for themselves." [74]

[74] Lucian W. Pye, *Politics, Personality, and Nation-Building* (New Haven: Yale University Press, 1962), p. 55.

After citing the preceding passage and backing it up with references to John Locke, Devine went on to present data from polls taken in 1948 and 1964 which indicate, he felt, a substantial consensus that "most people can be trusted." In fact, he found the sense of trust on the increase, with a 66 percent agreement in 1948 supplanted by a 77 percent agreement in 1964.[75]

Using the methods of depth psychology rather than those of survey research, Lane found the same characteristics. The majority of his group were optimistic about human nature and trustful of their fellow men, a trait which other social scientists have also found clearly correlated with support for democracy.[76] They also were individualists and exhibited considerable ego strength, a factor on which Lane places the greatest reliance. In one place he goes so far as to remark that "only the strong egos can support a free society, can bear the burden of choice, can accept the responsibility for internal control in the absence of social control." [77] Lastly, they displayed a capacity for present enjoyment—the pursuit of happiness, to which democracy gives priority over the aristocratic values of honor and glory.

Personal Experience and Political Culture.   What experiences account for the presence of these personality traits in the American democrat? History or tradition alone is hardly an adequate explanation. Many, perhaps most, Americans came from families who brought here, some very recently, the traditions of central and eastern Europe or the Orient, not those of Great Britain, the "home" of civic culture attitudes. In these cases tradition would be a negative factor, and one would have to examine the experience of daily living to find the social ground of civic culture traits in these men.

Robert Lane found important support for democracy in the experience of his "Eastporters," despite the fact that a quick glance at that experience seems to point in the opposite direction. None of these men had lived on the frontier, owned land or other real property, and none had succeeded as entrepreneurs. Few of them had parents or other

---

[75] Devine, *op. cit.*, p. 99. A poll reported on the following page, however, in a table giving cross-national comparisons for several years, gives a figure of 53 percent for 1964 and 62 percent for 1968. This discrepancy between the findings of these two polls may result from different wording of the question. The poll that registered the higher agreement in 1964 asked simply, "Do you think most people can be trusted?" The one that showed a lower level of agreement gave as an alternative, "You can't be too careful in your dealings with people."

[76] See Morris Rosenberg, "Misanthropy and Political Ideology," *American Sociological Review*, 21 (1956), 690–95; Abraham Kardiner *et al.*, *The Psychological Frontiers of Society* (New York: Columbia University Press, 1956), pp. 345–50.

[77] Lane, *op. cit.*, p. 54. We shall return frequently to this theme in the succeeding chapters in discussing the psychological background of totalitarianism.

relations who were successful small businessmen. As Catholics, their experience of Church government in the 1950s furnished no support for democracy, nor did the eastern or southern European origins of most of them. Nor did their childhood family experiences furnish support for freedom and for the participatory ideal.

One experience which Lane found important was the social and economic position of his respondents relative to that of their parents. With two exceptions they were markedly more prosperous than their fathers. And they had done well economically in respect to their own expectations. They were, after all, *upper* working-class people. Another experience which Lane found significant was their experience of small group democracy. The large majority of them had been participants in veterans organizations, unions, PTAs, and the local community council of "Hilltop." In these groups they had had a satisfying experience of democratic procedures. In Lane's findings we have a partial empirical confirmation of the hypothesis put forward on the basis of historical evidence by Frederick Watkins, which we discussed in Chapter 2, that the democratic habits needed to sustain democracy in the large world of distant representative government must be inculcated as a political ethic in the small face-to-face groups of daily life if our liberal democratic institutions are to be sustained. Almond and Verba found a similar correlation between organizational participation and civic culture traits.

The researchers discovered that "joiners" are to be found in higher proportion among British and American citizens than among citizens of the other three cultures. Fifty-seven percent of the American sample and 47 percent of the British belonged to some organization or other. In all countries economic interest groups are represented. Social organizations were mentioned by more than 10 percent only in the United States, Britain, and Germany. Only in the United States did 10 percent or more also mention religious, civic-political, and fraternal organizations. This indicates the persistence of associationism as a special characteristic of American political culture to which Tocqueville gave emphasis as far back as the 1830s. He interpreted our penchant for forming voluntary groups as a counteragent to the atomizing tendencies of our individualism and as a response to the natural need of an egalitarian society to find a substitute for the aristocrat as a sponsor of special programs. Almond and Verba relate joinerism to a high sense of civic competence. They conclude that "pluralism . . . may indeed be one of the most important foundations of political democracy." [78]

The authors of the "civic culture" project also hypothesized that democratic role playing in school and home would be primary socializ-

---

[78] Almond and Verba, *op. cit.*, pp. 309, 322.

ers for democratic attitudes at the national political level. The American and British interviews yielded the highest percentage of persons who remembered that they had had some influence on the making of family decisions when they were small, (73 and 69 percent). A similar result was found for remembering freedom to protest family decisions and actual protests made. Percentages were lower and closer together across the board on the question of freedom to discuss unfair school treatment. On the question of freedom to participate in school discussions and debates, Americans scored 40 percent, higher than any of the others, and the British, surprisingly, ranked much lower along with the others (16 percent). British and Americans ranked highest in consultation on job decisions. Job, schools, and family participation were shown to be of importance for developing civic culture traits in that area. Cumulative experience in the three areas was found more productive of democratic attitudes than experience in only one area.

The data showed that for all nations there was a tendency over time for more opportunity to participate both in home and in school decisions. In family decisions the increase was gradual both in the United States and in the United Kingdom. In school participation there were two dramatic increases in the United Kingdom following each of the two world wars—possibly a testimony to loss of authority by aristocratic elements of British political culture as a result of those two catastrophes. The increase in the United States has been a gradual one. The researchers connect these phenomena with continuing urbanization and industrialization, with rise in educational levels, with decline of the extended patriarchal family and rise of the nuclear family, with the emancipation of women, and with the development of greater individual autonomy.

Comparisons were made of democratic attitudes in a variety of subcultures in the five polities studied. Differences were measured among class groups, sex groups, ethnic groups, religious groups, age groups, and educational groups. Contrary to what one might expect, religion was not a chief differentiator. Of all of the subcultures measured, the educational was found to be *the* great differentiator of political attitudes. In all five political systems educated persons have more civic culture attitudes than the less well educated. National differences are markedly reduced by education. This bears out empirically a long-standing assumption of liberal democratic political philosophy and of popular democratic thought that developed reason and the capacity for informed reflection are intimately connected with the healthy operation of a modern democratic order.

Devine has pointed out that income and educational levels are closely associated with the willingness of Americans to trust one another.

Experiences of the kind we have described do not of themselves apparently produce an outgoing and trusting nature. Financial rewards and schooling are crucial. He found that although all class levels have a majority opinion in favor of the liberal tradition on most cultural measures, the lowest class (approximately 20 percent of the population) rejects trust in large numbers, with only 40 percent of them indicating that they trust their neighbors and fellow citizens.[79]

Psychological Factors.   Socializing factors in the environment alone may not induce the characterological supports of democratic culture. Lane found three men in his group of fifteen Eastporters whom he categorized as "undemocrats." Unlike the majority, the three undemocrats were intolerant of conflict and confusion. "I like to hear different points of view—up to a certain point," said one of them. "When it reaches the saturation point, it begins to get boring and meaningless." [80] Asked at this juncture whether he preferred to have expert opinion settle a matter, he was unwilling to accept this alternative and instead made excuses about his low saturation point and limited capacity, about both of which he felt guilty. One of the majority, much less well informed than this man, liked to make up his mind and felt far more confident in the face of confusion. The undemocrats are persons who fulfill Mannheim's prophecy that men of their social station are incapable of coping with the pressures of the open society. Yet it is clear that personal rather than class factors are the determining cause of this response, for the majority who could cope were of the same social background.

The undemocrats also feared social freedom. They were the only ones who believed that acts of violence were the result of greater freedom and fewer restraints. "They would do anything they want—they would steal, they would kill, and nobody would stop them. . . . You have to have laws to keep the people in bound or else they're going to run away with themselves." [81] Lane interpreted this as a reflection of these men's fear of themselves, a doubt of their ability to control their own passions if faced with greater freedom. Sex-tension tests confirmed this theory for two of them, as did a finding that these men were more prone to experience excessive anger than the others. The third exhibited extraordinary consumption impulses—for alcohol, food, cars, clothing—things which kept him constantly worried about money.

The three men with problems of self-control—which, according to Lane, accounts for their fear of freedom—exhibited the weakest ego strengths of the fifteen persons interviewed. And this appeared to Lane

[79] Devine, *op. cit.*, p. 263.
[80] *Ibid.*, p. 33.
[81] *Ibid.*, pp. 42–43.

to be the root cause of their desire to "escape from freedom," albeit not into the warm arms of community (as one would expect from Eric Fromm's interpretation of such escape), but rather into the repressive regulations of society. In a day of increasing social freedom, these men, lacking internal controls of strong conscience and a close and compelling moral code, retreat into the police power. Coercive authority, not community, is the refuge of the weak ego.

Lane found that ego weakness correlated in all these men with a great loss of identity—ethnic, religious, sexual. They were also the most withdrawn of the group, the least participant, socially and politically. Isolated, they belonged to no voluntary groups. With all this they displayed a romantic unrealism and a belief in the "philosopher's stone." They liked to fantasize about a golden age.

Unlike the majority, the three undemocrats also mistrusted the processes of democracy and found them illusory. They were pessimistic about the possibility of controlling public power and all subscribed to a conspiracy theory of government which Lane labels "cabalism"—the view that everything is manipulated by "a secret association of a few designing persons." [82] The cabals might be both high and low in status, made up of international bankers one moment, of Communists the next. One source of their cabalism Lane found in the need of these men to restore some agent of public authority to society in order to compensate for the destruction of democratic power and authority resulting from their cynicism. The most important explanatory factor he found to be the weak egos and lack of internal controls with which he elsewhere accounted for their fear of freedom and of situations of ambiguity.

Lane does not see the relationship of low ego strength to cabalism as psychodynamic but as cognitive and experiential. The undemocrats do not know the meaning of control in their own lives, and they can conceive it for society only as illegitimate and self-seeking conspiracy, not as rightful rule.

It would appear that personal rather than social factors must account for the cabalism of the undemocrats, which the trusting majority do not evidence. Nevertheless, Lane finds in the general social and political order as well as their specific life situations social explanations of their cabalistic beliefs. In our vast and complex society of separated, balanced, and federalized powers the agencies of control are obscure. The mysteries of the market economy are similarly unfathomable to most men, and the manipulative element in modern life, so prominent in advertising, as well as the traditional American fear of "being taken for a sucker" lend further credence to the cabalistic syndrome.

[82] *Ibid.*, p. 114.

In the specific situation of Lane's "Eastporters," feudal images carried over from recent European origins also contribute to cabalism. "Kuchinsky is, in particular, a transplanted peasant with a peasant's superstitution. The political order of Poland was seen as part of the natural or divine order of things, where events are established beyond peradventure of control; indeed, the idea of controlling events is hardly admitted to the peasant mind." [83] Shades of Mannheim's misgivings! Added to this, anxiety about Americanism still unachieved may lead to denunciation of the enemies of hundred-percent Americanism—Communists and Jews—as conspiratorial groups. And finally, Lane sees in the persistence of magical ways of thinking carried over from a formerly religious and now secularized culture another possible root of cabalism.

With all of these negative factors at work, one may well wonder why only three of the fifteen "Eastporters" turned out to be "undemocrats." Lane gives special emphasis to the willingness of the majority to participate, to leave the fantasy world which their social background tends to engender and move out into society, and to find an inoculant against the cabalistic myth in the satisfying transactions of this world of democratic participation.

It should be noted that Lane found no connections between the cabalism of his three undemocrats and an active authoritarianism. Nor did he find a desire for changes in the rules of the game, inadequate as they were perceived to be. "I think I'm pretty well satisfied," "I'm happy the way I am," said two of the three. In the statements of two of the most withdrawn respondents, there was a hint that a charismatic hero with magic formulas might be the solution to difficulty; but it was only a hint—"a rather faint trace, visible, a little disturbing, but in perspective, not a search for a great man to replace a worn-out constitution." [84] Only in their utopias, which were detached from aspiration or efforts to achieve actual political change, did the undemocrats delineate a simple and authoritarian mode of government. In later chapters we shall discuss in detail the social and political conditions under which the fantasies of men like Lane's undemocrats become politically active.

Conclusion.   We have seen that empirical social science can add several dimensions to the historian's explanation of the causes and conditions of liberal democratic political culture. In addition to ingrained historical habit arising from the continuity of our tradition, there are both characterological and sociological supports for liberal democratic values. There appears to be something that can meaningfully be called the "liberal personality"—the strong and self-reliant ego whose manner

[83] *Ibid.*, p. 128.
[84] *Ibid.*, p. 174.

is generous, trusting, and outgoing. We have seen that an authoritarian pattern of historical conditioning in an individual's family history can be canceled out by the contemporary experience of democratic role playing in a variety of face-to-face decision-making groups. All of these empirical findings have validated theories long held on purely intuitive grounds.

6. How Stable Is "Established Liberal?"

We have examined the salient elements of liberal democratic culture in the United States and outlined some of its preconditions. Due to the paucity of empirical information available, we probably have not accounted for all, or perhaps even the crucial preconditions. Nor have we been able to demonstrate that the preconditions we have described will be constant in the future. In view of these gaps in our information, what shall we take as a measure of the stability of the culture we have described?

Measuring Public Confidence.   A useful measure would appear to be the confidence that Americans display in the institutions of the political regime. These are the carriers of the values and beliefs we have been examining, and it seems reasonable to suppose that a loss of confidence in them might, at least in the long run, erode confidence in the ideal with which they are associated. Decline in institutional authority might well induce deep-rooted cultural strain of the kind Geertz has described, ultimately producing an ideological revolution. On the other hand, the result might well be a reaffirmation of the old system of values and beliefs and a movement to reinvigorate or replace institutions which have failed to give them life. An estimate of this second possibility may be in order after we have examined in the next three chapters the ideological systems on the right and the left that are pitted against the existing order. We shall have to discover whether they are opposed to the institutional order or also to basic value and belief patterns.

Many of the empirical studies we have reviewed contain recent evidence about levels of confidence found among Americans in their major institutions. McClosky's findings are at first glance contradictory. Replies by the followership sample to questions about faith in government policies and about the amenability of government to popular influence and control revealed considerable confusion and division. Half the sample perceived the government as inaccessible and unresponsive, while at the same time almost 90 percent were confident that government would do the right thing. As McClosky sums up this finding, "They may be cynical about the operation of the system, but they do not question its legitimacy." [85] The explanation of this phenomenon may lie in the American tradition of mistrust of government grounded in the history of the American Revolution and in frontier individualism.[86] By contrast, the active stratum registered far less cynicism and suspicion and virtually achieved consensus in this area. They also scored lower on cynicism and suspicion in the scale scores and far higher on the social responsibility scale. McClosky also found that among the electorate the respondents with college educations and those who had achieved high status occupations were significantly more positive about government than others, and also had a greater sense of social and political responsibility.

Almond and Verba's finding of a widespread sense of civic competence in the United States—that is, a sense of one's capacity to control public decisions—is an indirect measure of institutional confidence. So are the "givenness" thesis of Boorstein and the promises of "homogenizing" themes of the national purpose essay of the 1950s. Devine, citing an SRC poll first taken in 1958 and repeated in 1964, 1966, and 1968, shows a level of confidence ranging from 56 to 62 percent for each year except 1966, when the figure was down to 48 percent. More recent surveys carried out in 1971 and 1972, however, show a sharp downturn in confidence not only in governmental institutions, but in all the major institutions of American society.

In the fall of 1971 the Harris Poll asked a national cross-section sample: "As far as the people running these institutions are concerned, would you say you have a great deal of confidence, only some confidence, or hardly any confidence at all in them?" A list of major social and political institutions followed. It included large corporations, organized religion, education, organized labor, the press, medicine (both physical and mental), television, banks, the scientific community, the advertising industry, local retail stores, the executive, legislative, and judicial branches of the federal government, and the military.[87] Only one institution in sixteen commanded majority support—medicine. In comparison with the figures resulting from a similar poll in 1966, *every* institution had lost a large measure of support. Six of seven which had commanded a majority in 1966 had lost it by 1971. In the cases of major companies, education, banking and financial institutions, advertising, the presidency, and local retail stores half or almost half of the previous level of trust had been lost. Congress and the military lost substantially

[85] McClosky, op. cit., p. 371.

[86] Devine (op. cit., p. 102) has pointed out that Locke also emphasizes a suspicion of government in power.

[87] Harris Survey, reported in the Rochester Democrat and Chronicle, October 25, 1971.

more than half their previous support. Only in our doctors did a majority of people have "a great deal" of confidence. Less than 20 percent of the sample registered a "great deal" of support for organized labor, the press, the Congress, and the advertising agencies. "Obviously," concluded Lou Harris, "these are not comfortable times for any sector of the American Establishment, judged by the almost universal skepticism of the U.S. public toward the leaders of their principal institutions." [88]

Another poll conducted periodically by the Harris Survey has attempted to develop measures of general alienation through responses to such statements as "The rich get richer and the poor get poorer"; "What you think doesn't count very much"; "The people running the country don't really care what happens to people like yourself"; "People who have the power are out to take advantage of you"; "You feel left out of things around you." Taken together, these seem to measure an individual's sense of social and political competence and general level of satisfaction. Computing an average for responses to the several statements, Harris found that general alienation had risen from 24 percent of the population in 1966 to an all-time high of 47 percent in 1972. The index had risen by 6 percent between 1966 and 1968, by 5 percent between 1968 and 1971, and by 12 percent in the single year from 1971 to 1972! Among blacks, the aged, big-city residents, union members, and those with the least education and income in the country the alienation figure surpassed 50 percent.[89]

The data just reviewed indicate a widespread disenchantment with American society by its members just prior to the end of the Vietnam War. The effects of that war and of the Watergate scandal have yet to be measured. Chapters 4 to 6 may help us to decide whether these things are likely to lead to a general ideological and cultural revolution or, instead, to a renewal of our institutions on the basis of traditional American ideals and beliefs that remain authoritative.

Bibliography

ARIELI, YEHOSHUA, *Individualism and Nationalism in American Ideology*. Cambridge, Mass.: Harvard University Press, 1964.

Articles on Liberalism in *Annals of the American Academy of Political and Social Science*, November 1962.

[88] *Ibid.*

[89] Harris Survey, reported in the *Rochester Democrat and Chronicle*, July 2, 1971 and June 19, 1972. Also, for a detailed analysis of the alienation phenomenon, see Arthur H. Miller, "Political Issues and Trust in Government: 1964–1970," a paper delivered at the convention of the American Political Science Association, Washington, D.C., September 1972.

BACHRACH, PETER, "Elite Consensus and Democracy," *Journal of Politics*, 24(3), August 1962: 439–52.

BELL, DANIEL, *The End of Ideology: On the Exhaustion of Political Ideas in the Fifties*, rev. ed. New York: The Free Press, 1962.

BOORSTIN, DANIEL, *The Genius of American Politics*. Chicago: University of Chicago Press, 1953.

DAHL, ROBERT A., *A Preface to Democratic Theory*. Chicago: University of Chicago Press, 1956.

DEVINE, DONALD, *The Political Culture of the United States: The Influence of Member Values on Regime Maintenance*. Boston: Little, Brown & Company, 1972.

DOLBEARE, KENNETH M., and PATRICIA, *American Ideologies: The Competing Political Beliefs of the 1970s*. Chicago, Markham, 1971.

FREE, LLOYD A., and HADLEY CANTRIL, *The Political Beliefs of Americans*. New Brunswick, N.J.: Rutgers University Press, 1967.

FRIED, ALBERT, ed., *The Jeffersonian and Hamiltonian Traditions in American Politics: A Documentary History*. Garden City, N.Y.: Doubleday & Company, Inc., 1968.

HANDLIN, OSCAR, "The American Immigrant and Ideologies," *Confluence*, 2(3), September 1953: 95–104.

HARTZ, LOUIS, *The Liberal Tradition in America: An Interpretation of American Political Thought Since the Revolution*. New York: Harcourt Brace Jovanovich, 1955.

HOFSTADTER, RICHARD, *The American Political Tradition and the Men Who Made It*. New York: Alfred A. Knopf, 1948.

KAMMEN, MICHAEL, *People of Paradox: An Inquiry Concerning the Origins of American Civilization*. New York: Alfred A. Knopf, 1972.

LANE, ROBERT, *Political Ideology: Why the American Common Man Believes What He Does*. New York: The Free Press of Glencoe, 1962.

LOWI, THEODORE J., *The End of Liberalism: Ideology, Policy, and the Crisis of Public Authority*. New York: W. W. Norton & Company, Inc., 1969.

McCLOSKY, HERBERT, "Consensus and Ideology in American Politics," *American Political Science Review*, 58(2), June 1964: 361–82.

MONSEN, JOSEPH, and MARK W. CANNON, *The Makers of Public Policy: American Power Groups and Their Ideologies*. New York: McGraw-Hill Book Company, 1965.

NOBLE, D. W., *The Paradox of Progressive Thought*. Minneapolis: University of Minnesota Press, 1958.

NORTHROP, F. S. C., *The Meeting of East and West: An Inquiry Concerning World Understanding*. New York: The Macmillan Company, 1953, Chaps. 3 and 4.

PETERSON, MERRILL D., *The Jefferson Image in the American Mind*. New York: Oxford University Press, 1960.

PETTEE, GEORGE S., "Ideology in America," *Confluence*, 2(2), June 1953: 69–80.

President's Commission on National Goals. *Goals for Americans*. Englewood Cliffs, N.J.: Prentice-Hall, Inc., 1960.

PROTHRO, JAMES W., and CHARLES M. GRIGG, "Fundamental Principles of Democracy," *Journal of Politics*, 22(2), May 1960: 276–94.

REJAI, MOSTAFA, ed., *Decline of Ideology*. Chicago: Aldine-Atherton, 1971.

ROOSEVELT, JAMES, ed., *The Liberal Papers*. Chicago: Quadrangle Books, 1962.

SUTTON, F. X., et al., *The American Business Creed*. Cambridge: Harvard University Press, 1956.

DE TOCQUEVILLE, ALEXIS, *Democracy in America*, Phillips Bradley, ed. 2 vols. New York: Alfred A. Knopf, 1945.

WAXMAN, CHAIM I., *The End of Ideology Debate*. New York: Funk & Wagnalls, 1968.

WOLFF, ROBERT P., *The Poverty of Liberalism*. Boston: Beacon Press, 1968.

4

Conservatives versus Liberals:
Cleavage within Consensus

"The Liberal establishment has been shaken to its foundation!" This might well be a "New Left" taunt, but as a matter of fact it was uttered by a Conservative, the Monroe County Vice Chairman of the Conservative Party of New York, exulting over the victory of James Buckley in the 1970 senatorial election.[1] Is this evidence that Conservatives are outside the ideological consensus of Established Liberalism that we disdiscussed in Chapter 3? No; the language is simply misleading. The Conservative spokesman is not talking about "Established Liberalism," the abstract consensus described in Chapter 3, but about the very specific conceptions of governmental purpose espoused by Welfare Liberals (or Neo-Liberals—see Chapter 2) which have dominated policy-making at the national level since the first administration of Franklin Roosevelt.

1. The Area of Liberal-Conservative Disagreement

Within an overarching agreement on the broad ends of public policy and on the principles of democratic procedure, Liberals and Conservatives disagree on the kinds of policies which are most effective to achieve those ends and on the institutions which should principally be charged with their implementation. Liberals with a capital "L"—"The Liberal

[1] *Rochester Democrat and Chronicle,* November 4, 1970, p. B1.

116

Establishment"—are today those persons who believe in the importance of wide-ranging national welfare legislation to improve the lot of the poor, the handicapped, and the aged, and in the need for extensive national intervention in the economy to insure full employment, a stable currency, and general economic health and prosperity. They also expect the national government to play a large role in helping minority groups get integrated into the mainstream of American life. Conservatives, like Classical Liberals a century ago, stress the importance of private initiative and local government responsibility for the achievement of all these goals. And they are very strongly attached to the work ethic. (The New York State Conservative Party recently adopted the beaver as a party symbol.) The Liberal-Conservative disagreement is, therefore, one which has largely to do with the efficiency of means rather than with the legitimacy of ends or basic philosophic principles.

2. Ideological Coherence and Incoherence in Mass Publics: The Liberal-Conservative Dimension

Another fact that mitigates the divisive force of the Liberal-Conservative cleavage is that Liberalism and Conservatism, as self-consistent ideological positions, seem to be embraced only by elites. The public in general cannot consistently over time be divided into distinct Liberal and Conservative groups on the dimensions indicated, although the 1960s showed some evidence of polarization. Nor is the balance of support in the electorate for the two sets of elites constant over time. Moreover, the ideological elites are more perfectly committed than the pragmatic followers to the large principles of liberal constitutional process that form the conception of authority that in turn underpins the political system as a whole.

Survey Findings on Ideological Coherence.   These conclusions are based on the results of survey research carried out by Philip Converse, Herbert McClosky, Lloyd Free, Hadley Cantril, and others over the period running from 1956 to 1968. Using data collected in 1956, 1958, and 1960 by the Michigan Survey Research Center, Converse attempted to test the popular idea that in the 1950s the American people moved from a Liberal toward a distinctly Conversative ideological position. He did this by measuring for the presence in the respondents' minds of a "belief system," which he defined as "a configuration of ideas and attitudes in which the elements are bound together by some form of constraint or functional interdependence. In the static case, 'constraint' may be taken to mean the success we have in predicting, given initial knowledge that an individual holds a specified attitude, that he holds certain further ideas and attitudes." So, for example, if a person is opposed to expanding social security one would deem him a Conservative and predict that he is probably also opposed to such things as nationalizing private industries, federal aid to education, and a sharply progressive income tax. For the most part Converse measured for psychological rather than logical contraints; the latter, he finds, play only a very minor role in belief systems.[2] His general conclusion was that only 10 to 17 percent of the population can be said to have a "contextual grasp of 'standard' [i.e., Liberal and Conservative] belief systems."[3]

The 1956 Michigan SRC survey collected data on popular responses to the two presidential candidates of that year, Dwight Eisenhower and Adlai Stevenson. Using both structured and open-ended questions, the surveyors sought to discover how respondents evaluated the candidates in terms of their liberalism and conservatism and in terms of their positions on particular policy questions that implied a liberal-conservative continuum. (No effort was made, however, to test for consistency from issue to issue.) The responses of a random national sample of 1500 persons indicated the existence of five groups of people. "Ideologues" and "Near Ideologues," the first two groups, who answered questions with specific references to liberalism and conservatism, made up respectively 2½ and 9 percent of the panel. A third category of response was classified as "Group Interest" (42 percent), given by persons who identified policy positions with such expressions as "good for people like us," or good for "the common people," or good "for union members." Converse remarks of these people that "unless an issue directly concerns their grouping in an obviously rewarding or punishing way, however, they lack the contextual grasp of the system to recognize how they should respond to it without being told by elites who hold their confidence."[4] A fourth group of responses was labeled "nature of the times" (24 percent). These people praised or blamed parties and candidates on the basis of their association with general social states such as war or peace, depression or prosperity. A fifth category of responses contained no policy significance at all (22½ percent); they appeared to have been made at random. The survey did not seem to support the "revolt of the moderates" hypothesis about political change in the 1950s, for key defections from the Democratic to the Republican party occurred in the two bottom groups, for whom the "liberal-conservative" continuum was a meaningless expression.[5]

In the 1958 survey Converse defined the liberal-conservative op-

---

[2] Philip E. Converse, "The Nature of Belief Systems in Mass Publics," in David Apter, ed., *Ideology and Discontent* (London: Free Press of Glencoe, 1964), p. 207.
[3] *Ibid.*, pp. 213, 222.
[4] *Ibid.*, p. 216.
[5] *Ibid.*, p. 218.

position basically in terms of "big government" versus "small government," and measured for consistency among positions taken by respondents on a variety of issues involving these factors. In this survey the responses of an elite sample of congressmen were compared to those of a mass sample. Respondents were asked whether the federal government ought to intervene in the economy to guarantee full employment, whether it should aid state educational programs, whether there should be federally subsidized housing, and similar questions. Constraints, (which indicate a coherently defined ideological position) were found to be far higher among responses from the elite sample than among responses from the mass group. With regard to domestic issues, for example, the degree of constraint for elites was .53 and for the mass .23.[6]

In 1960, the year of the Kennedy-Nixon presidential race, the original sample of 1956 was reinterviewed by Professor Converse's team. This time the question was asked, "Would you say that either one of the parties is more *conservative* or *liberal* than the other?" Affirmative replies were followed up by questions about what the respondents had in mind in arriving at their conclusions. The responses were classified in a code resembling but more detailed than the one used in 1956. The results revealed that 17 percent of the sample had a fairly sophisticated conception of the distinction between "liberal" and "conservative." Another 37 percent had an entirely vague conception of the difference. The remaining 46 percent fell into two groups: those who engaged in guesswork to make the ideological distinction and those who, despite a fairly clear grasp of the matter, could put only a rather limited number of connotations on either of the ideological labels.[7]

Coherence in Elite Opinion.   A 1956 study by Herbert McClosky, aspects of which we discussed in Chapter 3, appears to bear out Converse's finding that elites have more coherent ideological positions than followers on the liberal-conservative dimension. McClosky's leadership data were drawn from a survey of three thousand political actives among the delegates and alternates who attended the Democratic and Republican conventions of 1956. The followership data derived from a Gallup survey of a representative national sample of 1500 adults from the general population.[8] The same questionnaire was administered to both groups.

Measuring for consistency, McClosky found that influentials are more likely than followers to have opinions on public issues; are able to classify themselves accurately as liberal, middle of the road, or conservative; name the issues that divide the parties; indicate a level of

---

[6] *Ibid.*, p. 229.

[7] *Ibid.*, pp. 219, 220, 223.

[8] See Herbert McClosky, "Consensus and Ideology in American Politics," *American Political Science Review,* 58 (2), June 1964, 361ff.

government they are most interested in; and express opinions on party discipline, desirable levels of party control, and similar questions. A corollary of this is the finding that elites are both more consistent and more partisan in their issue orientation than the electorate in general. On a scale measuring orientation toward fourteen liberal-conservative issues, the influentials were ranged at either end of the liberal-conservative spectrum whereas the electorate grouped toward the center. A large number of voters simultaneously scored high on both a right wing and a liberal issues scale and held outlooks that were otherwise discrepant with one another.

Beginnings of Polarization.   Later data analyzed by Lloyd Free and Hadley Cantril indicates that Converse's and McClosky's findings about mass ideological incoherence may have been conditioned in part by the atmosphere of the 1950s. The data used by Free and Cantril derived from a national opinion survey carried out in 1964, the year of the Johnson-Goldwater race, by the Gallup Poll and from more limited and special surveys conducted at the same time by both the Gallup and Harris organizations. The country had moved from the quiet fifties into the middle of the turbulent sixties. Both subjective and objective tests of ideological cohesion were employed, and respondents were asked to identify themselves in terms of a liberal-conservative dichotomy. They were also asked to respond to a number of questions about specific policy areas, which were designed to reveal ideological dispositions.[9]

On the subjective scale, the results of the polling showed that "few Americans classify themselves as either very liberal or very conservative; the tendency is towards the center." In only three special groups did a plurality call themselves unqualifiedly "liberal": Blacks, Jews, and people of Eastern or Central European origins. Nevertheless, the number of persons giving themselves an ideological label was higher than predicted by either Converse's or McClosky's findings about consistency. Six percent called themselves "very liberal" and another 6 percent "very conservative." This seems to square with the other research. However, 20 and 24 percent labeled themselves respectively "moderately liberal" and "moderately conservative." Thirty-four percent said they were "middle of the road," and 10 percent didn't know what they were.[10]

In another part of their study Free and Cantril asked questions about federal housing programs, federal grants for urban renewal, the federal role in reduction of unemployment, a broad federal aid to education program, and the federal "Head-Start" program in education, federal antipoverty programs, and compulsory public medical insurance.

---

[9] Lloyd A. Free and Hadley Cantril, *The Political Beliefs of Americans* (New Brunswick, N.J.: Rutgers University Press, 1967).
   [10] *Ibid.*, pp. 41–42.

The list, which was quite similar to the one used by Converse, tended to measure response to the idea of "big government" versus laissez-faire. A respondent who gave a favorable answer to all propositions was classified as "completely liberal." If all answers were negative he was deemed "completely conservative" (the modern conservative in America being identical with the Classical Liberal). In-between categories were worked out for responses in other proportions. The results showed that "about two-thirds of the public qualified as 'liberal' with respect to the operational level of Government programs, and the category of 'completely liberal' outnumbered the 'predominantly liberal' by more than two to one."[11] Middle of the road responses totaled only 12 percent, and predominantly and completely conservative only 7 percent each. The findings imply considerable ideological constraint in each grouping. A study of the 1964 election by J. O. Field and R. E. Anderson suggests that the way in which the election was conducted contributed to this result in the electoral mind. They found a correlation between the number of people who made ideological evaluations and the stimuli presented by the campaign itself. In another analysis of the same election, John G. Pierce concluded that the "entrance of an ideological candidate . . . into the political arena increased the salience of ideological concerns among the entire electorate."[12]

The limited trend toward polarization of the electorate on the liberal-conservative dimension continued at least down to 1968, the year of the Nixon-Humphrey election. Theodore Anagnoson, in a study of Survey Research Center data for 1956, 1960, and 1968 comparable to the one carried out by Converse in 1958, found levels of mass consistency resembling those of Converse in the 1956 and 1960 data. But by 1968, he reported, in the domestic and between domestic and foreign categories, his "cross-section sample closely resembles Converse's elite in consistency. Especially in the domestic/civil rights areas, the 1968 electorate is much closer to the 1958 elite than to the 1958 electorate."[13]

The import of these findings for the future salience of ideological cleavage in the general public on the liberal-conservative dimension is not at all clear. The growing polarization discovered in 1964 and 1968 may represent either a temporary divergence from a nonideological norm, or it may indicate an important secular change in the character of American politics. Of itself even the latter development would not

[11] *Ibid.*, p. 16.
[12] J. O. Field and R. E. Anderson, "Ideology and the Public's Conceptualization of the 1964 Election," *Public Opinion Quarterly*, 33, Fall 1969: 38–98; and John G. Pierce, "Party Identification and the Changing Role of Ideology in American Politics," *Midwest Journal of Political Science*, 14, February 1970: 25–42.
[13] Theodore Anagnoson, "Ideology and the American Electorate, 1956–68," unpublished research paper, University of Rochester, December 1972 (mimeographed).

imply a dangerous decay in ideological consensus at the more abstract level of basic principle, nor a threat to the continued observance of the rules of the democratic game. After all, elites who consistently have been divided into Liberals and Conservatives over the years have been the chief carriers of respect for those rules.

3. Goldwater's Ideological Manifesto

In some Conservative elite circles the long exclusion of their number from the presidency through the whole period from the inception of the New Deal in 1933 down to 1964 (the Eisenhower era was dominated by Liberal, not Conservative, Republicanism) has had a notable effect on ideological images. The nature of the effect can be measured clearly in Barry Goldwater's book, *The Conscience of a Conservative*, which was written by or ghost-written for the senator in 1960 and widely distributed in paperback during the 1964 presidential election campaign. The effect can be summed up as the dogmatization of outmoded legal rules as though they were fixed principles of Natural Right, and the repudiation of pragmatic judgment in favor of a pure logic of abstractions. In some areas an argument against welfare liberalism is mounted in purely philosophical terms.

Goldwater writes that Conservatives believe in the "absolute differentness" of every individual "from every other human being." They reject the ideal of the "common man" because the nation has grown great through the exertions of "uncommon men." [14] This *could* be an example of Burkean elitism—the aristocratic ideal of European Conservatism— were it not for the fact that the Burkean ideal was more a functional and class ideal than one of "rugged individualism." The individualist character of Goldwater's statement makes it appear more like a principle of Classical Liberalism, which put its faith in the "uncommon man" and believed that the few rather than the many would rise to the top, especially in economic endeavor. Why would the defense of property rights be the primary object of government if there were not fear of depredations by the propertyless? Politically relevant Conservatism in America has a Classical Liberal, not Burkean, root. It also fits the world view of the Social Darwinist Liberal, a species of the Liberal persuasion very common in the United States in the late nineteenth century, as we have seen.

Conservatism as Classical Liberalism.   The Classical Liberal character of the next sentiment enunciated by Goldwater, which indirectly

---

[14] Barry Goldwater, *The Conscience of a Conservative* (New York: Hillman Books, 1960). Copyright 1960 by Victor Publishing Co. Quotations with permission.

states a conception of purpose, is unmistakable. "Every man, for his individual good and for the good of his society is responsible for his own development," Goldwater writes. "If the Conservative is less anxious than his Liberal brethren to increase Social Security benefits, it is because he is more anxious than his Liberal brethren that people be free throughout their lives to spend their earnings when and as they see fit." [15] Here we begin to see man as a free and independent individual, autonomous and self-reliant for his own development. Burke wrote rather of the radical dependence of the individual on society for his proper development and of the educational—that is to say, the moral shaping and molding—function of the social order. He also placed the economic obligations of the individual to the common good above the claim to be free to spend one's earnings with complete freedom. The latter sentiment is wholly Lockean and implies the absence of a principle of social justice in the use of property.

The final theme of the introduction to Goldwater's volume, another conception of purpose, also stands wholly within the Classical Liberal *Weltanschauung*. It is the idea that the Conservative looks upon politics as the art of achieving the "maximum amount of freedom for individuals that is consistent with the maintenance of the social order." [16] Individual freedom, not virtue or the common good, is made the first principle of justice—the central value of the Liberal way of ideas. Burke, by contrast, as Leo Strauss has pointed out, "was still too deeply imbued with the spirit of 'sound antiquity' to allow the concern with individuality to overpower the concern with virtue." [17] According to Goldwater, however, "The Conservative's first concern will always be: *Are we maximizing freedom?*" [18]

Following this general introduction we find a series of chapters which deal with specific aspects of the Conservative conception of purpose—the need to achieve individual freedom by limiting the functions of government, especially at the national level. The central theme is the idea that "government has proved to be the chief instrument for thwarting man's liberty"—the "freedom from" theme of that Classical Liberalism which presided over the dissolution of the omnicompetent system of traditional regulation.[19] It stands in sharp contrast to the Neo-Liberal ideal of "freedom for," which views the role of government positively rather than negatively in the enhancement of individual freedom. Goldwater enumerates the legitimate functions of government as the mainte-

[15] *Ibid.*, p. 12.
[16] *Ibid.*, p. 14.
[17] Leo Strauss, *Natural Right and History* (Chicago: University of Chicago Press, 1953), p. 325.
[18] Goldwater, *op. cit.*, p. 14.
[19] *Ibid.*, pp. 16–17.

nance of internal order and external defense, the administration of justice, and the removal of obstacles to the free exchange of goods—the Classical Liberal canon.

To Senator Goldwater, the principal purpose of the Constitution is to provide "a system of restraints against the natural tendency of government to expand in the direction of absolutism." [20] It is therefore not the Populist or participant aspects of the Constitution that bulk largest in his view, but rather the limiting principle, after the persuasion of the Classical Liberal. In Goldwater's view, the theory of the Constitution is also expressly antidemocratic in being antimajoritarian. In other words, limited government is seen as incompatible with democratic government, an opposition *not* stated in the writings of Classical Liberals like Locke, though found indeed in the thought of some of our Founding Fathers—for example John Adams, who was opposed by Thomas Jefferson on the issue. "Was it then a *Democracy* the framers created?" Goldwater asks. "Hardly. The system of restraints, on the face of it, was directed not only against individual tyrants but also against a tyranny of the masses." [21]

Populist Counterpoint.   The sequel of Senator Goldwater's argument is that since the Founding, the restraints have been relaxed through the expansion of the functions of the federal government. "The result is a Leviathan," he laments. But then an unexpected note is sounded, for the "Leviathan" is described as "a vast national authority out of touch with the people, and out of their control. The monolith of power is bounded only by the will of those set in high places." [22] Here the argument is turned completely around. The threat to freedom emerging from big government in Washington is not a democratic threat, a "tyranny of the masses," but a conspiracy of the few, "the will of those set in high places." Having sounded the alarm from the position of John Adams, Senator Goldwater shifts to the opinion of Thomas Jefferson or some Populist thinker in the Jeffersonian tradition. He wishes to embrace at one time both of the main traditions of American political culture and is not concerned with the strain placed upon his logic by the way in which he does this.

Strict Constructionist Conception of Purpose.   In one part of his book the senator attacks federal grants in aid as devices which have brought federal controls into areas of legislation formerly occupied solely by the states. Taking a strict constructionist view of the Tenth Amendment, he argues that these areas have been wholly *reserved* to the states. In the

[20] *Ibid.,* p. 18.
[21] *Ibid.*
[22] *Ibid.,* p. 20.

course of developing this argument, he assails the more philosophical interpretation of states' rights given by the Liberal Republican (Neo-Liberal) writer Arthur Larson, who argues that with states' rights go corresponding duties, and that when states fail to fulfill these duties they lose their rights. Senator Goldwater, emphasizing the legalist character of his own argument, says that Mr. Larson would treat "the Constitution of the United States as a kind of handbook in political theory." "The Tenth Amendment," he points out, "is *not* 'a general assumption' but a prohibitory rule of law." [23] He neglects, however, to come to grips with the fact that the Supreme Court long ago rejected the strict construction of the Tenth Amendment. In *McCulloch versus Maryland* (1819) the Court said that whatever powers are not given to the federal government are indeed reserved to the states, but that the Amendment does not specify what is in fact given. The latter has been a matter of changing interpretation over the years. Here we have a good example of the Mannheimian view that "ideology" (conservative or reactionary theory) is out of touch with manifest realities, the expression of a dream world.[24]

In discussing federally defined civil rights enforcement against the states, Senator Goldwater again takes his stand with law against philosophy. He rejects the idea that civil rights are "human rights" or "natural rights" and contends that "unless a right is incorporated in the law it is not a civil right and is not enforceable by the instruments of the civil law." [25] The argument in effect is that much federal civil rights legislation is *ultra vires*. On the matter of school integration he says: "No power regarding education was given the federal government." [26] Although he does not overlook the fact that the Supreme Court has found such a power within the Fourteenth Amendment, he rejects the idea of judicial supremacy in Constitutional interpretation. "The Congress and the States, equally with the Supreme Court, are obliged to interpret and comply with the Constitution according to their own lights," he says.[27] But here he neglects the fact that on the matter of school integration Congress and Court are in agreement, the Court sustaining federal legislation in this area. This leaves the states as the only interpreters with different ideas, and it would seem that the Civil War definitively rejected the compact theory of the Constitution. Again, we find in Goldwater's conservatism the dream character of Mannheimian "ideology." A glimpse of Classical Liberal atomism is also seen in this

[23] *Ibid.*, p. 29.
[24] See Karl Mannheim, *Ideology and Utopia: An Introduction to the Sociology of Knowledge*, trans. L. Wirth and E. Shils (New York: Harcourt Brace Jovanovich, Inc., 1936), pp. 96–97.
[25] Goldwater, *op. cit.*, p. 34.
[26] *Ibid.*, p. 35.
[27] *Ibid.*, p. 37.

section of the book when the senator remarks that what Mississippi and South Carolina do about the integration of blacks, in which he affirms a personal belief, "is their business, not mine." [28] By implication there is no national moral community with a "general will." There is only an aggregate of self-sufficient, morally unconnected individuals.

Moving on to agricultural policy, Mr. Goldwater uses once more the argument about federal usurpation of power, but supplements it here with a philosophical principle. "Farm production, like any other production," he writes, "is best controlled by the natural operation of the free market." In this connection he refers to the "natural laws of economics." [29] Unable to find in the Constitution the "rights of man," he nevertheless manages to find somewhere a set of natural laws of free competition.

In the chapter on labor legislation Goldwater also rises from the law to the abstract heights of philosophical argument, invoking "freedom of association" as "one of the natural rights of man." "Right to work laws derive from the natural law: they are simply an attempt to give freedom of association the added protection of civil law." [30] By this point he has apparently forgotten that he had earlier denied to Mr. Larsen the right to place philosophical principles above the Constitution. Similarly, in discussing taxes and spending, where not even an old interpretation of the Constitution can serve him, Senator Goldwater says that "one of the foremost precepts of the natural law is man's right to the possession and use of his property." The senator supports his argument against the Neo-Liberals on this point by invoking *both* the Constitution *and* natural law. The Neo-Liberal aim, he writes, is "an egalitarian society—an objective that does violence both to the Charter of the Republic and the laws of Nature. We are all equal in the eyes of God but we are equal *in no other respect*." [31]

Hint of a Conspiracy Theory.   Senator Goldwater's chapter on the welfare state brings into play still another kind of argument—the "conspiracy theory," a device which usually is absent in the political polemics of Established Liberalism but frequently is found in the literature both of the Radical Right and the Radical Left. Mr. Goldwater speaks of a mysterious and unnamed group of people whom he dubs "the collectivists" whose ultimate aim is "to subordinate the individual to the state," apparently because they simply are devilish enough to want to. Having found that in America the success of free enterprise has made it impossible to accomplish this by fomenting a class struggle leading to the

28 *Ibid.*, p. 38.
29 *Ibid.*, pp. 42, 44.
30 *Ibid.*, p. 50.
31 *Ibid.*, pp. 61, 64.

introduction of state socialism, they have chosen another strategy which they have found "more compatible with the political processes of a democratic society." [32] This new strategy involves the introduction of the concept and practice of the "welfare state." Goldwater's argument is only a very modest version of the conspiracy theory, for we shall see it used more extensively and more dramatically as we move further to the right and then later as we look at the "New Left."

Senator Goldwater's chapter on foreign policy sounds a militaristic note and reveals an attitude of uncompromising rigidity toward the maintenance of established American positions. Our relations with the Soviet Union he sees as deeply antagonistic, virtually a condition of undeclared war. Neither alliances, negotiations, disarmament, nor the processes of the United Nations are of any use to sustain the position of the United States. We can rely only upon our own national military power and should not hesitate to encourage disaffection among the peoples of the Soviet bloc, to withdraw recognition from Communist regimes, and in all ways to act like a great power. Victory, not peace, must be the aim of our foreign policy.[33] This seems to be the natural external counterpart of the domestic "communist conspiracy" theme in Senator Goldwater's ideology.

4. Conservative Elites and the Established Liberal Consensus

We have described a major ideological statement by an American Conservative leader. Does Senator Goldwater's book also express the beliefs and values of his elite supporters in the 1964 election? James McEvoy III, for example, has analyzed the responses of early Goldwater supporters to questions from the Survey Research Center's studies of the 1964 election. His intention was to examine the "character and degree of attitudinal and ideological constraint among [the] opinions, behaviors and attitudes" of these persons.[34] The sample was drawn from relatively high socioeconomic strata and constituted the elite echelon of the Goldwater movement. They contained a remarkably high percentage of college graduates, of persons with incomes over $10,000 per year, of professional people, and of self-employed businessmen and managers.

The 1964 Election.   McEvoy found that the single most crucial issue of domestic policy for the early Goldwaterites he examined was segrega-

---

[32] *Ibid.*, p. 72.
[33] *Ibid.*, pp. 123–35.
[34] See James McEvoy III, "Conservatism and Extremism: Goldwater Supporters in the 1964 Presidential Election," in Robert Schoenberger, ed., *The American Right Wing* (New York: Holt, Rinehart & Winston, Inc., 1970), pp. 241ff. Copyright 1969 by Holt, Rinehart & Winston. Quotations with permission.

tion—particularly federal intervention in the area of civil rights, as manifested by the Civil Rights Act of 1964. They were distinctly opposed to federal intervention in this area and evidenced considerable approval of segregation and other anti-black attitudes.[35] In the case of federally directed school integration, the Goldwater group ranged thirty-three percentage points above the early backers of Lyndon Johnson. On other civil rights issues not related to federal control over traditional local matters there was also a difference between the two groups but it was not as great.

Although the integration position of the early Goldwaterites could be accounted for by the overrepresentation of the South in their ranks, it is significant that the opinion of the later supporters of the senator, among whom southerners were underrepresented, was not significantly different. Both groups also showed a tendency to favor segregation in general, to oppose open occupancy, and to perceive the civil rights movement as violent rather than peaceful. McEvoy points out, however, that the segregationist views of the Goldwater supporters were not an autonomous factor but were rather clearly tied in with opposition to the extension of federal power into formerly local matters. These people clearly responded to and agreed with Senator Goldwater's ideology of decentralization and strict constructionism that we described above.[36] Racism was present, however, and the Survey Research Center's "feeling thermometer," an evaluative measuring technique, showed a "general pattern of antagonism toward Jews, Catholics, and Negroes on the part of the early pro-Goldwater group." [37] None of these things was found in Senator Goldwater's own statement of ideals.

In foreign policy matters, both groups of Goldwater supporters ranked above the Johnson supporters on disapproving American involvement in Vietnam, with early Goldwaterites scoring fourteen points higher and later Goldwaterites seven. To solve the problem of the war the early supporters of the senator favored escalation of the conflict, including the invasion of North Vietnam, by a factor of two to one over the Johnsonites, and the later Goldwater group was only slightly less aggressive. These opinions seem to be in line with those of the senator, who engaged, as we have seen, in a certain amount of saber rattling in *Conscience of a Conservative*.

The early Goldwaterites also scored high on an "Anti-Communism Index" employed by the opinion surveyors, which measured aggressive interventionism in Communist countries. They were twenty points above the later group of Goldwaterites on this index and forty points above

[35] *Ibid.*, p. 247.
[36] *Ibid.*, p. 249.
[37] *Ibid.*, p. 250.

the Johnson supporters. This is congruent with the strong anticommunist ideology of the senator himself.

On social welfare questions the survey researchers found a similar marked difference between Goldwaterites and Johnsonites. As in the civil rights, anti-Communism, and militarism areas, the early supporters of Goldwater were more extreme in their opinions than the latecomers. The latecomers, for example, were eighteen percentage points higher than the earlier group in support of Medicare, ten points higher in favorable attitudes toward aid to the unemployed, and nine points higher in their approval of educational aid than the early Goldwaterites. The differences, however, were comparatively small when both groups are set over against the Johnson people. The finding here, as in the other areas of ideology and social policy, shows a strong congruence between Senator Goldwater's personal confession of faith and the beliefs and sentiments of his supporters, who tend to take, if anything, a more extreme stance than the senator.

A "Half-Ideology."   Journalist Richard Rovere and others have hypothesized that Goldwater supporters would vary significantly from Liberals on their support for basic constitutional procedures as well as on domestic and foreign policy issues. They expected in particular to find deep doubts about the effectiveness of the three national agencies of representation—Congress, the major political parties, and elections. The evidence, however, did not strongly support an interpretation of general alienation and hostility to the forms and institutions of American political life, McEvoy found. This result is also congruent with what we found to be the structure of the senator's own "half-ideology." He and his supporters do not stand outside the national consensus on rules of the game; rather, they represent simply one far pole among policy alternatives among which the public chooses by using those rules.

5. Senator Buckley: Back Toward Pragmatism

Other politically active self-identified Conservatives who have moved to the center of the stage since the failure of Senator Goldwater have maintained an ideological position in many ways similar to the one we have described, but also different in crucial respects. James L. Buckley, the Senator from New York and the first person to be elected to national office on the Conservative ticket, reviewed the elements of his political philosophy in a press interview shortly after his election in 1970. He described his Conservatism as "more a frame of reference in analyzing problems than an adherence to a set of principles which have to be applied to every new situation." [38] The framework, he went on, features prominently a disposition against drastic change without a careful analysis of the likely consequences of such change in order not to jeopardize the overwhelmingly healthy parts of an institution in an effort to cure ills in other parts. It also emphasizes problem-solving by smaller rather than larger units, and by private persons rather than public jurisdictions. Senator Buckley opposes the concentration of power, both economic and political, and is a believer in the principle of "subsidiarity," which holds "that every function should devolve to the lowest level of government that in fact can competently handle it." It is interesting that the philosophy of St. Thomas Aquinas should be invoked by this Catholic Conservative as authority for ideas which secular Conservatives derive from the ideologues of Classical Liberalism.

A Moderate Stance.   Senator Buckley readily accepted the label of "strict constructionist" suggested by his interviewer, and said that he had agreed with Barry Goldwater on the Civil Rights Act of 1964. His opposition, he said, was based not on the end but on the means employed, and he would not today desire to undo the achievement of this desirable goal. He would "enforce the laws we have and see to it that, for example, the unions don't discriminate against people trying to get into apprentice programs because of race." With recent "strict constructionist" Supreme Court decisions in other civil liberties areas Senator Buckley expressed mild disagreement because of their tendency to make it difficult to cope with modern criminality. In outlining his views on the handling of the problem of poverty, the senator avoided any flat repudiation of welfare programs or of federal responsibility in the area and concentrated rather on the question of effective kinds of federal legislation. He favors an emphasis on general education and special training programs rather than traditional welfare or the family income approach to the cure of poverty. A question about the need for a "strong, anticommunist foreign policy" he turned aside with a remark that in earlier years Conservatives were the most isolationist of Americans but today the least, and that he himself was "not prepared to turn [his] back on the rest of the world." All in all, Senator Buckley's presentation of his Conservative frame of reference was a much toned down, even muted version of the themes that we found so militantly set forth by Senator Goldwater. To some extent this may be explained by the fact that at the time of the interview he had just been elected to the Senate and was looking forward to the necessity of cooperating there with "Establishment Liberals" of the Republican Party.

[38] See David S. Broder, "Buckley Speaks on Senator Buckley," *Rochester Democrat and Chronicle,* January 10, 1971.

6. The Second Nixon Administration

In January 1973 a vast program of national welfare legislation that had been built up over forty years came suddenly under attack by President Richard Nixon. It was announced that the Office of Economic Opportunity would be dismantled and its functions parceled out among other governmental agencies. Many of its programs were terminated. A billion-dollar program to put the hard-core unemployed to work in public service jobs was dropped. Job-training programs were handed over to local governments, who were granted discretion as to which programs to retain. Urban Renewal and Model Cities programs were to be phased out. Money already appropriated by the Congress was impounded and a moratorium placed on housing subsidies. The family assistance plan for a minimum annual income was given up. It was also announced that farm price supports would be cut.[39]

The watchwords of national domestic policy had suddenly become "decentralization" and "economy." The Conservative dream of dismantling the vast federal bureaucracy was at last being realized by a Republican President who had been returned to power with an overwhelming electoral majority. A new Federalism had been proclaimed. The same political processes that had installed the welfare state had now, apparently, declared its dissolution—a fact which offers eloquent testimony to the importance of the abstract value consensus described in Chapter 3.

Richard Nixon had decided to enact Barry Goldwater's program, but not for Senator Goldwater's reasons. Nowhere in the rhetoric accompanying the sweeping policy changes was there found any reference to sacred principles of law, either positive or natural. The entire reasoning of the Administration was pragmatic. The welfare state simply had not worked. Money appropriated for welfare programs was not reaching its intended beneficiaries, and inefficiency within the federal bureaucratic structure had reached catastrophic proportions. The only possible cure was administrative surgery and the return of service functions to the states and localities.

The continuing strength of the basic consensus on Liberal Democratic constitutional principles was tested in ensuing weeks. Decisions in federal courts slowed the pace of the Nixon "revolution" by holding that the president could not arbitrarily impound moneys appropriated by the Congress for specified purposes. In general, it was made clear that the apparent mandate for change in policy direction given by the

39 See *Time*, February 5, 1973, p. 5.

presidential election process had to be validated by strict adherence by the Chief Executive to the principles of constitutional decision-making in other forums. The ensuing, though unrelated Watergate revelations demonstrated further the primacy for the nation of that procedural consensus. Senator Goldwater's severe strictures on the Administration and his insistence that the entire truth about the break-in and subsequent cover-up be made known regardless of political consequences made it clear that he valued that procedural consensus over the policy goals embodied in his private reading of the Constitution. Principled Conservatism and the Liberal Democratic value consensus stood together against an unprincipled pragmatism. It had been dramatically demonstrated that in a functioning Liberal Democracy there were parameters laid down for pragmatic politics. We shall see that this is not the case in our consideration of Fascist and Communist political cultures.

7. Varieties of Conservatism

To this point we have implied that the concept of Conservatism is more or less the same as "Business Liberalism," the small-government, laissez-faire values of Classical Liberalism. Nothing could be further from the truth. A summary and analysis of the writings of prominent Conservatives such as William F. Buckley, Jr., David Lawrence, Leonard Read, Clarence Carson, Henry Hazlitt, and others would seem in order at this point. And a comparative study of a number of such works would no doubt reveal a much broader range of ideas than we have reviewed, and many nuances of difference among them. The writings of Conservative intellectuals are also specialized in particular areas of social theory. People like Frederick von Hayek, Milton Friedman, Henry Hazlitt, and Ayn Rand specialize in economic theory. Willmoore Kendall, Frank Meyer, and James Burnham devote themselves to political themes. There are also theological or religious conservatives, like Eric Voegelin, Elton Trueblood, and John Hallowell. And finally there are the social conservatives, such as Russell Kirk, Robert Nisbet, and Whittaker Chambers. The variety of themes and of tones raises a question as to whether all of these people are really concerned with the same vision of the good society or with the same practical goals.

Burke and Conservatism.   Historically, we associate the beginnings of Conservative thought with the intellectual reaction to the French Revolution. A well-known history of Conservative thought by a leading American Conservative polemicist, Russell Kirk, is subtitled *A History of Conservative Thought from Burke to Santayana,* and in the learned world Burke is commonly known as the "Father of Conservatism." Yet we know that Burke was the articulator of an aristocratic, organicist, and in a sense theocratic philosophy. As Louis Hartz has pointed out, echoing Tocqueville, American political culture *never* contained the principles of feudal aristocracy and in that sense has been Liberal from the beginnings. Locke, not Burke, stands at the wellspring of political thought in America. Conservatism in this context, it would appear, should be something rather different from its European cousins. It should seek to conserve ideas and attitudes which are fundamentally Liberal—the original Classical Liberalism which in Establishment thought has been reshaped into Revised or Welfare Liberalism. And an examination of the writings of politically active Conservative ideologues and polemicists shows that this is indeed the case. Nevertheless, Burkean overtones are to be found here and there among their formulations, an anomaly that requires explanation. There is also a group of Burkean social critics of whom we shall have to give an account.

Even the introductory chapter of Senator Goldwater's *Conscience of a Conservative*, a prime example of Business Liberalism, contains a brief statement of "beliefs" (in the Beer and Ulam sense) which could have been formulated by Edmund Burke himself, or, for that matter, by a Tudor bishop:

> Conservatism puts material things in their proper place—[it] has a structured view of the human being and of human society, in which economics plays only a subsidiary role. . . . Conservatives take account of the *whole* man, while the Liberals tend to look only at the material side of man's nature. The Conservative believes that man is, in part, an economic, an animal creature; but that he is also a spiritual creature with spiritual needs and spiritual desires. What is more, these needs and desires reflect the superior side of man's nature, and thus take precedence over his economic wants. Conservatism therefore looks upon the enhancement of man's spiritual nature as the primary concern of political philosophy.[40]

Here is a world view very different from the atomistic economism of the original Classical Liberalism, whose *Weltanschauung* dominates Senator Goldwater's book.

Conservatives themselves have recognized and articulated the discordance and variety of Conservative doctrines. In an essay on the definition of Conservatism William F. Buckley, Jr., editor of the *National Review*, pointed up differences in tone between the dogmatic and dictatorial "objectivism" of Ayn Rand and his own prudential, situation-oriented approach. He also made it clear in describing the circumstances of Max Eastman's resignation from the editorial board of *National Review* that while his own Conservatism is God-oriented, this is not true of all

[40] Goldwater, *op. cit.*, pp. 10–11.

who properly call themselves Conservatives. In a final paragraph Mr. Buckley concludes that

> The freeway remains large, large enough to accommodate very different players, with highly different prejudices and techniques: from Frank Meyer, with his metaphysics of freedom, to Russell Kirk, with his traditionalist preoccupations; from Brent Bozell with his vision of the church-centered society to Garry Wills and his insuperable wall of separation; from Willmoore Kendall and Ernest van den Haag with their emphasis on the consensual society to Milton Friedman and the Open Society—the differences are now tonal, now substantive; but they do not appear to be choking each other off. The symbiosis may yet be a general consensus on the proper balance between freedom, order, justice, and tradition.[41]

Social Conservatives.   The general consensus, however, still remains only a possibility and has not been realized. And if it is to be a logical consensus, there are numerous anomalies to overcome. Social critics like Russell Kirk, Peter Viereck, and John Hallowell, for example, do not have a clear political objective. Their critique is aimed rather at our democratic culture. Its keynote is "a revulsion from the society and culture produced and shaped by America's politically and economically emancipated masses." It is an "aesthetic and visceral" rejection of mass society, as Philip Chapman describes it.[42]

Social critics of this ilk see in the Burkean variety of Conservatism an articulate philosophical reply to the democratic and equalitarian philosophers whom they regard as the authors and exponents of mass society. Inasmuch as there has been no indigenous opposition to the growth of democracy since the Jacksonian era, they need to import one from abroad. Unable to fit the Burkean model of aristocratic political order to American political culture, which never was feudal, they have produced no political prescription. Chapman argues that none of them have ever come to grips with specific problems of political philosophy: the nature, responsibilities, and limits of political authority, the rights and obligations of citizens, or the ideal form of leadership and government. Their total message is to reject the American present and to seek to stimulate the individual to have a change of cultural heart. Were they to develop a clear political theory they would have to abandon Burkean ideas about prescription and continuity and come out for drastic reform. The other alternative, in logic, is to abandon their aristocratic dream and reconcile themselves to the present character of American society. Neither alternative is acceptable to them.

[41] William F. Buckley, Jr., "Notes Toward an Empirical Definition of Conservatism," in Frank S. Meyer, *What is Conservatism?* (New York: Holt, Rinehart & Winston, Inc., 1964), p. 226.

[42] Philip C. Chapman, "The New Conservatism: Cultural Criticism of Political Philosophy," *Political Science Quarterly* 75 (1), March 1960: p. 21.

Without a clear philosophical objective in politics, many of the conservative cultural critics have nevertheless become politically active. In general they have supported the aims and strategies of the conservative political activists. Frequently this has led to intellectual anomalies, for political Conservatives like Goldwater and economic Conservatives like Friedman are really Classical Liberals, as we have noted. Their world view is precisely that against which Burke himself inveighed as destructive of high culture and civilization!

Harry Jaffa, a student and colleague of Leo Strauss, who is known as an exemplar of a kind of Neo-Platonist or more generally Neo-Classical political theory, was among the speech writers employed by Senator Goldwater in his presidential race. But the philosophical position of Mr. Jaffa contains a sharp critique of our entire Lockean political culture. Leo Strauss has described the Lockean world view as fundamentally Machiavellian, in that it has reduced the traditional view which saw moral perfection as the purpose of political society to a hedonistic preservation ideal. And in Goldwater's atomistic individualism we find a splendid example of the Lockean philosophical standpoint. But despite these anomalies, Conservatives of all stripes do tend to hang together in the political battle. We must therefore ask whether there is something that they have in common of a basic sort which makes them see one another as allies despite these large differences.

Is There a Unifying Theme? An attempt to discover the ties that bind various strands of Conservatism together—if indeed such ties exist —was made a few years ago by Professor Samuel Huntington in an article in the *American Political Science Review*.[43] Professor Huntington sketched out three theories of Conservatism as an ideology. The first is that it is purely and simply an aristocratic theory uniquely associated with a single historical moment—the reaction to the French Revolution and the Liberal ideas embodied in it. A second is what Huntington calls an "autonomous theory" of Conservatism which is popular among the new cultural conservatives. This runs to the effect that the essence of Conservatism is a body of eternally valid social ideas which is unconnected with the interests of a particular group or with the outlook of any particular age. The third is a situational definition, which sees Conservatism as that ideology which arises from a distinctive but recurring type of historical situation in which a fundamental challenge is posed to established institutions. Its essence is to affirm existing institutions whatever they are. Huntington opts for this last explanation, claiming that the conservatisms of all ages can play this role because they share

43 Samuel Huntington, "Conservatism as an Ideology," *American Political Science Review*, 51(2), June 1957: 454–73.

the following principles: (1) Conservatism declares that man is basically a religious animal who finds a religious foundation for civil society, which implies a divine sanction for the existing social order; (2) Conservatism views society as a natural, organic product of slow historical growth; its institutions are understood to embody the wisdom of generations; (3) man is seen as a creature of instinct as well as of reason, which leads to the judgment that experience and prejudice are better guides than reason in the appraisal of social orders; (4) Conservatism views the community as superior to the individual, and derives rights from social duties; evil is found to be rooted in human nature, not in governmental institutions; (5) men are unequal, says the Conservative, and society is a complex and necessarily hierarchical organization, requiring leadership; and (6) Conservatism argues that there is a prescriptive presumption in favor of the existing system.

Huntington claims that this is the common currency of all conservatisms and that the principles adumbrated can be used to justify any kind of social order. Huntington points out that with regard to England Burke defended a commercial society which was gradually becoming an industrial one whereas when he spoke about India and the American colonies he pleaded for the established order which was very different from the order in feudal Europe. Similarly, he finds that Tudor theologians, American Federalists, and Southern planters before the Civil War all subscribed to his list of six principles. And he thinks this is also true of contemporary American Conservatives like Kirk and Rossiter. He says of this group as a whole that some of them "appear uncertain as to what they wish to defend. Some simply continue the old identification of Conservatism with business liberalism. Others are radical aristocrats, ill at ease and disgruntled with American society as it exists today."[44]

That the six criteria Huntington lays down fit the belief systems of the social and cultural critics is clear. That they also embrace the "business liberalism" of people like Goldwater is less clear. We have seen indeed that some of the ideas have been absorbed by that business liberal creed, even though they were not there to begin with. The connection between religion and morality on the one hand and sound social order on the other was emphasized by Senator Goldwater throughout his campaign, along with the alleged moral decay of America attributed indirectly to the shortcomings of the Democratic administration. We also found traces of organicism in Goldwater's *Conscience of a Conservative* even though these were incongruent with the rest. This organicist strain also shows up in the writings of politico-economic

[44] *Ibid.*, p. 471.

Conservatives, in whose work it fits ill. Frank Chodorov, for example, who writes frequently for *The Freeman*, the organ of the Conservative Institute for Economic Education, tells us that modern (welfare) economics is an "atomistic approach, seasoned with relativism that characterizes the modern school of economics." [45] To "atomism" (which actually characterizes the Classical Liberal world view from which his own economics derives) Mr. Chodorov presumbly opposes a healthy "organicism," which doesn't fit with that world view at all.

It is not clear, however, that the "business liberal" characteristically prefers instinct, experience, and prejudice over reason. Reason usually is associated with the abstract idea of "natural law," and in the same breath that he condemns "atomism" Chodorov praises "natural law" and tells us that it is "the business of the economist . . . to apply himself to the study of nature." [46] He criticizes the kind of economics he dislikes as a "study of how men make a living under prevailing laws" and says that this kind of economist "rejects . . . the possibility of absolutes." [47] But Burke, in opposing experience to abstract reason *also* criticized abstract "principles" and an abstract natural law, to which Chodorov here seems attached.

The fourth criterion of Huntington's list—the primacy of the community over the individual as a focus of value—fails to fit the business liberal at all. We already have reviewed Goldwater's disdainful comment on the idea that one can derive rights from obligations, and his individualism, not his sense of community, is what predominates in *Conscience of a Conservative*. That men are seen as unequal (Huntington's fifth criterion) plainly fits Mr. Goldwater's theory, but it hardly could be said that he argues in favor of the existing system, as the fifth criterion also stipulates. His case is rather in favor of an old and superseded system, to which he would like to return from the present "Leviathan" state, which he abhors. We end up wondering, then, whether all men who call themselves Conservatives *do* share a common fund of theoretical opinions. Perhaps the most that we can discover is a common stance or attitude—a preference for the old against the new.

8. What Makes a Conservative?

How do we explain why some people become Conservatives while others do not? Is there anything which distinguishes a Conservative, either

[45] Frank Chodorov, "The Penalty of Disregarding the Natural Law," in A. G. Heimsohn, Jr., ed., *Anthology of Conservative Writing in the United States, 1932–60* (Chicago: Henry Regnery, 1962), p. 393.

[46] *Ibid.*

[47] *Ibid.*, p. 392.

psychologically or socially, from the Welfare Liberal? A variety of studies have been done to answer these questions. None of them, however, has been sufficiently exhaustive, carefully executed, or comprehensive to give a definitive answer. The findings of some of these studies are suggestive, however, and represent an important contribution to ideological research. But others have produced badly misleading results. Let us start with an example of the latter.

A Psychological Explanation.   In the mid-1950s Professor Herbert McClosky, whose excellent analysis of established liberalism we discussed in Chapter 3, attempted to discover whether there was something that could be called a "Conservative personality" type. To investigate the matter he developed a set of propositions which he thought constituted the chief elements of a Conservative world view. Some were statements of "belief," others of "value," as we have been using those terms. Here are some examples;

1. Man is a creature of appetite and will, "governed more by emotion than by reason."
2. Society is ruled by "divine intent."
3. Men are naturally unequal, and society requires "orders and classes."
4. Order, authority and community are the primary defense against the impulse to violence and anarchy.
5. Private ownership of property is necessary if we are to have a strong nation.[48]

Most of these statements were drawn from the writings of eminent Conservatives like Edmund Burke. But we already have seen the problem of simply equating the Burkean type of Conservatism with the Conservatism which is a factor in American politics.

With his set of statements as a standard of Conservative doctrine, McClosky interviewed two samples of persons drawn at random from a population living in the vicinity of the Twin Cities of St. Paul and Minneapolis. His results were checked by an independent survey covering the entire state of Minnesota. The interviews tested for agreement and disagreement with McClosky's list of Conservative doctrines and for correlative social and psychological factors such as social class, education, and personality traits. The surveys showed that "Conservative" beliefs are found most frequently among the uninformed, the poorly educated, and the least intelligent, not among the intelligentsia. Persons

[48] Herbert McClosky, "Conservatism and Personality," *American Political Science Review*, 52 (1), March 1958: 27–45.

agreeing with the statements also scored at the "undesirable" end of the distribution measuring certain personality characteristics. These people were low in sense of security and belonging. They felt isolated, with little social support, worthless, and inferior. They displayed a submissive and timid manner, were self-accusers, and lacked personal strength. (The reader will recall that Lane found traits like these among his "undemocrats.") There was also a certain correlation between "Conservative" belief and clinical personality traits; that is, the "Conservatives" in the sample were mentally ill to a degree. In addition, a correlation was found with mysticism and religiosity. But, most significantly, no correlation was found with party affiliation, attitudes on economic issues, or preference for candidates for office.

Problems.   McClosky has no doubt found a group of people on the psychological and social margin (or "ragged edge") who agreed with his "Conservative" propositions. But there was no correlation at all with what one could call Conservative political behavior. And this is our interest. Under these circumstances to claim that he had discovered a "Conservative personality" is misleading. All he had turned up was a group of sick outcasts who agreed with certain "Burkean" ideas. But they were not members of Radical Right organizations, of the Conservative Party, or even of the right wing of the Republican Party. Politically they were indistinguishable from those who disagreed with the statement and were normal and socially integrated persons.

Another Approach.   Andrew Hacker, also a political scientist, used a different approach to the social and psychological identification of the American Conservative. Using a variety of evidence, variously collected, Hacker examined the man who identified himself as a Conservative during the Goldwater campaign for the presidency. What he found was a person "neither philosophical in temperament nor maladjusted in personality," by rather an individual holding "the outlook of quite ordinary men and women." [49] At a Goldwater rally he found people "bearing smiles rather than sullen countenances." Most Conservatives, Hacker found, are employees, not employers, and many work for large corporations—as engineers, salesmen, and junior executives. They are "organization men." For the most part their incomes, homes, and backgrounds are unspectacular.

What sort of beliefs do Hacker's Conservatives hold? The common characteristic is a sense of being a superior individual. They see themselves as upwardly mobile and they are persuaded that they have gotten where they are by personal efforts. They feel "superior to those who

[49] Andrew Hacker, "Inquiry into the New Conservatism," *New York Times Magazine,* February 16, 1964.

have failed to get as far as they have." On economic questions they have distinct opinions. They dislike unions, which represent the "mass man" and are "led by 'crooks' (Hoffa) or 'Socialists' (Reuther)." They identify with management and they fear the political power of the unions in the belief that organized labor wishes to tax hard-working people like themselves in order to establish a welfare state for those "unwilling to provide for themselves." (Shades of Classical Liberalism!) Hacker's Conservatives have little or no compassion for Blacks or other minorities and they believe that if individual Blacks work hard they will succeed. They mistrust the legislative approach to improving the lot of the black man. In foreign policy they are proponents of a hard line, with a military focus. Many are isolationist, and they have no sense of an American responsibility to raise the standard of life of colored persons around the world.[50]

Why are these people Conservatives? Hacker offers in explanation a number of "educated guesses." These men, he writes, "realize the traditional middle-class ethic was created for an age of entrepreneurs, rather than themselves." Like the earlier entrepreneur, however, they are individualists, and they believe that they "can protect their individuality by embracing the Conservative mood." Conservatism is thus an escape into an ideal individualism from the marked constraints of the life style they are compelled to adopt—the life style of the "organization man." It is an ideological counterpart to their physical flight to the suburbs. Hacker also reports that his Conservatives are upwardly mobile socially, and that many of them are of recent immigrant stock. He accounts for the "hawkish" nationalism of these people as a means of accelerating their social assimilation. Implicit in Hacker's analysis is the idea that his Conservatives are anxious about their newly-won status because they feel that it is a tenuous affair, a thesis advanced by a number of other students of the subject.[51]

Hacker distinguishes between the personality of the Goldwater variety of Conservative and the member of the Radical Right. Although anxious and insecure, the former is mentally healthy, whereas "the distorted image of political reality, generally involving conspiracies, harbored by the typical right-wing extremist is a neurotic condition that cannot be changed by rational discussion."[52] He does not tell us upon what research this judgment is based.

A Survey Approach.   James McEvoy presents still other evidence from his analysis of the 1964 Election Studies as to what kind of people

[50] *Ibid.*

[51] *Ibid.* See Daniel Bell, *The Radical Right* (Garden City, N.Y.: Doubleday & Co., Inc., 1963).

[52] Hacker, *op. cit.*

become Conservatives. Among Senator Goldwater's early supporters McEvoy found an unusually large percentage of persons of high socio-economic status. More than one-fourth of them had a college education, half of them held professional or technical occupations or were self-employed, and there also were a large number of managers. (They were not predominantly "organization men" as Hacker hypothesized; almost 30 percent were self-employed.) Almost 40 percent had incomes of more than $10,000 per year.[53] Late supporters generally held a lower socio-economic status, but were still several cuts above the Johnson supporters.[54]

McEvoy also found, contrary to Hacker's theory, that vertical social mobility does not explain Conservatism. Discrepant conditions which imply either upward or downward mobility (e.g., as between educational level and income) were distributed about equally among the early Goldwaterites, late Goldwaterites, and Johnson supporters. Nor did McEvoy find more evidence of status anxiety among the Goldwater people than among the Johnson voters. In addition, they showed a considerable sense of political efficacy, were politically active, and possessed high levels of political information.[55]

Measuring for regional concentration, the analysis of the 1964 election showed a slightly small-town southern bias in the early Goldwater group, but its slightness is what must be emphasized. And there was no overrepresentation of rural voters. Indeed, the early Goldwaterite was more likely than either a late Goldwaterite or a Johnson supporter to have grown up on a farm and more likely to have come from a city of more than 250,000 population. Religious fundamentalism, which correlates strongly with right extremism, was not disproportionately represented among the early Goldwater supporters. Interestingly, measurement of their political orientation did not show that "19th-century Liberals" were very strong in the early Goldwater group.[56] High socio-economic status seems to be the most significant correlate of the Goldwater variety of Conservatism.

A Study of Conservative Party Members.   To this point we have been looking at persons who voted for a Conservative candidate for President who ran on the Republican ticket, and who were themselves largely Republican. What about those who are members of the Conservative Party? Are they a different and special group, demographically and psychologically? An answer to this question has been attempted by a young political scientist named Robert Schoenberger. In connection with his

[53] McEvoy, op. cit., pp. 244–71.
[54] Ibid., p. 245.
[55] Ibid., pp. 272, 259.
[56] Ibid., pp. 274, 275.

doctoral work at the University of Rochester, Schoenberger interviewed a sample of registered Conservatives and Republicans in Monroe County, New York.[57] He was unable to differentiate Conservatives from Republicans or from a cross-sectional sample on authoritarianism and misanthropy, a clear indication that McClosky's clinical "Conservative" was not a political animal. He also found no status anxiety among his sample. Demographically, the Conservatives were almost exclusively middle- and upper middle-class Caucasians, of high educational attainment, holding high-status occupations, and with high incomes. The sample was largely status-stable rather than upwardly mobile. Those of the respondents who were upwardly mobile could not be differentiated from status-stable respondents on political and psychological measures. The majority were older Americans, though a large minority (31 percent) were first or second generation citizens. They displayed no propensity for fundamentalism, and there were more avowed atheists and agnostics than fundamentalists in the samples. They were found to be involved in political and civic activities, and their sense of political efficacy was high. "Young, ambitious, well-paid, well-situated in business or professional hierarchies, it is their personal and social stability which most impress[es] the observer," Schoenberger writes. In other words, they very closely resembled McEvoy's early Goldwaterites.

Measuring their political opinions, Schoenberger found that his Conservatives were more libertarian than Republicans on the Bill of Rights. What especially distinguished them as Conservatives and consistently differentiated them from the Republican sample was their uniformly negative attitude toward government intervention in the economy and toward social welfare legislation. Only a minority supported right extremist political assertions or offered verbal support for radical right organizations. In sum, Schoenberger found Conservatism to represent a rational middle-class position, not related to special psychological or social factors.

Despite the evident divergences from Hacker's explanation of the Conservative syndrome, Schoenberger agreed with Hacker's major explanatory hypothesis. He found that the life style of most of his Conservative respondents was that of the organization man within the framework of a standardized and bureaucratic system, but that the Conservative's verbal style was highly individualist. These respondents uniformly approved the qualities of daring, resourcefulness, innovativeness, creativeness, and self-sufficiency. This is not congruent with McEvoy's findings

---

[57] See Robert Schoenberger, "Conservatism, Personality and Political Extremism," *American Political Science Review*, 62 (3), September 1968: 868–77, for a brief statement of the chief findings of this doctoral project.

about Goldwaterites and may be a special Conservative Party phenomenon.

Despite the special characteristics we have described, Conservatives share with Welfare Liberals the Liberal personality traits as well as the basic Liberal procedural commitment described in Chapter 3. McClosky's effort to identify neurotic pessimism with a specifically Conservative personality was a failure, as we have seen. On the other hand, Schoenberger's study of self-avowed Conservatives showed them to be rational, active, optimistic persons, integrated members of the American polity, not distinguishable from any other carrier of the "civic culture," the culture of Liberal Democracy.

Bibliography

Articles on Conservatism, *Annals of the American Academy of Political and Social Science,* 344, November 1962.

BASU, A. K., "Correlates of Political Conservatism," *Western Political Quarterly,* 21(4), December 1968: 725–30.

CAIN, EDWARD, *They'd Rather Be Right: Youth and the Conservative Movement.* New York: The Macmillan Company, 1963.

CHAPMAN, P. C., "The New Conservatism: Cultural Criticism v. Political Philosophy," *Political Science Quarterly,* 75(1), March 1960: 17–34.

HART, JEFFREY, *The American Dissent: A Decade of Modern Conservatism.* Garden City, N.Y.: Doubleday & Company, Inc., 1966.

HUNTINGTON, SAMUEL, "Conservatism as an Ideology," *American Political Science Review,* 51(2), June 1957: 454–73.

KENDALL, WILLMOORE, *The Conservative Affirmation.* Chicago: Henry Regnery, 1963.

KIRK, RUSSELL, *The Conservative Mind.* Chicago: Henry Regnery, 1953.

MACDONALD, H. M., "The Revival of Conservative Thought," *Journal of Politics,* 19(1), February 1957: 66–80.

MCCLOSKY, HERBERT, "Conservatism and Personality," *American Political Science Review,* 52(1), March 1958: 27–45.

MEYER, FRANK S., *What Is Conservatism?* New York: Holt, Rinehart & Winston, Inc., 1964.

ROSSITER, CLINTON, *Conservatism in America.* New York: Alfred A. Knopf, 1955.

SMITH, DEAN, *Conservatism: A Guide to Its Past, Present and Future in American Politics.* New York: Avon, 1963.

5

Challenge from the Right

Moving further to the right from the ground marked out by Conservatives, we arrive at the extreme of the spectrum which has been labeled "the Radical Right." If theoretical detail, sophistication, and consistency are not characteristic of Conservatism, we find them even less characteristic of opinion on the extreme right. The concepts are few and stereotyped, the language crude and harsh. The underlying conception of good order is an extreme version of "business liberalism." A typical example of this literature is found in A. G. Heimsohn's introduction to his anthology of conservative writing:

> There are only two ways to make a living—to work for a living or to "ride a gravy train." . . . Since there are those who prefer to live by seizing instead of working (robbers, confidence men, etc.) government is necessary to protect those who work from the predatory acts of those who prefer to live by stealing. The prime function of government is to protect each member of the community and to insure the safety of his life and possessions. . . . Laws [are] designed to protect life, liberty, and property.[1]

Mr. Heimsohn describes welfare taxation as "money seized by force from

[1] A. G. Heimsohn, Jr., *Anthology of Conservative Writing in the United States, 1932–60* (Chicago: Henry Regnery, 1962), pp. 12–13.

others . . . with legal sanction and in a sanctimonious manner." [2] "Undreamed of 'social services' . . . are imposed by force upon the people," he writes. "Thus by stealth and fraud, the unprincipled politician has reduced the nation of free men, trusting in God and individual effort, to a bewildered, cynical, divided mass of humanity forced to pay in about one-third of their total production to the public feed trough and then compelled to fight like hogs in an effort to get back as much as they can." [3] The established system is thus pictured as one of pure exploitation, a gang of thieves relying on force and fraud. It is the same picture as the one painted by the Radical Left.

Also characteristic of the Radical Right is the extensive use of a conspiracy theory to explain what is happening under the aegis of Established Liberalism. One scholar in fact takes this as the decisive characteristic of the "extreme rightist," which allows for some coherence in the application of the idea. Terms like "extremists," "super-patriots," and "radical rightists" have been used so indiscriminately "that a potpourri of organizations and individuals advocating views ranging from classic laissez-faire economics (the American Economic Foundation) to openly promulgated racial hatred and violence (the American Nazi Party, the Ku Klux Klan) have all fallen under the rightist label." [4]

1. Radical Right Organizations and Leaders

Robert Welch and the Birch Society.   A classical example of the conspiracy literature is *The Politician* by Robert Welch, the founder of the John Birch Society. Mr. Welch describes the purpose of his book as the presentation of a basic understanding of the "Communist conspiracy." The author's favorite metaphors in describing the nature of the work in which he is engaged are military rather than political. He finds his efforts at unmasking assaulted from all sides, and writes of the "salvo . . . fired by some eager beavers of the Left," and of "the real barrage." Opposition to him he describes as single, monolithic, and organized from a common center—world communism. The anti-Birch campaign began with the Communist People's World of San Francisco, he tells us, and soon "*Time* magazine hastened to fall in step," followed by "the whole Liberal-slanted press of America." All criticism is amalgamated to the left, as communist or communist-inspired.

The conspiracy is depicted as of long standing. The American

[2] *Ibid.*, p. 14.
[3] *Ibid.*
[4] Ira S. Rohter, "Social and Psychological Determinants of Radical Rightism," in Robert Schoenberger, *The American Right Wing: Readings in Political Behavior* (New York: Holt, Rinehart & Winston, Inc., 1969), pp. 193–94.

government from 1933 on is described as devoted to sustaining the policies of the Soviet Union. Remarkably enough, Welch's chief whipping boy in tracing the development of the "conspiracy" is the moderate Republican, General Dwight D. Eisenhower. He came into the office of President in 1953 when Americans were beginning to "wake up to the extent of Communist infiltration into our government and into every segment of our public life." For a while he "talked a good brand of anti-Communism. But the Communist influences which completely controlled him kept the reins of that control tight and effective. Subtly, cleverly, always proclaiming otherwise and finding specious excuses for what were really pro-Communist actions, these Communist influences made him put the whole diplomatic power, economic power and recognized leadership of this country to work on the side of Russia and the Communists, in connection with every problem and trouble spot in their empire. You have only to look at where we stand today, five years later . . . to realize the truth of the assertion and the extent of this Communist success." We could not have lost so much ground by sheer stupidity. "The word is treason." [5]

Characteristic of the conspiracy theory is the argument that nothing is what it appears to be. This being the case, it doesn't matter what is said or done. The author claims a secret insight into the real pattern behind the appearances—which is always a pattern of treasonous conspiracy. The object of the explanation is, of course, to account for real difficulties into which the country has fallen. Many alternative explanations are possible. But the only one that makes sense to the member of the Radical Right, who does not believe that America could legitimately fail or falter in a major undertaking, is a diabolical conspiracy.

The beginning of Eisenhower's involvement in conspiracy is traced back to his days as a young lieutenant colonel, when "some very sinister but powerful forces had already put their marks [on him] as a pliable tool of the future." In the meantime Franklin Roosevelt, the Democratic hero, was a captive of these forces. Roosevelt is represented as having encouraged the Japanese in their ambitions and as having made it easy for them to strike the first blow so that he could fight a glorious war to satisfy his hunger for power. The legislation of the New Deal is described as "Communist inspired," its central ideas having been advanced first by the late Earl Browder, the avowed Communist leader.[6]

In the development of his conspiracy theory Mr. Welch betrays a certain sympathy with other groups with an extreme right orientation. He laments, for example, the Russian rape of Berlin as the worst thing

5 Robert Welch, *The Politician* (Belmont, Mass., 1963), p. x.
6 *Ibid.*, pp. 5–6.

ever suffered by "Christian Europe." The Nuremberg trials of Nazi war criminals are described by him as a "heinous crime." Moreover, an anti-black bias shared with the German Nazis is revealed in a statement to the effect that black French troops as well as Russians were guilty of worse things than their enemies ever perpetrated. Welch also has hard words for Israel.[7]

This, then, is the characteristic extreme right conspiracy theory. In brief, it holds that the established political system does not work to secure either the special values which the rightist holds dear or more generally shared national values. Its failure can be adequately accounted for only by the simplest of explanations which cuts through all the complexity of empirical reality and moral right—an overarching conspiracy by a secret cabal of all-powerful opponents, who are identified with a cause which is deemed opprobrious by Americans far from the ranks of the Radical Right itself.

Wallace. Another sort of simplistic radical right ideology and one with a long history is overt racism. The most prominent political leader with whom it is associated today is George Corley Wallace, Governor of Alabama. Racist sentiments have been given a new impetus by the policy of busing school children which was adopted at the end of the 1960s as an expedient for black integration into white American society. Racism can be defined as "the persuasion that there is an innate, generic, permanent difference between the races in all the traits that describe humanity." [8]

Wallace has commented on the charge that he is a racist in the following cryptic terms: "Let 'em call me a racist. It don't make any difference. Whole heap of folks in this country feel the same way I do. Race is what's gonna win this thing for me." [9] It is not clear from this statement whether Wallace fully identifies with racism as a value system or whether he simply finds it a useful instrument in the pursuit of political power. Is he prompted to espouse the cause of white supremacy because he believes in its truth, because it helps him cope with social or cultural strain, or because it serves his interest? Or for all three reasons? The passage is revealing of the reflective character of elite ideology even when it is crude and simplistic, for Governor Wallace is capable of suiting his ideological message to the audience in front of him. "I'm not the demagogue they have tried to make me out to be," he is reported to have said when told that Edmund Muskie said he hated

[7] *Ibid.*, pp. 11–16.

[8] Marshall Frady, *Wallace* (New York: The World Publishing Company, 1968), p. 7.

[9] Quoted in *ibid.*

what Wallace stands for. "I want to say to Senator Muskie that I am a candidate for all the people." [10]

Intimately tied in with Wallace's racism is a species of populism which has received many articulations in American history. It is not the empathic and smiling populism of a Jefferson, nor is it the outgoing, confident sense of civic competence measured by Almond and Verba, both of which are described in Chapter 3 as characteristic elements of American Established Liberalism. We associate it rather with phenomena like Nativism, the "Know-Nothing" movement, the demagoguery of Huey Long, and McCarthyism.[11] Wallace sees himself

> as the very incarnation of the "folks," the embodiment of the will and sensibilities and discontents of the people in the roadside diners and all-night chili cafes, the cabdrivers and waitresses and plant workers, as well as a certain harried Prufrock population of dingy-collared department store clerks and insurance salesmen and neighborhood grocers: the great silent American Folk.[12]

"Power comes from the people," he proclaims," and if my health holds up I'm gonna change things in this country." [13] The role of "folk oracle" we shall find in a later chapter to be characteristic of the leader in that warped brand of Liberal culture we call Fascism. As played by Wallace, as well as the Nazi-Fascist leaders, the role also looks nostalgically back to a past political culture. In the categories of Almond and Verba, Wallace's world view is distinctively parochial. His biographer tells us that he understands the world as a sort of extension of Barbour County, Alabama, where he grew up. He projects the mentality of that rural county onto the world, instead of going out to meet the world on its own terms. Connected with this is a certain emotional tribalism, which builds politics on common feelings rather than on impersonal reasons.[14]

The elemental and primitive character of his style diminishes the

[10] *Rochester Democrat and Chronicle*, March 15, 1972.

[11] The startling variety of populism in American political culture is well displayed in the following passage from an article by Richard Reeves entitled "The New Populism and the Old: A Matter of Words": "It was just another week in American politics, 1972. John Lindsay called George Wallace a 'phony Populist.' George McGovern called John Lindsay a 'Park Avenue Populist.' Hubert Humphrey called himself 'The People's Democrat,' explaining at impressive length that the slogan meant he was and always had been a Populist. A New Jersey advertising man named Daniel Gaby went to an abandoned hotel ballroom in Newark to announce that he was the Populist candidate for the Democratic nomination for U.S. senator, 'running to defeat what is defeating this country: the concentration of great wealth and power in the hands of fewer and fewer people.' Jack Newfield and Jeff Greenfield, who used to compose the rhetoric for Robert F. Kennedy, published a book called *The Populist Manifesto*. Populism is in." (*Saturday Review*, April 8, 1972.)

[12] Frady, *op. cit.*, p. 9.

[13] *Ibid.*, p. 12.

[14] *Ibid.*, pp. 10–11.

role of ideas and abstractions in Wallace's approach to politics. His ideology at times boils down to pure action. "Now, we don't stop and figger, we don't think about history or theories or none of that. We just go ahead. Hell, history can take care of itself." [15] Once more the Fascist parallel comes to mind. Witness Il Duce's rejection of ideology in favor of action in a reflection on his revolution:

> Fascism was not given out to the wet nurse of a doctrine elaborated beforehand round a table: it was born of the need for action; whoever rereads, in the now crumpled pages of the time, the account of the constituent assembly of the *Fasci di Combattimento* will not find a doctrine, but a series of suggestions, of anticipations, of admonitions. . . . The doctrine itself must be not words but an act of life. Hence the pragmatic vein in Fascism, its will to power, its will to be, its attitude in the face of the fact of "violence" and of its own courage.[16]

The action called for is the action of the political struggle. Here again we are reminded of the European counterpart. Wallace declares, "Life's basically a fight," just as Adolf Hitler told his followers that "struggle is ever present and will remain so," that struggle "is the father of all things in the world." [17]

The Followership.   Surveys have been made of membership opinion in Radical Right organizations which give an indication of the degree of congruence between leadership and followership ideology at the far right of the American political spectrum. In 1965 a mail survey was made of a sample of the national membership of the John Birch Society.[18] The persons in the sample remained anonymous to researcher Fred Grupp, for his contact in the Birch Society undertook to do the mailing and to open the returned questionnaires. Thirty-five percent of the mailing was returned. There was evidence that better educated, higher status, and more involved Birchers were overrepresented in the sample.

Testing for issue orientation, Mr. Grupp found a rather comprehensive dissatisfaction with all aspects of federal policy among the members of the Birch sample. Domestic social policies were described as too liberal or "socialistic." There were calls for the reduction of the size of the federal government and for tax reduction, running from elimination

15 *Ibid.*, p. 13.

16 Benito Mussolini, "The Doctrine of Fascism," in Michael Oakeshott, *The Social and Political Doctrines of Contemporary Europe* (Cambridge: Cambridge University Press, 1939), p. 169.

17 Adolf Hitler, speeches reported in *Völkischer Beobachter*, Nov 21, 1927 and March 17, 1929, in Carl Cohen, ed., *Communism, Fascism, and Democracy*, (New York: Random House, 1962), pp. 409, 410.

18 Fred W. Grupp, Jr., "The Political Perspectives of Birch Society Members," in Schoenberger, *op. cit.*, pp. 83–118.

of the graduated income tax to the elimination of all taxes. It was urged that government cease competing with business and that there be a return to the "free operation of the law of supply and demand." Increased anti-union legislation also was urged. The largest single expression of discontent concerned United States foreign aid and trade policies. In the area of constitutional questions, the Birchers expressed a desire for either a weakened Presidency or a strengthened Congress. There was an even more widespread demand for less activity by the Supreme Court, which was seen as having "usurped" power, and for changes in the system of recruitment and tenure. Interestingly, despite the urging of the top leadership, only 7 percent called for the impeachment of Chief Justice Earl Warren. Only a small number were concerned with the civil rights area, though there was expression of support for states' rights.

Mr. Grupp writes that "the sharing of [a] conspiratorial view of social causation is probably the most common denominator among the Birch respondents."[19] He connects this with the marked individualism of the respondents, "associated with the Protestant Ethic and other traditional American values."[20] Because Birchers see the individual as alone responsible for his behavior, the importance of impersonal social forces is discounted or not seen. Thus conspiratorial explanations, which see calculating individuals behind social events, become especially attractive. In view of their conspiratorial frame of reference, it was therefore surprising that only 8 percent of the sample thought it necessary to weed out subversives from the ranks of government employees. Overall, the problem of disloyalty was cited less often than five of seven other areas of concern, although the few who were worried about internal subversion did indeed see it as of the utmost importance. The majority, however, were more concerned with the government's policy outputs. This is discrepant with the emphasis of the leadership, who stress the conspiracy theme above all else. It is also interesting that the survey revealed little strong support for the specific programs of the leadership for dealing with the alleged conspiracy, such as promotion of the Liberty Amendment, the impeachment of Earl Warren, getting the United States out of the United Nations, and "exposing the civil rights fraud."

An explanation of the discrepancy between leadership priorities and perceptions and those of the followership is found in Mr. Grupp's discovery that many Birch Society members are action-oriented rather than goal-oriented. They achieve large satisfaction from belonging to an organization of like-minded persons in which they experience the sense of *doing something.* But they are not concerned to achieve partic-

[19] *Ibid.,* p. 117.
[20] *Ibid.,* p. 94.

ular ideological goals, and as the membership of the Society has expanded, according to Mr. Grupp, the ideological fanaticism of the organization has moderated. This may be mirrored in a recent change in policy at the top, which has converted the specifically Communist conspiracy into a wider and more generalized conspiracy, of which the Communists are depicted as only an instrument. Accompanying this has been the departure from the Society's leadership of the more zealous anti-Communist ideologues who are more oriented to specific anti-Communist action goals than the average member.

The Christian Anti-Communism Crusade.   A study of the political attitudes of members of Dr. Fred Schwarz's Christian Anti-Communism Crusade carried out at a "school" of the Crusade in the San Francisco Bay area in January 1962 provides data for comparison with the findings about the Birch Society. The study, conducted by Professor Raymond Wolfinger and members of a political science seminar at Stanford University, showed that fear of a Communist conspiracy in American life is a dominant characteristic of rightist opinion, as the Birch study also showed. Ninety-one percent of the Crusaders thought Communists had great influence in colleges and universities, and 50 percent thought they were influential in the Democratic Party, though only 20 percent saw a like threat in the Republican Party. Seventy-one percent of the respondents said that domestic Communists were a greater danger to the United States than the Soviet Union or Communist China. Nevertheless, when it came to specifics, the surveyors found that there was great diversity of opinion on how to deal with the Communist problem. The same pattern was found in other areas. Although Crusaders expressed a general feeling that the federal government is too bountiful, some 40 to 60 percent of them took liberal positions on specific items. Thus two-thirds were opposed to the Southern position on desegregation and more than half were in favor of some federal aid to education. All of this indicates that Crusaders depart from the Established Liberal consensus at a very abstract level of ideological commitment, but that specifics appear to be still within this consensus.[21]

Consensus or Dissensus?   In a study of a second Crusader "school" held in the Bay area at the end of 1963, Sheilah Koeppen addressed herself specifically to the question of whether rightists can be said to fit within the American consensus or not.[22] The Birch Society and first Crusader studies give only indirect evidence on the question. According

21 Raymond E. Wolfinger *et al.*, "America's Radical Right: Politics and Ideology," in Apter, ed., *Ideology and Discontent*, pp. 262–93.

22 Sheilah Koeppen, "The Radical Right and the Politics of Consensus," in Schoenberger, *op. cit.*, pp. 48–82.

to Koeppen, consensus exists when citizens "(1) trust in the government, (2) support the values and abide by the procedures whereby political conflict is resolved, and (3) limit the range of alternative solutions they will consider in any dispute over public policy."[23] These tests she derived from a large body of behavioral literature on the consensus question. To measure trust in the government she asked questions about the existence of Communist influence in particular agencies of government, ranging from local city councils to the California State Legislature, to the State Department, the Congress, the Supreme Court, and the White House. She hypothesized that to a group of persons preselected because of their concern about Communism, a belief that Communist influence was not present in a particular agency would indicate trust in that agency, and that direct questions about Communist influence would be more indicative than generalized questions about trust. The results showed a picture "of pervasive distrust of American government, whether the governmental unit is elective or appointive, national or local."[24]

The results of the findings on responses to the second group of questions indicated that Crusaders do not withhold support from democratic procedures to the extent that they mistrust the government, but also that those most distrustful of the government did fail to support democratic procedures. The respondents showed themselves overwhelmingly supportive of the norm of universal suffrage. Even those who were certain that Communists have penetrated both Congress and the White House were more in favor of universal suffrage than the college-educated sample in a random poll of voters in another study.[25] By contrast, the Crusaders were found not to be supportive of free speech, another basic procedural rule of democracy. Both these findings seem to fit with the Crusaders' espousal of the conspiracy theory, which attributes evil intentions not to the many who are average citizens but to a few influential persons in high places who have great persuasive powers.

The Crusader response to Koeppen's last criterion also put them outside the consensus, for the survey indicated an espousal of extreme solutions to problems of domestic and foreign policy, such as abolition of the income tax, cessation of foreign aid, and relinquishment of membership in the United Nations. Distrust of the government correlated strongly with support for extreme policy solutions, as it did with refusal to support free speech.

---

[23] *Ibid.*, p. 63.
[24] *Ibid.*, p. 65.
[25] See James W. Prothro and Charles M. Grigg, "Fundamental Principles of Democracy," *The Journal of Politics*, 22, 1960: 270–94.

Koeppen's finding that Crusaders are nonconsensual seemed to fit badly with another result of her survey, the finding that Crusaders massively continue to support and trust the Republican Party, though not the Democratic, and continue to engage actively in Republican partisan politics. Indeed, it was found that persons most active in the Crusade movement were also most active in Republican politics. Crusaders thus "reverse the usual correlation between greater political participation and increased support for democracy." [26] The surveyor tried to explain this discrepancy with the argument that the Crusaders' participation is negative in that it is aimed at forestalling what they most fear, Communist subversion. The researcher noted also that the Crusaders' high educational and socioeconomic level provided the self-confidence needed to bring them to participate actively in a system which they distrust.

The adequacy of Koeppen's negative explanation may be questioned. Would Crusaders really work actively within a system which they fundamentally mistrust and believe is incapable of producing values for them? An alternative is to ask whether the statements about mistrust of specific agencies of government are to be taken at face value. These statements were not coupled with assent to specific action proposals aimed at changing the situation. Thus, they may function in the same way as the generalized conspiracy theory we found among the Birchers who, when quizzed about policy positions, exhibited more interest in particular economic and financial measures than in Communist witch-hunting schemes. Is consensus better tested at the level of abstract, generalized attitude or at the level of commitment on specific policies, which are much closer to the realm of political action? The reader will recall the finding of Professor Lane reported in Chapter 3 that the authoritarian fantasizing of his "undemocrats" failed to eventuate in undemocratic political behavior. On specific questions these men appeared no different from the "democrats" and had no plans to change the existing system. It would seem more appropriate to conclude from the study of the second Crusade "school" that Crusaders are consensualists in the area of our participant and majoritarian norms, but not in certain libertarian norms. They are, therefore, only partially dissident from Established Liberal political culture. (It could easily be shown that such partial dissidence has been a theme running through American political history. We also have suggested that there is a certain logical conflict between the majoritarian and libertarian elements in the culture.) We are here of course dealing only with certain segments of the American right wing. The alienation of groups like the American Nazi Party and the Minuteman groups might well be much more absolute than that of the John Birch Society or the Christian Anti-Communist Crusade.

2. Social and Psychological Background of the Radical Right

Are members of the Radical Right more easily distinguishable than Conservatives from established Liberals in their psychological and social makeup? The well-known sociologist Daniel Bell, citing Seymour Lipset and Richard Hofstadter, asserts in *The End of Ideology* that Right extremists characteristically display status anxiety connected with social mobility. And in a book of essays entitled *The Radical Right*, edited by Bell, this theme is developed in detail.[27]

Contradictory Findings.   A number of attempts at empirical verification of hypotheses of this kind have recently been undertaken. Their results have been mixed and to a degree contradictory, revealing clearly the problems of adequate method which continue to beset behavioral political science. We already have had occasion to mention two of Dr. Fred Schwarz's Christian Anti-Communism Crusade, a right-wing organization, during two successive "schools" conducted by the organization in the San Francisco Bay Area during 1962. In neither survey was there an effort to employ random sampling techniques. During the first "school," participants were interviewed by members of a Stanford University political science seminar who selected their subjects with an eye to representativeness in terms of age, sex, and style of dress. One hundred eight participants were interviewed and forty others refused to give interviews. More than one-third of mail questionnaires distributed to 625 persons attending the school were returned to the researchers: Approximately two thousand persons attended the Crusade. The second study relied entirely on revised questionnaires which were distributed to the "school" audience after sessions. The rates of return were 58 and 45 percent.

The populations of both surveys were very similar in demographic characteristics. All respondents were white, although the population of the Bay Area is 12 percent black and Oriental. And they were predominantly an upper status group, well educated with high status occupations and higher than average incomes. Respondents from the first Crusade included proportionately twice as many businessmen and professionals as are found in the Bay Area. Approximately 90 percent of respondents from both Crusades were born in the United States, and most were of long-established American families. Over 90 percent of

---

27 See Daniel Bell, ed., *The Radical Right* (Garden City, N.Y.: Doubleday & Company, Inc., 1963), especially the essay by Lipset, p. 436.

those whose grandparents were foreign-born stemmed from Northern Europe. In both these characteristics they are vastly disproportionate to the population of the Bay Area in general. In party preference both groups of the Crusaders were staunch Republicans, and from the Conservative end of the Republican spectrum.

Professor Wolfinger and his colleagues measured for "alienation" among the respondents of the first Crusade, an alleged characteristic of extremists mentioned frequently in the speculative literature on the right wing. If alienation is taken to be a correlate of political and social isolation, the Crusaders are not alienated people. Their level of membership in organizations of all kinds—civic, church-oriented, veterans groups, and so forth—is somewhat higher than that of the business, professional, and white-collar respondents of the 1952 Survey Research Center study. As to sense of political efficacy, another measure of "alienation," they scored higher than white college-educated northerners. Nor did it turn out that they are frustrated by the American two-party system, for 98 percent had voted in the 1960 presidential election and 54 percent had sent letters, cards, and other communications to government officials during the previous year. They also were extremely active participants in political campaigns. Koeppen noted a high percentage of political activists among the respondents from the second Crusade. By all the standard measures, therefore, the members of the Christian Anti-Communist Crusade are not alienates.

Data also were obtained during the first Crusade on the alleged right-wing characteristic of "status anxiety" as a function of social mobility. In a comparison of the occupations of the fathers of businessmen and professional Crusaders with the occupations of fathers of northern businessmen and professionals interviewed in the 1956 SRC election study, Crusaders manifested at least an equal status stability. Moreover, the status-stable were much more likely than the upwardly mobile to choose Conservative positions on attitude measures. It was found that there were few downwardly mobile persons in the Crusader sample. Nor could it be shown that Crusaders affirm a Radical Right position for psychological reasons—either to "naturalize" themselves or to wreak revenge on old-family liberals who reject them—for they were overwhelmingly of old American stock, not recent immigrants. With regard to two other characteristics often mentioned in the speculative literature, no evidence of marked "status discrepancy" was found among the Crusaders, nor could small-town resentment of the social, economic, and cultural dominance of large urban areas be correlated with Radical Rightism in the Crusade sample.

One correlate of Radical Right attitudes frequently mentioned in the literature that was discovered to hold for the Crusaders was religious fundamentalism. Why should there be such a connection? "Belief in the literalness and purity of Biblican teachings," Wolfinger writes, "makes fundamentalists resistant to social and cultural change; they are affronted by moral relativism, increasingly lenient sexual mores, the decline of parental authority, and other aspects of the secular modern world. The fundamentalist sees 'the world as strictly divided into the saved and the damned, the forces of good and the forces of evil.'" [28] Conservative attitudes in religion are thus translated into political and social terms, and the battle of cosmic good and evil is rendered into a conflict between super-patriots and traitorous Communists. Three-quarters of the sample at the first Crusade were Protestants, and 26 percent of these were members of fundamentalist denominations. But even here we are dealing only with a minority of the sample.[29]

A group of forty-three respondents who attended the Crusade because of church influence was isolated in the fundamentalist minority. These people turned out to be less well educated, from more rural backgrounds, and more devout and active in their churches than the rest of the Crusaders. They were also more liberal than the others on domestic questions, such as segregation, medical care for the aged, and federal aid to education, and by very large factors in each case. The appeal of the Crusade to these people had, therefore, little if anything to do with economic self-interest but was largely a function of their religious beliefs. Communism represented to them an earthly manifestation of the devil.[30]

To measure for a correlation of rightism with resentment of bureaucratic organization in modern society, Wolfinger and his colleagues adopted a test for the "19th-century liberal" syndrome which had been developed in an earlier study of rightist politics.[31] On this dimension again only a minority of Crusaders were found whose attitudes correlated with the hypothesized syndrome. Seventeen percent of the sample tested as "19th-century liberals," and it was found that these people were politically intolerant, had a low sense of political efficacy, were low in political participation, and believed there was no difference between the two major parties—a very different picture from that presented by the typical Crusader. None of the usual sociological-psychological propositions put forward to explain Radical Rightism

[28] Wolfinger et al., op. cit., pp. 281–82.

[29] Scott McNall, in a study of the John Birch Society in California (Schoenberger, op. cit., p. 128), found no relationship between religion and rightism. Grupp's national Birch study, however, showed an overrepresentation of fundamentalist Protestants in the Society. (Grupp, op. cit., p. 91.)

[30] Wolfinger et al., op. cit., p. 282.

[31] See Martin Trow, "Small Businessmen, Political Tolerance, and Support for McCarthy," American Journal of Sociology, 64, November 1958: 270–81.

were thus found to hold for the great majority of the members of the Christian Anti-Communist Crusade. "The Crusaders' beliefs about the extent of internal subversion may be regarded as paranoid, but, despite the deviant quality of some of their political attitudes, they are functioning members of society," Wolfinger concludes.[32]

Other social scientists have substantiated Wolfinger's findings about the demographic and psychological correlates of Radical Rightism, and in other ways have discredited earlier hypotheses. A study of forty adult volunteers from Dallas, Texas, carried out by Alan C. Elms in 1966, for example, showed no unusual mobility as compared with liberals in a control sample, nor did the respondents show unusual anxieties about status or job. They did not place themselves in the category of the "dispossessed" in terms of property, status, or moral position. Elms also found that his rightists were not unusually authoritarian, and that although they were dogmatic, they did not "convey the impression of real fanaticism or 'True Believerism.' "[33] Personality disorder seemed ruled out by the study as an explanation of rightist attitudes, and the researcher thought more reliance needed to be placed on environmental circumstances. "Individuals without unusual personality needs or strong predispositions toward authoritarianism, dogmatism, or normativism," writes the author of the study, "may adopt an extreme rightist posture, because a set of political opinions of any kind would be functional for them (in helping to explain complex public events efficiently, for example); because through personal experience or parental training a conservative political position is most acceptable to them; and because community standards make an extreme rightist position as acceptable as most other positions."[34] He also shows that a similar study of 143 midwesterners labeled as "super-patriots" by the researchers produced similar results. (Characteristics of "super-patriots" were given as patriotic and nationalistic conservatism, vigorous anticommunism, and a clear commitment to action.[35]) The authors of the study found that their respondents were not psychotic or severely disturbed personality types and that they did not suffer from excessive anomie or feelings of powerlessness. Like Elms' subjects, they scored above the median on the dogmatism scale, but not on the F scale for authoritarianism. The median income of the super-patriot group was somewhat higher than the national average, which dovetails to a degree with Wolfinger,

[32] Wolfinger *et al.*, *op. cit.*, p. 285.

[33] Alan C. Elms, "Psychological Factors in Right-Wing Extremism," in Schoenberger, *op. cit.*, p. 157.

[34] *Ibid.*

[35] See Mark Chesler and Richard Schmuck, "Social-Psychological Characteristics of Super-Patriots," in Schoenberger, *op. cit.*, pp. 164–92.

Koeppen, and Grupp's findings that rightists tend to be well-to-do persons.

The findings of the studies we have just reviewed have been contradicted by other recent analyses of the Radical Right, however. In 1965 Ira Rohter collected data on a group of 169 rightists and a nonrightist control group of comparable size, chosen from among people living in the Pacific Northwest.[36] Selection was made of persons who had given some public evidence of a Radical Right orientation—mention in the newspapers as a prominent Birchite, authorship of letters to the editor with a rightist accent. The nonrightist control sample was chosen in a similar way from politically active persons. Analysis of the data showed that rightists were drawn disproportionately from occupations of decreasing social prestige [37] and that they displayed much more status mobility than the nonrightists in the control sample. Their mobility was mostly downward. They were also on the average older and had less education than the nonrightists. Subjectively, the rightists tended to overrate their social position, claiming two-to-one to be "upper class," despite the fact that objective measures showed that twice as many nonrightists as rightists were in the highest group. They also suffered from feelings of lack of esteem, seeing themselves as outsiders, "discriminated against in a closed society run by an elite." [38] This is, of course, a view of things quite consistent with the rightist conspiracy theory. Twice as many rightists as nonrightists replied "No" to a blunt query as to whether people gave them as much respect as they felt they deserved. (According to Rohter, the rightist political association of these people helps them compensate for their feelings of inferiority and social resentment by virtue of its identification with "true Americanism," which induces honor and respect.) The survey sample also displayed a sense of powerlessness, with its members being significantly more alienated from the political system than the nonrightists.

Rohter attempts to square his findings with those of Wolfinger by noting that only 25 percent of the adult participants in the Crusade were willing to answer the survey questions. He also suggests that the Crusaders might simply not be a typical rightist population. The Crusade is, however, a typical right-wing organization with a typical Radical Rightist ideology.

[36] Rohter, in Schoenberger, op. cit.

[37] Grupp, in his study of Birch Society members, also found that individuals in his sample were engaged in occupations of declining prestige. He reported that Birchers had more status discrepancy between educational and occupational rankings than his control group. Those with occupations outranking their educational achievement were more alienated from the political system than the control group, and also more than those with the opposite kind of discrepancy.

[38] Rohter, op. cit., p. 223.

In measuring for personality factors, Rohter's results diverged from those of Elms and of Chesler and Schmuck discussed above. His data revealed a significant correlation between rightist dogmatism and general personality traits. Compared with nonrightists, Rohter's subjects were found to be "characteristically more intolerant of ambiguity, opposed to compromising their beliefs, and generally closed-minded and opinionated." [39] He found that they displayed as well an "extrapunitive" style of personality. All of these things are measures of authoritarianism. [40]

Reconciling the Contradictions. The discrepant findings about the social and psychological correlates of Radical Right behavior that we have just reviewed show clearly that Radical Rightism is produced by no single cause or single set of causes. Persons both rich and poor, well educated and poorly educated, status-stable and downwardly mobile, politically integrated activists and passive alienates, with liberal and with authoritarian personalities become enthusiastic participants in right-wing organizations. If it has been demonstrated that in some instances the correlation of social mobility, alienation, and authoritarian personality traits with rightism reveals causes of rightism, what shall we say about the rich, the well-born, the able, and the "normal" who are also rightists? Several of the studies we have reviewed suggest that if neither the social status nor personality makeup of an individual indicates a cause, one may be found in certain sociological and political characteristics of the particular geographical area in which a person lives.

Wolfinger notes that Radical Right activity is peculiarly intensive in regions like southern California and the Southwest in general and of much less importance and vitality in areas like the Northeast. His hypothesis is that "the right seems to be more successful in those states that are undergoing both major economic growth and marked changes in economic bases, life styles, and cultural geography." Rightism may be a function of "strains produced by the interpersonal and institutional instability that comes with rapid economic growth." [41] Anxiety, he argues, is as likely to be induced, among both oldtimers and newcomers to an unusually dynamic area, by the rootlessness that flows from this sort of "lateral social change" as by "vertical" mobility. In addition, the major political parties in these areas are, by comparison with the Northeast, weakly organized, lacking in established leaders with adequate resources to safeguard their positions against right-wing challengers. [42]

Wolfinger's observations are supported by other students of rightist

[39] *Ibid.*, p. 230.
[40] *Ibid.*, p. 235.
[41] Wolfinger *et al.*, *op. cit.*, p. 286.
[42] *Ibid.*

phenomena. Murray C. Havens reported in 1964 that it was in those southwestern cities where population growth was most rapid that the Radical Right had been most successful in seizing local political power.[43] Grupp's study showed that the eighteen states whose population increased between 1960 and 1965 more rapidly than the national average of 8.5 percent contained 55 percent of the membership of the Birch Society, but only 35 percent of the population of the United States.[44] He notes also that it is in the growing small communities that the Society has been particularly well received—communities of less than 50,000 population—rather than in the large cities.[45] It is his guess that this may have something to do with the "association of rural and small-town life with the Protestant Ethic," and also with the threat to the "old middle class" of these communities flowing from the fact of social change.[46] Grupp also notes that Birchers in the South and West concentrate in those states where the political parties are most poorly organized and are therefore unable to control dissident forces. Parties in these areas tend to be factions gathered around personalities rather than continuing bureaucratic organizations.[47]

George Wallace's biographer believes that it is the changing character of southern society, combined with the resentment of past defeats, that has given Wallace his special appeal there:

> In his transition from the gentle earth to the city—the filling stations, the power lines, the merciless asphalt, near Jumboburger drive-ins—the southern yeoman has acquired a quality of metallic ferocity. At the same time, the central fact about the south continues to be its defeat in the Civil War.[48]

Scott McNall, in an effort to relate Birch Society strength in California to social disorganization, found a very strong correlation between immigration as a measure of disorganization and membership in the Society in a county study. In focusing the analysis on differences between census tracts within a given city, he found still another explanatory factor, also related to social disorganization. Persons predisposed to deviant behavior joined the Birch Society in large numbers in those areas where there were no other organizational alternatives for persons seeking assimilation into the community. "The Birch Society is successful in California," McNall concluded, "because there was not a series of older

43 Cited in Grupp, op. cit., p. 89.
44 Ibid., p. 89.
45 Chesler and Schmuck, op. cit., p. 170, report a similar finding.
46 Grupp, op. cit., pp. 89, 90.
47 Ibid., p. 101.
48 Frady, op. cit., p. 19.

established groups to which people with deviant impulses could be attracted." [49]

Although the details of the picture are by no means fully clear, it appears from the evidence we have reviewed that espousal of Radical Right ideology is the result of a variety of kinds of stress and strain in modern American life, and that the act of espousal functions as a means of relieving stress and pressure. Strain may be the product of a variety of causes; in some instances the cause is anxiety provoked by declining social stature, at other times it is psychological stress related to personality structure. In still other cases an explanation is found in the strains created by rapid social change and the social disorganization accompanying such change.

3. Conclusion

How great a breach with Established Liberalism is represented by the ideologies we have just reviewed? If Conservatism remains only a "half-ideology," the same cannot be said of the Radical Right. Although the symbols of authority employed by the Radical Right remind us of those of Established Liberalism, the ones selected for emphasis appear as caricatures of the consensual model. What, for example, has the populism of George Wallace to do with that of Thomas Jefferson? In level of belief and of emotional attitude there are important differences from the general culture. Racism, as a belief that gives rise to important substantive and procedural values, has nothing in common with Established Liberalism, despite its compatibility with certain tenets of the Social Darwinist version of Liberalism. Nor has the conspiracy theory any place in Liberal culture. The closed-in, hostile, and resentful state of mind that its entertainment implies is incompatible with the empathic optimism of the bearer of the "civic culture."

Negative Character of Rightist Ideology.   Despite these differences from Established Liberalism, however, the Radical Right does not present an alternative system of ideas. The purely ideational element is almost nil. The Radical Right is ideologically a negation, not an affirmation of a better way. It is a call to an emotional rejection of the existing system, an almost pure cry of pain. It is a register of social strain, but not a set of norms and purposes for overcoming cultural strain.

Our presentation in the preceding chapter of evidence on the difference between Established Liberal elites and followers indicates a large potential for recruitment by rightists in the American center. Populism, defined as direct action, has a large attraction to the average

[49] McNall, *op. cit.*, pp. 137–38.

American. With this in mind, it is possible that the alarming figures on alienation in 1971 and 1972 that we reported in Chapter 3 are harbingers of more than a rejection of existing institutional leadership. The anger involved could lead to large-scale rejection of basic Liberal values. Nevertheless, the symbols of the center continue to be very tenacious. A Harris survey of April 1972 showed a marked decline in the willingness of voters to describe their political philosophy as "conservative" in the years between 1968 and 1972 (from 37 percent to 29 percent). A majority preferred the labels "middle of the road" and "liberal" (35 percent and 19 respectively).[50]

Bibliography

BELL, DANIEL, The Radical Right. Garden City, N.Y.: Doubleday & Company, Inc., 1963.

ELLSWORTH, RALPH E., The American Right Wing: A Report to the Fund for the Republic. Washington: Public Affairs Press, 1962.

JANSON, DONALD, and BERNARD EISMANN. The Far Right. New York: McGraw-Hill Book Co., Inc., 1963.

LIPSET, SEYMOUR M., The Politics of Unreason: Rightwing Extremism in America, 1790–1970. New York: Harper & Row, 1970.

SCHOENBERGER, ROBERT, The American Right Wing: Readings in Political Behavior. New York: Holt, Rinehart & Winston, Inc., 1969.

[50] Harris Survey, reported in the Rochester Democrat and Chronicle, April 20, 1972.

6

Challenge from the Left

The left end of the American ideological spectrum has been occupied through the course of its history by a number of rather different groups. Within the motley array we can distinguish, however, two main traditions. One tradition, culminating in Norman Thomas's Socialism, is native American and has its origins in Jeffersonian and Jacksonian egalitarianism. The other is a foreign-born Marxism, imported into this country from Germany in the mid-nineteenth century, which has subdivided since then into a number of forms. Elements of both the native American Socialist tradition and of European Marxism mingle with Anarchism and with Liberal values to form the world views of the groups which make up today's "New Left."

1. Native American Socialism

Norman Thomas.   The spirit of the native American old Left in its culminating form is perhaps best revealed in a description of the life and thought of its last and foremost leader, Norman Thomas. Thomas was born in 1884, the son of a Protestant minister who was himself the son of a minister, an emigré Welshman who came to the United States in the 1860s. On his mother's side Thomas was of seventeenth-century WASP ancestry.

Marion, Ohio, the town where Norman Thomas was born and raised, is described by Thomas' biographer Murray B. Seidler as much like Muncie, Indiana, which the Lynds have characterized in their study *Middletown* as a middle-class midwestern city, embodying all the typical ideas and attitudes of the "Established Liberal" political culture of the time.[1] His family situation was an unusually harmonious one, and Norman Thomas grew up with a great respect and admiration for his parents. Both of them were deeply involved in civic affairs, and the Thomas home was a real school of social responsibility. In school Thomas was a model for all his peers—president of his class, academically outstanding, and a leading athlete. He attended Princeton University, where his favorite professor was Woodrow Wilson, and where Raymond B. Fosdick, later president of the Rockefeller Foundation, was a classmate. In 1910 Norman Thomas married the granddaughter of a wealthy New York banker, an associate of John Jacob Astor, and from then until his death enjoyed a long and incredibly happy marriage.

Liberal Personality and Socialist Commitment.   Thomas's personality was that of a well-adjusted member of Almond and Verba's "civic culture"—open, trusting, optimistic about human nature and about the possibilities of cooperative endeavor. His biographer writes of his "overabundant faith in his fellow man": "He has been very receptive to the influence of others because he has usually, and frequently mistakenly, assumed that the integrity and honesty of other people equal his own." [2] A happy life at the heart of the Establishment and a liberal personality seemed to offer no ground for protest and rebellion.

Three events of his mature life led Norman Thomas out of the Establishment Liberal world of his upbringing into Socialism. One was his experience in social service work that he began upon graduating from Princeton in 1905. Another was the influence of the social teachings of Walter Rauschenbusch, a Protestant theologian and social reformer with whom he came in contact at Union Theological Seminary. Social criticism was strong at Union, where the young seminarians were taught the incompatibility of Christianity with capitalist materialism. A third event was the coming of World War I.

It was only gradually that Thomas's work with the poor led him toward Socialism. Shortly after taking his first job at the New York Presbyterian Settlement House, in fact, he considered writing a book refuting Socialist doctrine. But his experience later as pastor of the East Harlem Presbyterian Church, from 1911 to 1918, pointed him in the direction of Socialist commitment. In a letter of 1916 he wrote:

---

[1] Murray B. Seidler, *Norman Thomas, Respectable Rebel* (Syracuse, N.Y.: Syracuse University Press, 1961), p. 3. This section follows Seidler closely.
[2] *Ibid.*, p. 295.

There is no such thing as creating the type of church life we desire in New York either among the very rich or among the poor (or for that matter among the middle class) so long as unchristian conditions characterize industry, housing, and amusements. These unchristian conditions will not be conquered simply by a general feeling of good will but require definite and well thought out plans of action by which good will may be made to work.[3]

World War I confronted Thomas with still another problem of conscience —the morality of bearing arms in modern warfare—and he became a pacifist. In 1918 Thomas resigned his pastorate to protest the complacency and absence of concern for reform that he found prevalent in the Christian churches. The Socialist Party appeared to him a better vehicle for registering his concern in a meaningful way.

Democratic Reform.   What kind of protest against the established system would a man of this sort make? It would at no point involve advocacy of force or violence to overthrow existing institutions. Thomas's vision of a cooperative commonwealth—a more perfectly equal and free society than the present one—required that he live and act after the manner of that commonwealth now. He would set up no dichotomy between one set of rules to effect change and another set for behavior after change had been accomplished, like the revolutionary Marxist whose vision of good social order was much like his own. "There is no promise that out of convulsion you will get salvation," he said. He remained capable of invoking the "American ideal of democracy as government of the people, by the people, for the people." And he did not reject but rather embraced the existing machinery of democratic government as an instrument for gradually and peacefully reworking the economic and social order to a more equal condition which would constitute the basis for the good life of the free man. Thomas never lost faith in the capacity of the system to perfect itself; he simply wanted to make it work a little harder in that direction.

As a result of this outlook it was quite in order that Thomas associate himself with the Socialist Party, which was largely an outgrowth of the native American liberal and egalitarian tradition, a party committed to the fulfillment of the American dream and the Christian vision of equality by the method of practical reform within the structures of democratic capitalism. The Socialist Party, whose banner he carried time and again into the race for the presidency, was formed in 1901 through the fusion of two other groups. The major partner was Eugene Debs's Social Democracy, an outgrowth of midwestern Populism with roots in the egalitarianism of Jeffersonian and Jacksonian democracy. Debs's

[3] Quoted in *ibid.*, p. 16.

group emphasized practical legislative reforms of the economic system (e.g., hours legislation, public works) and the founding of socialist colonies in the west. The organization with which this group fused was a reformist or pragmatist faction of the Marxist Socialist Labor Party under Morris Hillquit, which had broken with its parent party on the issue of meliorism versus ideological absolutism.

The long-range program of Thomas's Socialist Party included extensive practical reform of American capitalist structures plus a limited socialism. It envisaged such things as public control of utilities, public control of basic industries, freedom for labor to organize and bargain collectively, job security for the working man, public housing, public assistance to the old and the needy, and unemployment insurance. A short-range program consisted of twelve immediate demands which constituted the Socialist platform for the election of 1932. These included federal appropriation of relief money to supplement state and local relief, federal appropriations for public works, reforestation, slum clearance, public housing to supplement state and city programs, a six-hour day and a five-day work week without reduction of wages, compulsory unemployment compensation, old-age pensions, health and maternity insurance, adoption of minimum wage laws, the abolition of child labor, and federal aid to farmers and small businessmen. Thomas received 800,000 votes—his most successful campaign—but the Democrats incorporated most of his program in theirs and won hands down. Virtually the entire Socialist short-run program was enacted by the New Deal government of Franklin Roosevelt.

Decline of the Socialist Alternative.   With the resolution by the New Deal of the large social issues of the day, the fortunes of the Socialist Party declined rapidly. It appears that despite the practicality of his legislative program, Thomas's continued emphasis on his vision of a democratic and socialist utopia worked against him. The American working classes were not interested in utopias but in immediate and concrete bread-and-butter benefits that they could enjoy, not dream about. In addition, the Socialist Party—the leadership group—remained, as its antecedents had been, a prey to debilitating factionalism. Moreover, Thomas's personality was not suited to building a strong organization. He was an intellectual, not a practical organizer. Seidler reports an exchange between Thomas and Franklin Roosevelt in 1935, when Thomas went to the White House to complain about the inadequacy of the Agricultural Adjustment Administration to meet the needs of sharecroppers. The President did not defend his program but simply said, "Norman, I'm a damn sight better politician than you." A man who knew him well and worked with him in many causes put the matter this way:

He has figured primarily not as an exponent of socialist principles, but as a critic of the parties in power and of big business. . . . But he is not an organization man. He is an evangelist, a crusader, a leader of dissenting opinion. . . . That he has been the candidate of a party is irrelevant; the party was Thomas.[4]

In his individualism Thomas was more the perfect Liberal whose work was to prick the conscience of a Liberal America than the Socialist reformer.

Toward the "New Left."   A link between Thomas's Socialism of the 1930s and the "New Left" is established in a book entitled *Great Dissenters*, which Thomas published in 1961, seven years before his death. The book's theme is the paramountcy of Truth:

> For different purposes we belong to different groups and we live by our loyalties, among which loyalty to the search for truth does not rank as high as it ought. The secret of a good life is to have the right loyalties and to hold them in the right scale of values. The value of dissent and dissenters is to make us reappraise those values with supreme concern for the truth.
>
> History is full of occasions when the higher loyalty of the dissenter has made him a rebel against not only particular conventions but the established order in church and state.[5]

It is interesting that Thomas makes no plea for socialism but simply for dissent from the established order of things. Unlike the Established Liberal, he does not call us back to "1776," when the Truth was settled once and for all, but rather to an abstract "Truth" which, as such, stands beyond our tradition. The book is a negative comment on the quality of our national life, on our loss of principle and ideal. Thomas's call for dissent remains, however, within the Liberal tradition in his advocacy of peaceful modes of dissent. He rejects "rebellion per se," the "*criminal* defiance of authority," and a purely "negative cynicism."

Thomas tells us that we have become apathetic conformists and that a "military-industrial complex" has skillfully employed both carrot and stick to make us so. The carrot is the good material life guaranteed to the conforming organizational man. The stick is fear of the consequences of a general war in a world of sovereign national states. Sounded initially by President Eisenhower, this theme is today the leading battle cry of the "New Left."

Thomas criticizes most of the dissent that has taken place as "con-

---

[4] Quoted in *ibid.*, pp. 2, 299.

[5] Norman Thomas, *Great Dissenters* (New York: W. W. Norton & Company, Inc., 1961), p. 13.

formity of criticism and exhortation without advocacy of specific sub-stitutes for our present conformities in personal or social morals or political customs." [6] As "conforming critics" he mentions intellectuals both of the Right and the Center—Barry Goldwater, William Buckley, Walter Lippmann, Archibald MacLeish. And he adds that he also dis-likes the "beatnik phenomenon" (the forerunner of the "Hippie") as another "conformity of protest" whose positive value he is "too much of a 'square' to appreciate." [7] But he has good words for the demonstrators of the Civil Rights Movement of 1960, both black and white, and he expresses his pleasure that after all, "socially concerned dissent is alive in conformist America." [8] It was from the Civil Rights Movement that the "New Left" was to emerge during the sixties.

2. Imported Marxism: The Doctrine and Appeal of the Socialist Labor Party

A rather different kind of socialism is represented by the Socialist Labor Party. This is a Marxist organization which grew out of the International Workingmen's Association (the First International, whose founder was Karl Marx himself) after its transfer from London to New York in 1872. A Social Democratic Workingmen's Party of North America was founded in 1874 and in 1877 received the party's present name. Its support came largely from workers of German origin who had begun to emigrate to this country after the revolutions of 1848. The party was particularly active in Chicago and St. Louis, where it won some electoral victories in local politics. Its fortunes declined with the wave of prosperity from 1880 to 1883, however. In the latter years the membership was down to 1500 persons.

The Leadership of Daniel de Leon.   In 1890 Daniel de Leon became the leader of the Socialist Labor Party and held this post to 1914. It was during this period that the ethos of the party as it exists today was developed and the basic outlines of party strategy evolved. De Leon was a talented ideologue, born in Curacao of Jewish parents and educated in Germany and in the Netherlands. He came to New York City in 1872 and in 1878 joined the faculty of Columbia Law School, where he ex-perienced frustration and a degree of failure in his teaching career; he was never given a full professorship. The high point of the party's for-tunes was the year 1892, when it had a presidential candidate on the

[6] *Ibid.*, p. 15.
[7] *Ibid.*
[8] *Ibid.*

ballot in six eastern states. In that election 21,512 votes were cast for the SLP candidate, 17,956 of them in New York.

The Socialist Labor Party has always remained a small splinter of the American left wing. An effort to infiltrate the Knights of Labor (a forerunner of the American Federation of Labor) failed miserably, and the party never attained a significant electoral position. It continues to persist as an organization, however, and it typifies the Marxist tradition as it exists in American political culture.

Millenarian Expectations. A leading characteristic of SLP Marxism is its "millennialism." In this context the idea expresses a concentration of attention on the final good society of perfect liberty and equality which will be brought about by a force beyond human agency. As the early Christians expected that God would one day suddenly destroy the old order and institute the thousand-year reign of Christ, so millenarian Marxists expect an economic catastrophe, flowing from the inner contradictions of capitalism, to be the trigger cause which ushers in a utopia of decentralized worker-owned cooperatives and the abolition of coercive political order.

As millenarians, SLP members are not interested in limited reforms within the capitalist system. Their eye is only on the order of perfection. But millennialism also allows them to be good democrats. There is no need for revolutionary activity to destroy the old order, for "history" as a *deus ex machina* will see that it falls apart of itself. When the economic cataclysm comes, it is expected that masses of people simply will troop to the ballot boxes and peacefully vote in the socialist utopia. Armed with this confidence, they tend to think of revolutionary Communists as "unprincipled": "The workers of America have more than the necessary numbers to vote capitalism out and Socialism in," says one of their handbills.

For many years the SLP predicted the coming of a terrible depression which would signal the fall of capitalism. More recently the "coming of the Kingdom" has been expected as a result of the ill effects of automation upon the system. *"The moment of truth on automation is coming* —a lot sooner than most people realize. The shattering fact is that the U.S. is still almost totally unprepared for the approaching crisis." These are the apocalyptic words of a recent handbill, quoted, ironically, "from the most conservative capitalist source imaginable—the Research Institute of America, Inc." After the cataclysm, however, we are told that automation, now a bane within the capitalist system, will become a blessing.

> The Socialist Labor party reminds the American workers that it is not automation as such that threatens them with degradation and misery in permanent unemployment; it is capitalism's use of automation for the

purpose of increasing profit. If the industries and services are owned by society, which is to say, by all the people collectively, and if they are administered democratically by the workers' own industrial union councils, then automation will become an unqualified blessing for it will be employed in the people's interest. The abolition of poverty, the production of an abundance for all with the leisure in which to enjoy it—these can be the blessed fruit of science and technology once industry is freed of the incubus of private ownership.[9]

SLP Approach to Reform.   The end of the "state" as organized political force is as central to the SLP conception of the good society as is the socialization of the economy. And this ideal makes them as critical of the Russian version of Marxist socialism as of American capitalism. In fact, they put the two together, saying that "the social and economic system of Soviet Russia has absolutely nothing in common with Socialism, It has, however, a great deal in common with capitalism." [10] They see the Russians as heretics and themselves as the true exponents of the gospel. "It was a basic principle with Marx and Engels that, once capitalist rule is overthrown, the State 'DIES OUT.' Marx stated unequivocally that 'the existence of the State is inseparable from the existence of slavery.'" [11] A similar hunger for a freewheeling liberty, a stateless society, is discernible in the communitarian dreams of today's "New Left."

Their millenarian emphasis on a utopian future has made the SLP not only uninterested in gradual reform of capitalism but positively mistrustful of such an approach to social improvement. Reformism is seen as compromising with essential evil, and as a policy which leads to the moral corruption of the reformers. "If you allow your own members to play monkeyshines with the party, the lookers on . . . will justly believe that you will at some critical moment allow capitalism to play monkeyshines with you," wrote Daniel De Leon.[12] Inasmuch as they believe that the critical moment will be produced automatically by the inner workings of capitalism, the SLP millenarians emphasize doctrinal purity and keeping the faithful uncorrupt until the "Day of Judgment," rather than action and strategy. "In all revolutionary movements, as in the storming of fortresses," writes De Leon, "the thing depends upon the head of the column—upon that minority that is so intense in its convictions, so soundly based on its principles, so determined in action that it carries the masses with it, storms the breastworks and captures the fort." [13] Right attitudes rather than practical methods are the important thing.

9 "Automation Crisis!!" Socialist Labor Party handbill.
10 "Socialism versus Soviet Despotism," Socialist Labor Party handbill.
11 "Which Would You Choose?" Socialist Labor Party handbill.
12 Quoted in Howard H. Quint, *The Forging of American Socialism* (New York: Bobbs-Merrill Co., 1964), p. 148.
13 *Ibid.*, pp. 147–48.

Lack of Mass Appeal. Millenarianism also accounts for the failure of the SLP ever to develop mass appeal among American workers. De Leon's passion for doctrinal purism and for an uncompromising opposition to the capitalist system led him to adopt a policy of systematically weeding out reformists from the party ranks. The result was that he diminished the number of his active cohorts by over half. The policy was unintelligible to the rank-and-file worker, who was interested in material benefits now, within capitalism, rather than in a future socialist order. And under the auspices of welfare Liberalism the worker found himself increasingly enjoying these benefits. Engels was right when he observed to the German revolutionary Friedrich Sorge, who had settled in Hoboken, that the enormous strength of "bourgeois prejudices . . . [is as] strongly rooted in the working class" of America as among entrepreneurs.[14] In addition, the Marxist stress on class antagonism was antithetical to an American tradition which is basically solidarist and which rejects the concept of class as a divisive idea and opts instead for belief in a universal middle-class identity. The very foreignness and doctrinaire utopianism of the SLP, seen in the context of the tradition of "givenness" of which Professor Boorstin writes, also made it suspect to the American worker.

There is little point in discussing in detail the ideology of the Communist Party of the United States, which formed in 1919 out of a splinter of the Socialist Party. It has never had even the limited popular appeal of the Socialist Labor or Socialist Party. Theodore Draper also tells us that it was early "transformed from a new expression of American radicalism to the American appendage of a Russian revolutionary power." [15] In a later chapter we shall detail the story of Soviet Russian Marxism.

3. The New Left: Definition and Origins

After two decades of unusual domestic calm, the United States experienced in the 1960s a sudden surge of radical dissent which has been attributed to the so-called "New Left." The use of a common name for the phenomenon implies more unity than it actually has had, however. For the "New Left" is not a single organization, like the Socialist Labor Party, but rather a congeries of groups, some local, some national, some quite ephemeral, others more permanent. Its adherents are mostly young radicals, on and off college campuses, committed to achieving a variety of changes in the political and social order by direct action. They have

[14] Clinton Rossiter, *Marxism: The View from America* (New York: Harcourt, Brace & World, 1960), p. 5.
[15] Theodore Draper, *American Communism and Soviet Russia, the Formative Period* (New York: Viking Press, 1960), p. 395.

organized themselves in such groups as Students for a Democratic Society (SDS), the Progressive Labor Party, the Student Nonviolent Coordinating Committee (SNCC), the Women's Liberation Movement, the Gay Liberation Movement, and others. Sometimes the expression "The Movement" is used to designate the entire motley aggregate.[16] The Black Liberation Movement, almost totally identified with the white radicals between 1960 and 1965, has become an entirely separate affair since the development of the "Black Power" concept, beginning in 1966.[17]

The "New Left" is also to be distinguished from left Liberals working for change within the system—the "New Democratic Coalition," which includes such people as Allard Lowenstein, and the "New Party" of Dr. Benjamin Spock, Christopher Lasch, and others. These Liberal groups are committed to electoral politics within the established rules as their primary instrument for change, whereas the New Left stresses direct action—protests, demonstrations, interruptions, and, at the extreme end of the spectrum, physical violence.[18]

Decline of the Old Left.   The old Left, weak and small in its best days, virtually disintegrated during the war years and the 1950s. The rise of Stalin to absolute power in the Soviet Union had been a severely

---

[16] See Massimo Teodori, ed., *The New Left: A Documentary History* (Indianapolis: Bobbs-Merrill, 1969), pp. 4–5, for definitions of "New Left," "Movement," and associated terms. Copyright 1969 by Massimo Teodori. Quotations with permission of the publisher.

[17] *Ibid.*

[18] Kenneth and Patricia Dolbeare, however, say that the New Left "covers a spectrum running from reform Liberalism to the hippie or Yippie perspective in which the individual's commitment to a radical new life style often precludes what is traditionally thought of as political action." *American Ideologies* (Chicago: Markham, 1971), p. 145. In *The New Radicals* (New York: Random House, 1966), Paul Jacobs and Saul Landau devote a chapter each to the Student Nonviolent Coordinating Committee (SNCC), and to the Students for a Democratic Society (SDS) as the most important and characteristic New Left groups, in terms of aim and style. Brief attention is given, in a chapter entitled "The Leftovers," to a number of groups of lesser significance, which are Marxist in orientation: the Progressive Labor Party (PLP), the W. E. B. Du Bois Clubs of America, the Young Socialist Alliance, and the Young People's Socialist League. More ephemeral and local groups discussed include the Free Speech Movement (FSM) at Berkeley and Vietnam Day Committees (VDC) at Berkeley and elsewhere. Teodori, *op. cit.*, emphasizes the same groups, though he organizes his presentation chronologically and around protest themes, rather than around groups. He also mentions the Committee for Non-Violent Action (CNVA), the War Resisters' League, (WRL), the Spring Mobilization Committee, the Women's Liberation Movement, the Movement for Democratic Society, and the Peace and Freedom Party, which became active after the publication of the Jacobs and Landau volume. Staughton Lynd, a leading New Left publicist, in an introduction to Priscilla Long, ed., *The New Left: A Collection of Essays* (Boston: Extending Horizons Books, 1969), discusses only SDS and SNCC. He also refers to a "White New Left" and a "Black New Left," whereas Teodori reserves the label "New Left" for white activism, calling black activism the "Black Liberation Movement." The Long volume, however, is devoted wholly to essays by white radicals.

disillusioning experience to many left intellectuals, and with the coming of the Cold War many of them came to identify with the Western bloc and its major institutions.[19] The fifties were indeed a decade of "the end of ideology." The most significant left position during these years was occupied by Americans for Democratic Action and the American Civil Liberties Union. Youth during the fifties was apathetic, indifferent, or very conservative, concerned primarily with career preparation and with "getting ahead."

During these years there did appear small groups of young people in revolt against American society, but for the most part they struck an apolitical stance—the "Hipsters" and "Beatniks" of Greenwich Village, of San Francisco's North Beach, of New Orleans, Chicago, Los Angeles. They were, however, a harbinger of things to come. Teodori sympathetically sums up their "program" as "rejection of industrial society and its many aberrations; irrational response to the congenital irrationalism of that society; individualism and communal living; liberation of sexual energies, with natural acceptance of homosexual and bisexual as well as heterosexual behavior; desecration of the traditional values of family, work, flag, religion and uprightness; Negro jazz and folk music; marijuana; freedom in dress and general appearance."[20]

A New Beginning.   If mass action had to wait for the sixties, the fifties were, however, important as a seedtime of New Left ideas, both in the United States and abroad. In England university intellectuals in 1957 brought out two radical journals which in 1959 were merged as the *New Left Review*. Marxist in orientation, the *Review* emphasized themes which had been dear to Marx in his youth but which had had no development within Soviet Russian Marxism: the themes of alienation and humanism. In the United States radical intellectuals at the University of Wisconsin and the University of Chicago brought out two publications with similar emphases: *Studies on the Left* and *New University Thought*, which were followed by the appearance of other new journals on campuses all over the country.[21] At the same time, C. Wright Mills, William Appleman Williams, and Paul Goodman were publishing books which were to be seminal for the coming Movement: *The Power Elite, The Tragedy of American Diplomacy,* and *Growing Up Absurd*. The leading theme of this literature was utopian activism.[22]

It is generally agreed that one important beginning of what became the "New Left" is found in the Civil Rights Movement in the South

---

[19] The account of the development of the New Left relies principally on Teodori, *op. cit.*

[20] *Ibid.,* p. 10.

[21] Jacobs and Landau, *op. cit.,* pp. 9–11.

[22] Lynd, *op. cit.,* p. 4.

beginning in 1960, when numerous idealistic young white people from the North went South to help southern Blacks in their drive for integration. It was in the Civil Rights Movement that the characteristic "New Left" style of confrontation politics was developed, albeit it was then under pacifist direction, carried on in alliance with Established Liberals and tied to specific and recognized rights. In April 1960 SNCC—the Student Nonviolent Coordinating Committee—a chief component of the Black New Left, was created for the purpose of coordinating the activities of groups participating in sit-ins. In SNCC we find the characteristic feature of "New Left" organizational structure and style: (1) open and flexible organization; (2) lack of a permanent and highly developed bureaucracy; (3) stress on "participatory democracy" in decision making; (4) a refusal to bind its people to a fixed ideological position; and (5) an affirmation of nonviolence (which now characterizes only *some* New Left groups).[23]

Radical Alienation.   The parting of the ways for SNCC with reform Liberals came after 1963, following upon its leaders' disillusionment with the gradualist Liberal approach in the federally backed voter registration campaign in the South. It is only at this point that SNCC adopted the full "New Left" position by moving wholly outside the "system" and its procedures for accomplishing objectives. The new attitude of radical alienation from the Established Liberal order was stated clearly by SNCC leader John Lewis, in a speech in Washington in August 1963:

> We cannot support the Administration's civil rights bill, for it is too little, and too late. . . . We are now involved in a serious revolution. This nation is still a place of cheap political leaders who build their careers on immoral compromises and ally themselves with open forms of political, economic and social exploitation. . . . The party of Kennedy is also the party of Eastland. . . . The party of Javits is also the party of Goldwater. Where is *our* party?"[24]

It was natural that movement entirely beyond the borders of the system would bring with it invocation of the theme of "revolution." Thus Lewis continued:

> The revolution is a serious one. Mr. Kennedy is trying to take revolution out of the street and put it in the courts. Listen, Mr. Kennedy, listen Mr. Congressman, listen fellow citizens, the black masses are on the march for jobs and freedom, and we must say to the politicians that there won't be a "cooling off" period.

[23] See Teodori, *op. cit.*, pp. 14, 15, 99–100.
[24] Quoted in *ibid.*, pp. 100–101.

All of us must get in the revolution. Get in and stay in the streets
. . . until true Freedom comes, until the revolution is complete.[25]

The Peace Movement.   A second large area of "New Left" concern
has been world peace. The beginnings of the Peace Movement were the
San Francisco Peace March of 1960 and the formation of the National
Committee for a Sane Nuclear Policy (SANE). As with the Civil Rights
Movement, the early days of the Peace Movement saw people of a
variety of persuasions, with very different general orientations to the
Established Liberal order, working together—Liberals, religious pacifists,
Communists, democratic socialists, and others. The focus of activity was
on propaganda to have nuclear weapons banned, and tactics included
appeals to governments and other action within the system.

Movement outside the system began to develop after 1959, with the
appearance of the Student Peace Union, whose program emphasized civil
disobedience and demonstrations against bomb shelters and against the
civil defense program. In February 1962 some five thousand students
picketed both the White House and the Soviet Embassy. Following the
signing of the Nuclear Test Ban Treaty in 1963 the Movement broke up,
if only temporarily. On its revival in the late sixties, a function of the
United States' dilemma in Vietnam, it was in certain of its branches a
full-blown "New Left" phenomenon.

Social Transformation.   A third focus of incipient New Left activity
was the ghetto transformation program, exemplified by the "Economic
Research and Action Project" of the Students for a Democratic Society,
initiated in August 1963. Chief inspiration for the project was Michael
Harrington's book *The Other America* (supported, ironically, by Established Liberalism's Center for the Study of Democratic Institutions, directed by Robert M. Hutchins), which showed that amidst the general
affluence of American society there were millions of poor and under-
privileged persons who constituted over 16 percent of the country's population. Like the Civil Rights Movement, the SDS project involved
principally college youth who went into inner cities, this time in the
North, to organize poor whites and blacks around a number of social
transformation goals—rectification of building code violations by slum-
lords, reasonable rents, more equitable and efficient welfare administration, the creation of job opportunities. By the summer of 1964 there were
ten such projects going in such widely separated places as Chicago,
Newark, Boston, and Oakland. Typically, the activists left their campuses
to go live in SDS community centers in the target ghettos, which also

---

[25] *Ibid.*, pp. 101–2; see also Jacobs and Landau, *op. cit.*, Chapter 3, "SNCC—
One Man, One Vote," and associated documents; and Howard Zinn, *SNCC: The New
Abolitionists*, 2d ed. (Boston: Beacon Press, 1965).

served as meeting places, offices, and organizational centers. In this area as in the others we have described, coalitions were formed with Liberals and the prime objective—the creation of a more efficient welfare state— was decidedly within the established order.[26]

The radical political strategy behind these projects has been articulated by Tom Kahn, executive director of the League for Industrial Democracy.[27] Kahn points out that although radicals traditionally have turned to the labor movement for support in transforming society, this was not possible for American radicals of the 1960s. The working class in the United States had become a vested interest of the Established Liberal order, not at all concerned with the integrationist aims of blacks and other depressed groups. Looking for a substitute force, the young radicals realized that the universities were an overlooked seat of power and influence. University populations had supported radical movements from time immemorial in Latin America and Europe, and there was an American university population of four and one half million persons to draw upon. Moreover, they were concentrated in huge schools like the University of Michigan, the University of California at Berkeley, and the University of Wisconsin, each with a population of over thirty thousand. The radical intellectuals realized, however, that this was not a sufficient force to accomplish extensive social change, and that allies would be needed; hence the attempted coalition with the poor and with reform Liberals.

Working with Liberals, however, soon produced disenchantment in the radical wing of SDS. Tom Hayden, an SDS leader, decided that the coalition with Liberals simply turned the poor over to the Establishment. The poor, he said, was "the only group in society not corrupted" (shades of De Leon's purism), and bureaucratic welfarism simply made them worse off. Gradually, therefore, on the SDS left wing, an alternative strategy of building counter-institutions began to take form. The ultimate aim was no less than the creation of a counterculture of "revolutionary garrisons" within the established order. This remains today a major "New Left" approach to social change, and we shall discuss it further below.[28]

The Academic New Left.   A fourth and last focus of New Left concern has been the mentality and the structure of the modern university. The psychological cramp involved was first signaled on a major scale by the Berkeley Revolt at the end of 1964. It amounted to a rejection of the conception of the university as a "knowledge factory" operated as

---

[26] Teodori, op. cit., pp. 25–29; see also, Jacobs and Landau, op. cit., Chapter 4.
[27] Tom Kahn, "The Problems of the New Left," Commentary, 40, July 1966: 30–38.
[28] Ibid., p. 33.

a bureaucratized, impersonal structure. Teodori has succinctly described aspects of the "multiversity" from which the protest stemmed:

> The University of California at Berkeley had a "modern" structure quite different from that of the feudal institutions which still dominate much of Academia in Europe. Its atmosphere was "liberal", and its machinery efficient and well organized. But it was the very "liberal" and apparently open character, as President Clark Kerr's theory had conceived it, which aroused opposition and revealed the actual substance of certain kinds of liberalism. The multiversity had become a service open to government, industry, finance, labor, and national defense, with expanded facilities dedicated to the preparation and training of personnel qualified to ensure the smooth functioning of a society increasingly subservient to science and technology. On the inside, the mechanism of the university was supposed to be administered in a managerial spirit like that of other units of production, with administrator-entrepreneurs capable of continuously making the program of study and scientific research meet the demands of outside customers. It seemed that there could be no place for the needs and desires of students or for the autonomy required by professors. Above all, there was no place for critical, as opposed to specialized training or for self-government of the institution. The multiversity was "a mechanism held together by administrative rules and fed by money." [29]

The university had become an exemplar, perhaps a caricature, of the type of rationalized, bureaucratized social structure which has become the chief end product of the revolution of modernity. It is not strange that the chief officer of its Berkeley embodiment manifested, to a heightened degree, the Protestant Work Ethic which from the beginning has been a catalyst and carrier of that revolution. Witness the following brief description of Clark Kerr by A. H. Raskin:

> Kerr is not a man for rich living, even though his salary of $45,000. a year puts him $900. ahead of Governor Edmund Brown as the state's highest paid official. He is frugal even of time. If Kerr gets to an airport and discovers the plane will be 15 minutes late, he is furious at the lost time. But if it will be an hour late, he is contented; he will sit quietly in a corner of the airport, begin writing memos, speeches, articles or even a chapter for a book.
> Kerr works with the same intensity at home. . . .
> The commander's invariable uniform is a navy blue suit and white shirt.[30]

The "New Left" challenges the rational work ethic values of the modern ideological revolution in the name of the humanity, freedom, and community norms which also are an integral part of that revolution.

[29] Teodori, *op. cit.*, p. 30.
[30] A. H. Raskin, "The Berkeley Affair: Mr. Kerr vs. Mr. Savio & Co.," *New York Times Magazine*, February 14, 1965, p. 89.

4. Radicalization of the Movement: Call to Revolution

We have described the origins of "New Left" activity in four areas of protest. In the three involving the general society, we saw radical activists working at first with reform Liberals, still hoping to use successfully the procedures of the Established Liberal system, such as the electoral process. But we also saw a gradual disillusionment with Liberal gradualism and compromise politics as the sixties unfolded, and an increasing separation of the "New Left" as a distinct and autonomous political phenomenon, characterized by bitter alienation, utopian purism, and a commitment to direct action as the only acceptable way of doing politics —in short, a commitment to revolution.

The New Peace Movement.   During 1965 the Johnson Administration escalated the war in Vietnam by instituting systematic bombing in the north and by increasing the American troop commitment from 35,000 to 200,000 men. This was a signal for the reactivation of the Peace Movement and for the appearance of a more vocal and strident "New Left" than that of the early sixties. With its activities more broadly coordinated over all areas of concern, it was able to gain a very wide hearing among college students in general. Antiwar teach-ins were held at hundreds of universities during 1965, which also saw two self-immolations, by a Catholic and a Quaker pacifist. In November SANE organized a march to Washington with SDS participation, and in January 1966 SNCC passed a resolution condemning war and encouraging resistance to military service. The following year brought two huge national demonstrations organized by a specially created mobilization committee linking together the efforts of the many and diverse "New Left" groups. Another Washington march in October was accompanied by acts of civil disobedience. By 1968 not only peace in Vietnam but the entire American foreign policy had become a target of criticism, and the word "revolution" was heard more frequently and loudly in "New Left" circles.

Draft resistance, beginning with the activity of small groups such as the "We Won't Go" group in 1964, became a mass movement between 1966 and 1968. In December 1966 the SDS National Council approved a proposal for organizing communities of draft resisters on the local level. In April 1967 the first large-scale public violation of a 1964 law making draft-card burning a crime occurred in Central Park, New York, where 175 young men burned their cards prior to a march organized by the Spring Mobilization Committee. Draft resistance groups appeared in numerous major cities around the country during 1967, and in October of that year 1,400 draft cards collected in eighteen cities were returned to draft boards. During antidraft weeks in 1968 over two thousand cards were sent back. Demonstrations before induction centers ended in confrontation with the police, and "New Left" groups turned more and more to tactics of guerrilla warfare.

Student Power. "Student power" (sometimes articulated in terms of syndicalist theory) has been the second great concern since the mid-sixties. In many instances it has been linked with antiwar protest. The student revolt at Columbia University in April 1968, for example, focused in part on a demand that the university end ties with the Institute for Defense Analysis. In other places student uprisings have been associated with demands to end ROTC programs and to prevent war manufacture firms such as Dow Chemical from recruiting employees from among the student body.

From 1965 to 1970 "New Left" activism was increasingly accompanied by acts of violence, against both person and property. On college campuses deans were summarily ejected from their offices, record files destroyed or scattered by occupying student bands, and fences torn down. Draft files have been rifled and scattered. Buildings have been bombed and burned, both on and off campuses. In confrontations with authorities—sometimes the police, sometimes National Guard units—students have been gassed and clubbed and policemen and Guardsmen injured.

The culmination of "New Left" protest to date occurred in the spring of 1970 following the announcement of an American invasion of Cambodia. It brought a massive wave of civil disobedience, rioting, and a variety of other violent and nonviolent protest actions on college campuses, including sit-ins, building seizures, and acts of bombing and arson, leading to numerous early school closings. The thousands involved were many times the number of actual hard-core New Lefters. Most of them were "Established Liberals." In all, there were a thousand demonstrations, on two hundred campuses in thirty-seven states.[31] Some of this was a reaction not only to the Cambodian affair but also to the killing of seven students on two campuses—the most appalling violence which has so far resulted from the challenge from the Left.[32]

The Ideological Stance. To this point we have concentrated on a description of New Left behavior—its activism and its methods. After a

[31] "What's Going on Inside America," *U.S. News and World Report*, May 25, 1970, p. 18.

[32] The periodization of New Left activity described above is drawn chiefly from Teodori, *op. cit.* For a somewhat different view see James O'Brien, "The New Left, 1967–68," *Radical America*, November-December 1968, pp. 42–43. See also Jerome H. Skolnick. *The Politics of Protest* (New York: Ballantine Books, 1969), especially Chapter III.

fashion this has also been a comment on its ideology, which almost can be reduced to a call for action, a call for revolution. Except in certain segments, such as the Progressive Labor Party (a disciplined Leninist group whose members dress "straight" and eschew the hair and tatters that are the uniform of most New Left protesters), the New Left repudiates ideology. They want to have nothing to do with elaborate, highly unified, and rationalized schemes of utopian reform set in detailed *Weltanschauungen* which explain the whole of reality. And, of course, they reject the latent ideological sets that we found characteristic of the "Established Liberal" of the American Center. Their stance is voluntarist, not rationalist, as is well epitomized in the title of a book by one of their chief leaders, Jerry Rubin's *Do It!* So far as they find conceptual behavior useful, they are eclectic. Jack Newfield, for example, tells us that New Left ideas are an "ecumenical mixture" of competing traditions—"anarchism, socialism, pacifism, existentialism, humanism, transcendentalism, bohemianism, populism, mysticism, black nationalism." He says of himself that he believes in the "democracy of Jefferson, the nonviolence of Camus, the radical empiricism of William James. I believe in liberal values and radical action." [33]

While Newfield emphasizes the concepts of Liberalism, other New Lefters make large use of language that we usually associate with Marxism—exploitation, oppression, class struggle, imperialism, socialism versus capitalism. The cult of Mao Tse-tung and his "cultural revolution" are, of course, well known. Nevertheless (again, except for PLP), it cannot be said that the New Left is *essentially* a Marxist movement, if for no other reason than that Marxism is a highly elaborate, structured, rationalistic system of ideas. If any ideological model is an appropriate standard for identifying the New Left outlook, it is rather European anarchism or anarcho-syndicalism than Marxism. As one scholar puts it:

> The current brand of radicalism in style and circumstances comes much closer to that of the Sorelian 1890s than it does to the Marxist 1930s. . . . The mood is one of passionate voluntarism rather than dogmatic rationalism. Instead of creedal conviction, there is doubt and searching, as in the restless eclectic end of the century. . . . The last place you can "do your own thing" is in a Communist cell. Personal heroics, militancy, violence, passion, independence and romanticism are *de rigeuer*.[34]

Although its concepts are thus eclectic and indistinct, and although its world view cannot be identified with any of the grand ideologies associated with the revolution of modernity, the New Left has had

---

[33] Jack Newfield, *A Prophetic Minority* (New York: New American Library, 1966), pp. 22, 24.

[34] Edward Cain, "The New Left: If Not Marx, What?" Paper read at New York State Political Science Association convention, Vassar College, April 1969.

theoreticians of a sort who have stated its ideas and values more systematically and comprehensively than the average activist. I shall discuss three articulations of New Leftism in particular.

5. Philosophers of the New Left

One-Dimensional Man was written by a professor of philosophy, Herbert Marcuse. It appeared in 1964, early in the history of the New Left, and has been both an inspiration and a summary of New Left concerns. A second New Left classic, composed in the heat of the battle—Jerry Rubin's *Do It!*—is a cruder statement of the same themes, perhaps closer to the spirit and mentality of the average activist than the elegant abstractions of Professor Marcuse. A third, Charles Reich's *Greening of America*, which appeared after the political denouement of May 1970, points away from politics toward cultural revolution and displays some points of similarity between the New Left and the New Right in their common antagonism to the Established Liberal order.

One-Dimensional Man.   Herbert Marcuse is Professor of Philosophy at San Diego State College in California. He is a native German, born in Berlin, who was a refugee from Nazism during the 1930s. Marcuse is a prolific writer whose works include a first-rate study of Georg Wilhelm Friedrich Hegel (whom Marcuse interprets as a Liberal), a Freudian view of the present state of things entitled *Eros and Civilization,* and several volumes on New Left themes. The earliest of Marcuse's New Left writings was *One-Dimensional Man,* which, ironically, was supported by grants from the Rockefeller Foundation, the Social Science Research Council, and other "Established Liberal" funding organizations.

The central theme of *One-Dimensional Man* is that the United States today is a bureaucratized industrial state that is manipulated by a small elite who contrive to give everyone, except an exploited margin of poor, a false sense of satisfaction, comfort, and "freedom" while at the same time destroying the possibility of "true" individual freedom and self-development. The system also purchases a precarious peace with the constant threat of holocaust. It is therefore radically exploitive of human values, but is not *seen* as such, for the whole affair is managed by technical sleight of hand rather than by terror. (The similarity between the epistemological structure of the book and that of the "conspiracy" literature of the extreme right is interesting; in both cases the writer argues that the average American is aware only of an apparent truth, while the real state of things, into which the writer has insight, is hidden from him.)

In a strange agreement with "Established Liberals" such as Boorstin and Bell, Marcuse tells us that ideology has indeed been absorbed into the experience of life in America, but his conclusions differ from theirs. Whereas for these other writers the "end of ideology" means giving up dangerous utopian visions in exchange for actual happiness in a socially healthy environment, for Marcuse it means losing our power to appraise critically a dangerous and unhealthy situation which has been imposed on us without our being aware of it.

The bulk of the book catalogs and details the new forms of control by which the hidden elite manages to narcotize us into the illusion of freedom and contentment. A chapter on "Economic Controls" argues that the achievement of affluence has produced a social conformity which is antithetical to the original freedoms on which America was founded—freedom of thought, of speech, and of conscience, which create a critical individualism. Nonconformity today is seen as socially useless. Similarly, freedom of enterprise, once central, has given way to a highly organized corporate economy in which all economic forces are mobilized by those who control the political system. Coupled with this is control by the secret elite over the entire communications system, a power which enables them to produce the "euphoria in unhappiness" that characterizes our society today. We are thereby rendered unconscious of our servitude to "external powers over which the individual has no control." (This sense of alienation in "powerlessness" is not unlike that found among some of the Radical Right and among Lane's "Undemocrats." This theme contrasts strongly with the Established Liberal's sense of control and power over his situation, emphasized by Almond and Verba.) The effect of all this, according to Marcuse, is a kind of totalitarianism. "Mass production and mass distribution claim the *entire* individual." [35]

A chapter called "Closing the Political Universe" connects the welfare with the warfare state. The need to fight an external Communist enemy produces the collusion of business with labor groups. Class struggle is attenuated by the external threat, and the social ranks close up. The mechanization of industry also assimilates nearly everyone into the white-collar class and produces one standard way of life. With this comes the end of what Marcuse considers a healthy opposition of groups and classes and a "one-dimensional" political behavior which in America takes the form of bipartisanship.

Still another chapter details the destruction of "higher culture." The arts, ideally, are set apart from society, antagonistic to and critical of reality. Today in America they have become flattened and reduced to a commodity, to a part of the material culture, like everything else,

[35] Herbert Marcuse, *One-Dimensional Man: Studies in the Ideology of Advanced Industrial Society* (Boston: Beacon Press, 1966), p. 10.

and rendered thereby meaningless. Marcuse has in mind the mass production of prints of great paintings and of Beethoven symphonies on tapes and records. By contrast a high culture is essentially alien and critical:

> The artistic alienation has become as functional as the architecture of the new theaters and concert halls in which it is performed. . . . Unquestionably the new architecture is better, i.e., more beautiful and more practical than the monstrosities of the Victorian era. But it is also more "integrated"—the cultural center is becoming a fitting part of the shopping center, or municipal center, or government center. Domination has its own aesthetics, and democratic domination has its democratic aesthetics.[36]

A chapter on "Closing the Universe of Discourse" laments the loss of moral standards set apart from practice. "Values" are no longer cognitive standards of right to be employed to criticize "facts," but are studied only as a *kind* of fact. The facts have become tremendously satisfying, so that the difference between the ideal and the real has disappeared. Hence meaning and moral significance have been abridged. "Right" and "truth" are simply names for what *in fact* goes on. Marcuse attempts to demonstrate the point with a critique of the concept of "operationalism" in the philosophy of science, which reduces the meaning of terms to descriptions of empirical processes or procedures. The loss of criteria of moral judgment in political analysis he illustrates with a discussion of the work of Morris Janowitz and Dwaine Marvick, who employ a definition of democracy derived wholly from what is observed to take place in a society which is simply *called* a democracy.[37]

Three more chapters focus on the loss of a concept of truth distinct from empirical reality, as manifested in the vogue of "analytical philosophy," which entails the loss of a sense of transcendence. Yet three more deal with the possibility of alternatives to the present sad state of things, but at the end Marcuse concludes that there really is no alternative. He finds no "bridge for transcendence," only a negative "great refusal" to go along on the part of those who remain outside the narcotic grasp of the system—the poor and exploited.

Do It!   A balder attack on the technological rationality of "Established Liberalism" is found in *Do It!: Scenarios of the Revolution.* Its author, Jerry Rubin, is the leader of the "Yippies" (Youth International Party), a young American who in his "straight" days was a college student and sports reporter. Since dropping out of college he has spent his time as a Movement organizer and agitator, bent on destroying the University of California and other elements of "the system," and in

---

[36] *Ibid.*, p. 65.
[37] *Ibid.*, pp. 114–15.

building a counterculture. He was indicted with seven others of the "Chicago Eight" for attempting to break up the Democratic National Convention of 1968. The "Yippies" are a link between left radical political activism and the cultural revolution of Hippiedom.

Like Marcuse's book, *Do It!* is a general assault on all aspects of modern industrial Liberal culture. "We are not protesting issues," he writes; "we are protesting Western Civilization." [38] A major target of the book is the Protestant Work Ethic and the derived idea that material success is the measure of human meaning. He brings the attack right into his own family circle:

> Dad looked at his house and car and manicured lawn, and he was proud. All of his material possessions justified his life.
> He tried to teach his kids: he told us not to do anything that would lead us from the path of Success.
>
> WORK *don't play*
> STUDY *don't loaf*
> OBEY *don't ask questions*
> FIT IN *don't stand out*
> BE SOBER *don't take drugs*
> MAKE MONEY *don't make waves*
>
> We were conditioned in self-denial:
> We were taught that fucking was bad because it was immoral. Also in those pre-pill days a knocked-up chick stood in the way of Respectability and Success.[39]

He takes a special crack at the manifestation of the Work Ethic in today's college life:

> The University is a place for making it, a high-pressured rat race. Competition for grades, degrees, books, recommendations, getting into graduate school and getting a good job.
> The academic world is a hierarchy, and everybody's always kissing the ass of the guy on top of him.[40]

Rubin also sets himself against rationality and critical thinking. This seems paradoxical, inasmuch as it was precisely the decline of critical thinking in America that Marcuse lamented. At a closer look, however, the two writers seem to be talking about different things, though even so it is difficult to see how they might both be right.

---

[38] Jerry Rubin, *Do It! Scenarios of the Revolution* (New York: Simon & Schuster, 1970), p. 105. Copyright 1970 by Social Education Foundation. With permission of Simon & Schuster and Jonathan Cape.

[39] *Ibid.,* pp. 17–18.

[40] *Ibid.,* p. 25.

Marcuse deplores the absence of normative rationality—the ability to stand aside from experience and critically examine its goodness in the light of rationally held values that are in some way apart from that experience so that they can serve as standards for conduct. The rationality he desires is action-oriented; it is essentially a guide for moral action. On the other hand, Rubin condemns the prevalence (especially in Academia) of a purely theoretical and passive rationality that stands apart from action, not for the purpose of gaining bearings for action, but detachedly for the purpose simply of understanding, and even here making the assumption that "the whole" will never be disclosed. This seems to be what the following passage is trying to say:

> "Critical" or "abstract thinking" is a trap in school.
> Criticize, criticize, criticize.
> Look at both sides of the argument, take no action, take no stands, commit yourself to nothing, because you're always looking for more arguments, more information, always examining, criticizing.
> Abstract thinking turns the mind into a prison. Abstract thinking is the way professors avoid facing their own social impotence.[41]

As Rubin sees it, the malady is not a thoughtless, un-self-conscious attachment to norms immanent in conventional action, but rather a rationality that stops action altogether.

There is another kind of rationality that Rubin also finds to be characteristic of the Established Liberal order. This second type of rationality is in fact action-oriented, but only in a purely technical, manipulative way. He is referring, of course, to the scientific rationality of psychological conditioning:

> Dig Pavlov and his dog Spot:
> Ring the bell and then give Spot food.
> Soon Spot salivates when you ring the bell.
> Conditioning.[42]

Scientific rationality, Rubin contends, destroys personality and human freedom by reducing behavior to an aggregate of conditioned reflexes. All of this adds up, for Rubin, to an oppressive and repressive reality which, borrowing his spelling from Kafka, he dubs "Amerika."

The rules of the Liberal political order cannot be used to change it. An extension of its technical rationality, they are simply instruments used by elites to manipulate the system to produce their ends. Of academic negotiations at Berkeley—an instance of the process of democratic bargaining and compromise—he writes: "The fucking deans were

41 *Ibid.*, p. 23.
42 *Ibid.*, p. 186.

using 'negotiations' as a dodge to wear us out. Talk, talk, talk while the rules against political activity stood strong. We got very pissed off." [43] Rubin sums up his disillusionment with the result of a mayoral election in Oakland in which he was a candidate with the statement that "To succeed in electoral politics you must be dishonest. Our new society is honest. . . . I will never put on a gold suit and vest again. Fuck electoral politics. LIVE the revolution." [44]

The only solution to the problem of impotent *cum* manipulative rationality, according to Rubin, is to pull down the system which incorporates them. We are enjoined to engage in one great, nihilistic action, aimed at destruction of the system. "*When in doubt*," writes Rubin, "*burn*. It may have to be violent action. Fire is the revolutionary's god. Fire is instant theater. . . . Politicians only notice poverty when the ghettos burn. The burning of the first draft card caused earth tremors under the Pentagon. Burn the flag. Burn churches. Burn, burn, burn." [45]

The attack is not aimed at realizing a more moral order worked out ahead of time; it is not based on critical rationality in Marcuse's sense. The action called for is irrational in a strict sense, for it is not goal-oriented:

> Goals are irrelevant. The tactics, the actions, are critical.
> If we had to decide beforehand what our goals would be, we'd be arguing about the future society for the next 1,000 years. Let's worry about that bridge when we come to it. *The goal now is to blow up the bridge just behind us.*
>
> Do. DO. DO. The movement gets its unity around tactics. We become a community through collective action. [46]

Marcuse calls for noncooperation, a "great refusal." Rubin demands that the Liberal system be destroyed. Much of *Do It!* is the story of actions taken by Rubin and his cohorts to stop the workings of the American political system: holding up a hearing of the House Un-American Activities Committee, a demonstration at the Pentagon, the attempted disruption of a Democratic National Convention.

The voluntaristic character of Rubin's recipe for revolution implies that he is not interested in forensic ideology-building, in discursive reasoning to construct goals and methods. He is in fact quite explicit

---

[43] *Ibid.*, p. 23.
[44] *Ibid.*, p. 51. This was written before the election of 1971, in which New Left candidates won seats on the Oakland City Council. One wonders how this result fits into Rubin's world view as expressed in the above quotations.
[45] *Ibid.*, p. 127.
[46] *Ibid.*, p. 125.

in his rejection of ideology. A section entitled "Ideology is a Brain Disease" contains the following passage:

> The revolution is *now*. We create the revolution by *living* it.
> What would happen if the white ideological left group took power: Communist Party, Trotskyites, Progressive Labor, Independent Socialists, Outer Mongolian Proletarian Internationalists and the rest of the alphabet soup?
> The hippie streets would be the first cleaned up by the "socialist" pigs. We'd be forced to get haircuts and shaves every week. We'd have to bathe every night, and we'd go to jail for saying dirty words.
> Sex, except to produce children for the revolution, would be illegal.
> Psychedelic drugs would be capital crimes and beer-drinking mandatory.
> We'd have to attend compulsory political-education classes at least five nights a week.[47]

We are in effect told that *any* kind of thought out, structured, organized pattern—*any* rational order, even the order of a Communist society—is oppressive and destructive of human freedom, which Rubin defines as pure spontaneity. Rubin nevertheless seems to recognize a need for *some* guide to action, in the form of myth, for he writes:

> Myths offer kids a model to identify with. Amerika's myths—from George Washington to Superman to Tarzan to John Wayne—are dead. Amerikan youth must create their own myths.
> The myth of yippie will overthrow the government. The myth makes the revolution. Marx is a myth. Mao is a myth. Dylan is a myth. The Black Panthers are a myth.
> Peoply try to fulfill the myth; it brings out the best in them.[48]

Here "myth" stands for "authoritative personality," something personal and concrete to imitate and follow, an existential personal reality rather than an abstract and impersonal program. Of course, one might well ask whether the particular personality embodying the Yippie myth does not represent an idea and an ideal, and hence an implicit program. Personalities are, after all, not interchangeable. But Rubin wants to disabuse us of this conclusion, for in the next sentence he tells us that "the secret to the yippie myth is that it's nonsense. Its basic informational statement is a blank piece of paper."[49]

Despite the rejection of ideology and the enigmatic qualification of the idea of myth, does not Rubin have *some* concrete conception of a good political and social order to put in the place of the one he

47 *Ibid.*, p. 113.
48 *Ibid.*, pp. 82, 83.
49 *Ibid.*

wishes to destroy? Must he not have *some* values in mind in order to know that he does not like the values implicit in the existing Liberal system? We have in fact already discovered one of them—individual freedom defined as spontaneity, unhampered by restricting rules and prohibitions. He wants to affirm the importance and reality of the flesh-and-blood individual and the individual's uniqueness, as over against the impersonal world of roles and rules. Rubin's concern is existential, as comes out clearly in his description of a "Be-in."

> If it had been a political demonstration they would have asked, "What are the issues? What are the demands? Why should we go?"
> But this time everybody knew.
> The purpose was just to *be*.
>
> > Golden Gate Park:
> > Rock music.
> > Grass.
> > Sun. Beautiful bodies.
> > Paint.
> > Ecstasy. Rainbows. No strangers!
> > Everybody smiling. *No picket signs or political banners.*
>
> Our nakedness was our picket sign.[50]

In a sense Rubin is here committing the sin that Marcuse attributed to the Established Liberal, for he is letting himself become uncritically wrapped up in values immanent in experience, he is living a way of life without thinking about it, he is a captive of convention. The difference, of course, is that the experience that Rubin celebrates is not the conventional, but the unconventional. It is not, however, a celebration of an ideal that takes one above and beyond convention. It is, rather, a going back to the preconventional, to the primitive, the original, the "natural." We are reminded of Rousseau's "child of nature." The ideal way of life to Rubin is simply existential reality seen as preconventional primitivism, simplicity. Here being simple is the way to be a free individual; it is also the way to true human community—"No strangers!" On the next page he adds, "We could see one another, touch one another and realize that *we* were not alone."[51] Elsewhere he writes of "the love and brotherhood of a community" as a primary value.[52]

The "Be-in" also represents for Rubin the end of all forms of alienation—not only that of man from man, but also that of every man

---

[50] *Ibid.*, pp. 55, 54–55.
[51] *Ibid.*, p. 56.
[52] *Ibid.*, p. 125.

from himself, from his work, from his environment. It signifies a satisfying and fulfilling wholeness, the perfection of human life:

> It was a new consciousness.
> Instead of *talking* about communism, people were beginning to *live* communism.
> The fragmented life of capitalist Amerika—the separation between work and play, school and fun, property and freedom—was reconstituted by the joyous celebrants.
>
> ————
>
> Revolution meant a new life.
> On earth.
> Today.[53]

Here we have a theme that was developed in the writings of the young Marx, before he became committed to dialectical materialism. It is a dominant New Left concern. It is a theme that has been sidetracked, played down in the making of actual Communist revolutions, which have been preeminently industrializing and rationalizing. But as we shall see, it is being sounded today throughout the Communist as well as the Liberal world, as a protest against the restrictive commonalties of industrial society wherever it is found and under whatever ideological banner. Its formulation has much in common with the original democratic dream of liberty, equality, and fraternity as found in the work of Rousseau and others. It is also a secular restatement of the old Christian apocalyptic dream of "a new Heaven and a new Earth." It contains as well the dream of versatility, which is as much a part of the ideals of Renaissance humanism as of the Marxian vision of the final phase of Communist society. "Communist society will usher in Universal Man," writes Rubin. "The economy will be a game of musical chairs. Everybody will drive a cab, sell shoes, grow feed on a farm, work on a newspaper. The expert-specialist will be a museum piece." [54]

Another "New Left" value that comes across clearly in Rubin's book is the hunger for adventure and romance. "We want to be heroes, like those we read about in the history books," he writes. "We missed the First Amerikan Revolution. We missed World War II. We missed the Chinese and Cuban Revolutions. Are we supposed to spend our futures grinning and watching TV all the time?" [55] Again we have an instance of the cramp that derives from the structured, impersonal rationality of modern society. Allied with this is the hunger for the mysterious, the holy, the transcendent, which have little place in the

[53] *Ibid.*, p. 56.
[54] *Ibid.*, p. 128.
[55] *Ibid.*, p. 87.

efficiency of industrial rationality. Marcuse speaks forlornly of the loss of the transcendent in philosophical terms, and Rubin too uses religious terminology. In *We Are Everywhere,* for example, he writes: "The revolution is nothing if it is not spiritual but the spiritual revolution by itself is nothing," and "Judaism as well as Christianity have universalized into Yippie." [56]

These are all primarily social and cultural values. Does Rubin also set forth any specifically political ideals? "Participatory democracy," the New Left expression for direct democracy in decision making, is graphically illustrated in an anecdote Rubin relates about the celebration of the first Vietnam Day, which included a march aimed at shutting down the Oakland Army Terminal. Twenty thousand radicals were pouring through the streets of Berkeley toward the Oakland city limits when rumors filtered back through the crowd that the National Guard planned to use gas on them. Rubin writes of the discussion that followed about what to do, and the way the decision was taken:

> Debate broke out within the steering committee: what to do? turn left into Oakland? sit down? charge the lines? turn right back to Berkeley?
> Behind us people shouted: *"Turn left! Turn left! Oakland! Oakland!"*
> *We can't turn back, I said. "This is the greatest night in Amerikan history!"* . . .
> *"Let's leave it up to the crowd," a militant said. "The nine of us can't decide for 20,000 people. Let's stop the march, get the loudspeaker and let the people debate what to do."*
> "'That's completely dogmatic. How can you have democracy in the streets with 20,000 people when you're going to be tear gassed any minute? The people who shout the loudest will get their way," replied the conservatives.
> The chanting grew more insistent: TURN LEFT! TURN LEFT! TURN LEFT! . . .
> The vote was 5–4 to turn back to Berkeley.
> The banner swung to the right.
> I fell back into the crowd, tears welling in my eyes. . . .
> It became a funeral march.
> Sad and solemn.
> Fuck "leaders." Fuck "steering committees."
> A movement that isn't willing to risk injuries, even deaths, isn't for shit.[57]

Elsewhere Rubin writes: "Yippies are a participatory movement. . . . Write your own slogan. Protest your own issue. Each man his own yippie." And again, "There's no such thing as a YIPPIE FOLLOWER.

[56] Jerry Rubin, *We Are Everywhere* (New York: Harper & Row, 1971), pp. 158, 76.
[57] Rubin, *Do It!,* pp. 41–43.

There are 646½ million different kinds of yippies, and the definition of a yippie is that he is a LEADER. Yippies are Leaders without followers." [58]

Except in its minor segments, such as the disciplined and elitist PLP, the New Left is devoted to the ideal of participatory democracy. The cry at New Left meetings is "Let the people decide!" No one is voted down, and dissident minorities carry out their own programs. Teodori has catalogued the elements of participatory democracy as: "(a) decentralization and multiplicity of structures and actions which serve the movements . . . ; (b) direct method of self-government at all levels, rather than delegated authority and responsibility; (c) abolition of institutionalized political bureaucracies and of the division of political labor between leaders and those who carry out the leadership's policy; (d) nonexclusionism." [59]

Whether such an ideology of decision making is compatible with effective organization is, of course, a large question. Jack Newfield, an important New Left personality, has decried its detrimental result for clarity and efficiency in policy making and action. It discourages the crystallization of opposing views and produces a debilitating factionalism and fragmentation of the movement. [60]

The Greening of America.   Charles Reich, a Professor of Law at Yale University, has given us another variation on the themes developed by Marcuse and Rubin. *The Greening of America* postdates the year of the great New Left battles—1970—and seems to point away from politics toward a kind of Socratic approach to cultural change. Let us first review the "cooling off" of New Left activity, which was the setting for the book's appearance. [61]

The incidence of bombings by the extremist "Weatherman" faction of the SDS declined after March 1970 when one of their bomb factories in a Manhattan brownstone blew up, killing three of their people. In December Bernardine Dohrn, a Weatherman leader who is a fugitive from the police, issued a manifesto entitled "New Morning —Changing Weather." It said that the explosion in March had forever destroyed the Weathermen's belief "that armed struggle is the only real revolutionary struggle. It is time for the movement to go out into the air, to organize, to risk calling rallies and demonstrations, to convince that mass actions against the war and in support of rebellions do make a difference." [62] That August Father Daniel Berrigan, a pacifist and the

---

[58] *Ibid.*, p. 84.
[59] Teodori, *op. cit.*, p. 37.
[60] Newfield, *op. cit.*, preface.
[61] The following account relies heavily on "The Cooling of America," *Time*, February 22, 1971.
[62] *Ibid.*, p. 11.

chief exponent of the Catholic New Left, sent the Weathermen a letter warning that "no principle is worth the sacrifice of a single human being." Since then throughout the Movement there has been evidence of a general revulsion against violence.

Time magazine suggests that behind the revulsion lies not only moral horror at human lives destroyed but an increasing fear of governmental repression and a sense of frustration. A Texas radical is quoted as saying: "Why try at all if all you are going to do is maybe get busted and bring on the far right?" An underground newspaper editor says: "You work your ass off for years and nothing comes of it." On the part of college students approaching graduation there is also fear of not finding jobs in a slackening market. And perhaps most important, there has been a realization among utopian radicals that the "objective conditions" for successful revolution do not exist. Herbert Marcuse writes that "It is becoming increasingly costly to use forms of confrontation which were still possible a year ago. What is required is a wholesale re-examination of the strategy of the movement." [63]

With campus radical groups, especially the SDS, either splintered or entirely defunct, action for change has swung back into the old channels provided by the Established Liberal system. Black activist Stokely Carmichael has declared: "We must seek and create a new system through a scientific and systematic program. We must be preoccupied with building, not destroying." Former SDS President Carl Oglesby is now writing songs and lecturing at MIT. John Lewis, co-founder of SNCC, whose disenchantment with the processes of the "system" we described earlier, is now directing voter education campaigns in the South. And in Berkeley several radicals were elected in April 1971 to the town council. Much radical organizational work continues to go forward among Marxist groups, Maoist groups, Trotskyites and others, but its objective is education—the long-run radicalization of the population—rather than the immediate disruption of the Established Liberal order through confrontation politics in its various forms. Some activists have become entirely private men, even such former firebrands as Jerry Rubin. In February 1973 Rubin announced: "The 1960s are over; the movement as we know it is dead. It's time to begin life anew. I am totally into self-development now, almost completely working on my body, on my mind. I do yoga, go to massage school, run every day, am into bioenergetics (study of the natural rhythms of the body). I want to lead a quiet life." [64]

[63] Psychology Today, February 1971, cited in ibid.
[64] Article on Carmichael in Rochester Democrat and Chronicle, Jan. 28, 1973; article on Rubin, ibid., Feb. 25, 1973.

From Political to Cultural Revolution. Professor Reich opens *The Greening of America* with a sketch of the present moral condition of America. He finds lawlessness and corruption in all our major institutions and a pervasive irresponsibility and hypocrisy. Our immorality is reflected in the Vietnam war, in poverty amid great affluence, in an unjust tax structure, and in an unplanned economy controlled by private centers of power.[65]

The burden of Reich's lament is decidedly cultural rather than political, for it is not a smug and smirking ruling class that is singled out as the chief devil in the works, but rather the organizational principles and ethics of modern industrial society. Our technology and our system of production "pulverize everything in their path: the landscape, the natural environment, history and tradition, the amenities and civilities, the privacy and spaciousness of life, beauty, and the fragile, slow-growing social structures which bind us together. . . . Organization and bureaucracy increasingly dictate how we shall live our lives, with the logic of organization taking precedence over any other values." [66] The logic of the system, which requires decision by experts, has eroded our democracy, and liberty has been eroded by bureaucratic discretion and the repression of dissent. Work has become meaningless, and much is produced which is socially useless or harmful. The bureaucratic industrial order has destroyed community, making of America "one vast, terrifying, anti-community." [67] (This is an assertion, it will be recalled, which an apologist of the Established Liberal order like Daniel Ball flatly denies.)

Of greatest distress to Professor Reich is his belief that the system has produced a loss of self. This is felt most keenly by the segment of today's youth that joins the New Left. This loss of self culminates in a general sense of powerlessness, of being trapped by an alien environment, something that Reich believes is felt even within the elite of the Established Liberal order. "We seem," he writes, "to be living in a society that no one created and that no one wants. The feeling of powerlessness extends even to the inhabitants of executive offices." [68] (One wonders on what data the finding is based, for none are proferred to the reader, who will recall that the survey data collected by Almond and Verba just a few years earlier found a sense of power and control over his destiny to be a characteristic mark of the bearer of the "civic culture," who inhabits the broad "Established Liberal" center of the American political culture,

---

[65] Charles A. Reich, *The Greening of America* (New York: Bantam Books, 1970), pp. 4–5.
[66] *Ibid.*, pp. 5–6.
[67] *Ibid.*, p. 7.
[68] *Ibid.*, p. 8.

especially its elite echelons.) What is chiefly responsible for the Leviathan system which is destroying our moral being? And what must be changed if it is to be reformed and reordered on more human lines? Reich considers the problem in terms of what he calls "consciousness," which he defines as "a total configuration in any given individual, which makes up his whole perception of reality, his whole world view." [69] In short, he finds the fault to lie with Established Liberal political culture.

Reich tells us that America, since its beginnings, has had two "consciousnesses," or two different political cultural sets. "Consciousness I" was what we have been calling Classical Liberalism. "Its reality centered on the truth of individual effort." [70] Reich tells us that this "consciousness" is still prevalent today among certain groups in American life—e.g., farmers, owners of small businesses, and immigrants with a sense of nationality. It figures today, therefore, as what we have called "conservatism." But its beliefs do not describe things as they really are today; they are at variance with the corporate reality of American society.

Reich then begins to speak of this new reality as a subversion of the American way, of "the original American ideal." Created by the Vanderbilts, Carnegies, Harrimans, and Fords, "the real socialists, collectivizers, subversives," the new corporate society has "cut down on democracy, independence, and the pursuit of happiness" while fostering "a new managerial order, a hierarchy of power and privilege that replaced communal values with antisocial success and with inhuman science." [71] It is a strange thing to witness an apostle of the New Left sharing the nostalgia of the New Right for the values of the older America—while at the same time misinterpreting them (young America was surely individualist, not communal in its ethos).

Before turning to "Consciousness II," which is the ideological counterpart of the corporate Leviathan state, Reich talks about the efforts of welfare Liberals (or Neo-Liberals) to remedy the abuses of Consciousness I. The forces of reform, however, succeeded in coping only with the Depression of the 1930s; they did not remedy the fundamental problems of the system. In fact, the cure was in a way worse than the sickness, for it caused the creation of a giant public regulatory state, which was to become a coercive monster. "The lasting product of the New Deal era was . . . a new consciousness that believed primarily in domination and the necessity for living under domination." [72] Note again the remarkable agreement between Left and Right on the vices of the "Established Liberal" order!

---

[69] *Ibid.*, p. 13.
[70] *Ibid.*, pp. 21, 23.
[71] *Ibid.*, p. 35.
[72] *Ibid.*, p. 60.

Reich identifies the people who share "Consciousness II" as businessmen of the new type, liberal intellectuals, educated professionals and technicians, suburbanites, labor union leaders, supporters of Eugene McCarthy's bid for the presidential nomination in 1968, blue-collar workers with new houses, old-line leftists, and (of all people) members of the Communist Party of the United States.[73]

We are then given a description of the essential characteristics of "Consciousness II": "Reason" in Consciousness II has produced a technological elitism. Its carrier abdicates personal responsibility to the impersonal organization, he accepts unthinkingly the premises of society, and he is always ready to defer to experts. He favors reforms, but he will not fight for them if they threaten to jeopardize his status. (Reich is talking about the same man whom Almond and Verba describe as the carrier of the "civic culture," but we are hard pressed to recognize the similarity.)

The man of "Consciousness II" has been victimized by a cruel deception, says Reich. Material well-being has produced in him a false consciousness of contentment. But it has destroyed his capacity for "awe, wonder, mystery." The corporate state has thus separated him "from his sources of meaning and truth." [74] There is an unmistakable echo here of Marcuse's lament for transcendence and of Rubin's paean to romantic adventure and spirituality.

Other evils are set forth in detail. The school system of the corporate society destroys the student's capacity to think and trains him in obedience. Sex life, culture, political thought and activity are all closely controlled in the name of the national interest. The competitive race has rendered its citizens fearful and suspicious of one another. They are fearful of economic obsolescence. They are commanded to buy and consume. The family has become merely a consumption unit, the environment has been put in jeopardy by the irrationalities of the corporate society, and freedom has been reduced to the single dimension of consumer freedom —freedom to buy anything and to go anywhere.

In reaction to the vacuousness of "Consciousness II," Reich finds a new political culture, a "Consciousness III," beginning to emerge. This corresponds to what we have been describing as the culture of the New Left. Its bearers see an enormous discrepancy between what is and what could be. "The promise of America, . . . somehow has been betrayed." [75] They stand aghast at the emptiness of their parents' lives. To witness his conversion to a new way, the man of "Consciousness III" grows his hair long and changes his style of clothing and of life in general. This sym-

[73] *Ibid.*, pp. 69–70.
[74] *Ibid.*, pp. 90, 140.
[75] *Ibid.*, p. 236.

bolizes his freedom to create his own philosophy and life style, "his own culture." [76]

The new man affirms himself. The individual, not society or something called "the public interest," is the only true reality. This represents a "return to the earlier America." [77] (Again, how close we are in this "rugged individualism" of the left to the outlook of conservatism and the Radical Right!) The bearer of "Consciousness III" understands that it is a crime to let oneself be used, manipulated. He also rejects competition as a way of life. He celebrates energy, enthusiasm, happiness, hope. His clothes express his newfound freedom; there is only one set for all kinds of activities. He values community, as an ideal composed of respect for the uniqueness of the individual plus the idea of "together." And he seeks to restore human consciousness, to recover "self."

The life of the new consciousness is a tenuous one, however, according to Reich. It is expressed only by a segment of contemporary youth, and unless it reaches further into society it will fail. What levers does it have on the future? Reich thinks there are possibilities in what he sees as the real dissatisfactions of middle-class life. He reiterates the theme of "powerlessness" and tells us that most middle-class people hate their work. Their wives do no real work and have no independence. They are disappointed in the workings of democracy and in society's priorities, and they are convinced that someone else is on the gravy train. Yet there is neither in the youth culture nor among the black militants a model adequate for them, one which defines new values for happiness. And the middle class has no idea of "self" to be recovered.

Reich weakly suggests that one possibility for a beginning of change among the middle class lies in the search for origins, a search for one's ethnic identity, in the manner of the militant blacks. How to encourage this or where to go from there, however, he does not say.

Reich expressly rejects a political road to the new society. Liberal reform, he believes, has already proven itself to be illusory. And an SDS-type revolution he sees as hopeless. The revolution must come *first* in consciousness, but how this is to occur Reich does not say. Presumably by preaching and teaching and the force of example—a cultural crusade by the true believers in the new way. "There is a revolution coming," Reich concludes. "It will originate with the individual and with culture, and it will change the political structure only as its final act." [78]

[76] *Ibid.*, p. 241.
[77] *Ibid.*, p. 242.
[78] *Ibid.*, p. 2.

6. The Psychology and Sociology of the New Left

Numbers.   How many New Lefters were there in the country? And who were they? What attracted them to the "Movement?" These questions, like the similar ones we raised about the Right, have not been fully answered. Let us review the evidence that is at hand.

As to numbers, SDS in 1968 claimed 7,000 national dues-paying members and 35,000 members in several hundred local chapters.[79] Richard Peterson of the Educational Testing Service found "student left" organizations on 46 percent of the nation's campuses in the same year.[80] Some estimates for the New Left as a whole have run as high as 250,000.[81] There is difficulty here, of course, in distinguishing between constant, hard-core members and those otherwise "Established Liberals" who can be mobilized by the activists from time to time on particular issues, such as the Vietnam War.

In any case, the overall number of committed New Left activists represents a small, though very vocal, proportion of the American college population as a whole, and an even smaller segment of the entire youth population. A 1968 election analysis by the Michigan Survey Research Center, based on 1,600 interviews, showed that voters under thirty years of age were overrepresented in the Wallace constituency, including areas outside the South, which indicates a perhaps even stronger youth movement to the Right than to the Left. The best evidence available shows, indeed, that the new generation of American voters tend to polarize in a way not characteristic of their parents. They do not accept as readily traditional party allegiances and are found moving away from the "Established Liberal" center in considerable numbers. Precisely *what* those numbers are, however, is not clear.

Social Background Factors.   An early theory explaining the New Left in terms of the "generation gap" has been quite thoroughly discredited by empirical research. Reviewing the evidence in an essay of 1966, the political sociologist Seymour M. Lipset argued rather that radical Left students "are acting out in practice the values which they have been taught by ideologically liberal parents." [82] He cites a study of civil rights

---

[79] *Life*, October 18, 1968, cited in Skolnick, *op. cit.*, p. 89.
[80] Richard E. Peterson, *The Scope of Organized Student Protest in 1967–68* (Princeton: Educational Testing Service, 1968).
[81] Newfield, *op. cit.*, p. 23.
[82] Seymour M. Lipset in *Comparative Education Review*, June 1966, p. 331.

workers in SCOPE which showed that parents supported their children's efforts in the summer program. Only 5 percent of the young people reported feelings of hostility toward their parents. Lipset also tells us that many of the Berkeley protesters were found to be the children of former radicals. A 1969 report by Jerome H. Skolnick, Director of the Task Force on Violent Aspects of Protest and Confrontation of the National Commission on the Causes and Prevention of Violence, includes the statement that empirical studies find that "student activists . . . come from politically liberal families whose values can be described as 'humanist.'"[83]

In 1970 Richard Flacks, a professor of sociology at the University of Chicago, summarized the findings of a large body of empirical research on the various social correlates of New Left activity.[84] He reports that "Movement" people tend to come from the most selective universities and institutions of higher education in the country—the major state and private universities and the prestigious liberal arts colleges. This may, he suggests, involve a self-selection of the protest-prone, for these schools tend to be associated with more liberal attitudes than others. The protesters are rarely students with low grades, and there is some tendency for them to have disproportionately high grades. They are also more academically oriented then the non-activists, scoring higher on verbal aptitude tests and on scales of aesthetic and intellectual interest, but not on mathematical aptitude tests.

As to social background, Flacks finds that the student protesters come from high income families and that both parents have four-year college degrees and are employed in occupations requiring advanced education—that is, intellectual and professional occupations. They especially tend to have highly educated mothers. The children of white-collar and blue-collar workers, of executives, and of the self-employed entrepreneur are underrepresented. As to size of community and region, they are predominantly urbanites and suburbanites, rather than people from small towns, and from the east and west coasts rather than from the Midwest or South. This is the modal picture which does not hold uniformly for all New Lefters.

Flacks also reports that protesters tend to come from secular rather than religious families, although a significant minority of them have strong religious backgrounds, especially Quakers and Unitarians. Protestants are found in proportion to their number in the general population, Jews are overrepresented, Catholics underrepresented.

In terms of political commitment, activists' parents are Democrats,

[83] Skolnick, op. cit., pp. 80–81.
[84] Richard Flacks, "Who Protests: The Social Bases of the Student Movement," in Julian Foster and Durward Long, eds., Protest! (New York: William Morrow, 1970), pp. 134–55.

in contrast to the majority of college students, who come from moderately Conservative or Republican homes. A small number of parents of activists had been converted from conservatism to a more liberal position, and a few were left wing or liberal activists.

Flacks also reports on life style. The parents of protestors read more than the average, attend more concerts, and engage in more aesthetic pursuits. They foster autonomy and self-expression in their children rather than the norms of conventional morality, and they are permissive. Flacks emphasizes, however, that the parents of activists were not found to be overly permissive or indulgent to their young. These parents also are people who have social ideals and wish to contribute to social betterment.

Social backgrounds factors such as this, according to Flacks, only help explain why certain people rather than others are *initially* attracted to New Left politics. Once the student is engaged, however, they do not help to predict his behavior. The "Movement" itself socializes and radicalizes its members.

Social correlates, of course, do not constitute an explanation; they merely identify social origins. But Flacks does attempt an explanation of the data he has presented. It is an especially useful one because it helps us to identify the precise character of the ideological set we have described as "New Left" and to relate it in a meaningful way to the Liberal political culture we have dealt with earlier. He argues that the dominant values of the "Movement" can be traced back to nineteenth-century writers and artists reacting against middle-class values. Their reaction stemmed from their problem of establishing an identity for themselves in the midst of the dominantly commercial ethos of their society. They were beset especially with the question of how to retain their spontaneity and how to find leisure for creative work in a fully rationalized world. American intellectuals, he points out, have always been alienated from the general culture.

Why this alienation now manifests itself, for the first time, in a political movement Flacks explains by citing the recent numerical growth of the professional and intellectual classes, the recent internalization of humanistic values by a large section of the American midde classes. With this must be combined, as "trigger events," the Civil Rights Movement, the Vietnam War, and urban racial crises. These events furnished a context for the public pursuit in a dramatic way of ideals formerly acted out privately.

Skolnick attempts to explain in his report how it can be that student protest today threatens the stability of advanced industrial societies, whereas historically student revolutionary movements have been features of societies in the process of transformation from traditional agrarian order to modern industrialism. He tells us that "while educated youth in developing countries experience the irrelevance of traditional, religious, prescientific, authoritarian values for modernization, industrialization and national identity, educated youth in the advanced countries perceive the irrelevance of commercial, acquisitive, materialistic and nationalistic values in a world that stresses human rights and social equality and requires collective planning." [85]

One may well add that the values of individual spontaneity and humanistic creativity always have been a central part of the intellectual tradition of Liberal Democracy and, along with the work ethic and economic rationality, can be traced back to the beginnings of the Western European revolution of modernity in the Renaissance and Reformation. Usually they also have gone hand in hand with the equalitarian and communitarian values with which they are associated in New Left protest, and which have for a long while been an integral part of Liberal culture.

Tensions in the Political Culture.   How, then, does New Left activism become a revolutionary movement aimed at pulling down the entire fabric of Established Liberal society? The answer seems to be the growing incongruence of two aspects of Liberal culture as it develops in the post-industrial phase, the more evident and the sharper competition between its economic rationality and its humanistic components. That the New Left represents a "civil war" within Liberal Democratic modernity also explains why it does not appear as "ideology" and why its adherents (except for committed Marxist-Leninists) do not find the notion of "ideology" appealing. In its forensic form, ideology means an entirely new world view—new conceptions of purpose and authority and a new "belief" system set over against the established order in a radically contradictory and innovative way. This is what Liberal modernity in its beginnings represented in its challenge to aristocratic, theocentric, traditional society. The New Left, however, accepts the basic elements of the world view of the modern Liberal order. Its intention is to emphasize certain aspects of that world view and to question the legitimacy of others. It is interesting to note that the same can be said for American Conservatism and for the political culture of the Radical Right.

The intellectual source of New Left alienation, therefore, is not so much a clash of ideas and ideals as a felt discrepancy between theory and practice. Thus Tom Kahn describes it as a "revolt against the liberal rhetoric of their class, against the apparent fecklessness and hypocrisy of modernistic parents who always *stood* for progressive ideas but never seemed to act or *sacrifice* for them." [86] Or, as Jack Newfield puts it, the

[85] Skolnick, *op. cit.*, p. 85.
[86] Kahn, *op. cit.*, p. 35.

New Left represents "an ethical revolt against the visible devils of racism, poverty, and war, as well as the less tangible devils of centralized decision-making, manipulation, impersonal bureaucracies, and the hypocrisy that divides America's ideals from its actions from Watts to Saigon." [87]

Psychological Explanation.   We still have not provided a very adequate explanation as to why the moral revolt has occurred precisely today. Why has the discrepancy between ideal and practice been seen now rather than twenty-five or fifty years ago, when the gap cannot have been so very different from what it is today (or was, if anything, greater)? Flacks's suggestion that it has to do with the expansion of a a humanistic upper middle class in recent years, plus a series of trigger causes, is only partially satisfying. Why, for example, has it been the children rather than the parents who have engaged in the protest?

A more comprehensive attempt at explaining the New Left phenomenon has been presented by the Yale psychologist Kenneth Keniston, who has engaged in both intensive and extensive study of the social psychology of American youth. An important element of Keniston's explanation is his description of the new life situation of upper-class American youth. He points out that over the years, as a function of increasing economic abundance, young people have for an increasingly long period of time been afforded opportunity for leisure, for disengagement from the work-a-day routines of life. Prior to the nineteenth century one was considered an adult at twelve. The industrial revolution first made possible a period that we have called "adolescence," during which adult work could be deferred. Industrial society has now become so prosperous that we recognize still another period of disengagement from society that we call "youth," a period which for the society's elite continues well into the twenties. This new situation frees the maturing young mind from the necessity to swallow unexamined the assumptions of the past and to express his feelings more openly, unafraid of the sanctions of authority. In short, it has occasioned the development of a considerable group of highly critical citizens, free from the pressures of work.

This is one factor in the situation. Add to it the fact that post-industrial society has demonstrated the capacity to produce enough for all its members and you have an explosive situation. "Growing numbers of the young are brought up in family environments where abundance, relative economic security, political freedom and affluence are simply facts of life, not goals to strive for. To such people the psychological imperatives, social institutions and cultural values of the industrial ethic seem largely outdated and irrelevant to their own lives." Thus "self-discipline, delay of gratification, achievement . . . economic success and

[87] Newfield, *op. cit.,* p. 22.

productivity" cease to be authoritative norms and values, and the behavior and institutions with which they are associated lose moral authority. Youth become concerned with such things as equity in distribution and the search for meaning and significance.[88]

With moral legitimacy gone from the social system, the least request for loyalty or conformity is seen by the dissidents as a moral outrage, as a manipulative effort to co-opt one into the system. Hyprocrisy—objectively probably no greater than at any other time—is now seen everywhere. Moreover, precisely because so much has been accomplished by our society in the realization of widespread abundance and of the values of freedom and opportunity, the continued existence of marginal groups, black and poor white, appears unnecessary and therefore doubly outrageous. Thus the challenge to the system arises paradoxically from its success. "What used to be utopian ideals—like equality, abundance and freedom from discrimination—have now become demands, inalienable rights upon which one can insist without brooking any compromise." [89] And with the quantitative revolution over, the demand arises for a revolution of quality—hence the cult of "expansion of consciousness," with its stress on creativity, the personal development of the individual, and "meaningful human relationships." The whole person succeeds to the role-player of the past.[90] This is the ultimate intention of the New Left.

Bibliography

FEUER, LEWIS S., *The Conflict of Generations: The Character and Significance of Student Movements.* New York: Basic Books, 1969.

FOSTER, JULIAN, and DURWARD LONG, eds., *Protest!—Student Activism in America.* New York: William Morrow, 1970.

HAMALIAN, LEO, and F. R. KARL, eds., *The Radical Vision: Essays for the Seventies,* New York: Thomas Y. Crowell, 1970.

HOWE, IRVING, ed., *The Radical Papers.* Garden City, N.Y.: Doubleday & Company, Inc., 1963.

JACOBS, PAUL, and SAUL LANDAU, *The New Radicals.* New York: Random House, 1966.

LIPSET, SEYMOUR, ed., *Student Politics.* New York: Basic Books, 1967.

LIPSET, SEYMOUR, and PHILIP ALTBACH, eds., *Students in Revolt.* Boston: Houghton Mifflin, 1969.

[88] Kenneth Keniston, "You Have to Grow Up in Scarsdale," *New York Times Magazine,* April 27, 1969, 27–29.
[89] *Ibid.*
[90] *Ibid.*

LIPSET, SEYMOUR, and SHELDON WOLIN, eds., *The Berkeley Student Revolt: Facts and Interpretations.* Garden City, N.Y.: Doubleday & Company, Inc., 1965.

LYND, STAUGHTON, *Intellectual Origins of American Radicalism.* New York: Random House, 1968.

MARCUSE, HERBERT, *One-Dimensional Man: Studies in the Ideology of Advanced Industrial Society.* Boston: Beacon Press, 1968.

REICH, CHARLES A., *The Greening of America.* New York: Bantam Books, 1970.

RUBIN, JERRY, *Do It! Scenarios of the Revolution.* New York: Simon & Schuster, 1970.

RUBINSTEIN, RICHARD E., *Rebels in Eden: Mass Political Violence in the United States.* Boston: Little, Brown, 1970.

SEIDLER, MURRAY B., *Norman Thomas, Respectable Rebel.* Syracuse, N.Y.: Syracuse University Press, 1961.

SKOLNICK, JEROME H., *et al., The Politics of Protest.* Report of the National Commission on the Causes and Prevention of Violence. Washington: U.S. Government Printing Office, 1969.

TEODORI, MASSIMO, ed., *The New Left: A Documentary History.* Indianapolis: Bobbs-Merrill, 1969.

THOMAS, NORMAN M., *Democratic Socialism: A New Appraisal.* New York: League for Industrial Democracy, 1953.

PART TWO

REVOLUTIONARY

COLLECTIVISM

We have surveyed in general and abstract terms the characteristics of that modern ideology or Weltanschauung *we call "Liberalism" and have pointed out the salient differences between Liberal modernity and traditional European political culture. We also have examined in empirical detail what is perhaps the most natural (i.e., the most unalloyed) exemplar of that* Weltanschauung *as a living political culture, Established Liberalism in the United States of America. In its post-industrial phase this culture has been subjected to a variety of strains, both social and cultural, and to stressful conflicts of interest. We have displayed the ideological byproduct of these strains and conflicts in our description of right- and left-wing American political culture. At both ends of the spectrum of opinion we have found alienation expressed not in new symbols and values, but in sharp variations on themes already present in the culture, in new (or old) emphases, or in the clear articulation of ideas and attitudes that have been for the most part latent or suppressed in the main stream of the culture. Some of these expressions of alienation within Liberal culture we shall discover to be dominant concepts in the collectivist forms of modernity to which we now turn our attention.*

We shall look first at the experience of German Nazism, which like Liberalism was carried by urban middle classes that grew numerous and culturally prominent pari passu *with the commercialization and industrialization of European society. We shall see, in fact, that Nazism emerged from a failed effort at Liberal modernization, the Weimar Republic. We shall describe the special aspects of the pre-Weimar German historical experience and the kinds of stresses and strains within the tenuous Liberal order that brought the Nazi version of modern political culture into ascendancy.*

The other main form of political modernity, Marxist Communism, we shall examine in two contexts—the modernization experience of the Russians and of the Chinese. In both cases we shall see that the Communist transformation of traditional political culture occurred suddenly in basically agrarian societies in which urban, middle-class people were few and occupied a subordinate social and cultural position. Here, too, we shall attempt to relate the ascendance of the variety of modern political culture that emerged to special features of the Russian and Chinese historical experience and also to explain the kinds of social and cultural strains and conflicts of interest in the prerevolutionary society that precipitated a Communist mode of modernization.

7

The Nazi Version of Modernity

Nazism was not a uniquely German experience. A subclass of Fascism, it was part of an ideological movement that dominated many parts of Europe during the period between the two world wars and remains today an ideological system to be reckoned with. Two major continental powers and several minor ones enthroned Fascist regimes after 1918, and even in stable Liberal democracies there developed broad popular enthusiasm for the Fascist *Weltanschauung* during the interwar period.[1] Thomas Mann, following the capitulation of Neville Chamberlain to Adolf Hitler at Munich in 1938, writes of "the complete victory [of the] massive trends of the times, which can be summarized in the word fascism," and links this to "Europe's psychological preparedness for fascist infiltration in a political, moral, and intellectual respect." He calls it "a disease of the times . . . at home everywhere and from which no country is free."[2]

Fascist political culture took form amid the general political, social, economic, and moral collapse which followed World War I, and found its first embodiment in the codes and behavior of a plethora of paramilitary patriotic defense leagues. It was in the spring of 1919 that Mussolini formed the first *Fasci di Combattimento* in Italy, while in the same year

[1] See Ernst Nolte, *Three Faces of Fascism* (New York: Holt, Rinehart & Winston, Inc., 1966), pp. 3–10.

[2] Cited in *ibid.*, p. 7.

a collection of paramilitary *Freikorps* challenged the short-lived Soviet republic in Munich. Similar bodies appeared in Hungary, where Julius Gömbös was already using the label "National Socialist." In Austria the irregular *Heimatwehren* were formed to protect the new southern border against Yugoslav incursions, and by 1927 they had become a mainstay of Austro-Fascism. We find an "Iron Guard" in Romania, Degrelle's "Rexists" in Belgium, a Danish National Socialist Party, a French "Croix de Feu." The first Fascist formations do not appear until 1923 in stalwartly Liberal Democratic England, but by 1926 there were half a million of them. In America in the 1930s we find the Fascist "Silver Shirts" and a German-American Bund.[3]

Bred by one world war, Fascism's logical culmination was another, which also destroyed the regimes of its chief exponents. But the characteristic ideas and attitudes live on, in the German *Nationale Deutsche Partei* (NDP), in the American Nazi Party, in Colin Ross' British fascist group, and elsewhere. The conditions which produced their ascendance might well be reproduced at some future time. As Erik Erikson puts it, "It is our task to recognize that the black miracle of Nazism was only the German version—superbly planned and culpably bungled—of a universal contemporary potential. The trend persists; Hitler's ghost is counting on it."[4]

If individual freedom, power, and well-being have been the leading themes of Liberal political culture, Nazism has contrastingly stressed the freedom, power, and welfare of the group, specifically the group that is called "the nation." In all facets of Nazi political culture the individual finds meaning and self-expression only in radical subordination to the nation, which in fact means subordination to the demands and dictates of the charismatic leader who represents the group in historical action and who is credited with mystical insight into the nation's needs and destiny. The latter are expressed as territorial aggrandizement by force and violence and as imperial domination. These things constitute the totalitarian character of Nazi political culture.

As in Liberal political culture, the ideas and symbols of the ideological system correspond to underlying psychological realities. In the case of Nazism these are a deep-seated longing on the part of Germans for the bonds of community, stemming from an incomplete national identity, and an exaggerated hunger for power, status, and material well-being through national aggression attributable to a variety of social strains and economic frustrations, all associated with the special German

---

[3] *Ibid.*, pp. 12–15.
[4] Erik H. Erikson, *Childhood and Society* (New York: W. W. Norton & Company, Inc., 1950), p. 284. Copyright 1950 by W. W. Norton & Co., Inc. With permission.

pattern of industrialization and urbanization. The stresses and strains of post-industrial society have produced in Established Liberal culture alienated longings for community similar to those experienced by German Nazis, though they have been combined there with the humane and egalitarian values of revised Liberalism (the New Left). At the same time, in other parts of Liberal society (the right) these strains have given rise to an elitist and aggressive nationalism like that of German Nazism, but one combined with an atomistic individualism and a longing for independence rather than for community.

1. Nazi Ideology as Weltanschauung and Program

Unlike Liberalism in the United States, German Nazism does not appear as the established ideological habit of an un-self-conscious historical political culture, but as a self-conscious and revolutionary doctrine. We shall show later in this chapter that Nazi ideas were by no means novelties on the German political scene, but had deep roots in the German past, particularly in the culture of the industrializing nineteenth century. The peculiar constellation of notions and the extreme form that these ideas took, however, was a new reality. It stood in sharp juxtaposition to the *Weltanschauung*, and especially the concepts of legitimacy, that underpinned Weimar, the Hohenzollern Empire, and the looser preexisting German confederal political order. Nazi ideas certainly had nothing in common with traditional theories of aristocratic class privilege or divine right.

As a consequence, we shall not begin with an historical description of German political culture, but rather with an account of the Nazi ideas that were designed to produce new departures in German history. Inasmuch as the political program of the Nazis was shaped and determined at every point by the ideas and plans of one man, the Führer, Adolf Hitler, it seems fitting to start with the special *Weltanschauung* of this man. Some scholars have argued that Nazi ideology was an illogical baggage of mystical nonsense that did not serve to shape policy but was rather a psychological device to produce mass insecurity on the one hand and absolute dependence of the insecure masses on the charismatic leadership on the other. Still other writers have argued that the Nazi *Weltanschauung* can be clearly stated, and that it fully explains, if it did not determine, the main lines of Nazi domestic and foreign policy.[5]

[5] See C. W. Cassinelli, "The Totalitarian Party," *Journal of Politics*, 22 (1) February 1960, for the first thesis and Carl J. Friedrich and Zbigniew Brzezinski, *Totalitarian Dictatorship and Autocracy*, 2d rev. ed. (Cambridge, Mass.: Harvard University Press, 1965), for the second. The thesis that Nazism represents a self-consistent *Weltanschauung* and program is spelled out in detail in Eberhard Jäckel, *Hitler's*

The structure of Hitler's ideology, though simplistic, was nonetheless systematic, and we can find it clearly traced out in his two major books, Mein Kampf, which appeared in two volumes in 1925 and 1926, and the Secret Book, which was completed in 1928 but not published until 1962. According to one scholar who has made a careful analysis of Hitler's writings for the purpose of discovering an underlying Weltanschauung, the pattern consisted of three central themes. Within the schema we have been using, two of them can be described as conceptions of purpose—the acquisition of Lebensraum for Germany and the extermination of the Jews—and the third can be seen as a "belief" that envisaged history as the struggle of nations for survival and that subsumed an elitist conception of authority. The first two are only partially worked out, independently of one another, in Mein Kampf. Their full development, synthesis, and justification as a single program are found in the Secret Book of 1928.[6]

Foreign Policy Objectives: Lebensraum.   Hitler says in Mein Kampf that he became a German nationalist when he was still in secondary school.[7] The Habsburg Empire in which he grew up was still legitimated by the traditional, premodern principle of dynasticism, and remained so down to its destruction in 1918. But Hitler's heart was with the modern national monarchy in the north. The defeat of the Central Powers turned his generalized German nationalism first of all into a preoccupation with a revisionist foreign policy, the main aim of which was to undo the restrictions laid on Germany by the Versailles Treaty. This means among other things a return to the boundaries of 1914, to accomplish which Hitler was ready as early as 1920 to envisage a new war against France. Renewing the war would require allies, and this implied the need to cultivate Italy, between whom and France there were already notable frictions. It is significant that to achieve this Hitler was prepared to violate the first of the twenty-five points of the program of the newly founded National Socialist German Workers Party of February 23, 1920, which called for "the unification of all Germans into a Greater Germany on the basis of the right of all people to self-determination." It was

> necessary that Germany, clearly and unequivocally, renounce any claim to the Germans in Southern Tyrol. All that claptrap about Southern Tyrol, those empty protests against the Fascists, only hurt us because they

---

Weltanschauung: A Blueprint for Power, trans. Herbert Arnold (Middletown, Conn.: Wesleyan University Press, 1972). Copyright by Wesleyan University. The following account derives largely from Jäckel's book. Quotations are reprinted by permission of Wesleyan University Press.

    [6] Jäckel, op. cit.
    [7] Cited in ibid., p. 114.

alienate Italy from us. In politics sentiments do not count, only cold determination (*Kaltschnäuzigkeit*) counts.[8]

Hitler also thought of Great Britain as a potential ally when she dissociated herself from the occupation of the Ruhr in 1923.[9]

Revision of the Versailles Treaty, however, would not be an adequate foreign policy goal. Hitler held before himself the image of an everexpanding German population that had to be fed, an annual population increase of 900,000 persons.[10] Of the four policies he envisaged to cope with the problem, he was ready to reject three out of hand: birth control, internal colonization, and expansion of industries producing export goods, all of which are aspects of the Liberal pattern of modernization. "The acquisition of new land and soil"—*Lebensraum*—was the only acceptable alternative. And he even was ready to specify where territorial expansion would have to take place—Russia.[11] In this project, too, Hitler believed he could enlist the British as allies, for it would involve for Germany "giving up maritime trade and colonies, giving up overindustrialization, etc." In short, it would not put Germany in competition with Great Britain.[12] In the first book of *Mein Kampf* Hitler speculates on both the revision of Versailles and the project of Russian conquest, but at that time he had conceived of no way to dovetail them with one another, no way to work out the implicit inconsistencies between the two schemes. By the end of 1926, in the second volume of *Mein Kampf*, they have become a single, integrated plan. The destruction of France is now described as a precondition of and a prelude to the Russian adventure.[13]

Destruction of the Jews as Domestic Good. Hitler had formulated the goal of Jewish extermination even earlier than his foreign policy of revision and conquest. In a letter of September 1919 we find him writing:

> A rational antisemitism . . . must lead to the systematic legal fight against and the elimination of the prerogatives of the Jew which he alone possesses in contradistinction to all other aliens living among us (legislation concerning aliens). Its ultimate goal, however, must unalterably be the elimination of the Jews altogether.[14]

He had become steeped in anti-Semitism years earlier during his sojourn in Vienna, where anti-Semitic sentiment was deeply rooted.

[8] Quoted in *ibid.*, p. 30.
[9] *Ibid.*, p. 31.
[10] *Ibid.*, p. 34.
[11] *Ibid.*, pp. 34–35.
[12] Quoted in *ibid.*, p. 33.
[13] *Ibid.*, pp. 36, 37.
[14] Quoted in *ibid.*, p. 48.

In his speeches and other writings down to 1924 Hitler identifies the Jews with all the other whipping boys of his ideology, seeing them as antagonists in every area of political and cultural policy. They stand for international solidarity, and are therefore a threat to all efforts at national development and integration. They would denationalize the races of the world. They are egalitarians, whereas nature is elitist. They were responsible for the revolution of 1918 and for the establishment of the Weimar Republic. And they can be seen at work in financial circles of the Right as well as in the Marxist parties of the Left. Five of twenty-five points of the original Nazi program of 1920 were devoted to demands for anti-Jewish measures: the abolition of their civil rights and their right to hold office, their placement under jurisdiction applying to aliens, and their deportation.[15]

In *Mein Kampf* Hitler's anti-Semitism takes on an even more radical tone as it emerges as a universal missionary objective. In Volume Two he writes that freeing Germany of "Jewry" would liberate the world from the danger.[16] At this point he begins to draw connections between the anti-Semitic and the foreign policy themes. Russia is described as an easy mark, on the grounds that her Communist rulers were Jews who had no capacity for state building. On the other hand, the recalcitrance of the British toward the idea of a German alliance is explained as the result of Jewish influence.[17] In referring to methods for eliminating the Jews, Hitler's expressions become more violent. "No nation can dislodge the fist of the implacable world Jew from its throat except by the sword," he writes in Volume Two of *Mein Kampf*. And he wishes that during the war the Jews had been subjected to poison gas.[18] Later still, in a speech of 1939, we find Hitler predicting the "annihilation of the Jewish race in Europe." [19] During the years of National Socialism the policies actually adopted against the Jews accelerated in a directly parallel fashion, from deprivation of civil rights in Germany to physical extermination throughout Nazi-occupied Europe.[20]

A Philosophy of History: Racial Competition.   According to Eberhard Jäckel, Hitler's two chief policy goals—*Lebensraum* via conquest and the extermination of the Jews, both of which emerged as goals early in the development of his political thought—achieve meaning and coherence within the total context of his philosophy of history. This did not acquire detailed definition until the composition of the *Secret Book* in 1928,

[15] *Ibid.*, pp. 52, 50.
[16] *Ibid.*, p. 54.
[17] *Ibid.*, pp. 54–55, and *The Testament of Adolf Hitler*, quoted in *ibid.*, p. 57.
[18] Adolf Hitler, *Mein Kampf*, trans. A. Johnson *et al.* (New York: Houghton-Mifflin, 1939), p. 946.
[19] Quoted in Jäckel, *op. cit.*, p. 61.
[20] *Ibid.*

though some of its basic elements are found in *Mein Kampf*.[21] There Hitler describes history as a life-and-death struggle of races for existence.[22] He gives the term "race" no precise definition but uses it interchangeably with "people," "tribe," and "nation." [23] The struggle of the races of man he views as an aspect of a universal law of nature which decrees the struggle for self-preservation among all living things. The theme is repeated over and over: "the struggle for daily bread," "struggle for existence," "struggle for survival," "this world of eternal struggle." We are told that "the whole of nature is a continuous struggle between strength and weakness" and that this struggle constitutes in itself "the meaning of life," "the great rhythm of life." Hitler thus embraces as a basic principle a kind of Social Darwinism, which he derived from writers like Ernst Haeckel. Haeckel, for example, had written:

> . . . the theory of selection teaches us that organic progress is an inevitable consequence of the struggle for existence. Thousands of good and beautiful and admirable species of animals and plants have perished during those forty-eight million years, because they had to make room for other and stronger species, and the victors in this struggle for life were not always the nobler or morally more perfect forms.
> Precisely the same applies to the history of nations.[24]

It is interesting to note that the ideas of natural selection and survival of the fittest also play a role in some versions of Liberal Democratic ideology, such as that of Herbert Spencer, which had considerable vogue in the United States during the nineteenth century, when the "robber barons" were building a national economy and a national communications network. And we shall see that a conception of conflict and struggle is also a primary principle of Marxist metaphysics. We are thus dealing here with common currency of modern political culture as such. On the meaning, outcome, and modes of struggle, however, there are significant differences among the three systems. Spencerian Liberalism features chiefly economic competition, carried on within the confining parameters of democratic political process and culminating in a cooperative commonwealth when the forces of production have been brought to a certain level. Hitler's conception of struggle has no parameters. It was conceived not within a working liberal democratic culture but in the face of democratic collapse. It is therefore an unbounded concept, and the kinds of struggle envisaged by Hitler include the most crude and violent forms.

[21] *Ibid.*, p. 102.
[22] *Ibid.*, pp. 87–88.
[23] *Ibid.*, p. 88.
[24] Ernst Haeckel, "Social Darwinism," in Joachim Remak, ed. *The Nazi Years, A Documentary History* (Englewood Cliffs, N.J.: Prentice-Hall, Inc., 1969), p. 4.

The need for struggle arises from the scarcity of resources, chiefly the limited surface of the globe.[25] In the human struggle for living space, politics is the great instrument of nations and its chief end is the conquest and maintenance of living space. Both the politics of peace and the politics of war, both foreign and domestic policy, are directed toward this one overriding aim:

> Politics is the art of carrying out a people's struggle for its earthly existence.
> Foreign policy is the art of safeguarding the momentary necessary living space, in quantity and quality, for a people.
> Domestic policy is the art of preserving the necessary employment of force for this in the form of its race value and numbers.[26]

The upshot of this view is the constant need to engage in preparation for war, and, indeed, to make war. For if domestic policy allows a population to remain static or decline, it weakens the ability of the nation to defend its living space and invites attack. It therefore must decree an expanding population, which implies the necessity for more living space, and hence the necessity to struggle. What are the chief means of struggle? The emphasis is on fear, force, violence, and brutality. "I am restoring to force its original dignity, that of the source of all greatness and the creatrix of order." "The world can only be ruled by fear." "Yes we are barbarians! We want to be barbarians! It is an honourable title. We shall rejuvenate the world. . . . We must shake off all sentimentality and be hard." [27]

Numbers are only one element of power. More important is the "racial value" or "blood value" of a people. In some places, drawing on the work of Houston Stewart Chamberlain and the Comte de Gobineau, Hitler presents the concept as an ethnic one. The Chamberlain-Gobineau race theory rests on a mythical notion of the existence of a specially gifted race of blue-eyed, blond-haired people called "Aryans" who originated in early times in Central Asia, from where they moved out to colonize the world. As they went they built great empires—Assyria, the powerful city-states of Greece, the Macedonian Empire, Rome, and the barbarian peoples who conquered Rome. At the outset of each imperial venture they maintained themselves apart from the inferior peoples they conquered. Gradually, however, they intermarried with their subjects and lost both their separate identity and their original prowess and capacity. Today only in the Nordic states of Europe, the theory holds, does the

25 Jäckel, op. cit., p. 92.
26 Telford Taylor, ed. Hitler's Secret Book, trans. S. Attanasio (New York: Grove Press, Inc., 1961), p. 24.
27 Hermann Rauschning, The Voice of Destruction (New York: G. P. Putnam's Sons, 1940), p. 80. Copyright 1940 by G. P. Putnam's Sons. With permission.

Aryan blood remain relatively pure, and therefore still capable of creative power.

In describing the creation of culture Hitler adopted and adapted the Aryan theory in the following terms:

> Aryan tribes (often with a really ridiculously small number of their people) subjugate foreign peoples . . . and favored by the size of the labor force in the shape of people of an inferior kind now at their disposal, they develop the mental and organizational abilities which have slumbered within them. Often, in the course of a few millennia or even centuries they create cultures which initially bear completely the inner features of their character. . . . Finally, however, the conquerors deviate from the purity of their blood which they originally maintained, they begin to mix with the subjected natives, and thus end their own existence.[28]

Here the conception of racial superiority is cast in biological terms. Elsewhere Hitler converts it into a psychological and moral concept of self-conscious will to power, a quasi-Nietzschean notion.

> The importance of the blood value of a people . . . only becomes totally effective when this value is recognized by a people, properly valued and appreciated. Peoples who do not understand this value or who no longer have a feeling for it for lack of a natural instinct, thereby immediately also begin to lose it. Blood-mixing and lowering of the race are then the consequences.[29]

Elitism. The blood value of a people in Hitler's *Weltanschauung* depends on still another factor, that people's recognition of "personality value." In this concept is embodied an elitist conception of authority. It means that the rank and file of a nation must recognize in its midst the men of outstanding will-power and capacity and must accept their leadership in the nation's struggle for preservation and power. Only a few are supremely well endowed with physical and intellectual prowess. The rest are mass. And in the *Secret Book* he says that majorities have never

> wrought creative achievements. Never have they given discoveries to mankind. The individual person has always been the originator of human progress. Once a people installs the majority as the rulers of its life, that is to say, once it introduces present-day democracy in the Western conception, it will not only damage the importance of the concept of personality, but block the effectiveness of the personality value. Through a formal construction of its life it prevents the rise and the work of individual creative persons.[30]

[28] *Mein Kampf*, p. 400.
[29] *Secret Book*, p. 27.
[30] *Ibid.*, p. 32.

Here we have the expression of a rather fierce individualism which is in many ways a close counterpart to the individualism of Classical Liberalism and of Spencerian Liberalism in America. It also parallels to a degree the individualism of modern American conservatism.[31] It is important to emphasize this similarity in view of the common conception of Nazism as a dominantly collectivist doctrine. It was only the "mass-man," the average man, who was expected to yield to the collectivity and be shaped by its norms and values. The superior individual stood above the collectivity as its creator and as the author of its myths, not as its product.

The masses are seen as especially incapable of common action through democratic decision-making processes. They must be led by the nose and told where their interest lies. This disdain for basic democratic institutions is quite frankly expressed. Thus Hitler writes in 1924, "What concern of ours was universal suffrage? Was it for that we fought for four years? It was not with the cry of 'Long live universal suffrage' that the young regiments went to their death in Flanders, but with the shout of 'Germany above all else in the world.' " [32] Public opinion can only be the result of manipulation, and at the top of the system there must stand the one man who knows best the mystical "will of the people." This is the *Führer*, who is self-chosen and who assumes full responsibility for what happens under his direction (though it is never clear to whom or to what the responsibility is owed). All the subordinate elite abdicate their consciences to him. So, for example, when Hermann Göring was asked whether his conscience did not bother him for his part in the Reichstag fire, he is said to have replied, "Adolf Hitler is my conscience." [33]

A Populist Note.   Despite this frank elitism there is also, however, a strong populist strain in Nazism. All the little men are expected to be politically conscious and politically participant, though they also are expected to be obedient followers whose role is to demonstrate the solidarity of the *Volk* behind their leaders. Nazi populism is egalitarian and anti-class, in the traditional sense. All Germans are equal followers of the *Führer*. They are also anti-intellectual, for Hitler had great contempt for the professors. Both "nation" and "race" thus are leveling concepts.[34]

The Movement.   Formal structures of public government carried no authority in Nazi ideology. All authority vested in the "Movement" and

---

[31] Cf., e.g., Barry Goldwater, *The Conscience of a Conservative* (New York: Hillman Books, 1960), pp. 11–12.

[32] Nolte, *op. cit.*, p. 411.

[33] Rauschning, *op. cit.*, p. 78.

[34] See Hajo Holborn, "Origins and Political Character of Nazi Ideology," *Political Science Quarterly* 79 (4), December 1964, pp. 547–48.

in its Leader. The "Movement," i.e., the Nazi Party, is described by Nazi theoreticians as "bearing the state and the nation." It is in and by the Party that the nation's "general will" is formulated and expressed. The Party is also an educational institution, whose work is to create a sense of national solidarity and enthusiasm for the Leader's plans among the population as a whole. Hence the totalitarian principle that all aspects of life and culture are dominated by the Party to the end of forming the entire people into a ready instrument of the Leader's will. The Party monopolizes the individual's entire day. There are organizations for the young, both male and female, for women specifically, for workers, for farmers. There are sports clubs, hiking clubs, singing clubs, art clubs, all organized and controlled by the Nazi Party. Much mysticism is employed to legitimate the Party's work.[35]

Synthesis of Program and Weltanschauung. The concepts of racial value and personality value are spelled out in detail in the *Secret Book* and combined there with extensive reflections on the Jews as carriers of the antithetical notions of internationalism, egalitarian democracy, and pacifism. Throughout *Mein Kampf* Hitler had attacked the Jews as the champions of democracy and parliamentarism; they were, he claimed, interested in paralyzing the instinct of nations for self-preservation.[36] These ideas were both a cause and an effect of the fact that the Jews themselves had no state but lived throughout the world in other peoples' states. In the *Secret Book* of 1928 these ideas are worked into Hitler's philosophy of history. Eberhard Jäckel summarizes the result as follows:

> History is the peoples' life struggle for living space. In this . . . the Jewish people cannot participate since it has no territory which it could either preserve or increase. It thus obscures the clear battle lines of history, it runs counter, as it were, to the basic idea of nature, it throws out of joint the world as it should be and as it actually is in every other respect.[37]

All this does not mean that Jews have no desire for self-preservation and power. Rather, they are viewed as carrying on their struggle in an unnatural way, as parasitic forces within the bodies of other nations. From these considerations logically derive the major goals of Hitler's subsequent domestic and foreign policy. He must exterminate the Jews in order to restore meaning to history. And within the restored natural struggle for existence he must conquer new living space

---

[35] See documents in Carl Cohen, ed. *Communism, Fascism, and Democracy* (New York: Random House, 1962), pp. 396ff.

[36] Jäckel, *op. cit.*, p. 101.

[37] *Ibid.*, p. 103.

for Germans. In Jäckel's words,

> Each of these tasks was inextricably linked to the other; indeed they
> were the mutually necessary preconditions for each other. Unless the
> Jews were annihilated there would very soon no longer be any struggle
> for living space, nor therefore any culture, and consequently nations
> would die out; not just the German nation, but ultimately all nations.
> But if, on the other hand, the German people failed to conquer new
> living space, it would die out because of that and the Jews would
> triumph.[38]

Although the Nazis aimed ultimately at world domination, the
process of struggle as they conceived it has no end, no final stage. "We
are a movement," Hitler declares. "Nothing could express our nature
better. Marxism teaches that a vast upheaval quite suddenly changes
the world. . . . But we know there is never a final stage, there is no
permanency, only eternal change. Only death is unchanging. . . . The
future is an inexhaustible fount of possibilities of further development." [39]

The Private Doctrine.   Hitler's ideology is not one but two overlapping
sets of ideas and images. One set was ordained for general consumption by the average German. Another, in some ways rather different creed
was meant for the Nazi elite. In studying Liberal culture, despite our
discovery that leaders and followers emphasize different aspects of the
ideology, we did not find a sharp and self-conscious dichotomy, nor
anything like a secret creed. Even the most bloodthirsty of the ideas
that we have described in reconstructing Hitler's *Weltanschauung* appeared in written public statements. Beside them in Hitler's published
written works, and in the most public of all his statements, his speeches,
there appeared other more conventional and moderate statements that
tended to mitigate the overall violence of tone. An effort was made to
take over usable Christian ideas and symbols and to amalgamate them
to nationalist ideals and symbols, which we found also to be the practice
of certain groups of the American Radical Right. Thus in his inaugural
speech as Chancellor we find Hitler in February 1933 saying that "the
National Government . . . will preserve and defend those basic principles upon which our nation has been built. It regards Christianity as
the foundation of our national morality, and the family as the basis of
national life." [40] In private, however, Hitler was already at that time
speaking of his intention ultimately of "tearing up Christianity root and

---

[38] *Ibid.*, p. 106.
[39] Rauschning, *op. cit.*, p. 187.
[40] Proclamation to the German Nation, February 1, 1933, in Raoul de R.
de Sales, ed. *My New Order* (New York: Reynal & Hitchcock, 1941), p. 144.

branch, and annihilating it in Germany." And in reporting a conversation of Hitler's in 1934, Hermann Rauschning gives us a picture of morality very different from anything that could readily be described as "Christian" underlying Hitler's plans for the education of a new Nazi elite:

> In my *Ordensburgen* a youth will grow up before which the world will shrink back. A violently active, dominating, intrepid, brutal youth—that is what I am after. . . . It must be indifferent to pain. There must be no weakness or tenderness in it. I want to see once more in its eyes the gleam of pride and independence of the beast of prey.[41]

Hitler's theories of Aryan racial superiority, as we have recounted them above, even in those statements where "will" rather than ethnic inheritance is determinative of "blood value," all appear as theories of German nationalism. Although the state appears as a purely instrumental value, a means, the value of the national cultural group seems to be an ultimate one. Similarly, mass propaganda always emphasized the centrality of the nation in the Nazi world view. Thus we find such passages as the following from the official Nazi Party newspaper repeated over and over:

> Our goal is that the German people should again acquire honor and conviction, that it should again bow in adoration before its own history, that it should respect those things which formerly gave it significance, and that it should curse that which damaged its honor. We recognize only two Gods: A God in Heaven and a God on earth and that is our Fatherland.[42]

In the private doctrine Hitler speaks rather differently about the national idea. "The conception of the nation," he said to Hermann Rauschning, "has become meaningless. The conditions of the time compelled me to begin on the basis of that conception. But I realized from the first that it could have only transient validity. . . . The new order cannot be conceived in terms of the national boundaries of the peoples with an historic past, but in terms of race that transcend those boundaries."[43] But the race idea as well, conceived in ethnic terms, was for Hitler only a myth to be manipulated. For one thing, its strict application posed empirical problems. Neither Hitler himself, nor Goebbels, the propaganda minister, nor Himmler, the chief of the notorious SS, was a typical blue-eyed, blond-haired Aryan. Each was, in fact, rather short, slight, and dark. To avoid embarrassing questions on this score, Alfred Rosenberg, the party's chief theoretician, developed the formula that while Germans were 89 percent of the Nordic types, some members

[41] Rauschning, *op. cit.*, pp. 49, 252.
[42] *Völkischer Beobachter*, September 23, 1928, in Cohen, ed. *op. cit.*, p. 411.
[43] Rauschning, *op. cit.*, pp. 231–32.

of the Aryan race would display their Nordic blood in their actions rather than in their appearance.[44] A moment's reflection would tell one, of course, that such a way of presenting the race idea makes it absolutely meaningless as an ethnic concept.

In the private doctrine Hitler called the race idea frankly a myth:

> I know perfectly well . . . that in the scientific sense there is no such thing as race. . . . As a politician I need a conception which enables the order which has hitherto existed on historic bases to be abolished and an entirely new and anti-historic order enforced and given an intellectual basis. Nations are the outward and visible forms of our history. So I have to fuse these nations into a higher order if I want to get rid of the chaos of an historic past which has become an absurdity. And for this purpose the conception of race serves me well. . . . France carried her great Revolution beyond her borders with the conception of the nation. With the concept of race, National Socialism will carry its revolution abroad and recast the world. . . . Our own revolution is a further step, or, rather, the final step in the rejection of the historical order and the recognition of purely biological values.[45]

By "biological values" Hitler here means simply things like physical size and strength. The "master race" would consist of all men of violence and capacity whom he could attract to his system. In this sense the Nazis indeed took the race idea seriously. It was, for example, a policy of the SS troops who occupied the conquered countries of eastern Europe to carry off the vigorous and able-bodied children of the vanquished to be raised in Germany as recruits for the elite of the succeeding generation.

What all this seems to mean is that the Nazi private doctrine was a purely Machiavellian code of elite power. The sole irreducible end was the indefinite expansion of the scope and degree of dominion by Hitler and the other Nazi leadership. The German people as well as all other peoples were simply instruments of the will to power of a self-recruited and self-perpetuating elite of domineering and ruthless men of capacity. This is not to say that all of the Nazi elite were frank subscribers to the doctrine of power for the sheer sake of power. Heinrich Himmler, for example, the SS chief, felt compelled to put an aura of transcendent mission around his organization. Albert Speer reports in his memoirs that Hitler used to make great fun of him for it:

> What nonsense! Here we have at last reached an age that has left all mysticism behind it, and now he wants to start that all over again. We

[44] Alfred Rosenberg, *The Myth of the Twentieth Century* (1930), in Cohen, *op. cit.*, p. 399.
[45] Rauschning, *op. cit.*, p. 232.

might just as well have stayed with the church. At least it had tradition. To think that I may some day be turned into an SS saint! Can you imagine it? I would turn over in my grave.[46]

Himmler also seemed to be irreducibly a German nationalist. He made an idol of the medieval German ruler Henry I and built something of a cult around him for the SS. He also devoted considerable attention to excavating and celebrating the pagan Germanic past. With all this Hitler himself had little patience:

> Why do we call the whole world's attention to the fact that we have no past? It isn't enough that the Romans were erecting great buildings when our forefathers were still living in mud huts; now Himmler is starting to dig up these villages of mud huts and enthusing over every potsherd and stone axe he finds.[47]

Speer reports that Goebbels, the propaganda minister, joined Hitler in ridiculing Himmler's romantic fantasies.[48]

In the bunker, in the last days of the war, Hitler remarked that Germany had failed him and should therefore be destroyed. "The future belongs solely to the stronger Eastern Nation," he concluded.[49] In his conversations with Rauschning, Hitler remarks: "we . . . are feverishly in pursuit of power. . . . We are madly keen on it. . . . For us the pursuit of power . . . the will to power . . . is . . . literally the whole meaning of life." [50] Hitler here and there speaks of the "development of humanity" as the function of struggle, adding that "struggle is the father of all things." [51]

These expressions appear to raise the idea to a level of spiritual gentility. But the catalog of things created by struggle is exhausted by works of art (especially music), technical inventions, and technology generally. The latter appear simply as instruments of physical power, not as significant in themselves. So "development" means for Hitler the creation of a class of domineering beasts of prey with technical capacity and aesthetic sense. Nowhere does the idea of "humanity" include the gentler virtues of soul and mind.

That private interest was in fact the operative code of the elite is

[46] Albert Speer, *Inside the Third Reich,* trans. R. and C. Winston (New York: The Macmillan Company, 1970), p. 141. Copyright 1970 by Macmillan Publishing Co., Inc. and Weidenfeld Publishers, Ltd. With permission.

[47] *Ibid.*

[48] *Ibid.,* pp. 174–75.

[49] H. R. Traver-Roper, ed. *The Testament of Adolf Hitler* (London: Cassell & Co., 1961), p. 24.

[50] Rauschning, *op. cit.,* p. 279.

[51] *Völkischer Beobachter,* November 23, 1927, in Cohen, *op. cit.,* p. 409.

well attested by the revelations of the various sets of memoirs that have been published since the war. Speer, in particular, well documents the narrow self-concern with his own power position of each of the chief leaders, describing in detail the intricate intrigues that each of these men carried on in an effort to undermine the other's status in order to build up his own. No joint concern for an irreducible common good, no matter how pervertedly conceived, mitigated the pattern of individual self-seeking:

> After only nine years of rule the leadership was so corrupt that even in the critical phase of the war it could not cut back on its luxurious style of living. For "representational reasons" the leaders all needed big houses, hunting lodges, estates and palaces, many servants, a rich table, and a select wine cellar. They were also concerned about their lives to an insane degree. Hitler himself, wherever he went, first of all issued orders for building bunkers for his personal protection. The thickness of their roofs increased with the caliber of the bombs until it reached sixteen and a half feet.[52]

"The Jew": A Metaphysical Antagonist.   A perfect Machiavellism excludes all notions of transcendence, both of transcendental right and transcendental power. And myths about transcendent forces are employed only as instruments to manipulate a gullible and superstitious followership. The Machiavellian leader stands outside all such myths and measures the world in terms of purely observable magnitudes of power and observable process. He is a pragmatist in the narrowest sense of the word. But there are indications that even in the private doctrine Hitler did not manage to abandon all ideas of transcendent power along with his abandonment of transcendent right. He was superstitious. The "Jew" was Hitler's transcendent bogeyman.

Hermann Rauschning speaks of Hitler's antagonism to the Jews as "metaphysical." By this he means that Hitler used the concept *Jew* as a label for all opposition to himself and his plans, whatever its source or character. And as such it took on the form of an abstract idea of an "anti-nature."[53] "The struggle for world domination," wrote Hitler, "will be fought entirely between us, Germans and Jews. All else is facade and illusion."[54]

At home the Jew is seen as the prime mover behind the enemies on the Left—Communists and Social Democrats—the organizers and leaders

---

[52] Speer, *op. cit.*, p. 290.
[53] Nolte says that Hitler learned this from the author of the notorious Ostara pamphlets in Vienna, the former monk, Dietrich Eckhart; *op. cit.*, pp. 328–30.
[54] Rauschning, *op. cit.*, p. 237.

of the working classes. Hitler describes him as the champion of the international as against the national idea. But he is also the enemy on the Right—the epitome of the big businessman and banker, greedy for money, unscrupulous in business, squeezing the honest German petit-bourgeois and worker. He is the exploiter. In this embodiment the Jew foments class war and thereby destroys national unity. With political and social ends in mind, he seduces or rapes Aryan German girls and deliberately corrupts their blood. He also introduces the black man into white societies.

Abroad the Jew is described as controlling all the governments opposed to Hitler. In *Mein Kampf*, published in 1925, Hitler writes of "the gigantic American colossus of states with enormous wealth of its virgin soil," and in the *Secret Book*, written in 1928 though published only after the war, he pays tribute to America in racial terms. America, he says, "felt itself to be a Nordic-German state and in no way an international mishmash of peoples." After Pearl Harbor, however, America is described in Hitler's secret conversations, published in 1953, as "a decayed country" without "much future," "half Judaized and the other half negrified." [55] England and America would not have opposed him had they not been "Jew-ridden," Hitler asserted. "Behind England stands Israel and behind France and behind the United States." [56] The Japanese are seen as loyal allies because they are not contaminated by Jewry. The last sentence of Hitler's *Testament* ends with the word "Jewry":

> The only peoples who will have the right to claim these qualities [the ability to suffer, to fight] will be those who have shown themselves capable of eradicating from their system the deadly poison of Jewry.[57]

This is not an expression of rational Machiavellism.

2. Operational Code: The Theory of Organization

Alongside the elements of *Weltanschauung* (both public and private) which explain reality, designate and justify ultimate goal values, and adumbrate general principles of authority, an ideological system contains an operational code. This consists of procedural rules for the making of decisions, a set of practical principles for the consolidation and

[55] Telford Taylor, ed. *Hitler's Secret Book*, Salvator Attanasio, trans. (New York: Grove Press, Inc.). Taylor's Introduction, pp. xxiii–xxiv.
[56] Rauschning, *op. cit.*, p. 237.
[57] *Testament*, p. 109.

use of power for the achievement of ultimate goal values.[58] Because the achievement of any political value requires the exercise of power, an operational code becomes first and foremost a logic of power.

In an established Liberal Democratic order the operational code consists of a broad range of things: the explicit rules and conventions of the constitution; the interpretations given to them by the legislative, executive, and judicial bodies which have the status of historical precedent or constitutional habit (actual usage), and rules and conventions of administrative practice. We did not attempt to discuss operational codes in the chapter on Established Liberalism in the United States, for it would have involved us in a description of the entire processes of government, a complete behavioral analysis of a highly decentralized political system, something that goes beyond the purview of this book. Our discussion was largely confined to the description of *Weltanschauung*, though an effort was made to relate principles of *Weltanschauung* to actual behavior, and therefore indirectly to operative or operational codes of political behavior.

In a working Liberal Democratic system an operational code does not have the autonomy that we observe it to have in totalitarian politics, where it is the property of a restricted elite. It is deeply informed and constrained by the Liberal *Weltanschauung*, and by the constitutional order and habits of the people, which carry the ideals of the *Weltanschauung*. To the extent that an operational code can be separately stated as an elite decision-making code, one finds the rules set down in books such as Anthony Downs' *An Economic Theory of Democracy*. In a system like that described by Downs the parameters within which an elite can maneuver are restricted indeed.[59]

In a totalitarian system it is much easier to distinguish operational code from the *Weltanschauung* in general, because of the revolutionary

[58] The notion of an elite "operational code" was coined by Nathan Leites and used by him to study the principles of decision-making inherent in the behavior of Russian Communist elites. See Nathan Leites, *A Study of Bolshevism* (Glencoe: The Free Press, 1953). His concern was to uncover basic strategic principles for the organization and development of power, both domestically and in foreign policy. In an article in 1969 Alexander George attempted to refine and detail Leites's analytic scheme, also within the context of a study of Russian Communist elite behavior. He broadened the definition of operational code, however, to include, besides "instrumental beliefs," a whole range of things that we have discussed under the heading of *Weltanschauung:* "the political actor's 'philosophical' beliefs . . . assumptions he makes regarding the fundamental nature of politics, the nature of political conflict, the role of the individual in history, etc." See Alexander L. George, "The 'Operational Code': A Neglected Approach to the Study of Political Leaders and Decision-Making," *International Studies Quarterly*, 13(2), June 1969: 191, 199. In what follows I shall employ the narrower meaning of strategic organizational principles aimed at the consolidation and articulation of power.

[59] Anthony Downs, *An Economic Theory of Democracy* (New York: Harper & Bros., 1957).

character of the political culture we are describing. The revolutionary *Weltanschauung* does not already exist as an established set of political habits, but has to be inculcated by the revolutionary elite. This elite itself, whether it consists of true believers or pure power-pragmatists, is not constrained by the *Weltanschauung* in its choice of means—that is, of organizational structures and procedures—to carry out the vague long-run goals of the ideology, but tends to move in an almost pure power-political realm, using the *Weltanschauung* (at least the public part) itself as a means rather than serving it as a set of ends. In the case of the Nazi private doctrine, whose central principle and goal was itself the acquisition and exercise of elite power, one would not expect any important discrepancy between *Weltanschauung* and operational code. Nevertheless, even in this case, we will see a certain difference between the two and an autonomous logic in the operational code.

A first principle of Hitler's operational code was that he always appeared to have fixed and unshakable convictions, with his mind once and forever made up on all the large questions of public policy. This seemed to him a prerequisite for retaining the absolute allegiance and trust of his followers, and hence a key principle for the maintenance of power. For this reason Hitler argued that a man should not become publicly active in politics before the age of thirty, before which time his outlook is likely to be flexible, still in process of formation. Otherwise it may happen

> that some day he will have to change his attitude toward vital questions, or, despite his better knowledge and belief, will have to uphold points of view which reason and conviction have long since rejected. The first case is very embarrassing for him, for now personally uncertain he has no longer the right to expect that his followers have the same unshakable belief in him as before; such a reversal on the part of the leader brings uncertaintly to his followers.[60]

Apparently Hitler intended more than the mere appearance of fixed conviction as requisite to charismatic leadership. The leader actually had to have his mind made up for good. Thus the operational code contained as a first principle the possession of a fixed and unchangeable *Weltanschauung*. Hitler wrote of himself that he acquired his at an early age, during his years in Vienna just before World War I.

> At that time I formed an image of the world and a *Weltanschauung* which became the granite foundation for my actions. I have had to add but little to that which I learned then and I have had to change nothing.[61]

[60] *Mein Kampf*, p. 85.
[61] *Ibid.*, p. 29.

It is not relevant to ask here whether in fact Hitler changed his mind or whether he built up his complete *Weltanschauung* later than his Vienna period. According to Jäckel, as we have seen, the ideological system was not complete until 1928. The important thing is that Hitler believed in the importance of a fixed world view, and that he believed he had achieved one early in his career.

The idea of unshakable convictions as the basis of charismatic power may be the root of what one scholar has described as the static character of Nazi political culture in general. Thus George Mosse writes that within Nazi culture "there is no progression, no development, for 'truth' was accepted as 'given,' laid down forever by the race—as eternal as the Aryan himself. . . . There was a static quality to this culture, and it would serve no purpose . . . to attempt to show any cultural development, for it did not exist." [62]

The Führerprinzip.   A key principle of Nazi organizational strategy was to substitute for the notion of impersonal legal authority, which by nature is structured and circumscribed, a conception of the unbounded authority of Adolf Hitler as a person. The idea of the legal state was identified with Weimar parliamentarism, which was made to bear the blame for all the ills of the German nation. It was also a dull and drab concept, hardly able to compete with the romantic conception of the *Volk* as the source of all authority, an authority summed up and expressed through the will of the Führer, Adolf Hitler.

Hitler actually came to power by legal means. In January 1933, as the leader of the largest party within the national legislature, the Reichstag, he was designated Reich Chancellor by President von Hindenburg. Although the March elections of that year gave him only 43.9 percent of the popular vote, he was able to establish control over the legislative process. Then, by a series of acts passed under the authority of Article 48 of the Weimar Constitution, which provided for emergency executive powers of an extraordinary character, he was able piecemeal to destroy every vestige of legal limitation of executive power prescribed by that constitution and to outlaw and drive underground all political opposition.

In August 1934 President von Hindenburg died, and the powers of the President were transferred by law to the chancellor. The title "Reich President" was abolished, and Hitler styled himself "Führer and Reich Chancellor." Even at this time the use of the title "Führer" indicated that authority was being claimed on some basis other than that of legal designation. In the later years of the Nazi regime the title "Chancellor"

[62] George Mosse, *Nazi Culture* (New York: Grosset & Dunlap, 1966), p. xxii. Copyright 1966 by George L. Mosse. Quotations reprinted with permission of the publisher.

was dropped altogether and official documents were signed simply "The Führer." Ernst Rudolf Huber, a Nazi ideologist, has set down in a study in constitutional law an explanation of the ground of Hitler's authority as Führer and the relationship of this authority to the legal offices Hitler had acquired:

> The office of Führer emanates from the National Socialist Movement. In origin it is not a governmental office. This fact must never be overlooked if the present political and legal position of the Führer is to be understood. Originating from the Movement, the office of Führer has grown its way into the Reich as the Führer has taken over in turn, first the powers of Reich Chancellor and then the position of Head of State. He remains, however, primarily the Führer of the Movement; as such he has drawn into himself the Reich's two most exalted political leadership functions, thus creating a new office, Führer of the German people and the German Reich.
>
> The Führer combines in his own person the entire supreme authority of the Reich; all public authority both in the State and in the Movement stems from that of the Führer. . . . Political authority is wielded not by an impersonal entity, the State, but by the Führer as executor of the united will of the people. The authority of the Führer is total and all-embracing; . . . it covers every facet of the life of the people; it is free and independent, overriding and unfettered.[63]

Three things stand out in this explanation. First, the revolutionary character of the new regime is underlined by the statement that the office of Führer, which emanates from the extralegal and unofficial Movement, had absorbed the primary legal offices of the governmental system and thereby created a new office. The revolutionary political movement had thus swallowed up and supplanted the legal system of Weimar. Second, we note the paradox that although the office of Führer emanates from the Movement, and thus has initially a representative character, it ends up superior to the Movement; a transfer of authority from *Volk* to Leader has occurred. And third, we observe that the authority of the Führer actually does not attach to a new office, though this expression is used, but to the person of Adolf Hitler, and that this personal authority is total and unbounded. Thus all legal authority is dissolved away in a system of purely personal authority resting wholly on itself.

Nazi Feudalism. We seem to have been describing the emergence of something like Byzantine absolutism as the operational system of Nazi Germany—a code that dovetails very well with the *Weltanschauung* and that does not display the autonomy we wrote of earlier. The fact of the

---

[63] Ernst Huber, quoted in Helmut Krausnick *et al.*, *Anatomy of the SS State*, trans. Richard Barry *et al.* (New York: Walker, 1968), p. 128. Copyright 1968 by William Collins Sons and Walter Verlag, A.G. With permission.

matter, however, was quite different. It has been cogently argued that the *Führerprinzip* that we have just described was the capstone of an operational code for decision making that in actuality was highly complex and decentralized, modeled more on the feudal organization of the old Holy Roman Empire than on the centralized order of either the ancient or the Byzantine Roman Empires.[64] The principle of personal absolutism, according to this view, was designed to substitute for a system built upon rational and impersonal rules founded on personal loyalty and man-to-man confidence. "The power of a leader was said to be proportional to the confidence and loyalty of his voluntary followers. . . . The *Führerprinzip* was 'the rediscovery of the basis of political power: loyalty.' And behind that loyalty lay the 'full and honest acceptance of responsibility' by the strong."[65] The idea is epitomized by the motto carried on the belt buckles of the members of the SS—"*Meine Ehre heisst Treue* (My honor is loyalty)."[66]

The idea of personal government stemmed from a critique of modern western industrial society as irresponsible in its anonymity and impersonality, as destructive of truly responsible behavior. We have seen that an essential element in the Liberal Democratic *Weltanschauung* is the idea that the just order rests on uniform and rational rules of political procedure. The Nazis claimed that in fact this system had become a cloak for irresponsibility in decision making. The attempt to create a modern nation-state on lines laid down by Liberal ideology, an effort that culminated in the Weimar Republic, they saw as a rationalistic nightmare—a superficially rational system imposed on an aggregation of contradictory class and regional interests. The upshot, in this view, had been the concentration of large police and administrative powers in Berlin, without the establishment of correspondingly clear lines of responsibility, and paired with irresponsible party power in parliament.[67] Uniformity and bureaucracy were the chief devils in the piece. And in the background was the image of the centralizing economic cartel, using the situation to expropriate both small businessmen and small farmers, the classes that formed the backbone of Nazi power.

The Nazi critique of Weimar reminds us of the critiques of post-industrial American society developed both by the New Left and the New Right that we studied in earlier chapters. There is present in each case the same mistrust of rational bureaucratic order as a disguise used by a sinister power elite to facilitate the exploitation of the little man.

[64] See Robert Koehl, "Feudal Aspects of National Socialism," *American Political Science Review*, 54(4), December 1960: 921ff. Copyright 1960 by the American Political Science Association. Quotations with permission.
[65] *Ibid.*, p. 922.
[66] *Ibid.*, p. 924.
[67] *Ibid.*, p. 922, n. 7, and p. 930.

The recipes for a better order, however—the New Left's "participatory democracy" and the Right's adulation of old-fashioned constitutionalism and individualism—are radically different from that used by the Nazis.

Although the New Left and the New Right in their models of reform employ symbols and ideas that, despite their diversity, derive from the modern Liberal Democratic tradition, the Nazis reached back into premodern German political life for their symbols of order. The authoritative model appears to have been the elective kingship of the Middle Ages. In theory elected for life by popular acclamation, Hitler was "in reality chosen and maintained in power by his paladins. They chose him for his personal qualities. In the form in which political battles are fought in the twentieth century, his prowess was supposed to outshine that of the fighters grouped around him." And as in feudal practice, the bond between leader and follower was an oath of personal loyalty.[68]

The substitution of "men for laws, personal judgment and responsibility for the rule-book and anonymity," was carried out throughout the entire Nazi system by a series of subinfeudations in which superior vassals invested inferior ones with rights and responsibilities cemented by mutual pledges of loyalty and confidence contingent upon a continuing demonstration of ability to get things done. The system remained throughout a highly fluid affair, with protagonists and antagonists in constant flux in an unending test of confidence and capacity.[69]

The feudal investiture and revocation of power took place within the organizational scheme of the National Socialist Party based on a system of regions called *Gaue,* in each of which preeminent power was wielded by a *Gauleiter* who held autonomous authority analogous to that of a medieval duke or count. At the center of the system, the chief vassals or *Reichsleiter*—men like Heinrich Himmler, head of the paramilitary SS formations and secret police, Paul Goebbels, chief of the propaganda network, and Hermann Göring, the airforce chief—constructed vast and interlocking systems of personal dependencies with ever-shifting borders.

Although the independent authority of the system of official government inherited from Weimar was undermined by the Nazis, the structures were not abandoned but were rather taken over by the new party elite and used as instruments of policy administration. The chief leaders functioned sometimes as deputies of the Führer, at other times as the heads of administrative departments. The actual structure of the chain of command became extremely complex and often difficult to discern in a system in which a subordinate official in a ministry could issue commands to a superior as the deputy of a party "lord" with general over-

[68] *Ibid.,* p. 925.
[69] *Ibid.*

sight over the ministry's policy area. "At any given moment a German with an ax to grind . . . had to ask, not 'what is the chain of command,' but who has the actual 'connections'—the nominal boss or someone else." [70] Albert Speer has left us some examples of the complexities that developed in this *ad hoc* system:

> On August 20, 1943, Heinrich Himmler had been appointed Minister of the Interior of the Reich. Until then, to be sure, he had been Reichsführer of the all-embracing SS, which was spoken of as a "state within a state." But in his capacity as chief of the police he had been, strangely, a subordinate of Minister of the Interior Frick.
>
> The power of the Gauleiters, constantly furthered by Bormann, had led to a splintering of the sovereignty in the Reich. . . .
>
> It was characteristic of Hitler's double-track way of running things that the Gauleiters in their capacity of party functionaries were under Bormann, while in their capacity as Reich Commissioners for Defense they were under the Minister of the Interior. Under the feeble Frick this double allegiance involved no danger to Bormann. Analysts of the political scene suspected, however, that with Himmler as Minister of the Interior, Bormann had acquired a serious counterpoise.
>
> I too saw it this way and was looking forward hopefully to Himmler's reign. Above all I counted on his checking the progressive fragmentation of the government executive power.[71]

A system of this sort encouraged overt feuds and private warfare, so that decision making took place in a kaleidoscope of shifting coalitions and juntas engaged in perpetual rivalry, requiring intricate systems of arbitration and adjudication to break deadlocks between rival empires and to settle disputes. Koehl describes the typical pattern of dispute settlement as follows:

> A kind of jury-trial resulted. The rivals each spoke in their own defense before the Führer, Lammers, Hess or Bormann, and some of the neutral bigwigs. Spokesmen were also heard from the opposing camps. Questioning began; from the neutrals, suggestions were made. The Führer speaks. He assigns the blame, and directs the character of the solution in broad lines. The contestants shake hands and agree to meet with each others' experts shortly. At the following negotiations a *modus vivendi* agreement [sic] was achieved. Sometimes this resulted in some institutional changes; often it led to the creation of some new joint agency, or in "personal union" of the rival agencies through a single executive officer. Both of these solutions increased the complexity of the network of loyalties. The new agency was inserted into the old channels with special authority—often given it directly by the Führer—to go over the heads of the line people in the rival parent organizations. The

[70] *Ibid.*, p. 926.
[71] Speer, *op. cit.*, p. 404.

executive with two hats was supposed to cut through red tape, but he also had two evenly matched bosses to worry about.[72]

One result of so elaborate a system of personal rivalry operating as a decision-making system independently of anything resembling fixed jurisdictional lines was that final judgment in large policy questions usually was pushed up to Hitler himself or to an immediate subordinate like his secretary, Martin Bormann. Hitler's personal power over policy derived, therefore, not so much from the formal attribution of absolute authority in Nazi ideology as from the need for a unifying figure in the complicated constellation of competing egos and viewpoints. The system nevertheless remained one of decentralized power. The chief vassals, through the control of units of economic power, could assert and defend considerable autonomy. And in the *Gaue* the increasing identity of the local party leaders with local interests over time decreased the ability of the central government to manipulate them at will.[73]

If the Nazis had found the operational code of Weimar Liberalism wanting on grounds of irresponsibility and inefficiency in the defense of national interests, their own dog-eat-dog system in time was to evidence even greater irresponsibility, incoherence, and inefficiency. For one thing, it admitted no principle of cooperative trust. Speer describes the atmosphere of decision making in the following terms:

> The world in which we lived forced upon us dissimulation and hypocrisy. Among rivals an honest word was rarely spoken, for fear it would be carried back to Hitler in a distorted version. Everyone conspired, took Hitler's capriciousness into his reckonings, and won or lost in the course of this cryptic game. I played on this out-of-tune keyboard of mutual relations just as unscrupulously as all the others.[74]

The incoherence of the system and the capriciousness of Hitler's mind combined to assure that no overall plan for the war was ever produced. Speer makes this comment in his memoirs, and also points up the inefficiencies and errors with which the system was rife. "From the start of my work as Minister of Armaments," he writes, "I discovered blunder after blunder, in all departments of the economy." [75] The ideology of anti-Semitism also affected rational policy. To his dinner companions, Speer reports, Hitler used to refer to nuclear physics as "Jewish Physics," which was no invitation to the Education Minister to support nuclear research.[76]

[72] Koehl, *op. cit.*, p. 927.
[73] *Ibid.*, pp. 926, 928.
[74] Speer, *op. cit.*, p. 350.
[75] *Ibid.*, p. 305.
[76] *Ibid.*

Thus in the final analysis the emphasis of the *Weltanschauung* on a *will* to power and dominion proved incapable of generating in its believers a *rational* operational code for the development and maintenance of power. Both the drive for national power and the effort of a new aristocracy—Himmler's SS—to establish itself by physical conquest and totalitarian terror failed amidst the incoherence of Nazi "feudalism." Perhaps the greatest irony of Nazi failure was the ultimate triumph in the midst of national defeat of the cartelized economic order, the financial and big business elite that had grown up during the Bismarckian Empire and Weimar Republic under the auspices of German Liberalism. An initial objective of the Nazis had been to save the small farmer, the craftsman, and the small businessman by a reorganization of the market economy of Liberal times on a corporative basis harkening back to medieval principles of economic order. The market was to be suspended as an allocator of economic values. Farmers were to have their debts remitted and then receive back their farms from the state as hereditary fiefs, subject to a law of entail. Industry was to be nationalized as an "industrial estate" whose units would be managed by their former managers and owners also as public fiefs, on something like a guild basis, with rules for recruitment to management positions from the lower echelons of workers and with limitations on production and competition.[77] The corporative grand design remained a dead letter, however, as an instrument of social and economic reform. Such corporative institutions as did come into being were used solely for purposes of wartime economics. A *Reichsnährstand* (an estate composed of all those engaged in the production of food) was organized, but its chief utility was to permit central mobilization of supplies for the war effort.

Similarly, the Socialist component of the ideology, featured in the name of the party and salient in the original Twenty-five Point Program of 1920, was only temporary window dressing. Point 11 called for the abolition of all unearned income, points 13 and 14 for the confiscation by the state of trusts and a state share in the profits of large industries. Point 16 demanded the nationalization of the large department stores and their rental to small tradespeople. But this entire program was gradually dropped, beginning in 1926. It proved not to be of interest to the groups on which Hitler's support ultimately rested, and no idea, save that of his personal power and that of the Party, was of irreducible value to Hitler. "All programmes," writes Alan Bullock, "were means to an end, to be taken up or dropped as they were needed. 'Any idea' [Hitler] says in *Mein Kampf*, 'may be a source of danger if it be looked upon as an end in itself.'"[78] Or as Hajo Holborn sums it up, the only

---

[77] Koehl, *op. cit.*, p. 924.
[78] Allan Bullock, *Hitler, A Study in Tyranny* (London: Odhams Press, 1960), p. 68.

ideas that were of interest to Hitler were those which proved usable in the building up of organizations. The growth of the "Movement" was to him a criterion of its truth.[79]

Hitler supposed, then, that an alliance with the economic forces of the old regime would serve his political interest in personal and national power better than any of the corporative or socialist schemes proposed by various of his early cronies. For a while, indeed, this seemed to be the case. And it is also true that the Nazis gained a certain upper hand over the industrialists during their heyday and entered into an economic partnership with the managers of the great cartels. But it is also the case that Nazi economic policy increased the power of the industrial and banking elite as the economy geared itself up for war. "These interlocking power systems did not fall victim to the revolutionists' axes because they were scarcely understood, scarcely visible. They continued to grow during the Nazi era, concealed by the elaborate romantic propaganda of the Nazis." [80] When the Nazi system of political power fell apart, the cartelized economy remained largely intact and the business elite remained ensconced in the seats of economic power. It is true, however, that a certain measure of social change had taken place during the Nazi years. The Nazi Party became a vehicle of upward mobility for large segments of the lower middle class. A notable increase in the numbers of well-to-do middle-class persons in the large urban centers occurred under Nazi auspices. But the economic and political future of this class were not to be what Hitler had envisaged. Willy-nilly he had helped produce the demographic basis for the present Liberal democratic German system, which we shall discuss briefly later in this chapter.

Operational Code and Circumstance.   The operational code of decentralized decision making and the accompanying decentralized and complicated organizational scheme that we have been describing do not seem to correspond very well to the logic of absolute power implied by the Nazi *Weltanschauung* that we outlined earlier in this chapter. Nor would it be proper to attribute it to the old Germanic feudal ideology we have described that was illogically crossed with the nineteenth-century Social Darwinist categories. It had a decidedly autonomous character *vis à vis* the ideological *Weltanschauung* and seems clearly to have derived from the necessities of political circumstance. It was certainly not seen as an ideal scheme for the efficient organization of power.

The relevant circumstances have to do with the sharing out of power in the early years of the Nazi Party and with Hitler's strategy for carrying out his revolution by using rather than destroying the established elite groups. The German Workers' Party of 1919 from which it

[79] Holborn, *op. cit.*, p. 544.
[80] Koehl, *op. cit.*, p. 931.

grew was organized before Hitler became associated with it, and when it later assumed its ultimate name, the National Socialist German Workers' Party, Hitler served first as propaganda chief before he became party leader. The first paramilitary formation of the party, the *Sturmabteilung* (SA), headed by Ernst Röhm, was not a palace guard of Hitler's nor was it in the early days even subordinate to the Party leadership. Röhm intended it to be an independent organization which would merely support the party in "military" actions.[81] Röhm had first encountered Hitler in the months immediately after the First World War when he was engaged in putting together a secret army to be run by former military officers like himself. His intention had been to use Hitler's demagoguery to rally mass support for his secret army, which would bring him, not Hitler, to power.[82] Later, when Hitler had clearly established himself as the Führer of the Nazi Movement, and after he had come to power as Chancellor, Röhm continued his efforts at maintaining an independent power position and aimed at a certain primacy by attempting to supplant the regular German Army, the *Reichswehr*, with the SA. In the early years, therefore, Hitler was only *primus inter pares* in the Nazi Party itself.

After the abortive Munich Beer Hall putsch of 1923, which resulted in two years' imprisonment in Landsberg, Hitler decided that the only safe and efficient road to power would be a legal one. This meant alliances with existing political forces that were willing to work with him, while in the meantime gradually building up his personal mass political appeal. Even after his designation as Chancellor Hitler found it important to ally himself with existing elite structures. There were, in addition to segments of the old aristocracy, the representatives of German big business, the officer corps of the Army, and the ensconced bureaucracy. All initially were established interests of the Hohenzollern Empire, and the latter two in particular were anxious to undermine the republican institutions of Weimar. When in 1934 Hitler moved to destroy his competitor Röhm and the power of the SA, this was not only to secure his personal power position but also to placate the regular army interests which were threatened by the prospects of a lower middle-class-based people's army taking over their power and prerogatives.

The Ultimate Operational Intention.   Hitler's ultimate intention nevertheless was a revolutionary one, which involved the elimination of the old elite structure and the creation of a new Nazi aristocracy resting on a mass base mobilized in such institutions as the Hitler Youth, the Work

---

[81] Hans Buchheim, in Krausnick, *op. cit.*, p. 140.
[82] Heinz Höhne, *The Order of the Death's Head*, trans. Richard Barry (New York: Coward-McCann, 1969), p. 17.

Service, and a host of other Nazi political and cultural organizations. As the new order took form, his own office presumably would become more absolute in fact, less a brokerage factor among semi-autonomous power centers. This would in large part be a function of the soldierly obedience norms of the new elite he had begun to create and of the success of his mass mobilization policies.

The budding aristocracy was the black-shirted SS which, unlike the SA, was from its inception a palace guard. Its beginnings are found in the Hitler Assault Squad (*Stosstrupps Hitler*), a bodyguard of 1923, reorganized as a Headquarters Guard (*Stabswache*) in 1925 as a counterweight to the SA, when it became clear that Röhm would not play the role of subservient disciple. Later that year it was renamed the "Protection Echelon" or *Schutz Staffel* (SS). It included only the most reliable of Party activists and, unlike the SA, was an integral part of the structure of Party organization, a "Party cadre to be used for any political, technical or strong-arm purpose." [83] Over the years the SS expanded in size and in the number of its functions and took on considerable organizational complexity. It came to include a pervasive political police system with functions both at home and in conquered countries and responsibility for the administration of concentration camps both in Germany and in the conquered eastern countries. At its core was the notorious Gestapo, a domestic and foreign intelligence service. To perform its various functions it took on the character of a full-scale military formation, a Party army, whose divisions also fought side by side with the divisions of the Reichswehr during the Second World War. So organized, the SS gradually came to function as a special executive machine for Hitler's will, unlike the regular Party officialdom, standing apart from and above the legal structures of the bureaucratic state inherited from Weimar. Hans Buchheim has described its evolving role in the following terms:

> To impose and implement the supra-State Führer will, a new executive machine was constructed from parts of the SS, a machine entirely independent of the State administration and, as a matter of principle, subject to no official norms. This Führer executive did not act in accordance with the principle of executive legality; it was guided solely by the will of the Führer. To this machine were allotted all those political tasks in which Hitler was really interested; in particular preservation of his own power, demographic policy, policy for the occupation of conquered territory, persecution of all actual and supposed opponents of the regime. . . . The Führer was able to invest this new executive from time to time with the rights, prerogatives and privileges of an official organization without at the same time subjecting it to established State rules.

[83] Buchheim, in Krausnick, *op. cit.*, p. 141.

Conversely, as happened in the case of the political police, official authorities could be divorced from the general administrative machine and transferred to the Führer executive. Thus as time went on the concept of the Führer's authority in its purest form became a reality and the process of "de-governmentalization" of public life gathered speed. The historic significance of the SS was that, in its capacity of Führer executive, it became the real and essential instrument of the Führer's authority.[84]

It is significant that the man Hitler chose to be the Reichsführer in charge of the SS organization was Heinrich Himmler, a man who, unlike many of the other Nazi chiefs, was prepared entirely to efface himself before Hitler and to subordinate himself to the Führer's will. In Hitler's presence Himmler always exhibited a certain shyness. His adulation of Hitler was extreme. It is reported, for example, that he used to hold murmured conversations with a picture of Hitler on his office wall, and that he admiringly referred to Hitler as the "greatest brain of all time." When speaking with the Führer on the telephone it was Himmler's habit to click his heels and come to attention.[85]

In building up his organization, Himmler fashioned in idea a model SS man who displayed just such single-minded devotion to the will of the Führer as he himself did. The SS were to be subservient, however, to no others, but were, under Hitler, to constitute a new aristocracy of "Nordic blood." Himmler envisaged the emergence of "the Völkisch elite of the future, the lords of the new Germanic tribes, the men of his SS Order." And they were to embody in their persons the perfect Nordic man of Nazi racial theories.

If Hitler was not a true believer in the racial myth, Himmler apparently was. He had been captivated by the version of it that was propagated by Richard Walther Darré, whom he met in 1924 when he was working with a nationalist back-to-the-land group with a "blood and soil" ideology and a program of driving Slavic farm workers out of east German farm areas. "We know," said Darré, "that almost all great empires in the history of the world and all the greatest cultures have been founded and maintained by men of Nordic blood. We know also that these great empires and cultures have fallen into ruins because the men of Nordic blood who had constructed them did not keep their blood pure." [86] In recruiting his SS men Himmler used most elaborate procedures to screen out persons with the slightest trace of Jewish ancestry, back to the year 1700. Efforts were made to find recruits who fit as closely as possible the Nazi stereotype of the blond Nordic superman.

[84] Buchheim in *ibid.*, pp. 139–40.
[85] Höhne, *op. cit.*, p. 43.
[86] Quoted in *ibid.*, pp. 47–48.

What all this adds up to is the suggestion that in time the operational code of feudal decision making would have given way to a logic of power much more in keeping with the centralized Machiavellism of the *Weltanschauung*. A detailed view of this other code's operation can be obtained by an examination of the kind of mentality that Himmler tried to instill in his SS men.

3. The Inculcation of Nazism

In Chapter 3, after describing the ideological formulas of Established Liberal intellectuals, we turned to a range of empirical studies designed to "excavate" from the American mind the latent ideological principles that in an established culture have the form of attitude and mental habit rather than self-conscious belief. The task of understanding a political culture in revolution, however, demands a different approach. Having surveyed the dual ideology of the Nazi leadership, as *Weltanschauung* and as operational code, we now must consider the ways in which that leadership attempted to inculcate the new way of ideas in the German people. Our concern is to understand modes of indoctrination and to measure success in political socialization, rather than to describe the morphology of an existing culture. Nazi culture in the 1930s, unlike American Liberalism, was not something "given" à la Boorstin, but a reality to be created.

Indoctrinating the New Elite.   The identity of the ultimate operational code with the pure power-pragmatism of the private *Weltanschauung* is revealed in the kind of training undergone by the recruits of the SS and especially in the mentality inculcated by that training. One writer tells us that "the body of ideological doctrine and theoretical dogma available in the SS was astonishingly meagre." [87] Some attention was indeed given to biological theory and to a bowdlerized German history focused on two disconnected periods—the pre-Christian old Germanic era and the Movement's "struggle period" after 1918. But this appears to have had little influence on the SS man's thinking, and there was "no strict ideological training or educational discipline, nothing which can even remotely be compared with that of the communists." All that was required was lip service to notions like the "Führerprinzip" and "racial purity." [88]

Another writer tells us that the SS did not possess "a coherent doctrine," that it did not have "any distinctive ideology," and that its officers complained of lack of interest in ideology among the men.

[87] Buchheim, in Krausnick, *op. cit.*, p. 319.
[88] *Ibid.*, p. 320.

Educational evenings were among the worst-attended SS gatherings. Gruppenführer Zech reported that even SS Commanders often found it more important to be present at the Wehrmacht's beer evenings than to attend the SS educational courses. In January 1939 Standartenführer Dr. Cäsar, Head of the SS Educational Office, complained that racial policy instruction was making little impact on SS men—"Boredom with these subjects is gradually becoming noticeable among the men and so instruction has been extended to cover the basic concepts of National-Socialist ideology." [89]

What was inculcated was a mentality and character that displayed the following qualities and attitudes:

His basic attitude must be that of a fighter for fighting's sake; he must obey unquestioningly; he must be 'hard'—not only inured to but impervious to all human emotions; he should be contemptuous of 'inferior beings' and arrogant towards all those who did not belong to the Order; he must show comradeship and 'camaraderie'; the word 'impossible' did not exist. [90]

"Outwardly and officially," writes Buchheim, "these were evidenced in 'soldierly bearing'," but "in day to day practice . . . pragmatism was the governing factor." [91] The SS man was inculcated with the qualities and attitudes of the pure power pragmatist.

The notion of "fighting for fighting's sake" derives from a conception of "heroic realism" set forth by the Nazi ideologist Werner Best in 1930. Best noted that in Nazi doctrine life was understood to consist wholly of tension and struggle, which were entirely nonteleological and also unceasing. The Nazi moral code, therefore, could not be directed toward any "purpose of fulfillment or completion." And its yardstick could not be a "what," but was of necessity a "how." Thus the important point was "not what we fight for, but how we fight." [92] In Best's theory this standpoint was intended to produce a disregard for any outcome at all, including success or failure in any particular engagement, and to focus attention entirely on the process of struggle. Of course, for the SS success and victory did indeed count, but adopting the ideology of struggle produced a lack of concern with analyzing and evaluating ends. Ends were concretely given, and the SS man was expected to do battle for the end, thinking only of his duty to carry on the fight. Thus "heroic realism and pragmatism are clearly closely related; it is quite understandable that an organization designed purely for a specific purpose should use as

---

[89] Höhne, *op. cit.*, p. 155.
[90] Buchheim, in Krausnick, *op. cit.*, p. 320.
[91] *Ibid.*, p. 321.
[92] *Ibid.*, p. 324.

a facade a purposeless ideology. The extreme subjectivism of the heroic fighter, who regarded any objective purpose as a matter of unimportance, can be made to serve any end whatsoever." [93]

In the end the SS doctrine of heroic realism became twisted into a doctrine of achievement for the sake of achievement. Purpose or justification did not matter; getting the work done as quickly and efficiently as possible became the norm. "It is typical that even in the dock in Jerusalem Eichmann prided himself upon the fact that his organization had worked so perfectly and run like clockwork." [94] The net result of all this seemed to be something like a distorted version of the work ethic which we met in our study of Liberalism and found to be central there. The norm of technical efficiency seems to be an important common currency of all modern political culture.

> "The impossible is the essence of the heroic." SS literature presented heroism as the quality which made possible the impossible; but where practical problems were concerned, SS orders and instructions placed a premium on the spirit of "efficiency." Only through this spirit of efficiency and only through ruthless pragmatism was the SS able to build itself up over a mere ten years into a colossal but nevertheless reasonably well functioning machine for the exercise of power.[95]

The efficient performance of his duty carried with it for the SS man the obligation to be totally self-effacing before his task. Thus an order of 1937 read, "We must teach our men unselfishly to forget that little bit of 'I,' so that when the time comes they will give themselves unreservedly and do their duty doggedly." This total surrender of the self, nevertheless, was seen as a free offering. "Our men have not been called up under some defence law; they have come of their own free will to serve the Führer. . . . This free will . . . is the basis of future achievements and future great deeds." [96] The coupling of self-sacrifice with the idea of a free giving appears as a strange parody of the traditional Christian model of dedication and self-sacrifice. Himmler had been raised a Catholic, and it is a wry fact that he had modeled the SS doctrine of obedience to organizational commands on that of the Jesuits. Hitler even referred to his SS chief as "my Ignatius Loyola." [97]

"Hardness" was another quality deemed essential to the character of the good SS man. Although all military organizations strive to one degree or another to inculcate this quality, among the SS it took on an extreme form. It meant being insensible not only to one's own pain but

---

[93] *Ibid.*, pp. 327–28.
[94] *Ibid.*, p. 328.
[95] *Ibid.*, p. 329.
[96] *Ibid.*, p. 331.
[97] Höhne, *op. cit.*, p. 144.

also to the pain and suffering of others, when they were Jews or foreigners. It meant the cultivation of a spirit of mercilessness and savagery in the execution of organizational commands. Himmler once remarked:

> For the SS man there is one absolute principle; he must be honest, decent, loyal and friendly to persons of our own blood—and to no one else. I am totally indifferent to what happens to the Russians or the Czechs. If there is good blood of our type to be found among these peoples, we will have it; if necessary we will take their children away from them and bring them up ourselves. I am interested in the question whether other peoples live in plenty or starve only in so far as we need slaves for our *Kultur;* apart from that, the question is one of complete indifference to me.[98]

It is interesting that to inculcate this kind of hardness in their people—in the public at large as well as among the SS—the Nazis found it necessary to represent non-Germans, and especially Jews, as creatures who were not really human. Being human and being German (or Nordic) came to be absolutely equated. Thus the SS were taught such expressions as "the Eastern subhuman" as a way of referring to Czechs, Poles, and Russians. In 1931 a Nazi speaker told a crowd that non-Nordic man held a place intermediary between Nordic man and the animal. Non-Nordic man was not completely a man and shared traits with the apes. In 1932 another Nazi propagandist compared Jews to bugs and urged their extermination.[99] One writer has compiled from the writings of Hitler the following catalog of inhuman epithets for the Jews:

> The Jew is a maggot in a rotting corpse; he is a plague worse than the Black Death of former times; a germ carrier of the worst sort; mankind's eternal germ of disunion; the drone which insinuates its way into the rest of mankind; the spider that slowly sucks the people's blood out of its pores; the pack of rats fighting bloodily among themselves; the parasite in the body of other peoples; the typical parasite; a sponger who, like a harmful bacillus continues to spread; the eternal bloodsucker; the peoples' parasite; the peoples' vampire.[100]

The perfect embodiment of "hardness" among the heroes of the SS was Reinhard Heydrich, Himmler's second in command, head of the infamous Gestapo, who as "Reich Protector" of Bohemia and Moravia earned the title "Butcher of Prague." One SS cadet wrote in his memoirs that nearly every room in the cadet school had a picture of Heydrich on

[98] Buchheim, in Krausnick, *op. cit.*, pp. 234–35.
[99] *Ibid.*, p. 321; George L. Mosse, *The Crisis of German Ideology: Intellectual Origins of the Third Reich* (New York: Grosset & Dunlap, 1964), p. 143.
[100] Jäckel, *op. cit.*, pp. 58–59.

the wall, and that what all admired most in him was his iron discipline and his "hardness." Another former SS man exemplifies this quality in his memoirs with the report that Heydrich had once said to him: "Abroad they take us for bloodhounds, don't they? . . . It is almost too difficult for some people but we must be hard as granite. Otherwise our Führer's work will come to nothing. Later people will thank us for what we have taken upon ourselves." [101]

Cameraderie was yet another quality of the good SS man, a trait that mitigated the demand for "hardness" at the price of loss of all standards. The term is not to be rendered as "comradeship," which implies community and moral solidarity. It meant, rather, an indifference to the individual's moral character and a willingness to make concessions to one another's failings and weaknesses, a spirit of indulgence within the "ingroup." It involved a willingness to cover up failures and derelictions both of the individual and of the group. It was a quality not found so much in line military formations, but rather in places where the SS were in absolute control of the situation and could lord it over others with impunity, as in the concentration camps. *Cameraderie* implied the extinction of all objective criteria of morality of any kind.[102]

Such was the ideal SS man, chief carrier of the ideology of struggle and power, who was to share with Hitler the domination of the "Reich of a Thousand Years." What was to be the role and ideal character of the average German? What aspects of the ideology were to be paramount for him, and how did the Nazi leaders attempt to mold him to their purposes?

Political Socialization of the Masses.   While ideological elite formation focused on molding the "hard" and intrepid fighter, the political socialization of the masses aimed at inculcating a sense of organic belonging. It was a belonging that was to be pervasive, so that in everything one did, one acted consciously as a member of the German *Volk*. Hitler spoke of this objective as the "nationalization of the masses." Because the Nazi party and its Führer were seen as the keepers of the national will and destiny, "nationalization" implied making the people radically dependent on both party and Führer, an objective to be accomplished through establishment of an intricate network of "national" organizations as the context for the individual's action in every moment of his waking life. Vocational party groups made one conscious of being a German on the job. And there were also organizations based on age, sex, and family role—youth organizations for boys, youth organizations for girls, a German mothers' group, plus a host of Party groups for leisure-

---

[101] Buchheim, in Krausnick, *op. cit.*, pp. 339, 340.
[102] *Ibid.*, pp. 343, 344.

time activities such as hiking and music. One's entire social and cultural life was nationalized. The purely private man was to be swallowed up in the German, a political animal in every facet of his life activity.[103]

Mass "nationalization" was to be an instrument of mass mobilization, the pooling of all German energies for the projects of national aggrandizement plotted out by the leadership. The very modern character of the concept is revealed in the metaphor used to describe the result sought—*Gleichschaltung*, the "equalization of the nation's gears." One could hardly find a more apt symbol for totalitarian endeavor in a technological age. "In an age of industrialization and class conflict man was to be integrated into his Volk; his true self would be activated and his feeling of alienation transformed into one of belonging." [104]

Forming the Volk Member.   We need now to ask how ideology figured in the process of "nationalization." What was communicated to the average German as the belief system of the good and loyal members of the *Volk?* And by what media was it communicated to him? Self-conscious doctrine was sparse and simple. Hitler had no high opinion of the ability of the average man to absorb abstract ideas, nor did he think an intricate doctrine was an important thing for his purposes. The vital thing was to form certain attitudes and to train will and instincts. In *Mein Kampf* he presents the following theory of ideological indoctrination:

> The great mass of a people consists neither of professors nor of diplomats. The small abstract knowledge it possesses directs its sentiments rather to the world of feeling. In this is rooted either its negative or positive attitude. . . . It is more difficult to undermine faith than knowledge, love succumbs to change less than to respect, hatred is more durable than aversion, and at all times the driving force of the most important changes in this world has been found less in a scientific knowledge animating the masses, but rather in a fanaticism dominating them and in a hysteria which drove them forward.

In another part of the book he sums up his view of the matter in these few words:

> A change in education is a further necessity: today we suffer from overeducation. Only knowledge is prized. The know-it-alls are the enemies of action. What is needed is instinct and will.[105]

The race myth formed the core of such doctrine as there was. It was disseminated in a variety of books, typical of which were the writings

[103] Mosse, *Nazi Culture,* p. xx. The following account relies heavily on this study.

[104] *Ibid.,* pp. xx, xxi.

[105] *Mein Kampf,* quoted in *ibid.,* pp. 8, 10.

of Hans F. K. Günther, a professor at the University of Jena who held the chair of "racial science" there, a chair that was established in 1930, before Hitler's rise to power. The Nazis at that time controlled the government of the province of Thuringia, under whose auspices the appointment was made. Günther's *Kleine Rassenkunde des deutschen Volkes* (*Short Ethnology of the German People*), first published in 1929, was distributed in numerous editions and sold 272,000 copies throughout the country between then and 1943. A major theme of the book is the Nordic "ideal type" as a physical stereotype. Although Günther denies that language groups or "peoples" are identical with racial types, and affirms that the various nations of Europe are made up of mixed races, he argues that nevertheless "in the mixture of one nation one or more races may be more strongly represented than in the race mixture of another nation." Hence even though Germans will vary in physical appearance, a tendency will be found for the Nordic to predominate. Günther describes the type as follows:

> The Nordic race is tall, long-legged, slim, with an average height, among males, of above 1.74 meters. The limbs, the neck, the shape of the hands and feet are vigorous and slender in appearance. The Nordic race is long-legged and narrow-faced, with a cephalic index of around 75 and a facial index above 90. . . .
> The cut of the face of the Nordic race—at least in the male—creates the effect of a unique boldness through three striking traits in the lines of the profile. . . .
> The skin of the Nordic race is roseate-bright and the blood shines through so that it looks specially enlivened, and at the same time mostly somewhat cool or fresh. . . .[106]

Certain qualities of character are supposed to go with the physical type, and Günther tells the reader that when an artist wishes to "represent the image of a bold, goal-determined, resolute person, or of a noble, superior, and heroic human being" he will create an image that approximates the Nordic type. This was the image that Hitler wanted Germans to have of themselves, and, in a heightened degree, of him. "Such features can be intensified in individuals within the Nordic race to a pronouncedly heroic disposition, to a transcendent leadership in statesmanship or creativity in technology, science, and art." [107] Surely Hitler hoped that when Germans read this last sentence they would think of him.

In the work of another Nazi racial theorist, Ludwig Ferdinand Clauss, racial qualities are tied into "landscape style." The Nordic man is pictured as someone who loves open spaces and prospects of distance in his landscape. The Nordic landscape is said to invite movement and

[106] Hans Günther, quoted in *ibid.*, p. 64.
[107] *Ibid.*, pp. 64, 65.

action. It is suited to the "accomplishment-oriented man." One is reminded by this phrase of the Protestant Ethic, which we found so central to the Liberal version of modernity. And indeed, activity like that of the good Lockean Liberal involved in the development of technology and the exploitation of the earth's resources is celebrated as the accomplishment of Nordic man: "To assert that the world becomes Nordic means that countless hidden values are being opened up and made useful and productive—mines of iron ore, oil wells, water power, as well as animal and man power." But there is also the suggestion that "accomplishment" means the literal conquest of terrain. "In the Nordic landscape everything points to places beyond and tempts the soul born of it, to cross the borders of this landscape. The Nordic soul has an innate urge to push on into the distance." Although the context is a discussion of travel, we are led to think of the drive for *Lebensraum*.[108] Clauss's book, first published in 1932, went through eight editions, with thirty thousand copies sold in its first five years.[109]

Alongside the celebration of things Nordic this literature also contained material to feed anti-Semitism in its pejorative images of the Jew. The Nordic man is depicted as a builder and a creator of culture, whereas the Jew is called a destroyer. "Considered in himself the Jew represents nothing else but . . . blind will for destruction, the insanity of mankind," writes Alfred Rosenberg, supervisor of ideological education of the Nazi Party from 1934 on. "It is known that Jewish people are especially prone to mental disease. . . . To strip the world of its soul, that and nothing else is what Judaism wants." [110]

Heroes to Imitate.   The attitudes and qualities of the good member of the *Volk* were presented by the Nazi propagandists in many other ways than in formal racial doctrine of the sort we have been describing. There was also a literature in which heroes, both historical persons and fictional characters, were presented for admiration. Frederick the Great, a person of slight physique, is celebrated for his strength of will and his fortitude:

> What is there to say of this Prussian will of Frederick's, this inflexible will to live? . . . Flaming sparks are ignited only . . . when the genius of a great man is engaged in desperate battle with unyielding Fate, when the harmoniously peaceful purpose of his planning is transformed into the stormy, roaring hurricane of his will.[111]

[108] Ludwig Ferdinand Clauss, quoted in *ibid.*, pp. 65, 67, 75.
[109] *Ibid.*, p. 58.
[110] Alfred Rosenberg, quoted in *ibid.*, p. 78.
[111] Quoted in *ibid.*, p. 120.

The authors of this literature did not worry about historical accuracy in their word-pictures, for the Prussian king of subtle and brilliant intellect, friend and patron of the *Philosophes,* is made to appear, like the Nazis, an anti-intellectual:

> There was hardly a man of his time, filled as it was with so-called philosophical speculation, who expressed his scorn and derision for them as strongly as did Frederick. . . . He avoided philosophical speculations which seldom can awaken the interest of active people. In fact, he hated them in his innermost soul.[112]

Ernst Röhm, in his widely distributed autobiography, eulogizes the qualities of the good soldier and emphasizes "a spirit of defiance, comradeship cemented with blood," passion, "fanatical love and hate." He comments negatively on the monetary values of the "hustling and sneaky trader who has made accursed gold his God." And he delivers a strange apostrophe to freedom that would perplex and horrify any good Liberal for whom "freedom" is a chief value word: he appeals to "the warrior who is struggling in the battle of life, who wants to win freedom and with it the kingdom of heaven." From the sequel it is plain that he is not thinking of individual freedom but of national aggrandizement. He writes, "I approve of whatever serves the purpose of German freedom. I oppose whatever runs counter to it. Europe, aye, the whole world, may go down in flames—what concern is it of ours? Germany must live and be free." [113]

Another favorite hero of the Third Reich was Albert Leo Schlageter, who was executed by the French for engaging in guerilla warfare with the French occupation forces when the Ruhr was seized in 1923 to compel the payment of war reparations. The Nazis presented him to the German public for adulation in several ways. A memorial volume of his letters was brought out. And on Hitler's birthday in 1933 a play entitled *Schlageter* by Hanns Johst was premiered before the Führer and performed throughout the country thereafter by a number of touring companies. The anti-hero or antagonist, the Jew, also was dramatically represented, notably in a play entitled *Jew Süss,* in which the author made lavish use of typical Jewish stereotypes in portraying the life of an eighteenth-century Jewish financier.

Fictional heroes of Nazi drama included Michael, a creation of propaganda minister Goebbels, and the hero of his only published novel, seventeen editions of which were purchased by the German reading public between 1929 and 1942. Michael was a soldier who after the war

[112] *Ibid.,* p. 121.
[113] Ernst Röhm, quoted in *ibid.,* pp. 101, 102.

became a student, but who soon tired of the intellectual life of the university, which he saw as a time-wasting, dilletantish affair, of no use to the *Volk* which was being strangled by the Jewish financier and the foreign conqueror. "Intellectualism is becoming a big bore to me. I feel nauseous at every printed word. I don't find anything in it that could redeem me. . . . The wisdom of university chairs will never be able to redeem us!" [114] Michael leaves the university to go to work with his hands, and finds great satisfaction in joining the class of simple workers, of whom he has a romantic vision as the saviors of the country. "Money has made slaves of us," says Michael. "But work shall make us free. With the political bourgeoisie we staggered on the edge of an abyss; but with the political working class we will achieve a resurrection." [115] He castigates the "bourgeoisie" over and over and with them the ideology of Liberalism, which "in its deepest sense . . . is the philosophy of money. Liberalism means: I believe in Mammon. Socialism means: I believe in work. . . ." [116]

We should be careful to realize that the word "socialism" here implies no affinity to Marxist doctrine, which the Nazis denounced (though, interestingly, many of them were converts from the Communist movement). Nor does the praise of labor mean solidarity with the international proletarian class. Goebbels makes Michael say explicitly, "Labor is not class. . . . It is a historical social estate." [117] It is an irony that such a glorification of the working class should circulate as "nationalizing" propaganda during a time when the Nazi coalition had come to rest on the middle classes, including the magnates of industry, and to rely heavily on numerous members of the old aristocracy, who also are explicitly castigated in the novel. The image conveyed was in effect not a class image, but a "blood and soil" romance of the *Volk* or nation, who are seen as simple men and brothers. For in one place Michael says, "No oak tree grows without soil, root, and strength. No man comes out of the unsubstantial. The people are his soil, history his root, blood his strength." He is here speaking of the origins and support base for the "geniuses" who are "the highest forms of expression of the national will," presumably the Nazi leadership. And he speaks of a "new aristocracy . . . being created on the basis of new law. Tradition is being replaced by ability. The Best One! This title is not inherited, it has to be earned." [118] What we have here appears to be a strange inversion of the Classical Liberal conception of achievement as the basis of status, combined with

[114] Joseph Goebbels, quoted in *ibid.*, p. 104.
[115] *Ibid.*, p. 107.
[116] *Ibid.*, p. 110.
[117] *Ibid.*, p. 107.
[118] *Ibid.*, p. 105.

the anti-intellectualism and praise of the simple life that have bulked so large in the ideology of the American New Left.

The middle-classness of the authoritative image of the good member of the *Volk* is very clearly revealed in the Nazi ideology of sexual morality, of the family, and of woman's role in it. Hans Anderlahn, the author of numerous books about the SA, casts the good SA man in the role of family founder and good father. His writings on this theme were a real effort at reform, for the brawling SA man of the twenties had been anything but a good family man. The family Anderlahn had in mind was the traditional German bourgeois family. Great attention was given to the role of the mother, whose place was that of childbearer and home-maker, the typical nineteenth-century middle-class German *Hausfrau*. The Nazis explicitly rejected the idea of equal rights for women and the emancipation movement. Woman's place was definitely in the home, playing her roles there in quiet obedience to her husband. Her beauty standards also conformed to nineteenth-century, middle-class models of "naturalness," which eschewed the artificialities of the beauty parlor.[119] Prolific motherhood, which produced soldiers for the Reich, was elaborately celebrated and rewarded by the Third Reich.

Mobilization of the Arts.   It was not only through the sale of particular series of books or by the performance of particular plays, like *Jew Süss,* or *Schlageter,* that the Nazis attempted to inculcate the image of the good *Volk* member, whom one widely used expression described as the "new man." After coming to power the Nazis exploited all the resources of the German literati and artists for propaganda purposes. In September 1933 the regime created a Reich Chamber of Culture organized in seven departments, each devoted to one medium of expression: literature, music, films, radio, theater, fine arts, and the press. By making membership in the chamber compulsory for all persons wishing to practice the various arts, the threat of denial of membership was a powerful inhibitor of the nonconformist. Lists of forbidden books were published by the Culture Chamber, and the Propaganda Ministry exercised a censorship over all new publication.[120]

By 1937 Goebbels was able to report:

> The purging of the cultural field has been accomplished with the least amount of legislation. The social estate of creative artists took this cleansing into its own hands. Nowhere did any serious obstructions emerge. Today we can assert with joy and satisfaction that the great development is once again set in motion. Everywhere people are paint-

[119] *Ibid.,* pp. 19–21.
[120] *Ibid.,* p. 135.

ing, building, writing poetry, singing, and acting. The German artist has his feet on a solid, vital ground. Art, taken out of its narrow and isolated circle, again stands in the midst of the people and from there exerts its strong influences on the whole nation.[121]

In the graphic arts the main thrust of the Nazi takeover was to abolish the schools of abstract art that had flourished from the turn of the century, and the forms of art criticism through which the members of the artistic world communicated with one another. All this was labeled as "degenerate," and the new popular art was required to be very literal in its renditions. Favorite subjects for representation were, of course, the "ideal type" Nordic man and woman, shown engaged in some patriotic work or in the family circle. The entire theater, opera, and film worlds also were brought into the work of "nationalization." The radio broadcasting network was carefully controlled to prevent all criticism of the Nazi regime and its ideas, and great use was made of barrages of political addresses and of the controlled news broadcast. Along with literature, the arts, and the communications industry, the Nazis also tried to work science into their system of *Gleichschaltung*, especially for the purpose of establishing their claims about racial hierarchy.

Political Liturgies.   Probably more important than the written word, the dramatic gesture, the art exhibition, or the dicta of science as media of inculcation were the vast participatory celebrations in which the subjects were actually made a part of the ideological drama. These were large-scale political rallies—party congresses and rallies held to mark specific political occasions—processions, and revived pagan Germanic religious ceremonies such as the celebration of the summer and winter solstices. These have been described as liturgical events, in which the feelings of awe, of spiritual uplift, and of fellowship and communion that accompany religious experience were transferred to political objects by the Nazi mythmakers and high priests. Elaborate settings, designed to enhance their solemnity, were created for these events. Emphasis was laid on size, with fixed banners the size of ten-story buildings behind the speaker's podium, massed marching flags in the thousands, massed torches. Even lighting effects were carried out on a colossal scale. Albert Speer, Hitler's architect, has described in his memoirs the "cathedral of light" that he created for the 1934 party rally in Nuremberg:

> The actual effect surpassed anything I had imagined. The hundred and thirty sharply defined beams, placed around the field at intervals of forty feet, were visible to a height of twenty to twenty-five thousand feet, after which they merged into a general glow. The feeling was of a

[121] Address by Goebbels, quoted in *ibid.,* p. 154.

vast room, with the beams serving as mighty pillars of infinitely high outer walls. Now and then a cloud moved through this wreath of lights, bringing an element of surrealistic surprise to the mirage. I imagine that this "cathedral of light" was the first luminescent architecture of this type.[122]

The liturgical forms in which these party spectacles were presented often borrowed from the forms of Christian worship with which Germans were familiar. Some interesting illustrations of these borrowings are found in a song book published in 1941 for use at Party meetings and festivities. It was brought out by the cultural office of the Reich Propaganda Administration. A section devoted to battle songs carries the following quotation from a prayer of the *Führer* as a prefatory thought:

> Almighty God,
> bless thou our weapons as we go forth.
> Be just, as thou always wast.
> Judge now whether we now deserve our freedom.
> Lord, bless our struggle!

This is simply a traditional invocation of divine help in battle. In other sections only the traditional form remains intact, however, and the substance is radically altered. Thus prefatory to the section containing Christmas songs is a statement entitled "Words of the Leader," which has the form of a Christian Creed, like the "Apostles' Creed," but the creedal references are to the German people rather than to the Divine Persons. It runs as follows:

> I am a German
> I believe in my People!
> I believe in her honor!
> I believe in her future!
>
> I believe in her right,
> and I will stand up for her right!
>
> I will stand up for her freedom,
> and thereby I stand up
> for a better peace
> than the peace of adversity
> and of hate of the past.
>
> This I believe,
> and this I confess
> in the name of my People.

The title page of the section, which shows a lighted candle on the branch of a fir tree, also revolutionizes substance while retaining elements of

[122] Speer, *op. cit.*, pp. 97–98.

traditional form. The caption reads, "High Night of the Clear Stars—Winter Solstice—People's Christmas (*Volksweihnacht*)." The carols have nothing to say about the birth of Jesus, but celebrate rather the rebirth of the sun after the shortest day in the year—an ancient pagan German festival!

In an epilogue the editor notes that the book is put together "according to the order of the political year, beginning with the day of the seizure of power and running to the People's Christmas," an imitation of the traditional Christian breviary.

The kinds of feelings evoked by such solemnities are graphically revealed in an account of one of these celebrations in the diary of an SA man's wife.

> At twelve-fifteen finally came the great moment. The order came to march off and the torches were lighted. We marched with joyful song, accompanied by lutes, through the streets of the little town. After a short time we were to top marching form. As we entered the market square, there was a roar of "Heil!" There stood Flight Captain Hermann Göring, his hand raised in the Hitler salute, and he reviewed the long line of marchers, while shouts of "Heil!" echoed in the square. After we left the town, the road led us up into the mountains toward the solstice fire. It was a splendid sight. The road led to the mountain in serpentine twists and turns. From the top we could look back on the long marching columns. The brilliant glare of the torches in the night was glorious. It was an overwhelming sight. My words are too poor to portray this experience. For a long time we let this picture enter our thirsty souls to their uttermost depths until our eyes were focused on one mighty flaming fire. It was our solstice celebration.

The author next tells that she fell into conversation with one of the young SA men present, who asked her about her reasons for joining the party and what National Socialism meant to her. She replied at length, and then:

> He was silent for a while, turned his head, and looked thoughtfully into the flames of the solstice fire. Slowly he turned his face to me, looked deep into my eyes, and, shaking my hand, said in all seriousness: "You have truly grasped what National Socialism is!" . . . We looked silently and seriously into the fire. Then Wolfgang Jensen said admonishingly, almost solemnly, to me: "Don't ever forget the solstice fire. Let it flame in your heart and let its rays reach out to your racial comrades. Then you will truly help in the great work of Adolf Hitler." [123]

Schools and the Youth.   The school was of course a prime focus of National Socialist efforts at political socialization. For if they could mold

[123] Gudrun Streiter, quoted in Mosse, *Nazi Culture*, pp. 125, 126.

the young to their will they guaranteed their future power. Again, even in the school, the emphasis was not so much on teaching doctrine as on molding attitudes. "The German school is not an institution devoted only to the transmission of knowledge. . . . The task of the German educator is to form human souls." [124] As with the adult population, festivals and ceremonial assemblies played a large role. These included flag raisings, massings of colors, and celebrations of national holidays such as The Day of the Reich, The Day of the Führer, The Day of Labor, The Day of the Farmer, Heroes' Memorial Day, The Day of the German Mother, The Day of German Volkdom, and a light celebration at Christmas. In addition to such special occasions there was a weekly Festive Hour that was used for the purpose of Volkish indoctrination. At a special annual flag raising at the opening of the school year, the usually brief ceremony of song and recitation was embellished with pledges of faith and an admonition from the Führer read by a teacher. The latter dwelt on the usual themes: standing "solidly on the ground of your soil" and being "hard so that this flag does not slip from you." [125]

The transmission of knowledge as a means of indoctrination was of course not ignored. Racial biology was made a required course, and the teaching of German history and literature was emphasized at the expense of other things, including the science curriculum. The overall meaning of education was the training of little soldiers for the Reich, and as though to give emphasis to this, five hours per day were devoted to physical education.[126] Individuality was suppressed at every point, and the student was taught instead to find satisfaction in the fellowship of the "racial community" defined as a "fellowship of battle." [127] After school hours the administration of further discipline and indoctrination was taken over by the extensive programs of the Hitler Youth and the Federation of German Girls.

Measures of Success and Failure. How well did the Nazis succeed in their elaborate program of ideological indoctrination and the shaping of souls and wills? To what extent were the values and attitudes that made up Nazi culture implanted as habit in the average German? Unfortunately, we have no survey data available like that discussed in the chapters on American political culture, to give us a detailed empirical measure of these things. Nor are there psychological studies like Lane's extant. The evidence we have to work with is at once less comprehensive, less systematically collected, and more impressionistic in character.

Some of the systematic evidence that is extant derives from the re-

[124] Hermann Klauss, quoted in *ibid.*, p. 127.
[125] *Ibid.*, pp. 128, 129, 130.
[126] *Ibid.*, p. 263.
[127] *Ibid.*, p. 265.

searches of the Nazis themselves. One of the departments of the Reich Security Main Office, established after the war began in 1939, was mandated to "explore the public frame of mind," and employed a network of confidential agents in every walk of life "to build up a general picture, so that a mosaic of impressions becomes a valid survey of the entire Reich." [128] One report drawn up by this organization contained a survey of the reading tastes of the German public taken a little more than a year after the war had broken out. One of its findings was that there had been a rise in the popularity of religious literature as compared with the prewar period. It was also discovered that there was a wide interest in travel books, Russian literature, and crime novels. One might well conclude that the experience of *Volk* community provided by the regime did not give an adequate release from anxiety for the average German, and that he sought distraction from his troubles and solace in the non-Volkish pastimes listed. The whole collection of reports also makes clear that from the very outset of hostilities, the German people had little enthusiasm for the war and that there was a widespread yearning for peace. In addition, "there were early doubts that Germany would win the war, and after the summer of 1942 these doubts grew into certainty." [129] One could well conclude from these findings that the Nazis had failed in their efforts to inculcate hardness, iron determination of will, and abiding irrational devotion to the expansionist goals of German nationalism.

Albert Speer's memoirs contain a similar finding, although the evidence he presents is less direct. He contrasts the spontaneous enthusiasm displayed for Hitler in the early days of the regime, before the indoctrination program had gotten well underway, with the cooler mentality of the war years. As an example of the first, Speer decribes a Hitler motorcade from Weimar to Nuremberg one autumn day in 1934. The progress was extremely slow, due to the pressure of well-wishers all along the way who crowded in to smile and cheer and demand autographs of the Führer. Shortly thereafter, Hitler decided it was more economical of his time to travel by railroad. The cause of all the adulation in these days appeared to have little to do with true belief in German Volkdom or inculcated discipline and everything to do with success and a generalized sense of well-being.

> This enormous popularity was only too easy to understand. The public credited Hitler and no one else with the achievements in economics and

128 Felix Kersten, *The Kersten Memoirs, 1940–45*, C. Fitzgibbon and J. Oliver, trans. (New York: The Macmillan Co., 1957), p. 213.
129 Arthur L. Smith, Jr., "Life in Wartime Germany: Colonel Ohlendorf's Opinion Service," *Public Opinion Quarterly*, 36(1), Spring 1972: 6, 7.

foreign policy of the period. They more and more regarded him as the leader who had made a reality of their deeply rooted longing for a powerful, proud, united Germany. Very few were mistrustful at this time. And those who occasionally felt doubts rising reassured themselves with thoughts of the regime's accomplishments and the esteem it enjoyed even in critical foreign countries.[130]

Later in his book Speer describes the deterioration of morale during the war years. A decline was noticeable at the very outset, in 1939, when it was necessary "to organize cheering crowds where two years earlier Hitler had been able to count on spontaneity."[131] He writes of Hitler's preoccupation with security measures growing out of a fear that popular discontent might lead to uprisings. He also describes Hitler's reluctance, for fear of adverse public reaction, to enact an austerity program in order to conserve resources for the war effort. "It remains one of the oddities of this war that Hitler demanded far less from his people than Churchill and Roosevelt did from their respective nations. The discrepancy between the total mobilization of labor forces in democratic England and the casual treatment of this question in authoritarian Germany is proof of the regime's anxiety not to risk any shift in the popular mood. The German leaders were not disposed to make sacrifices themselves or to ask sacrifices of the people."[132] This is tantamount to a confession by the leadership that all the indoctrination in "hardness" and military stoicism was an utter failure. It was the liberal democratic leaders who could expect and receive support for a program of "blood, sweat, and tears," not the totalitarian "Führer."[133]

The solidary racial community, a "nationalized" *Volk*, a conception of purpose at the heart of the public doctrine, also never became a moral or psychological reality. Speer writes of the increasing compartmentalization of life within the comprehensively organized Nazi society, "the way people were immured in isolated, closed-off areas of life. . . . The disparity between this and the *Volksgemeinschaft* proclaimed in 1933 always astonished" him, he reports. What actually developed was a "society of totally isolated individuals."[134]

Another mark of the failure of the Nazi program of ideological remolding is found in Hitler's reluctance to mount an all-out attack on the Christian churches in Germany. As the years of the Third Reich wore on, there was increasing pressure from the second echelon of the Nazi elite for a complete break with traditional Christianity and an outright de-

---

[130] Speer, *op. cit.*, p. 105.
[131] *Ibid.*, p. 218.
[132] *Ibid.*, pp. 287, 336.
[133] *Ibid.*
[134] *Ibid.*, p. 65.

nunciation of the old religion. Hitler's secretary, Martin Bormann, wrote in a secret instruction to all Gauleiters in July 1941:

> The consequences of the irreconcilability between National Socialist and Christian views is that we must refuse to strengthen existing Christian denominations or to sponsor new ones. . . . More and more the people must be wrested from the churches and their ministers.[135]

Hitler, however, feared an open break and temporized about the matter to the end.

4. The Roots and Origins of German National Socialism

Although the ultimate ideological objectives of the Nazis were never achieved, we still have to explain why Nazism emerged at all in German political life and how it mustered the power that it did. How did a regime which was to bring about a Second World War and the virtual extermination of a people get installed and remain in power for a dozen years? Historians, psychologists, and political scientists have attempted to answer these questions with a variety of scholarly methods.

Ideological Precursors.   Recent historical scholarship has argued that the ideas and attitudes that were to become Nazi political culture were long present in German society and had become familiar ideological currency long before they were put together in the ultimate Nazi form in which they became an official political program. "Their ideas were eminently respectable in Germany after the First World War, and indeed had been current among large segments of the population even before the war," writes George Mosse.[136] Some of them can, indeed, be traced as popular ideas well back into the nineteenth century. These include racial thought, Pan-Germanism, the idea of a Germanic Christianity, Volkish nature mysticism, anti-Semitism, and even the Führer principle.
    Three nineteenth-century writers in particular display the form of the emerging Germanic or Volkish ideology and its relationship both to traditional and to Liberal political culture. These were Paul de Lagarde, Julius Langbehn, and Arthur Moeller van den Bruck. Fritz Stern entitles a study of the three men *The Politics of Cultural Despair*, for he sees their writings as a pathological reaction to a situation of acute cultural and social strain produced by the special historical experience of Germans during the nineteenth century, an experience we shall describe later in

---

[135] In Remak, *op. cit.*, p. 104.
[136] Mosse, *The Crisis of German Ideology*, p. 1.

this chapter. "Unable to endure the ills which they diagnosed and which they had experienced in their own lives, they so got to become prophets who would point the way to a national rebirth. Hence, they propounded all manner of reforms, ruthless and idealistic, nationalistic and utopian. It was this leap from despair to utopia across all existing reality that gave their thoughts its fantastic quality." [137] All three were acclaimed by the Nazis as spiritual forebears.

In each of the writer's lives personal strains combined with the general cultural disarray which they came to express and prescribe for in their work. All three writers experienced tragically unhappy boyhoods, which were reflected in the rest of their restless, neurotic, lonely lives. Lagarde's mother died at his birth, and he grew up hated by his father as the cause of this misfortune. Langbehn was the son of an impoverished and disappointed scholar who had been forced for political reasons to leave his native Schleswig, in 1851, when it was under Danish rule, but who received no recompense for his patriotism from German Holstein where he took refuge. Moeller was a rebellious youth, dismissed in adolescent years from his Gymnasium, rejected by his family, and a "draft dodger" who fled abroad to escape military duty.

It is interesting to note that the early lives of some of the top Nazi leadership revealed very similar patterns of unhappy family experiences, disappointment, frustration, and failure. Adolf Hitler was born in the provincial Austrian town of Braunau am Inn in 1889, the son of a minor customs official, who was barely able to scrape out a life style conforming to the norms of contemporary respectability. The pattern of parental influence involved a fundamental contradiction between the petty tyrannies of a martinet father and the overindulgence of a sentimental mother. The father died when Hitler was thirteen.

Disappointment and frustration Hitler experienced early and often. Most acute was his disappointment in being refused admission to the Vienna Academy of Fine Arts. He went nevertheless to the Capital in 1908 at the age of nineteen, where he led a Bohemian life, supporting himself by painting watercolors and by performing odd jobs. He was a failure and a social outcast.

The early life of Paul Joseph Goebbels evinces a similar pattern of failure and thwarted ambition. Born in 1897 in Rheydt, a Rhenish factory town, he was the son of a factory foreman of modest means. Because of a deformed foot he was rejected for military service and spent the war years pursuing a higher education. Considerable intellectual capacity won him scholarships at a number of schools, and in 1921

[137] Fritz Stern, *The Politics of Cultural Despair* (Berkeley: University of California Press, 1963), p. xi. Copyright 1961 by the Regents of the University of California. With permission.

he obtained a Ph.D. from the University of Heidelberg. Afterward, however, he could not find the niche in society that he desired. He wanted to be a writer, but his novels and plays were invariably rejected and returned to him by the publishing firms to which he sent them for appraisal.

Rejected by his family for his apostasy from Catholicism, Goebbels experienced a sense of total loss and alienation. The collapse of his private world took place, as with Hitler, in the context of public collapse following upon a lost war, revolution, and economic depression. The depth of Geobbels' alienation is graphically marked in diary entries of 1925 and 1926. "I have learned to despise the human being from the bottom of my soul. He makes me sick in my stomach. Phooey!" "Much dirt and many intrigues. The human being is a canaille." The converse of this is Goebbels' availability for ideological politics. A diary of 1926 bears the entry: "Weimar. Hitler spoke. About politics, the Idea, the organization. Deep and mystical. Almost like a gospel. One shudders as one skirts the abyss of life with him. I thank Fate which gave us this man." [138]

Most successful of the three nineteenth-century formulators of the German ideology, in terms of position and public recognition in his lifetime, was Paul de Lagarde, a Scripture scholar at the University of Göttingen. Having lost his faith in traditional Christianity early, he devoted much of his professional life to cultural criticism and to an effort to fashion a new semi-secular Germanic religion. Langbehn lived the life of a literary wanderer and recluse, supporting himself precariously with his pen, which like Lagarde's was devoted to criticism of contemporary German culture. Moeller similarly led the life of a wandering publicist, whose writings up to the First World War were in the area of cultural criticism, but which during the war took a political direction.

Difficult as it was for each of these men to relate well to his contemporaries in his personal relationships, all three of them achieved large notoriety for their writings, either during their lifetimes or soon afterward. Lagarde's work, strangely enough, appealed both to the leaders of Germany's cultural elites and to disestablished and disreputable political groups as well. There was both a "soft" and a "hard" side to Lagarde, and in this he foreshadowed Hitler's ability to garner both established and nonestablished political forces into his coalition. On the "hard" side Lagarde became the patron saint of the anti-Semitic Volkish movement. He also was hailed by various groups within the Protestant churches that were seeking to Germanize Christianity, groups

[138] Louis P. Lochner, ed. and trans., *The Goebbels Diaries* (New York: Eagle Books, 1948), pp. 17, 16.

which in the early 1930s gave their support to the Nazis. The Pan-German League espoused his ideas of a continental imperialism and an aggressive Eastern policy. And after the revolution of 1918 his name was invoked "by all those Germans on the right who hated the republic but had no desire to go back to what they remembered as the bad old days before 1914." [139] Langbehn's principal work, *Rembrandt als Erzieher,* became a literary fad in the year of its publication (1890). In two years' time more than forty printings were struck. After 1893 interest in the book declined, but it remained on the market and sales again soared during the 1920s. By 1945 the book had sold at least 150,000 copies, and had been brought out by four different publishers. The same anti-Semitic and German nationalist groups to whom Lagarde had appealed were also attracted by Langbehn. Like Lagarde, "he was one of the bridges between the rabble-rousing nationalists and anti-Semites and the highly respectable, culturally discontented, politically dis-interested groups in German life." [140] Moeller's principal influence, which dates from the years of collapse after 1918, was evident among mal-contents of all sorts, but especially among the urban middle classes and unemployed former army officers organized in a number of anti-party and anti-parliamentary groups. Moeller's best known political work, *Das Dritte Reich* was published in 1923, and ultimately provided the Nazis with a name for their revolutionary regime.[141]

Despite manifest traditional elements in the Germanic ideology, and despite the fact that it appealed to Conservative groups in German society, the doctrine put forward by Lagarde, Langbehn, and Moeller was eminently modern in its salient ideas. It was, indeed, antipathy to Liberal democratic culture that provoked the Germanic ideologists to thought. And in attacking Manchesterism and Rousseau they intended to assault the foundations of modernity. But the terms in which they mounted the attack were themselves modern ones. "Their animus blinded them to the fact that their best ideas on men, on nature, and education, on anti-urbanism, and antiparliamentarianism, were but distorted and intemperate adaptations of Rousseau's thought." [142] "Lagarde, Langbehn, and Moeller had no commitment to the past nor were they defending existing social privileges." [143]

The common point of departure for Lagarde, Langbehn, and Moeller van den Bruck was a common experience of cultural strain. Germany in the nineteenth century had lost her soul, her meaning in the world, they thought. Religion had become a lifeless and platitudinous

---

[139] Stern, *op. cit.,* pp. 84, 90, 92, 93.
[140] *Ibid.,* pp. 155, 168, 170.
[141] *Ibid.,* pp. 224, 253.
[142] *Ibid.,* p. 51 n.
[143] *Ibid.,* p. 268.

affair, and Germans had become a collection of isolated individuals contending with one another for material gain and lacking in all spirituality
and a sense of higher values. Self-seeking was the order of the day, and
the result was conflict and dissension. What Germans needed above all
was a new spiritual and cultural life, a new faith, and a new sense of
community. And this had to be achieved on a national basis. A new
national religion was imperative. "Not freedom but communal bonds"
with a spiritual content was the crucial need.[144]

All three writers attacked Liberalism as the cause of the trouble.
With its economic individualism they associated a rationalist and secular
view of the world which was cold, humdrum, and routine, lacking in
creative imagination and vitality. The embodiment of its spirit was for
them the burgeoning commercial and industrial center of the nineteenth-
century city with its scientific technology. The middle classes that dominated the life of the city "had become 'rootless,' alienated from folk and
nature, had lost its *Volksthümlichkeit* and childlike nature (*Kindlichkeit*)
and thus had forfeited the prerequisites of manhood and greatness." [145]
Their culture was one of mediocrity: "Liberalism has not the slightest
trait in common with freedom," wrote Moeller. "Its freedom is only the
freedom of the individual to become average humanity." In their hu-
manitarianism and charity Liberals preserved such an average humanity,
which was not worth the saving.[146] Leaderless democracy in the form
of a multiparty parliamentary regime within a purely pragmatic power
state (the Wilhelmine Empire) was seen as Liberalism's specific political
form.

All three were also anti-Semites who saw the Jews as the chief
embodiment of the Liberal ethos. Lagarde said they were "the carriers
of decay and pollute every national culture, they exploit the human and
material resources of their hosts, they destroy all faith and spread materialism and liberalism." [147] "The modern Jew has no religion, no character, no home, no children," wrote Langbehn. "The aspiration of
present-day Jews for spiritual and material domination evokes a simple
phrase: Germany for the Germans." He especially hated Jews who had
become assimilated and called for their extermination. "They are a
poison for us and must be treated as such. . . . They are democratically
inclined: they have an affinity for the mob; everywhere they sympathize
with decadence." [148]

What did the authors of the Germanic ideology intend to substitute for the complex world of urban commerce? Like Rousseau, they

---

144 Hugo von Hofmannsthal, quoted in *ibid.*, p. xv.
145 *Ibid.*, p. 130.
146 *Ibid.*, p. 198.
147 *Ibid.*, p. 61.
148 *Ibid.*, p. 141.

extolled the simpler life of earlier times and one which emphasized will over reason and art over science. The return to simplicity would be a kind of return to childhood, and the virtues of simplicity were identified with those of the child. "Simplicity is the panacea for the evils of the present," wrote Langbehn. In his new Germany "the talents and joys of the child would be preserved in the adult; even now the 'genuine and pure' Germans had retained more of the childlike in their nature than had other peoples." [149]

We are reminded of Rousseau's simple and idyllic peasants gathered beneath an oak tree. But the authors of the Germanic ideology are selective in their use of Rousseau. Their simple peasantry are not themselves capable of conducting the public business, but, like very children, must be led. "And perhaps some day there will come a big child, that 'hidden emperor' who will revenge" all the miseducated children of today, wrote Langbehn.[150] Such a leader would do away with the anarchy of political parties and the chaos of parliamentary government. "Toward the end of his life, more and more insistently [Lagarde] called for a Führer who would so completely represent the people that in him they would be united and his command would be their will." [151]

The Führer to come, as the Germanic ideologists conceived him, would be a great artist-hero. He would fire the imagination and mold the will of his people; he would lead them to great deeds. It was not his task to educate their reason. "The core of man is not his reason, but his will," wrote Lagarde. "For like everything that is good, knowledge also enters through the will, whose wings are sensibility and imagination, and whose driving force is love." [152] The Germanic reformers would "destroy the supremacy of reason and establish a vital, populistic, primitivistic society." [153] Here was the other side of the Rousseauistic coin— the "Legislator" figure of the *Social Contract* who, from his genius, imaginatively creates a world of meaning and value for his people and leads them in romantic achievement.

The Germanic ideologists criticized Liberal individualism that manifested itself in economic activity. But they also criticized Liberal society for a lack of individuality of another kind. "Everything depends on the human being, and Germany lacks nothing so much as men; there is nothing toward which Germany . . . directs so much hostility as toward the individual, who alone can bring it life and honor," wrote Lagarde.[154]

The idea of equality he called a fraudulent myth. The recognition

[149] *Ibid.*, p. 129.
[150] *Ibid.*, p. 127.
[151] *Ibid.*, p. 58.
[152] *Ibid.*, p. 28.
[153] *Ibid.*, p. 179.
[154] *Ibid.*, p. 33.

of inequality was a psychological necessity. For "man's greatest joy is to revere other men. . . . To recognize other men above themselves."[155] The charismatic leader was an individual par excellence, using the force of his elemental and primitive strength of will to break out of all existing patterns. "The new individualism was a plea for the natural man, for the psychological and biological self that was to be delivered from the shackles of society and conventions."[156] Not every man, but the great individual of superior will and imagination needed to be liberated; he then could lead the *Volk* to its destiny. "An attempt is made," wrote Langbehn, "not to measure a man by his age—but an age, today's present —by a man."[157] It would be the work of this "hidden emperor" to draw material from the historic life of the people and mold it into a new living faith, "a new national religion that would somehow spring from the still uncorrupted German Volk, from the untutored classes."[158]

The work of national reconstruction was not conceived by the authors of the Germanic ideology as a quiet and peaceful affair. Imperialism was central to Langbehn's thought. The maxim that "the best shall rule applies to people too," he wrote, "and that is why the Germans have a calling to world domination."[159] "In the European state system she either dominates or is dominated. A third possibility does not exist. As long as she is unified she will dominate."[160] The basic justification of such an imperialism was to be culture, not the declining culture of his time, but the new one that the "hidden emperor" would make flourish from the uncorrupted resources of the simple people of Germany. We find him preaching the "spiritual annexation" of the Netherlands and Denmark, for their own sake, "so that they will not dullen because of the narrowness of their horizons."[161] Moeller also sounded the imperial theme in loud tones, tying it in with racialism: "Race is almost a metaphysical concept, but on a physiological basis. . . . Race is a power. Whoever feels that power in him, possesses it and exercises it." And he saw it as Germany's destiny "to represent Europe in the racial and world-continental conflicts of the future, to become synonymous with Europe." The road to such dominance might well have to be through war. "Does one want to make a pestilent heap out of humanity?" asked Moeller. "War has always been the national expression of the struggle for survival."[162] Lagarde, too, had written

[155] *Ibid.*, p. 29.
[156] *Ibid.*, p. 170.
[157] *Ibid.*, p. 118.
[158] *Ibid.*, pp. 35–36.
[159] *Ibid.*, p. 150.
[160] *Ibid.*, pp. 150–51.
[161] *Ibid.*, p. 151.
[162] *Ibid.*, p. 201.

many years earlier of the need of the young for an idealistic war, different from the cold pragmatism through which Bismarck had built the Second Reich. "They want to fight a war for a concrete ideal, they want danger, risk, sacrifice, and death." [163]

Surely it would be an exaggeration to say that the writings of Lagarde, Langbehn, and Moeller, despite their wide dissemination and popularity, were the cause, or even a chief cause of the popularity and familiarity of the Volkish ideology. We have described the ideas of these men at length mainly for the purpose of showing how extraordinarily complete an articulation of the leading ideas of National Socialism there had been during the century prior to the emergence of Nazism itself. We also have pointed out an aspect of nineteenth-century German society—a condition of cultural despair—out of which the Germanic ideology emerged. We shall say more about this shortly.

George Mosse, in a study of Nazi origins that parallels the work of Fritz Stern, describes, along with Stern's three major prophets, a host of minor novelists, poets, and academicians (many of them minor figures of the German Romantic movement) whose pens poured out a similar ideological fare from early in the nineteenth century. Mosse also describes a large number of movements and organizations which, between 1873 and 1918, were the carriers and systematic disseminators to their membership of the ideas and attitudes we have been describing. These included gymnastic groups, groups in the educational establishment, especially high school teachers and college fraternities, a boarding school movement, the Wandervögel (a youth movement), Pan-German cultural and political movements, and various paramilitary and veterans' organizations. Long before there was a National Socialism its component elements had been elaborately articulated, institutionalized, and inculcated in important segments of the public. The Nazi movement was simply the culmination of a long historical development.

The Problem of National Unity. What produced the condition of cultural despair that gave rise to Volkish ideas? One important factor was the way in which German unification was accomplished. When the Congress of Vienna produced a loose German confederation instead of a united German state, the German intelligentsia who wanted unity sought it in the surrogate form of cultural unity. This meant a self-conscious search for national roots and the hunting out of foreign influences one could oppose. When the effort at union under Liberal auspices proved abortive in 1848, the longing for cultural unity was intensified. Given the fact of marked regional differences in life style, the question of what the pivot or focus of cultural unity might be was

[163] *Ibid.*, p. 33.

a problematic matter. Hence the search for unity in distant times, the pre-Christian Germanic past, which could be mythologized in a consensual form. When political unity finally came as a product of Bismarck's *Realpolitik*, the psychological or moral dimension of union—a genuine and widespread feeling of brotherhood—was lacking. Cultural unity, which was needed to give moral élan to the new policy, remained to be won. The elites of the Wilhelmine Reich seemed to the intelligentsia more interested in making money than in cultural nation-building. The form of unity was there, but somehow the substance, in terms of feelings of togetherness, remained far off. Indeed, the very industrialization that was proceeding rapidly at the time of unification seemed to be destroying those vestiges of old German culture which seemed to be the natural raw material of cultural unity.

But we have dealt only with the problem of the intelligentsia. What about the average man? To a certain extent the cultural malaise filtered down to him in simplified form. What is more, the fact that he had to adjust his allegiances from a parochial to an imperial sovereignty also provided a source of stress.

Most significant of all were the social and economic strains attendant upon the industrialization that was in process during the period of unification. Beginning in 1873, Germany experienced a series of grave economic crises. The class structure was also in flux as a new bourgeoisie and proletariat grew up in burgeoning urban centers and the middle classes of the small cities declined. The drive for a more intense Germanic faith and a more "genuine" unity seemed to many a panacea for the problems resulting from economic growth and change. "In the end they called for a 'German revolution' to liquidate the dangerous new developments and to guide the nation back to its original purpose as they conceived it." [164] The Volkish ideology of hyper-nationalism and anti-Semitism thus can be understood as a national reaction to the social and cultural strains of political and economic modernization. The trauma of a lost world war and the economic disasters of the 1920s were simply the last occasions of strain in a mounting series. In this view of German history, Nazism represents a flight into a fantasy world to escape an unpleasant reality.

Oedipus.   Erik Erikson, the Harvard psychologist, echoes the historian's analysis. "Advancing civilization," he writes, "is potentially endangered by its own advance, in that it splits ancient conscience, endangers incomplete identities, and releases destructive forces which now can count on the cold efficiency of the super-manager." [165] In his exploration of this theme Erikson substitutes the analytical concepts of

---

[164] Mosse, *The Crisis of German Ideology*, p. 4.
[165] Erikson, *op. cit.*, p. 285.

Freudian clinical psychiatry for the common-sense social psychology of the historian.

Erikson's analysis of Nazism uses as its point of departure a psychiatric interpretation of the imagery Hitler employs in the first chapter of *Mein Kampf*. His basic thesis is that Hitler identified his personal "oedipal" situation with the national problems of the German people, and that the response which his personality elicited from Germans derived from the fact that his oedipal complex, though exaggerated, was nevertheless a typically German phenomenon. The personal-political identification Erikson finds illustrated in such passages as the one in which Hitler complained that the "beloved mother . . . the *young* Reich," through her "tragic alliance with the *old Austrian sham state* . . . herself sanctioned the slow extermination of the German nationality." [166] His own mother was twenty-three years his father's junior, and she was a woman who continued to respect and support the drunkard husband who beat her. As to the typicality of Hitler's personality, Erikson writes that "on the stage of German History [he] sensed to what extent it was safe to let his own personality represent with hysterical abandon what was alive in every German listener and reader." [167]

On what ground can Erikson assert that Hitler's oedipal situation was typical for German sons as a whole? He presents no empirical data to support the claim and in fact even says that "obviously, not all Germans had fathers of the kind Hitler had." Nor does he argue that the average German son of the early twentieth century was a clinical case. "The question . . . is," he writes, "whether the German father's position in his family made him act—either all of the time, or enough of the time, or at memorable times—in such a way that he created in his son an *inner* image which had some correspondence to that of the older Hitler's public image." [168] This suggests that there was just *enough* in common between the behavior of the older Hitler and that of the typical German father to make Hitler's story of his boyhood appealing and persuasive to "masses of Reichs-Germans." [169]

Father-Son Relations.   Erikson follows this with an "impressionistic version of what [he] consider[s] one pattern of German fatherhood." [170] He paints a situation of paternal oppression and of dutiful maternal compliance to the father's demands which eventuates in "that severe German *Pubertaet* which is such a strange mixture of open rebellion and 'secret sin,' cynical delinquency and submissive obedience, romanticism

[166] Quoted in *ibid.*, p. 286.
[167] *Ibid.*, p. 288.
[168] *Ibid.*, pp. 288–89.
[169] *Ibid.*, p. 288.
[170] *Ibid.*, p. 289.

and despondency, and which is apt to break the boy's spirit, once and for all." [171] Traditionally, German boys at the age of adolescence would engage in a period of "wandering," which allowed escape from paternal tyranny in the form of an apprenticeship in some distant place or a romantic vagabondage. This usually was followed by a return to the home town and acceptance of the routine responsibilities of family life. Reality "would finally make a *Buerger* out of the boy—a 'mere citizen' with an eternal sense of sin for having sacrificed genius for Mammon and for a mere wife and mere children such as anyone can have." [172] The total pattern exemplified a "regular split between precocious individualistic rebellion and disillusioned, obedient citizenship." [173] Here, clearly, is a pattern of political immaturity quite different from the happy balance of citizen and subject roles which Almond and Verba describe as the "civic culture" which provides the psychological foundation of working democracy.

Erikson derives the family role of the German father from prior psychological, political, and social facts. The psychological fact is the German father's "essential lack of true inner authority," which Erikson traces back to the absence of an "integrating cause" in German life. Germany historically had been a collection of disparate regions, each with its characteristic culture and characteristic manner. But this "did not assume an integrated meaning on a national scale as the imagery of the Reich became dominant and industrialization undermined the previous social stratification." [174] Here we have another echo of the historian's analysis. On top of this, Germany did not, like the other nations of the West, experience a deep-seated democratic revolution which, as a taking over of aristocratic privilege by the middle and working classes, also involved a fusion of aristocratic with democratic ideals. The new political culture in these other areas was embodied primarily in the concept of "the 'free man'—a concept which assumes inalienable rights, indispensable self-denial, and unceasing revolutionary watchfulness." [175] By contrast, the German father "came to represent the habits and the ethic of the German top sergeant and petty official who . . .would never be more but was in constant danger of becoming less; and who had sold the birthright of a free man for an official title or a life pension." [176] In short, fathers with weak and uncertain identities, as a result of their family role, beget sons with similar identity problems—problems which result in undemocratic and, indeed, destructive politics.

[171] *Ibid.*, p. 290.
[172] *Ibid.*, p. 293.
[173] *Ibid.*
[174] *Ibid.*, p. 291.
[175] *Ibid.*
[176] *Ibid.*

Erikson describes Nazism, the destructive phase of evolving German politics, as the political embodiment of the romantic, utopian irresponsible adolescent mentality with which Germans had come to identify freedom and happiness. In this state of mind "the world is experienced either as vastly superior in age and wisdom, the goal of eternal longing and *Wanderlust;* or as a mean, treacherous, encircling encampment of enemies living for one aim—namely, the betrayal of Germany; or as a mysterious *Lebensraum* to be won by Teutonic courage and to be used for a thousand years of adolescent aggrandizement." [177] (All of these perceptions reflect the ambivalent mother-images of the oedipal son.) As the "Führer" of his immature people, Hitler became the chief and "unbroken adolescent who had chosen a career apart from civilian happiness, mercantile tranquillity, and spiritual peace; a gang leader who kept the boys together by demanding their admiration, by creating terror, and by shrewdly involving them in crimes from which there was no way back." [178]

Erikson's explanation is attractive for its comprehensiveness and simplicity. With it one immediately "understands" Nazism. But its problems are, of course, manifest. For one thing, it rests on what he himself describes as "an *impressionistic* version of . . . one pattern of German fatherhood" (my italics), for which the author presents no empirical evidence at all, of either a qualitative or a quantitative sort. It is an impression only—albeit a brilliant impression.

A "Mass Man" Explanation.   Another interesting effort to explain Nazism is Hannah Arendt's application of the "mass man" thesis to the phenomenon. The "mass man" theory has been set forth by numerous authors to explain various problems of modern society, and there is, in fact, an entire "mass society" literature.[179]

The central notion of the "mass society" thesis is that industrialization, in uprooting people from small-city and rural environments and moving them into large urban centers, destroys an entire complex of social relationships which give life meaning and does not replace them with anything else. The new men in the cities constitute what David Riesman has called a "lonely crowd." [180] They are anomic—that is, having lost the old values which were carried in the institutions and way of life they have abandoned, they now find themselves with nothing

---

[177] *Ibid.*, p. 298.

[178] *Ibid.*, p. 295.

[179] See, e.g., William Kornhauser, *The Politics of Mass Society* (Glencoe: The Free Press, 1959). Daniel Bell's *End of Ideology*, it will be recalled, is in part a refutation of applications of the "mass man" idea to American society.

[180] David Riesman, *The Lonely Crowd: A Survey of the Changing American Character* (New Haven: Yale University Press, 1951).

to believe in, nothing to give life significance and importance. They drift about in a moral vacuum, without identity or purpose. They also experience an intense loneliness amidst the impersonality of their new surroundings. It is from such people as these, Arendt argues, that large numbers of Germans were recruited for Nazism, which, as a strong and emotional ideology, gave them something to believe in once more and a cause to work for. In the organizations of the Party they also found community, "togetherness" with like-minded souls, and in Adolf Hitler as the "Führer" a new authority figure to replace those that had been lost with their loss of tradition. We are dealing here with another instance of what Geertz calls "cultural strain" and the method Germans chose to overcome it.

Arendt argues that the "mass men" who became Nazis were not capable of being integrated into the democratic parties and pressure groups that formed the political basis of the Weimar Republic, because they were indifferent to the group interest appeals of those organizations. Masses, she writes, are "people who either because of sheer numbers or indifference or a combination of both cannot be integrated into any organization based on common interest." The Nazis "recruited their members from the mass of apparently indifferent people whom all other parties had given up as too apathetic or too stupid for their attention. The . . . majority of their membership consisted of people who had never before appeared on the political scene." Democracy, she concludes, works "only where the citizens belong to and are represented by groups or form a social and political hierarchy." "Masses grow out of the fragments of a highly atomized society whose competitive structures and concomitant loneliness of the individual had been held in check only through membership in a class." [181]

There is no doubt that many Nazi activists fit the picture of the declassé, nonparticipant "mass man" whom Arendt describes. We have empirical evidence that this is so. Arendt, however, overgeneralized her argument. She writes, for example, that totalitarian movements like Nazism demonstrate that "The politically neutral and indifferent masses could easily be the majority in a democratically ruled country." [182] Yet we have no evidence that the Nazis ever did constitute a majority in Germany, or that the bulk of the people who were either Party members or supported the Nazi Party with their franchise during the period of free elections were "mass men." She also argues that the electorate of the various parties went over wholesale to Nazism, which is simply not true: "The fall of protecting class walls transformed the slumbering

181 Hannah Arendt, *The Origins of Totalitarianism* (Cleveland: The World Publishing Company, 1958), pp. 311, 312, 317.
182 *Ibid.*, p. 312.

majorities behind all parties into one great unorganized, structureless mass of furious individuals who had nothing in common except their vague apprehension that the hopes of party members were doomed."[183]

There is also a question about the adequacy of Arendt's interpretation of the motivation of the German Nazi. She describes it wholly in terms of compensating for "cultural strain." Thus, for example, she takes at face value Heinrich Himmler's announcement that his SS men and the strata from which they were recruited were interested only "in ideological questions of importance for decades and centuries." Frequently she cites the writings of Hitler or other of the Nazi leaders to prove a point about the conceptual notions and motivation of the average Nazi or of Germans in general during the Nazi period.

Sociology and Survey Research. A more empirical approach to the explanation of Nazism is found in the work of the political sociologist Seymour Lipset. Using statistics of the last free elections in Germany, he attempts to disprove the interpretation of Nazism as a product of anomie and the general rootlessness of man in modern industrial society; instead, he puts forth an interpretation which appears to rest on what Geertz has called the "interest theory" of ideology. Using statistics for the 1928 and 1932 elections, Lipset shows that the Nazis gained ground not from all the parties indiscriminately, as Arendt says, but disproportionately from the Center and Liberal parties. Also, he found that it was not the areas dominated by the old Conservatives which initially supported Hitler, but those in which the middle classes prevailed. His conclusion is that Fascism appeals to the same strata as Liberalism, a mark of its peculiarly modern character whose significance we shall ponder at greater length later. In Schleswig, for example, Lipset's figures show that it was not the rural nobility or the rural proletariat but the small farm proprietors and the petit-bourgeoisie of the small cities which voted Nazi. These groups were not the declassé urban "masses" about whom Arendt writes, but established classes, in their original situation, who were undergoing severe economic pressure in a time of inflationary change. "The larger the city, the smaller the Nazi vote," Lipset writes. The federalist and regional autonomy parties which went over to the Nazis "gave voice to the objections felt by the rural and urban classes of provincial areas to the increasing bureaucratization of modern industrial society and sought to turn the clock back by decentralization of government authority." These "states' rightists" were attracted by the Nazis' ideological antagonism to "the 'big' forces of industrial society."[184] Lipset describes the ideal-typical Nazi voter in 1932 as "a middle-class

[183] *Ibid.*, p. 315.
[184] Seymour M. Lipset, *Political Man, The Social Bases of Politics* (Garden City, N.Y.: Doubleday & Co., Inc., 1960), pp. 140–49.

self-employed Protestant who lived either on a farm or in a small community and who had previously voted for a centrist or regional political party strongly opposed to the power and influence of big businessmen and big labor." [185] This reminds us of some of the analyses of support for American Conservatism, or, more especially, the American Radical Right.

Lipset does note that a good deal of support was indeed forthcoming for the Nazis from the ranks of the formerly apathetic and outcast, after 1930 and especially after Hitler became Chancellor in 1932. Arendt's "mass men" indeed did play a role in the story. But this was only one role, and a later one, and therefore not the entire explanation.

Philip Converse, of the University of Michigan Survey Research Center, argues that different explanations are needed for the behavior of the Nazi elite and the Nazi masses. In analyzing election returns for an explanation of the latter, what strikes Converse is the role played in the development of Nazi popular support by new young voters, former nonvoters, and the peasantry. All these groups, Converse notes, were peculiarly ill-informed about the Nazi *Weltanschauung* and he believes that their motivation was not ideological but economic (again, the "interest theory"). They believed the promises of the Nazis that they would declare a moratorium on debts. Converse goes so far as to say that if they had had political sense, the Communists as well as the Nazis could have reaped a harvest of votes in the country.[186]

A Synthesis.   An explanation which combines elements of the "interest," "cultural strain," and "social strain" theories, and which is therefore more comprehensive than any of those we have examined so far, is presented by Erich Fromm in *Escape from Freedom*. Unfortunately, this tends, like the work of Erikson and Arendt, to be a grand impression rather than an empirically grounded study like Lipset's and Converse's. It is nevertheless significant as a kind of synthesis of the findings of all these writers.

Fromm tells us that Nazism was peculiarly attractive to "the lower strata of the middle classes, composed of small shopkeepers, artisans and white-collar workers," the very groups among whom Lipset found marked early electoral support for Hitler's movement.[187] He then describes the specific characteristics of the petit-bourgeois as love of strength, hatred of weakness, pettiness, asceticism, and suspicion of

---

185 *Ibid.*, p. 149.
186 Philip Converse, "The Nature of Belief Systems in Mass Publics," in David Apter, ed. *Ideology and Discontent* (New York: The Free Press of Glencoe, 1964), pp. 253–54.
187 Erich Fromm, *Escape from Freedom* (New York: Farrar & Rinehart, 1941), p. 211.

strangers—all traits that go with a life based on the principle of scarcity. Always present, Fromm finds that these traits were intensified by the experience of World War I. Before this time, despite their declining economic position, the small businessman and the artisan had the monarchy, an authoritative church, and a stable family situation to lean on. That is, he lived still in a stable social and cultural system, which compensated for economic deprivation to a degree. Submission to existing traditional authorities satisfied his masochistic proclivities without producing an extreme of self-surrender. But the war destroyed the monarchy, and the depressions of 1923–24 and the one following 1929 destroyed his savings, which threatened in a very radical way his economic position. His prestige was threatened by the enhanced status of the urban worker. The old family authority structure, earlier so firm, had been threatened by the disruptions of the war. The combined package of personal frustrations thus generated was easily translated into feelings of national frustration following upon the defeat and the stern terms of the Treaty of Versailles.

Unfortunately, Fromm attempts to document many of his points in this interesting synthetic explanation of the Nazi followership with references to Hitler's self-image in *Mein Kampf,* which can only tell us authoritatively about the Nazi leader, rather than with electoral statistics or with survey data. His explanation is nevertheless an interesting and a cogent one which may some day be validated with more elaborate empirical data.

5. The Condition of German Political Culture Today

Several of the explanations we have just surveyed attribute the advent of Nazism either to what appear to be permanent and deep-rooted characteristics of the German personality or to continuing aspects of modern industrial society. This is true of the analyses by Erikson and Arendt. If these explanations are basically sound, we should find that democracy is today, as it was in the 1930s, in a precarious situation in Germany, especially after the long and systematic effort of the Nazi regime to expunge all liberal democratic norms from the mentality of the population. Yet we are faced with the fact of demonstrated democratic stability on the part of the West German regime since World War II. In contrast to the experience of the First Republic, the number of parties in German political life has declined markedly in the system governed from Bonn. Down to the period of the short-lived coalition, each West German government from 1945 on lived out four years in office, which contrasts sharply with with the kaleidoscope of governmental change during the 1920s. Under

Weimar, there was a total of twenty-one governments in fourteen years, while in a sixteen-year period Bonn saw only five. A partial explanation of the difference is of course found in the different constitutional machinery—e.g., the requirement under the Fundamental Law of a positive vote of no confidence if a government is to be dissolved. But this is certainly not a full and adequate way of accounting for the differences. One scholar actually finds in the policies of the Nazi regime a catalyst of social and economic changes which account for the stable democratic order today in West Germany. Hitler certainly never counted on so ironic an outcome of his work! [188]

Nazism and Democratic Revolution.   Charles Frye, of Bryn Mawr, has pointed out that certain Nazi measures, which were aimed at the mobilization of the German population for the achievement of government goals by destroying the authority of the paternalistic traditional family, eventuated in the democratization of the family structure. Holding a war production job, for example, yielded the German wife greater independence than she had enjoyed before and more of a voice in family affairs. Subjecting children to the authority of party organizations for the purpose of political indoctrination and the mobilization of national energies removed them from a formerly omnipresent parental discipline. Similarly, the encouragement of zealous children to spy on ideologically recalcitrant parents set up a conflict situation which resulted in a more equal balance of power in the family. During the Nazi years the extended family also gave way to the nuclear family as a function of mobilization policies and the war situation.[189]

Frye also underlines an indirect democratic result of the Nazi repudiation of class divisions in favor of "the national unity of the community of followers or the *Volk* and the unquestioned validity of the leader's decisions." This caused the emergence from the lower middle class of a new elite which in some cases replaced the traditional elites and in others came to dominate them. The social revolution thus accomplished was a lasting one. Lewis Edinger has pointed out that "most of the members of the 1956 elite of the German Federal Republic had followed their elite occupations in the Nazi era." [190] In bringing about this revolution the Nazis replaced ascription with achievement norms and encouraged a process of social mobility which outlasted the regime. The German rate of social mobility is now only slightly less than that of the United States. The overall result of these changes demographically

---

[188] Charles E. Frye, "The Third Reich and the Second Republic: National Socialism's Impact Upon German Democracy," *Western Political Quarterly*, 21(4), December 1968: 668–80.
[189] *Ibid.*, p. 673.
[190] *Ibid.*, p. 674.

has been to strengthen the middle class at the expense of both the proletariat and the aristocracy. Frye believes this has resulted in a decline in the number and magnitude of social antagonisms and in the reduction of ideological cleavages based on class differences. Frye also points out that the Nazis fostered industrial and urban growth at the expense of the farmer, even though strong support for their regime originally came from the countryside. An improved communications network, especially the new highway system, and the establishment of centrally controlled party newspapers and radio programs helped integrate the society by diminishing differences between rural and urban life. The Nazis also encouraged flight from the land as manpower problems increased. In addition, the war caused vast movements of people, both voluntary and forced migration, which disrupted traditional ties and traditional regional and particularist patterns of life.

Frye also notes that the experience of Nazism has politicized the German people and, indirectly, made pragmatists of them, as Almond and Verba have pointed out. (He neglects to explore, however, the implications of Almond and Verba's other finding of widespread political passivity among the German public.)

Frye concludes that the net result of the social and economic changes effected by Nazism and by the experience of the Second World War has been to create a society whose basic structure is much more compatible with the effective operation of democracy than was that of the Weimar Republic. These changes have moved Germany from the condition of an industrializing but still transitional order to a fully industrialized state. Today the choice between modernizing or preserving traditional and feudal patterns is no longer there, although many presumed that it was under Weimar. It is in the transitional state such as Weimar that the appeal of totalitarian ideology is greatest, as Frye sees it, because of the stresses and strains caused by the conflict of radically different value patterns with contradictory goals and norms. In such a confusing and stressful world, according to Frye, ideology simplifies the situation to permit coping with it. It curtails the flow of information into the system and the range of possible responses to a problematic world. The need for ideology is greatest when the range of real choice is exceedingly great, as it is when sweeping changes are occurring but no single pattern of organization is as yet dominant—which is precisely the situation that prevailed under Weimar. Although Nazism seemed to point against the rationalization and modernization of society, it actually helped complete that process in Germany, and thereby paved the way for its own demise and supersession by a consensual democratic regime.

Frye's thesis is a pregnant and challenging one, though not without problems. Does it imply that the final phase of German modernization *had* to occur according to a totalitarian pattern? Are the two things causally related, or simply concomitant events? Would West Germany have become democratic had it not been occupied by democratic states after World War II? May this outside influence not be more the cause of German democratic stability than the social changes wrought by the Nazis and the war? Does Frye's thesis imply that totalitarianism is *merely* a temporary aspect of modernization, which necessarily gives way at some point to democracy? We should keep these questions in mind as we continue our story of ideology and political culture in a modernizing world. Frye's thesis about the bases of modern German democracy implies that ingrained psychological patterns (if they exist) can be offset by changed sociological circumstances, as Lipset's and Fromm's analyses also suggest. Frye's study, however, does not deal directly with the question of psychic types. And neither Lipset's nor Fromm's work deals with the present democratic structure of Germany. In the work of Klaus Roghmann, a political sociologist at the University of Rochester, however, we have an attempt, using empirical data, directly to relate psychological to sociological variables in the explanation of ideological patterns.

The Authoritarian Personality Revisited.   In a study of 1966, Roghmann attacks the theories of T. W. Adorno and M. Rokeach, which held that in adult persons there are definite personality and opinion structures which are constant over a long period of time and which explain the largest proportion of the thinking and the behavior of these people.[191] Specifically, Adorno and others have argued that there are people who have "authoritarian personalities," and that when given the opportunity they will act out their personality patterns and become Fascists. This is held to be the cause of German Nazism. The parallel with the kind of argument presented by Erikson is clear.

Roghmann's work takes the form of a secondary analysis of data collected by Professor Eric Waldman, Professor of Political Science and Director of the Institute of German Affairs at Marquette University in the early 1960s. Two surveys were carried out which were designed to measure both residual totalitarian thinking and the degree of absorption of democratic values and attitudes among West Germans since World War II.

Roghmann, in his analysis of Waldman's data, attempted to corre-

[191] See Klaus Roghmann, *Dogmatismus und Autoritarismus: Kritik der Theoretischen Ansätze und Ergebnisse dreier Westdeutscher Untersuchungen* (Meisenheim am Glan: Verlag Anton Hain, 1966); T. W. Adorno et al., *The Authoritarian Personality* (New York: Harper, 1950); M. Rokeach, *Political and Religious Dogmatism; An Alternative to the Authoritarian Personality* (Washington: American Psychological Association, 1956).

late dogmatism and authoritarianism (as measured by scales developed by Adorno and the others) with social class, religion, social mobility, and political affiliation. A major finding of his work was that persons with authoritarian personalities do not, as Adorno holds, tend toward Conservative or Radical Right affiliations in West Germany today.[192] It was in the Social Democratic Party (SPD), a pillar of the democratic regime and the party of Chancellor Willy Brandt, that Roghmann found the largest cluster of persons with "authoritarian personalities." The German Party (DP), a conservative Lower Saxon party, by contrast showed the lowest concentration of such types. In a sample taken of members of the armed forces, those who belonged to the democratic Christian Democratic Union (CDU) showed the highest incidence of authoritarianism, and members of the conservative Free German Party (FDP) the lowest. Thus the majority parties were shown to attract persons of an authoritarian bent while the small minority parties attracted the most liberal persons.

Roghmann's explanatory hypothesis is that authoritarians are conformists. They want to be "where the action is." If democratic institutions (for whatever reason) appear strong and authoritative, they support democracy. If democracy appears weak (again, for whatever reason) they will orient to the charismatic leader. The hypothesis is borne out by an analysis of small-group studies in the West German Army which were a part of the investigation. These showed that in groups with strong and established norms, authoritarian persons conformed to them rather than to a leader. In groups where the norms were weak, they oriented to the leader instead. Tolerant persons always behaved the same, consistently orienting themselves to the norms, and were not influenced by the group structure. The small-group analysis also showed that tolerant persons gravitated to strongly coherent groups and avoided incoherent ones, which were populated solely by dogmatists (though some dogmatists also were found in coherent groups). This suggests that situations of social disorganization and anomie bring dogmatists and authoritarians to the fore, whereas tolerant persons will predominate in public affairs under conditions of social order (coherence). Overall, Roghmann's findings support the thesis that the incidence of authoritarian behavior will vary with the strength of democratic norms and the coherence of society. In a working democracy, authoritarians "go underground," as Lane's discussion of his four "undemocrats" in

---

[192] "Personality" is probably a misnomer here, inasmuch as Roghmann found that dogmatism and intolerance appear to be more a function of education than of anything else. The highest dogmatism values were found among SPD members with only an elementary education. The lowest were found among the highly educated minority of West Germans.

New Haven suggests. They may have authoritarian personalities, but their behavior will be undistinguishable from that of the democrats by whom they are surrounded. They will conform to the democratic structure, which appears strong and well-entrenched to them. By contrast, when society is disordered and democratic processes break down, persons with an authoritarian bent will emerge as political leaders and will in particular attract the support of those in the population with an authoritarian potential. The incidence of Fascist behavior and the popularity of Fascist ideology are shown, therefore, to depend not so much on personality structure as on the configuration of social circumstance. There are Democratic and Fascist "situations" rather than personalities.

The Sinister Configuration.   H. R. Trevor-Roper, an English historian who has written much on German Nazism, has listed five social conditions whose confluence, he believes, tends to engender Fascist behavior. These are: (1) an economic depression (such as the one that wiped out the savings of the German middle classes); (2) national humiliation and nationalist resentment consequent upon a lost war (such as World War I for the Germans); (3) the failure of existing institutions to cope with pressing social demands; (4) the organization of working-class forces to undertake a proletarian revolution; and (5) the presence of unassimilated foreigners which gives rise to racial tensions and the demand for a scapegoat (the role of the German Jews).[193] It seems evident that this complex of circumstances might develop in an established post-industrial democracy as well as in a newly democratic and transitional state. In such a case the democratic order would have nothing to protect it except historical habit, tradition.

Bibliography

ADORNO, THEODOR W. *et al.*, *The Authoritarian Personality.* New York: Harper & Row, 1950.

BULLOCK, ALLAN, *Hitler: A Study in Tyranny*, rev. ed. New York: Harper & Row, 1958.

CASSINELLI, C. W., "Totalitarianism, Ideology and Propaganda," *Journal of Politics*, 22(1), February 1960: 68–95.

GREGOR, A. JAMES, *The Ideology of Fascism: The Rationale of Totalitarianism.* New York: The Free Press, 1969.

HITLER, ADOLF, *Mein Kampf.* New York: Stackpole Sons, 1939.

————, *Hitler's Secret Book*, trans. S. Attanasio. New York: Grove Press, 1961.

[193] H. R. Trevor-Roper, "Rockwell Cannot Be a Hitler," *New York Times Magazine*, November 25, 1962.

HOFFER, ERIC, *The True Believer: Thoughts on the Nature of Mass Movements*. New York: Harper & Row, 1951.

INKELES, ALEX, "The Totalitarian Mystique." In Carl J. Friedrich, Jr., ed., *Totalitarianism*. New York: Grosset & Dunlap, 1954.

JÄCKEL, EBERHARD, *Hitler's Weltanschauung: A Blueprint for Power*, trans. Herbert Arnold. Middletown, Conn.: Wesleyan University Press, 1972.

KORNHAUSER, WILLIAM, *The Politics of Mass Society*. Glencoe, Ill.: The Free Press, 1959.

KRAUSNICK, HELMUT *et al.*, *Anatomy of the SS State*, trans. Richard Barry *et al.* New York: Walker, 1968.

MOSSE, GEORGE L., *The Crisis of German Ideology: Intellectual Origins of the Third Reich*. New York: Grosset & Dunlap, 1964.

——————, ed., *Nazi Culture: Intellectual, Cultural, and Social Life in the Third Reich*. New York: Grosset & Dunlap, 1966.

NOLTE, ERNST, *Three Faces of Fascism: Action Francaise, Italian Fascism, and National Socialism*, trans. L. Vennewitz. New York: Holt, Rinehart & Winston, 1965.

STERN, FRITZ, *The Politics of Cultural Despair: A Study in the Rise of the Germanic Ideology*. Berkeley: University of California Press, 1961.

VIERECK, PETER, *Metapolitics: From the Romantics to Hitler*. New York: Alfred A. Knopf, 1941.

8

Communist Modernity
in the Soviet Union

To this point we have mentioned Communist and Socialist ideologies only peripherally in our discussion of other kinds of political culture. We shall now turn our attention to the leading exemplar of Marxist ideology today, the Union of Soviet Socialist Republics. In doing so we shall examine an ideological system which is different not only in substance from those we have looked at to this point, but also in the manner of its origination. Its beginnings do not seem characteristically Russian, as the leading elements of American political culture are native American (i.e., Anglo-American) or the chief elements of Nazi ideology (with the exception of the influence of Gobineau) were predominantly German. Communism as the ideology of modern Russia at least *appears* to be a foreign import, inasmuch as all its leading concepts are derived from the work of Karl Marx, a German philosopher and economist who lived and wrote in England. This appearance poses the large question as to whether doctrines from abroad can revolutionize a political culture which is basically different from the one that engendered them. Or are revolutionary ideas attractive because they somehow "fit" the society in which they succeed, and are they shaped and formed by the traditional culture at whose transformation they are aimed? We must be able to give an adequate answer to this question if we are to understand what has happened both in the Soviet Union and in Communist China and if we are to be able to understand ideological behavior in the "Third World."

1. The Antiquity of Communist Ideology

The Communist ideal of social organization is as old as philosophy. The community of wives, children, and property that Plato decreed for his ideal ruling class is perhaps the first theoretical statement of Communism. And the communal life of early Christians may be the first practical Communist experiment. Alexander Gray indicates an even earlier origin in the subtitle to his *Socialist Tradition*—"from Moses to Lenin." [1]

Utopianism.   Do the various forms of Socialism and Communism have anything in common? For one thing, no matter what the origin or antiquity of the doctrine, they are all utopian, in the sense that they take as a leading goal value the perfection of the human being as an other-regarding, benevolent, empathic, social animal who can identify his interest with that of the whole society. For another, they all posit an intimate connection between the achievement of this value and the communal ownership and control of property.

Communist doctrines vary in their understanding of the causal connection between solidary utopianism and communist ownership. Plato held that the spiritual regeneration which he saw as the underpinning of utopian politics would be produced by a communal institutional order. For the early Christians, however, it was the spirit of love and brotherhood flowing from their religious commitment that was seen as the precondition of successful communal living. Christian monastic communities and sectarian communal societies seem to make the same assumption, and the Israeli Kibbutzim appear also to derive their viability from an initial spiritual and moral commitment.

Modern secular Socialists and Communists of all kinds, however, adopt a causal theory more like that of Plato than like that of the religious communities we have mentioned. They view private property, at least in the instruments of production, as the source of selfishness, social conflict, and exploitation of the weak by the strong. And they accept the corollary view that when property is brought under general social control, human nature will change and all will live happily and benevolently together.

The note of general abundance in Communist theory is specifically modern and more secular than religious in its origins. Platonic theory and the practice of the early Christian communities as well as that of

---

[1] Alexander Gray, *The Socialist Tradition: From Moses to Lenin* (New York: Longmans, Green & Co., 1946).

the monasteries and sectarian communes are preeminently ascetic. Although no one is expected to live in poverty and the commune provides for economic sufficiency, the ideal of life does not glorify material well-being. Modern secular Communism, however, stresses material abundance as a primary goal. Generalized economic well-being is seen as the immediate cause of healthy social behavior and of the flowering of individual personality.

2. Social Background and Beginnings of Modern Socialism

What are the historical conditions associated with the appearance of modern secular Socialist and Communist theories? To whom do they appeal? What are the main kinds? How do they relate to political behavior in the leading Communist states of the contemporary world?

The Industrial Revolution.   The first distinctively modern secular Socialist and Communist theorizing and the first modern Socialist movements are byproducts of the early phase of the industrial revolution in Western Europe during the first part of the nineteenth century. Classical Liberalism and Capitalism had promised universal bliss, individual freedom, and political democracy, but had failed so far as the European working class and the middle-class intellectuals who became their ideologues and leaders were concerned. The industrial revolution was well under way in Engand by the last quarter of the eighteenth century. By the 1830s England had become a leading industrial power and had begun the accumulation of an unprecedented national wealth through the development of coal and iron resources, the processing of imported cotton and wool into finished textiles, and the export of finished textile products, as well as the export of surplus capital for profitable investment abroad. Similar beginnings are found in France and Germany a few decades later.

With the industrial revolution came severe social dislocation and fantastic inequalities in the distribution of the new wealth which were made more illegitimate than otherwise by the equalitarian theme in Liberal ideology, which was penetrating everywhere. New industrial towns like Manchester and Birmingham mushroomed into existence as the new Capitalism evolved. Labor was treated simply as one commodity among others, and the new system gave no thought to worker safety, to adequate housing, or to decent living conditions for the new industrial workers. Long hours were worked for subsistence wages. The development of Capitalism required repeal of the traditional system of public economic control, and a new system which would sufficiently safeguard the values of the working class was slow to evolve.[2]

Social Protest and Utopian Socialism.   Widespread social protest was one fruit of the stresses and strains caused by the growth of the new economic system under the auspices of Classical Liberal politics. On the ideological side, a cluster of theories appeared calling in question the basic principles of the new laissez-faire, individualist capitalism with its assumption of an ultimate social harmony as the product of the pursuit of profit in a nightwatchman state. One approach to reform is illustrated by the work of the so-called "Utopian Socialists."

The "Utopian Socialists" received that name from Marx and Engels, who thought their conception of human nature "unscientific," by which they meant that it was out of keeping with empirical reality. Charles Fourier (1772–1837), a leading Utopian, for example, advertised in the newspaper the hours he would be at home to receive visits from capitalist entrepreneurs who might be interested in sponsoring his socialist schemes.[3] As Marx and Engels saw it, this was simply expecting them to act contrary to their nature as capitalists. Moreover, Fourier's expectation that his experimental socialist communities might be able to function successfully in a world still dominated by capitalist forms and by the sheer force of rationality might convince the capitalist world of their greater efficiency struck them as of the essence of utopianism. All these expectations ran quite contrary to the line of historical development decreed by the "scientific" law of the dialectic.

Fourier envisioned a society reorganized in small self-contained communities, each with about 1,800 members, which he called "phalanxes." The major emphasis was not on a uniform egalitarianism but rather on contributions to the common good by each member according to his peculiar talents. Things would be arranged so that each person would be able to do what he enjoyed. (This is also a feature of the future Marxian classless society.) Children, for example, would do the garbage collecting and other messy tasks, because they love dirt.[4] Emphasis was also placed on economies of size. Members of phalanxes would eat together in large dining rooms served by communal kitchens. It horrified Fourier to think of the great waste of millions of individual kitchens and private dining rooms all over the world. Efficiency also would be sought through organized competition among functional groups in which those doing the best job would receive special rewards. (Here

[2] See Edmund Wilson, *To the Finland Station: A Study in the Writing and Acting of History* (Garden City, N.Y.: Doubleday & Co., Inc., 1953), pp. 135–37.

[3] Gray, *op. cit.*, p. 195.

[4] *Ibid.*, p. 188.

we have something like a forerunner of the Russian "Stakhanovite" movement.) The product of the phalanx was to be divided into three parts, the largest share going to labor, the next to capital, the next to skill.

Forty phalanxes were ultimately founded in France, and the idea caught on in the United States in the 1830s and 1840s, promoted by men like Horace Greeley and Nathaniel Hawthorne. In all, thirty communities were founded, the most memorable of which was Brook Farm in Massachusetts.

Another leading "Utopian" was Robert Owen (1771–1858), a successful Scottish industrialist who bought up the grim Scottish town of New Lanark and transformed it into a modern factory community organized as a workers' cooperative. In 1824 Owen emigrated to the United States, where he founded the cooperative community of New Harmony, Indiana. Again, the Marxian critique was that these efforts flew in the face of the laws of historical development and could not be expected to succeed.

3. Dialectical Materialism

Marx and Engels ranged their own work under the banner of science, the leading conception of authority of modern time, and claimed that they had insight into the working of necessary historical laws governing the evolution of economy and polity. Classical Liberalism also had based itself on the idea of scientific law—in this case the natural laws of social harmony operating through a mechanism of enlightened self-interest once the "unnatural" encumbrances of feudal aristocracy and the guild system had been done away with. Rational man, as a benevolent and sociable though self-interested creature, would emerge as the model of human endeavor in a condition of political and social freedom, the "natural" context of normal humanity.

The principles of Dialectical Materialism, the name of the new Marxist "science," however, decreed a different pattern. Individual freedom and social harmony were not impeded by an irrational political order so much as by the organization of economic endeavor. Politics was not an independent realm but was underpinned by economics, and history called for a complicated process of economic development before the day of peace, freedom, and sociality could dawn. Struggle and conflict rather than the harmony of interests was therefore the order of the day.

Dialectical Contradictions.   The fundamental "belief" of dialectical materialism is a conception of reality as inherently contradictory. All things consist of opposite principles of order in dynamic tension. Here are some examples from Lenin:

> In mathematics: + and −. Differential and integral.
> In mechanics: action and reaction.
> In physics: positive and negative electricity.
> In chemistry: the combining and dissociation of atoms.
> In social science: the class struggle. . . .[5]

Engels even tried to give a dialectical explanation of sex:

> You, as a bridegroom, have a striking example of the inseparability of identity and difference in yourself and your bride. Take away the difference (in this case sex), or the identity (the human nature of both), and what have you got left? [6]

The actual movement from one dialectical pole to the other is represented by such phenomena as the heating of iron until it turns from a solid into a liquid and the metamorphosis of a chrysalis into a butterfly.[7]

Freedom and Determinism.   Society as well as nature, according to Marxism, is to be understood dialectically. What this means, however, varies markedly within the corpus of Marxist literature. Even in the writings of Karl Marx himself we find two very different formulations of the idea. The young Marx, under the influence of Hegel, gave singular importance to human consciousness as a creative force in the dialectical process. This made the individual to a certain degree free, or autonomous, even in the imperfect world of alienated existence predating the institution of communist order. The older Marx, as the collaborator of Engels, made determinate historical law the fundamental causal agent, and reduced human reality to a reflexive function of the historical process; until that process had produced a communist society, man was fated to be a creature of necessity. Engels wrote graphically of the ultimate transformation of human reality as the "ascent of man from the kingdom of necessity to the kingdom of freedom." [8]

It was the necessitarian Marx whose thought most influenced the makers of the Russian Revolution, so we shall confine our description of the Marxist view of historical reality to its formulation as Dialectical Materialism at this point. The writings of the younger Marx are only

---

[5] Lenin's Notebook, cited in Max Eastman, "Against the Marxian Dialectic," in Michael Curtis, ed. *Marxism* (New York: Atherton, 1970), p. 180.

[6] Frederick Engels, *Selected Correspondence*, cited in *ibid.*, p. 45.

[7] *Ibid.*

[8] Frederick Engels, *Socialism: Utopian and Scientific*, trans. Edward Aveling (New York: International Publishers, 1935), p. 73.

today coming into vogue in certain intellectual circles in the Soviet Union and elsewhere in the Communist world (as well as among Marxists in the Capitalist West). So we shall reserve our discussion of this rather different way of thinking about reality until we come to our consideration of contemporary Marxist developments.

Economic Base.   Dialectical Materialism as social philosophy proposes that we understand man primarily as an *"animal laborans,"* a worker, i.e., as a being defined by the activity of material production. The specific manner of his being is therefore determined by the way in which he ·carries on this activity. The first question one must ask in trying to understand a given society therefore deals with the character of its economy: "What is produced, how it is produced, and how the products are exchanged." [9]

The answers to these questions constitute a description of the mode of production of the society in question. When these answers are at hand one has the key to an understanding of all other things in the society, which are seen simply as byproducts of this primary reality. So the class order and the relations among classes, the character of the political system, of art, philosophy, religion—all the rest of human culture—are superstructure.

Superstructure.   According to Dialectical Materialism, every historical social order is radically exploitative because it is based on the principle of scarcity. In each society a few persons, organized as the ruling class, control the instruments of production which they use solely for their own well-being. Economic control yields political power, which also serves in turn to stabilize existing relations of production. The thought forms of a society—its philosophy and religion—are also at the disposal of the ruling class as instruments for stabilizing the system which serves their interests by giving it legitimacy. They do not give legitimacy in the sense of providing it with a basis of objective moral truth, which does not exist for the Dialectical Materialist. They are simply a device for duping the repressed classes into accepting their inferior status. This is not to say that the rulers consciously manipulate religion to keep the ruled in line. They believe the myth, but it is in them only a "false consciousness" because it does not conform to a real truth. Its reality is to be an "opiate of the people."

The Dialectic in History.   Marx and Engels believed that in the conception of the Dialectic they had discovered a scientific law determining the manner in which social systems, ordered as we have described above, change over time. As in physical nature so in society, movement means

[9] *Ibid.*, p. 54.

opposition and contradiction. The antithesis, or opposite principle, of any social order grows within that order until it negates and destroys it. Thus towns and a trading middle class develop during the later middle ages within the structure of a feudal system based on agriculture and aristocratic rule. At a certain point the older order, which becomes increasingly inefficient as the new principle develops within it, can contain the new system no longer. The new class (in this case the bourgeoisie), nurtured within the womb of the old system, rises up to overthrow the old ruling class and thus move society to a new stage of historical development.

Dialectical change in earlier societies is dealt with only sketchily by Marx and Engels. The bulk of their attention is devoted to analysis of the development and breakdown of capitalism, and the clearest, most graphic examples of oppositional change are drawn from this experience. It is pointed out, for example, that capitalism in its early stages stresses competition among many small, relatively equal enterprises. Over time, by the very logic of the competitive process, competition gives way to its opposite—monopoly—as the weaker producers are "driven to the wall" by the stronger (i.e., the more efficient). The capitalists who are driven out drop down into the ranks of the propertyless proletariat, a class which has been created by the capitalist system itself, and which is destined to become its "gravedigger." As time passes, the ranks of the proletariat grow larger and larger and those of the bourgeoisie smaller and smaller. At a crucial moment the proletariat, driven to distraction by their misery, rise up in revolution and seize control of the property which the capitalists themselves, by the creation of vast monopolies, have already socialized. Marx writes in Volume I of *Capital:* "Along with the constantly diminishing number of the magnates of capital . . . grows the mass of misery, oppression, slavery, degradation, exploitation; but with this too grows the revolt of the working class, a class always increasing in numbers, and disciplined, united, organized by the very mechanism of capitalist production itself." [10]

Paradoxical contradiction in capitalist evolution is also highlighted by Engels in *Socialism: Utopian and Scientific:*

> The means of production and production itself had become in essence social, but they were still subjected to a form of appropriation which presupposes the private production of individuals, under which, therefore everyone owns his own product and brings it to market. . . . This contradiction . . . *contains the germ of the whole of social antagonisms of today.* The greater the mastery obtained by the new mode of produc-

[10] Karl Marx, *Capital,* I, Chap. 32, in Karl Marx and Frederick Engels, *Selected Works* (Moscow: Foreign Languages Publishing House, 1962), I, 460.

tion . . . *the more clearly was brought out the incompatibility of so-cialised production with capitalistic appropriation.*[11]

Here is another example of change through contradiction. Capitalism is seen as the most productive economic system begotten by the historical process. Because history, in the Marxian world view, aims at the creation of a superabundant economy, the capitalist order actually warrants high praise. Thus, for example, we read in *The Communist Manifesto* that:

> the bourgeoisie, during its rule of scarce one hundred years, has created more massive and more colossal productive forces than have all preceding generations together. Subjection of nature's forces to man, machinery, application of chemistry to industry and agriculture, steam-navigation, railways, electric telegraphs, clearing of whole continents for cultivation, canalization of rivers, whole populations conjured out of the ground— what earlier century had even a presentiment that such productive forces slumbered in the lap of social labor? [12]

But at a certain point the contradictions set in. Capitalism, instead of continuing indefinitely to build up new economic forces, becomes a "fetter on production." In order to reap profits, capitalists begin to limit production and even to destroy plants they have built. During business crises "a great part not only of the existing products, but also of the previously created productive forces, are periodically destroyed. In these crises there breaks out an epidemic that, in all earlier epochs would have seemed an absurdity—the epidemic of overproduction." [13] Thus once again we have contradiction and opposition. Instead of becoming ever more productive, capitalism becomes less productive. The arrival of this moment also signals the imminent demise of the system, which has outlived its historical utility. "Centralization of the means of production and socialisation of labour at last reach a point where they become incompatible with their capitalist integument. This integument is burst asunder. The knell of capitalist private property sounds." [14]

The Profit Motive.   The basic motivating mechanism behind the rise and decline of capitalism as seen by Marx and Engels is the profit motive. The capitalist's behavior is determined at every point by the quest for profits, which consist of the portion of the worker's product over and above what the capitalist must pay him to subsist. All value is under-

---

[11] *Op. cit.*, p. 58.
[12] Karl Marx and Frederick Engels, *The Communist Manifesto* (New York: Appleton-Century-Crofts, 1955), p. 14.
[13] *Ibid.*, p. 15.
[14] Marx, *Capital*, I, Chap. 32, *op. cit.*, p. 460.

stood as solely the product of labor, and the value of capital goods is determined by the amount of "socially necessary labor"—that is, work already done—contained within them. Wages are held at a subsistence level because of the existence of a "reserve army" of labor fed constantly by the declassé entrepreneurs who lose out in the economic struggle.

It is the profit motive which also produces the ultimate contradictions within capitalism. Capitalists begin to limit production and destroy plant when they are unable to sell their products. Crises of overproduction result from the payment of subsistence wages and from the growth of the great reservoir of poverty-stricken unemployed. The limitation of production results from the consequent threat to profits.[15]

The Communist Revolution and After.   The transformation of Capitalism into Socialism is for Marx and Engels an apocalyptic moment. It heralds the end of social antagonisms, of exploitation and oppression, of suffering. Man ceases to be what he has been throughout the historical process—a narrow, greedy, individualist—and becomes a social animal—benevolent to others, cooperative. Classes and the class struggle are eliminated and all conflicts of interest cease. Society has reached a stage in which the "free development of all has become the precondition of the free development of each."

At the political level, the new order is characterized by the disappearance of the state which, like the class system, has ceased to have historical utility. As Engels puts it in *Socialism: Utopian and Scientific:*

> As soon as there is no longer any social class to be held in subjection . . . nothing more remains to be repressed, and a special repressive force, a state, is no longer necessary. The first act by virtue of which the state really constitutes itself the representative of the whole of society—that is, at the same time its last independent act as a state. . . . The government of persons is replaced by the administration of things, and by the conduct of processes of production. The state is not "abolished," it *dies out.*[16]

It is not, however, the bourgeois state that "dies out" but rather the proletarian "semi-state" which has succeeded the middle-class parliamentary order. In the *Critique of the Gotha Program* Marx says that "between capitalist and communist society lies the period of the revolutionary transformation of the one into the other. There corresponds to this also a

---

[15] This is a highly simplified account of Marx's very complicated discussion of the labor theory of value, surplus value, the rate of profit, overproduction, and so forth. There are very large problems about resolving differences between the account Marx gives of these things in the first volume of *Capital* and the account found in the posthumous third volume.

[16] *Op. cit.,* p. 70.

political transition period in which the state can be nothing but the revolutionary dictatorship of the proletariat." [17] In *The Civil War in France* he suggests that although it is a dictatorship, it will be (so far as the proletariat is concerned) democratically organized, on the model of the revolutionary Paris Commune of 1870. This was

> formed of the municipal counsellors, chosen by universal suffrage in the various wards of the town, responsible and revocable at short terms. The majority of its members were naturally working men, or acknowledged representatives of the working class. The Commune was to be a working, not a parliamentary body, executive and legislative at the same time. The police . . . was turned into the responsible and at all times revocable agent of the Commune. So were the officials in all other branches of the Administration. . . . Magistrates and judges were to be elected, responsible, and revocable.[18]

The revolution would be led, indeed, by a smaller group, the Communists, "the most advanced and resolute section of the working-class parties of every country, that section which pushes forward all others." [19] But the revolutionary government to be created by them would be under the democratic control of the entire proletariat. Marx even suggested in a late work that the new order might not necessarily in all cases have to be installed by a revolutionary act. Under special circumstances the middle-class parliamentary regime could be employed to achieve a peaceful transformation of Capitalist into Socialist society.[20] We shall see that on both these points—the structure of proletarian government (democratic or elitist) and the manner of ushering in the Socialist regime (revolution versus evolution)—there were to be, and continue to be, marked differences among the various Marxist factions.

We have reviewed in outline the salient elements of the original doctrine of Marx and Engels which was to be the raw material of future Communist ideologists. It consisted primarily of a detailed analysis of Capitalism and a prediction of its collapse. As such, it was an explanation of present reality within a roughly defined metaphysic or world view, Dialectical Materialism. Original Marxism, however, was manifestly sparse in prescriptive statement. It contained no detailed strategy of revolution and no clear picture of the organization of economy or polity in the Communist utopia to come. These things would have to be filled in by the activists who were to carry out Communist programs of socialist

---

[17] Karl Marx, *Critique of the Gotha Program* in Robert C. Tucker, ed. *The Marx-Engels Reader* (New York: W. W. Norton & Co., 1972), p. 395.

[18] Karl Marx, *The Civil War in France* in Tucker, *op. cit.*, pp. 554–55.

[19] Marx and Engels, *Communist Manifesto*, p. 23.

[20] Speech at the Hague Convention of the First International, 1872. See Harry W. Laidler, *History of Socialism* (New York: Thomas Y. Crowell Co., 1968), p. 156.

and communist transformation. We shall see now how V. I. Lenin, as the primary architect of the Russian revolution, used, reworked, and added to the materials bequeathed him by Marx and Engels.

4. Leninism

The increasing democratization of Western European society during the last part of the nineteenth century, which gave the working classes some leverage within newly established parliamentary governments, brought to prominence the evolutionary or "revisionist" version of Marxism. Capitalists were found willing to pay more than subsistence wages and to accept the public regulation of wages, hours, and conditions of labor. Writers like Eduard Bernstein developed in detail a gradualist theory of socialism to be won via the ballot box and of piecemeal economic reform that became the official doctrine of the leading European socialist parties. It has evolved today into the pragmatic and democratic socialism of leaders like Willy Brandt, West Germany's Socialist Chancellor. In Russia, however, industrialization did not get underway until the last quarter of the century, and its early phase produced dislocations and misery similar to the early Western European experience. Wages were low and working conditions oppressively poor. Having hardly been out of Russia before 1900, Lenin read Bernstein's work as a great lie and fraud. In his essay *What Is to Be Done?* we have a ringing denunciation of Bernsteinian "economism," which had achieved considerable vogue in Russia, and Lenin's own prescription for the effective organization of socialist reform.

The Cadre Party.   Marx had written of proletarian class consciousness as something which arises automatically from the sufferings of the class. It was the job of the Communist Party to lead the proletariat into the promised land, but it could count on the underlying motor force of an already existing proletarian consciousness and on preexisting revolutionary fervor. According to Lenin's analysis, however, workers if left alone could be counted on only to achieve a "trade union consciousness" which would be characterized by the revisionist mentality embodied in western European socialism which was ready to strike all kinds of bargains and compromises with capitalism. To shape them into a revolutionary force by making them aware of irresolvable class antagonisms, the workers needed outside leadership—ideological molding by the Communist intelligentsia. "Modern socialist consciousness," Lenin wrote, quoting Kautsky, "can arise only on the basis of profound scientific knowledge. . . The vehicle of science is not the proletariat, but the bourgeois intelligentsia. . . . Thus, socialist consciousness is something introduced into the proletarian class struggle from without, and not something that arose within it spontaneously." [21]

On the organizational side, the waging of successful revolution required, according to Lenin, the application of elitist principles. An entirely open and democratic party was cumbersome and a prey to penetration and harassment by the reactionary forces in control of the government of the day. Lenin recommended instead the adoption of an elitist and conspiratorial model, the creation of a party of disciplined, professional revolutionaries to carry out the revolution in Russia. The precepts adumbrated in *What Is to Be Done?* were to provide the organizational principles of the Russian Social Democratic Labor Party (Bolshevik), the party of Lenin, which made the November Revolution of 1917.

Imperialism.   Another important addition of Lenin to the corpus of Marxist doctrine is his essay of 1916 entitled *Imperialism: The Highest Stage of Capitalism.* This was to be of special significance for converting Marxism into an ideology with wide applicability to nonindustrialized, traditional societies where, by and large, it has flourished more than in the industrialized areas of Europe which gave it birth. Though of little importance for the making of a Communist revolution in Russia (itself in 1917 a backward area), Lenin's essay on Imperialism provided a basic rationale for Soviet policy toward the underdeveloped portions of the globe after World War II, which brought the radical retrenchment of European colonial empires.

Additions to ideological doctrine usually arise from the need to explain observed discrepancies between empirical reality and existing theory. In the case of Lenin's essay on Imperialism, the problematic reality was the nationalist behavior of European Socialists in 1914. Instead of rejecting their capitalist governments, the Socialists flocked with enthusiasm to the national banners and enthusiastically supported what, as Lenin saw it, they should have condemned as a capitalist war. Lenin's theory was that they had been bought off by the capitalist classes, who found that they could deal with the problem of failing demand by exploiting markets in the underdeveloped parts of the world—Africa, the Middle East, Asia, Latin America—through the creation of colonial empires. Having cooled the revolutionary fervor of their home proletariats with higher wages and better working conditions, capitalist governments developed an external proletariat among the primitive peoples of the world. Lenin interpreted World War I as a result of heightened competition among capitalist states who made their governments finally go to war to promote their colonial interests.[22]

[21] V. I. Lenin, *What Is to Be Done?*, in *Selected Works* (New York: International Publishers, 1967), I, 129.
[22] V. I. Lenin, *Imperialism: The Highest Stage of Capitalism* (New York: International Publishers, 1939).

Despite clear and manifest evidence that World War I was fought over intra-European questions, not over colonial empire, and that colonial trade by the European powers amounted to only a small fraction of domestic and intra-European trade, Lenin's theory has had great popularity in the backward regions. Relegated by colonial elites to an inferior status, the native peoples of these areas have found in Lenin's doctrine a ready vehicle for the expression of their natural resentment of foreign economic and political domination. Also, Lenin's prediction that the war would wear out the colonial powers and spark anticolonial revolution has had something of the character of a self-fulfilling prophecy.

Explaining the Revolution in Russia.   Our major present concern, however, is the Russian Communist Revolution and its ideological justification. Marx had never envisaged a successful Communist revolution as an autonomous event in an agrarian society, which was what Russia largely remained in 1917. He saw the European peasantry as a petit-bourgeois and reactionary force. The logic of the theory of capitalist development, which he so painstakingly delineated in three stout volumes, pointed to revolutionary outbreak in industrially developed Western Europe. Russia hardly had the makings of a proletarian class, let alone a proletarian social majority. How then could this extraordinary event have occurred?

Lenin, preeminently a pragmatist and opportunist in his political behavior, was ready to admit that from the point of view of existing theory his success was an anomaly. "That the revolution succeeded so quickly," he wrote, "is only due to the fact that, as a result of an extremely unique historical situation, *absolutely dissimilar currents, absolutely heterogeneous class interests, absolutely contrary political and social strivings have merged.*" [23] Not the theory, but a unique and therefore theoretically inexplicable historical opportunity accounted for his success. It is also the case that it was not the Communist ideology but the promise to supply basic material values that gave Lenin's party its appeal to the Russian peasant. " 'Bread, peace, and freedom'—these slogans were to be endlessly reiterated and emphasized, and they were to lift Bolshevism to power." [24]

After the fact of his success, however, Lenin was prepared to try to fit a theory to the events that had transpired. Purists insisted that the law of the Dialectic had to be observed, and that the most that Russian Communists could be expected to do was to support a bourgeois revolution, which commonly occurs in the early phases of industrialization. Lenin instead supplied a new theoretical principle which maintained that it was sometimes possible to telescope historical development to eliminate par-

[23] "Letters from Afar," in *Selected Works*, II, 5.
[24] Merle Fainsod, *How Russia Is Ruled* (Cambridge, Mass.: Harvard University Press, 1954), p. 63.

ticular stages. In particular, it was possible to go beyond "bourgeois democracy" in Russia, into "proletarian democracy" and socialism.[25]

Lenin nevertheless continued to worry about the possibility of maintaining a Communist regime in Russia unsupported by a general Communist uprising all over Europe. He liked to chart the possibility of various combinations of capitalist powers falling out with one another and bringing on another war which would further weaken their position. He developed no theory of "Socialism in one country" nor did the idea of "peaceful coexistence" occur to him as a way of relating to the external Capitalist world. It remained for Stalin to develop the one and Khrushchev the other of these two concepts, which, like the theory of the "weakest link," were not *a priori* notions, but rather theoretical derivations from what in fact was observed to be happening.

Post-Revolutionary Order.   The industrialization of Russia under Lenin also had to proceed without benefit of theory. After a disastrous experiment with utopian Communist forms of economic organization ("War Communism"), Lenin was ready to try a quasi-capitalist approach in the New Econome Policy instituted in 1921 and employed down to 1928. Limited private enterprise and the profit motive were introduced in certain areas of industry, and a new land law legitimated individual farming. In 1928 the institution of the Five-Year Plans and collective farming created a form of state capitalism.

Phases of Communist Development.   Only with the development of economic superabundance as the fruit of advanced industrialization could special incentives be done away with, as Lenin saw it. The evolution of Communist society would thus be characterized by two phases. In the first, or lower phase, perfect justice and equality were not possible, because of continuing scarcity. Although the exploitation of man by man would cease, rewards would have to be distributed according to product. Only in the higher phase would it be possible to employ the principle: "From each according to his ability, to each according to his needs."[26]

The problem of industrial development also had an important impact on forms of political control. In *The State and Revolution,* written on the very eve of the 1917 uprising, Lenin described the state of the proletarian dictatorship as "a very simple 'machine,' almost without a 'machine,' without a special apparatus. . . ."[27] Officials would be elected

---

[25] See "Theses and Report on Bourgeois Democracy and the Dictatorship of the Proletariat," First Congress of the Communist International, March 1919, in *Selected Works,* III, 128ff., and speech on the Fourth Anniversary of the October Revolution, 1921, in *ibid.,* p. 634ff.

[26] V. I. Lenin, *The State and Revolution,* in Arthur P. Mendel, ed. *Essential Works of Marxism* (New York: Bantam Books, 1961), p. 178.

[27] *Ibid.,* p. 173.

and subject to recall (once more, shades of the democratic Paris Commune) and would simply carry out the workers' instructions as a bookkeeping operation. After the revolution, however, Lenin "found himself obliged to establish a highly centralized administrative machine in Russia, finding that he could not govern without it." [28]

5. Theory and Practice: From Stalin to Khrushchev

Stalin's exegesis of the Marxian gospel evidences the same sort of empirical practicality as Lenin's. The success of the Russian Communists in consolidating their regime despite the nonoccurrence of a general European revolution produced the theory of Socialism in one country. Similarly, Stalin's theory of "capitalist encirclement" also yielded a justification for the continuance of a powerful state apparatus and the indefinite deferral of the "withering away of the state." Leon Trotsky, more of a theoretical purist, accused Stalin of substituting the dictatorship of the Communist Party over the proletariat for the dictatorship of the proletariat, for Stalin actually announced that whole epochs might pass before it would be possible to establish the "higher" or Communist phase of the socialist order.

Peaceful Coexistence.   Both Lenin and Stalin held as a basic tenet the idea of inevitable conflict between Capitalism and Socialism as Socialist power grew. Again doctrine dovetailed with experience, in this case the youth and isolation of Communist Russia. By 1961, however, after the experience of wartime cooperation with leading Capitalist states and following the appearance of another large Communist state on the Russian border—Communist China, whose location and political dynamism posed a more manifest problem for Russian security—we find Khrushchev ready to abandon the outworn theory of inevitable armed conflict with the Capitalist world. A justifying formula was ready to hand—the theory that the balance of force already had passed to Socialism, so that the end of Capitalism could be a quiet affair. "There is now a prospect of achieving peaceful coexistence," he told the Twenty-second Congress of the Russian Communist Party, "for the entire period in which the social and political problems now dividing the world will have to be solved." At an earlier Congress he had said that "countries with differing social systems can do more than exist side by side. It is necessary to proceed further, to improve relations, to strengthen confidence among countries and cooperate." [29] A

---

[28] John Plamenatz, *German Marxism and Russian Communism* (London: Longmans, Green and Co., 1954), p. 247.
[29] Robert C. Tucker, *The Soviet Political Mind*, rev. ed. (New York: W. W. Norton, 1971), pp. 244, 245.

corollary to this was the acceptance of the "Revisionist" idea that there might be alternatives to violent revolution, including parliamentarism, in the creation of Socialist societies. Here were examples of what Khrushchev called a "creative Marxism-Leninism." More recently three economists have received Lenin Prizes for contributions to economic theory which in effect deny the labor theory of value by recognizing the validity of charges for the use of capital and land, charges which amount to capitalist "interest" and "rent." Again experience was determinative—in this case, the crying need to rationalize fiscal procedures in the interest of economic efficiency.

How Theory Develops.   This brief sketch of the evolution of Marxist theory in the Soviet Union has shown us how an abstract *a priori* doctrine can be made to conform to political reality by a successful revolutionary regime. This raises two large questions: (1) how can large emendations of a highly developed abstract system be made credible to believers? And (2) if the official ideology does not rigidly determine policy making in such a regime, what does guide politicians in their day-to-day decisions?

To answer the first question, the ideology in its original formulation actually makes provision for its own periodic reworking. This is found in the dictum of Engels that "dialectics reduces itself to the science of the general laws of motion, both of the external world and of human thought." [30] Emphasis must be laid on the word "general." What Engels means is that although the overall historical trend can be discerned with the help of dialectics, no *particular* event can be either predicted or explained by the application of dialectical law. Even the appearance of Marx in the early nineteenth century, wrote Engels, was "not an inevitable event, following of necessity in the chain of historical development, but a mere happy accident." [31] Thus Engels himself leaves the way open for flexibility in policy making; indeed, *every* particular policy choice can be quite free of theoretical determination under this rubric. Engels does not tell us what of substance is left of the "general law" of the dialectic if no actual historical sequence is determined by it. Thus we have a theoretical or rational justification for the very suspension (or alteration) of the theory built into the system, which may serve to make shifts in the party line credible to some of the more philosophical minded (and gullible) of the "true believers." Other nonrational (i.e., psychological and sociological) grounds for the acceptance—and the nonacceptance—of theoretical shifts we shall deal with in a later section of this chapter.

[30] Frederick Engels, *Ludwig Feuerbach,* in Marx and Engels, *Selected Works,* II, 387.
[31] Engels, *Socialism: Utopian and Scientific,* p. 34.

6. Operational Code: An Ideology for the Elite

Soviet Pragmatism. Both Lenin and Stalin, who established the foundations of the Soviet Russian system and carried the country successfully through a perilous and exhausting world war, quite consciously adopted Engels's pragmatic rubric to explain their policy making. One scholar, in an analysis of the writings of both leaders, found that "although it is always asserted that the direction and end of a major historical development (e.g., the transition from capitalism to communism) is predictable, the length of time and the path such a development will take are not held to be predictable." [32] Detailed policy planning, therefore, tends to be shorter rather than longer in range, and is constantly subject to revision. Lenin, for example, espoused Napoleon's dictum that "one must first start a serious engagement and then see what happens. . . . Well, we started a serious engagement in . . . 1917, and *then* we saw such details of development (from the point of view of world history they are certainly details) as the Brest-Litovsk peace, the New Economic Policy, etc." [33] Elsewhere he writes that "there must be no doctrinaire attitude . . . against changes in strategy and tactics. . . ." The Party "must not blindly worship the particular phase in which it may find itself at any particular time or place." "If I pursue an enemy who does not move in a straight line but zigzags, then I too must zigzag in order to reach him." Similarly Stalin, writing in 1930 on the development of the Five-Year Plan, tells us that "only bureaucrats can imagine that the work of planning is *concluded* with the compilation of a plan. The compilation of a plan is only the *beginning of planning*. Real planned guidance develops only . . . in the course of the plan's application, by correcting it . . . rendering it more exact." [34]

Freedom for the Planners. Lenin and Stalin also believed that at many junctures of historical development various outcomes were "objectively possible." "Objective conditions" create "opportunities" which can be used or lost. The dialectic does not guarantee proletarian success in the short run. Careless planning may result in failure. In this way Lenin and Stalin stressed freedom and responsibility rather than determinism in their approach to policy making. This meant, of course, *their* freedom

[32] Nathan Leites, *The Operational Code of the Politburo* (New York: McGraw-Hill Book Company, 1951), p. 2. Copyright 1951 by The Rand Corporation. Quotations with permission of The Rand Corporation.
[33] Quoted in *ibid.*
[34] Quoted in *ibid.*, pp. 33, 34.

and that of the supreme decision-making bodies of the Communist Party, such as the Politburo. Not the underdeveloped and backsliding proletariat but the Party leadership were the proper agency for studying "objective conditions," for making estimates of path and timing, and for revising these estimates. This was not a self-evident affair but required "scientific" skill and judgment.

The effect of this way of doing things was to detach the Party from the rigorously determined chain of causes and effects of the dialectic and give it the kind of freedom to choose, to determine the future shape of the world which is accorded to the proletariat as a whole in the Marxist utopia of the classless society. "All the actors on the world scene are 'forced' into their parts through the pressure of historical developments. Only the Party, through its insight and dedication, acts freely." The Party "solves the problems that have been put on the agenda by history." [35] This way of adapting the theory of the dialectic to the understanding and manipulation of actual events produces on the part of the Russian leadership a constant effort to find a pattern in events and to plan for revolutionary change on the basis of the possibilities indicated by that pattern. It also makes for flexibility, for a willingness to change plans because of the assumption that the historical pattern is by no means fully determinate.

Rules of the Operational Code.   This discussion of leadership pragmatism leads us to our second question. If the ideology does not, after all, contain a detailed plan and prediction of the course of world history, what rules do the Soviet leaders observe in policy making and what practical goal values do they pursue? An attempt to provide an answer was made during the last years of the Stalinist period in a Rand Corporation study authored by Nathan Leites, a social psychologist. Professor Leites hypothesized that the operative rules for policy making might be discovered through a close analysis of the writings of top leaders such as Lenin and Stalin. Some rules or norms he found explicitly stated in this literature, and others he derived by clear inference from explicit texts. He also attempted to discover rules implicit in actually observed Russian political behavior, rules that "seem to be operative among Bolsheviks but might not be recognized easily by them." [36]

The basic policy-making rule discovered by Professor Leites is precisely the pragmatic rubric we have outlined above. It is a pragmatism characterized by moderateness of expectations in the outcome of the political game as well as by flexibility in planning. "Revolutionaries will perish . . . only if . . . they lose their sobriety of outlook," wrote Lenin.

[35] *Ibid.*, p. 1.
[36] *Ibid.*, p. xii.

"Bolsheviks do not believe in miracles." "We must formulate our program in such a fashion that we are prepared for the worst." "We must count on the worst." [37] This leads to the avoidance of extremely risky undertakings, which Lenin sarcastically labels political "adventures"; the Party ought not commit itself politically or militarily without sufficient forces available, expecting to make up the deficit during the operation.

Soviet pragmatism also involves the norm, "Respect your enemy!" Leites found that Lenin and Stalin granted the bourgeoisie political insight superior to that of the masses, though inferior to that of the Party. He writes that "this helps to explain why the Politburo keeps a respectful eye on 'Wall Street' while it regards its 'progressive friends' abroad with contempt." [38] The operational code also stresses control of feelings in policy making. Political activity is seen as "a most coldblooded . . . war." Even when there seems to be a spontaneous antidemocratic mood developing in a revolutionary stratum somewhere, unless "objective forces" promise success one should avoid giving in to optimistic and sympathetic feelings. "Revolutionary moods" alone are not enough.

Control of feelings also requires the simulation of good feelings toward an enemy and a willingness to bestow temporary advantages on him if it serves one's interest. Leites cites Lenin's willingness to make common cause with French monarchist officers in defeating Germany in 1918. Ideological animosity must not get in the way of practical interest. Control of feelings also involves avoidance of panic in unfavorable circumstances.

Another aspect of Soviet pragmatism, as the operational code of the Soviet Politburo (now called the Presidium), is the rule of concentrating fire at any given moment on the achievable rather than the desirable, "a modest taking into account of the probable and possible next conquest, instead of an 'unhistorical' . . . claim to win total victory." "The most important task" is "fighting the danger of being carried away by vast plans and tasks." [39]

Still another rule of the operational code is the injunction to hard work and perseverance—on the American model! Stalin, for example, wrote in 1924 that the Party should combine "the wide outlook of the Russian revolutionist" with "American practicality": "American practicality is that . . . spirit . . . that simply must go through with a job, once it has been tackled, even if it be of minor importance." [40] Stalin gave priority to the inculcation of this rule at all levels of Party activity as a means of offsetting what he saw as a characteristic Slavic trait, the lack

[37] Quoted in *ibid.,* p. 17.
[38] *Ibid.,* p. 19.
[39] *Ibid.,* p. 28.
[40] *Ibid.,* p. 30.

of perseverance. What we have here is an attempt to establish a counter-part to the Protestant Ethic, which we have seen has been a central pro-cedural norm of Liberalism as a modernizing ideology.[41]

The "hard work" rule of the operational code, unlike the other ele-ments we have reviewed, is not simply a norm of general political pru-dence, but is closely tied in with a leading goal value of official Marxist ideology—material superabundance based on industrialization—a value shared with the world of Liberal political culture. Here, then, is one im-portant point in which the official ideology does have direct implications for Soviet behavior without determining particular policies. We shall see in a later section how this Russian Marxist "work ethic," in its result like its Western Liberal counterpart, has produced widespread psychological stress and strain and has led in certain intellectual circles to a demand for emphasis on other aspects of the ideology.

Another rule of the operational code that appears to derive from the metaphysical abstractions of the official Marxist ideology is the rule that short-run planning be made on the basis of the long-range estimates of power relations between contending classes that the dialectic is ex-pected to produce. This rule has been of special importance in the making of Russian foreign policy. Thus, for example, in 1925 we find Stalin assess-ing the future role of China in world politics as follows:

> The forces of the revolutionary movement in China are immeasurable. They have not yet come into anything like full operation. The future will show how vast they are. The rulers of the west and of the east, who do not see these forces, who do not make sufficient allowance for their strength will find out when the time comes. We, as a state, cannot but take such forces into account.[42]

Whether it is the result of a self-fulfilling prophecy or of the inherent truth of Dialectical Materialism, Stalin's reading of the future in this instance was certainly a most accurate one. Ironically, the event that Stalin foretold has presented Russian ideologists with an almost insuper-able task (despite the leeway afforded by the "indeterminism" described above)—the task of reconciling the resulting Russian-Chinese conflict, an internecine antagonism within the Marxist world, with the basic ideolog-ical dogma of Socialist harmony.

The stress on continuous assessment of the balance of class forces may well account for the shift of the edge of Russian political pressure

---

[41] For an extended discussion of this parallel, see Reinhard Bendix, *Nation-Building and Citizenship* (New York: John Wiley & Sons, Inc., 1964), Chapter 5. We shall have more to say about this when we examine the sociological and psycho-logical characteristics of Russians in relation to the inculcation of Marxist ideology in the public as a whole.

[42] Quoted in Leites, *op. cit.*, p. 16.

from Europe to the underdeveloped areas of the world after the establishment of an equilibrium in Europe following World War II. As early as 1938, for example, Stalin seems to have recognized the potential for Soviet policy successes in such places as Latin America, Africa, and Asia, when he wrote:

> We must not base our orientation on the strata of society which are no longer developing, even though they at present constitute the predominant force, but on those strata which are developing and have a future before them, even though they at present do not constitute the predominant force.[43]

Another element of the Soviet operational code discovered by Professor Leites, which also may derive from the Marxist *Weltanschauung,* is the norm of constant action to keep the enemy off balance. This appears, quite simply, as a general prudential rule to the effect that policy must never be passive, because Communism represents and embodies the dynamic of history itself. By the decree of history, Capitalism is on the defensive and Communism is the wave of the future. It is therefore the role of Communists to probe for the enemy's weak point at every moment. As Stalin put it:

> . . . The whole of political life is an endless chain consisting of an infinite number of links. The whole art of politics lies in finding the link that can be least torn out of our hands, the one that is important at the given moment, the one that guarantees the command of the whole chain, and having found it, to cling to that link as tightly as possible.[44]

A final and central rule of the operational code is the norm of centralized and monolithic organization. Like the absence of the work ethic, disorder is seen as a weak point in traditional Russian culture. "Organized activity," writes Lenin, "was never a strong point with the Russians in general, nor with the Bolsheviks in particular." [45] Although it takes a markedly different form, the stress on self-consciously organized "rationalized" activity in juxtaposition to un-self-conscious traditional order (seen as "disorder") is also a characteristic aspect of Liberal political culture. As with the work ethic, the concern for organization in both Marxist and Liberal cultures, as an aspect of their modernizing and industrializing activity, has given rise to ideological countercurrents in the form of "New Lefts" in each culture calling for individual autonomy and spontaneous community, and the repudiation of organization as stultifying and destructive of basic human values. But more about this later.

[43] Quoted in *ibid.,* p. 16.
[44] Quoted in *ibid.,* p. 27.
[45] *Ibid.,* p. 37.

In Russian political culture, the modernizing emphasis on organization has implied the concentration of power in the top leadership. In 1902 we find Lenin writing: "Without the 'dozen' of tried and talented leaders . . . no class in modern society is capable of conducting a determined struggle." This is particularly essential because the Capitalist opposition is also seen as operating on the same principle, by concentrating power in the hands of "a narrow circle of individuals connected in one way or another with the big banks." [46] At the same time, stress is placed on the need for the leadership to maintain contact with the masses. Stalin uses the metaphor of the "barometer" in writing about this.

Power as Goal Value.   Given the unpredictability of realizing in any short run the ultimate values of the ideology, what serves as the central goal value of daily policy? The answer is power—the power of the Party, or, more strictly, of its central apparatus. This derives from the logic of Leninist epistemology—that is, from the idea that Party leaders alone have insight into the subtle meanderings of the dialectic, and the shrewdness and strength of will to exploit the opportunities which it from time to time presents. Left alone, the proletariat backslides and retards dialectical development. Thus, whatever contributes to the Party's control over society contributes *ipso facto* to the realization of the goal of history. This has been a basic premise of Soviet policy to date, though there recently have been ideological stirrings which indicate a growing uneasiness about it in Russian society, especially among the intelligentsia. But these stirrings require separate attention later in the chapter; we are focusing now on the operational code of Soviet Communism down to the death of Stalin.

Even institutions which appear to derive from a utopian blueprint are actually the product of the concern for Party power. Leites thus quotes Stalin as saying in 1933 that "from the point of view of Leninism, collective . . . farms are a weapon and a weapon only." [47] There are also no moral or constitutional principles of procedure in the ideology to limit the means whereby power may be acquired or exercised. Russian leaders, indeed, have frankly repudiated traditional ethical norms in their conduct of the "class struggle." Thus Lenin writes in 1920: "A Communist who says that one should never dirty one's hands . . . that he is going to build Communist society with clean . . . hands, is an empty phrasemonger." [48]

Philip Selznick, in another Rand study, *The Organizational Weapon*, published in 1952, has shown that the ideology itself—the metaphysic of

[46] *Ibid.*, pp. 38, 39.
[47] *Ibid.*, p. 9.
[48] *Ibid.*, p. 8.

class struggle, proletarian dictatorship, socialism, classless society, dialectical development, and so forth—has been reduced to an instrument in the establishment and maintenance of Party power.[49] "It is clear," he writes, "that the Communists do have a body of principles useful to them in the struggle for power. However, it is not clear that these principles are relevant beyond organizational structure . . . and organizational strategy and tactics. . . . It may be said that Stalinism has developed most fully the Leninist modification of Marxism—namely, the subordination of all doctrinal precepts to the needs of the struggle for power." [50]

Ideology, Selznick reports, is used to mobilize both the Party cadres —the activists who staff the apparatus—and the general public, "the masses." But it is employed in different ways. To the cadres the ideology is taught in its "pure" form, whose purity is determined not so much by the more subtle statement of dialectical reality as by the frank espousal of Machiavellian method and a thoroughgoing elitism. Thus the activists are taught that they must at times conceal the Party's aims from the masses. "The Vanguard must be prepared to adjust its use of symbols to the needs of the struggle." [51] In other words, cadres are taught how to manipulate the masses with the grand slogans of the ideology.

Thus, as with Nazism, we find in the Russian version of Communism a dual ideology—an esoteric, or private, doctrine for the few, and an exoteric, or public, doctrine for the many. Despite its large Machiavellian content, however, the private doctrine does not necessarily become for the Russian Communist elite purely and simply an ideology of personal and organizational power and glory, which it is in Nazism. It retained the original Marxist concepts of ultimate freedom, equality, and community. This portion of the doctrine, Selznick says, "plays the decisive role in fulfilling the morale function." It also provides categories of thought in such concepts as the theory of class struggle, the theory of the state, the theory of economic crisis, the theory of dialectical development—a "map" or "template," in Geertz' terminology.[52] But the central fact remains that these concepts and ideals are manipulated to serve Leninist aims of party unity, cohesion, and discipline.[53] Selznick also argues

---

[49] Philip Selznick, *The Organizational Weapon,* The Rand Series, (New York: McGraw-Hill Book Co., 1952). Selznick's book is an attempt to generate a general model of Communist organizational strategy rather than a case study of the Russian Party. Data are drawn from Communist practice in the United States, France, Germany, Great Britain, and elsewhere, as well as from the Russian experience. The principles of the model, however, are identified as Leninist and Stalinist, and the book was published at the end of the period in which the Russian Party had dominated the structure and goals of the international movement.

[50] *Ibid.,* pp. 38, 39.

[51] *Ibid.,* p. 9.

[52] *Ibid.,* p. 39.

[53] *Ibid.*

that the chief motivating force in the daily behavior of the cadres is institutional loyalty—loyalty to the Party and to the USSR as the "fatherland"—rather than to the original Marxist ideals. "Loyalty to abstract ideals such as 'Socialism' or even 'revolution' is always somewhat tenuous, since the individual's commitment is not sufficiently concrete to be readily and clearly defined. . . . Institutional patriotism . . . adds concrete meaning to the original ideological grounds for participation." [54]

Selznick's theory of the role of ideology as stated in these passages, however, appears to be generalized to political behavior as such, not simply to the behavior of Communists. It would seem to be as applicable to an explanation of the motives of Liberal Democratic as well as of Communist politicians, and to contain the proposition that all elite codes are basically alike in a common focus on considerations of power. As we noted in our discussion of Nazism, the work of theorists of games such as Riker and Downs reduces the operative ideology (or operational code) of Liberal Democratic politicians to a rational scheme for "winning," i.e., to a scheme for the acquisition and maintenance of power.[55] Richard Neustadt's *Presidential Power* suggests that such a motivation in the incumbent of the presidency is an absolute necessity for the public good as a whole.[56]

A Comparison.   In distinguishing Liberal Democratic political culture from Nazi and Communist culture perhaps we need to focus not on elite motivation but rather on the ideological and constitutional parameters to the motivation laid down by the general cultural set. Although their mouthings of libertarian and egalitarian slogans may be dishonest and their only aims may be personal and organizational power, they are compelled to pursue those aims through established procedures and processes which circumscribe the means they may employ in their pursuit. And they know, too, that large groups exist on whom they rely for support whose demand for values incorporated in the Liberal Democratic *Weltanschauung* must be met. These limitations on elite ends and means do not exist either for Nazis or for Communists, who can convince the general public (the "Folk," the "masses") of their superior knowledge and of the necessity to sacrifice and to accept discipline and hierarchical control to fend off the machinations of some devil, be he "Jew" or "Capitalist," who constantly threatens the present and future well-being of the holy "Folk" or "class."

[54] *Ibid.*, pp. 42, 43.

[55] Anthony Downs, *An Economic Theory of Democracy* (New York: Harper, 1957), especially pp. 25, 28, 29; William H. Riker, *The Theory of Political Coalitions* (New Haven: Yale University Press, 1962), especially pp. 22–23.

[56] Richard Neustadt, *Presidential Power* (New York: John Wiley & Sons, Inc., 1960).

7. Stalinist Transformism

During the Stalinist period the cult of elite power reached its apogee, culminating in an ideology of "transformism," to use the label given the phenomenon by Professor Robert C. Tucker of Princeton. This signifies the belief of Stalin and his henchmen that they could become absolute masters over all nature, both physical and human, and could transform empirical reality at will. At the purely intellectual level, Tucker sees "transformism" present for the first time in the discussions of 1948 at which the Michurin-Lysenko doctrine of heredity was officially accepted by the Central Committee of the CPSU and by Stalin himself.[57] Darwin, it was said, had explained evolution, but "I. V. Michurin made evolution," because, it was claimed, he had discovered methods for molding organic forms at will. The new doctrine repudiated the long-standing Mendelian theory of the relationship between an organism and its environment, a theory which gave primary weight to hereditary forces inherent in an organism as the chief causes of evolutionary development. The external environment had been seen only as a catalyst and limiting factor. Michurin and Lysenko substituted the notion that "controllable conditions in the environment" constituted the exclusive causal factor in evolutionary change. "Changing conditions make the unity of the organism with the environment a 'contradictory unity,' and the organism then resolves the contradiction by successive adaptations that become hereditary. Or else it falls by the wayside." [58] The doctrine implies that our control over the environment of plant and animal life, once established, permits development of them at will to suit our purposes. Human determination replaces natural selection through chance variations.

Professor Tucker sees this theory as the intellectual counterpart of policies of 1948 to 1953 aimed at the radical transformation of natural conditions in Russia. In 1949 the Party decision makers brought forth a "Stalin Plan for the Transformation of Nature," which involved, for example, costly irrigation and afforestation projects. There were also grandiose plans for the construction of dams, canals, and hydroelectric power stations. A project was launched to raise skyscrapers in Moscow to rival those of New York City. Tucker also finds a growing obsession with necessity and determinism in Stalin's last book of 1952, *Economic Problems of Socialism in the USSR*, and he sees lurking in the back of Stalin's mind the notion that his own ideas were natural necessities governing social development.

[57] See Robert Tucker, *The Soviet Political Mind* (New York: Frederick A. Praeger, 1963), Chapter 5.
[58] *Ibid.*, pp. 93, 94.

Physics as well as economics and biology were involved. Bohr's attempt to convert the law of preservation of energy from an absolute law into a statistical one was ridiculed by Soviet scientists, as was Heisenberg's principle of indeterminacy. The idea of western quantum theorists that electrons select their paths at random was laughed out of court. Thus, by an ironic twist, the original Leninist assumption of unpredictability and indeterminacy of political and economic events, which produced a sense of need for a disciplined and insightful party to guide a wayward historical process, is transmuted under Stalin into an assumption of absolute determinacy, of rigid law, which is, however, not the master but the servant of absolute political and scientific power.

Determinism also penetrated the sphere of human behavior. Efforts at the extraordinary manipulation of opinion and behavior by party organs followed upon a period of popular apathy and a certain withdrawal from governmental goals consequent upon the disillusionment that spread in the immediate postwar period when it became clear that the end of the war would not mean material improvement and the diminution of conflict with the outer world. Stalin saw the problem as one of mounting a gigantic propaganda effort operated through tightened controls over the intelligentsia—literati and artists—and their impressment in the work of manipulating the masses in the desired direction. Human perversity had to be conquered, not accommodated, and a scientific formula for psychological transformism seemed to be at hand. Such was the ideological end product of leadership pragmatism under the conditions of absolute power.

The formula for transforming human nature was found in the Pavlovian theory of the conditioned reflex. Its central principle was that man is a "reactive mechanism whose behavior, including all the higher mental processes, can be exhaustively understood through a knowledge of the laws of conditioning and can be controlled through application of this knowledge." [59] Beginning as a theory in physiology in 1949, it radiated out into the spheres of psychiatry, pedagogy, and psychology by 1952. The vogue of the doctrine was not a spontaneous affair, however, but was politically sparked and organized. In 1949 a special celebration was held of Pavlov's hundredth anniversary. In 1950 a convocation of the joint sessions of the Academy of Science of the USSR and the Academy of Medical Science was called to discuss Pavlov's physiological theories; in 1952 a conference on psychology was held in Moscow attended by over four hundred psychologists from all over the country.

With the Pavlovian revival was connected the development of a new science of semantics and linguistics in which words came to be treated

---

[59] *Ibid.*, p. 101.

only as having a signal function for action (and hence for the control of action), rather than also as object symbols which evidence conception. Linguistics thus became a policy science.

Retrenchment.   A countertrend began to set in the year after Stalin's death, 1954. A prominent physicist, S. I. Sobolev, was permitted to publish an article in *Pravda* saying that scientific progress is "always connected with the abandonment of preconceived points of view, with the bold breaking-down of old norms and conceptions." [60] It then was asserted in a variety of publications that there exists in human nature an independent subjective principle. Still later, during the period of de-Stalinization, it became fashionable to criticize the "dogmatization of Pavlov's teachings." The Pavlovian vogue had found its political culmination in the concept that propaganda can accomplish everything in the manipulation of popular behavior. There was no need to better the living conditions of the people. But the post-Stalinist period has witnessed numerous efforts to accommodate to the demand for some realization of the promise of Communist well-being and freedom. Some limitations have been introduced in the exercise of propaganda and physical methods of coercion as well, and there have even been experiments in economic organization which smack of capitalism, things which Tucker labels jointly as a "strategic retreat into the realm of possibility." As we have indicated earlier, such recent ideological developments and their policy concomitants will be treated in more detail later in this chapter.

8. The Social and Psychological Background of Marxist Appeal

We have reviewed the salient elements of the original Marxist ideology and have seen how Russian leaders have modified this doctrine, a foreign import, to fit the special circumstances of the Russian revolutionary scene. We also have observed that these leaders, like the Nazis, have evolved in their conduct of day-to-day government in Russia an esoteric operational code which is different from and in many ways independent of the Marxist *Weltanschauung*. We have seen that the original Marxist world view actually is manipulated by these leaders as a special instrument of social control, rather than as a map or blueprint for policy makers. The use of the ideology in this way implies a certain natural appeal to Russians, despite the fact that certain modifications had to be made in fitting it precisely to the Russian reality. We need to ask at this point what it was in traditional Russian political culture that matched the categories of this Western European doctrine to such a degree that it could evoke a positive response in the Russian east in this way.

[60] *Ibid.*, p. 115.

Christian Eschatology.   There is an entire literature which argues that Marxism appealed to Russians because it employs secular categories which parallel and are allegedly derived from the religious categories of Christian eschatology which have formed the matrix of traditional Russian political culture.[61] (Eschatology is the doctrine of the beginning and culmination of all things, a theory of the origin and goal of history.) In other words, Marxism appealed to Russians because its terms were actually familiar to them, although its secular formulation allowed it at the same time to negate the entire existing social, political, and religious order. The argument is of long standing and has been criticized by Marxists as so much conservative propaganda. The Russian Communist leader Nikolai Bukharin, for example, wrote: "One of the most widespread forms of ideological class struggle against Marxism is its treatment as an eschatological doctrine, with all its accompaniments of chiliasm, of soteriology, of myth. . . . All these analogies are playing with words." [62] The defenders of the thesis argue, however, that the structural and functional similarities of the two sets of concepts and the similarities of their psychological appeals are manifest. One scholar writes that "The Bolshevik testament is a Christian heresy where God is personified history, pronouncing judgment on the unjust in the thunder of revolution and the smoke of battle, and delivering them not in some far future but here, now." [63] Like early Christianity, he argues, it is a religion of the dispossessed, which asserts that the mighty shall be cast down and the lowly exalted, though *in* history rather than *after* it. The dictatorship of the proletariat, he claims, is functionally parallel to the Christian millennium, a time of justice without mercy. This is followed by the classless society of "truly human history," when the coercive state shall have been done away, a time of love and comradeship like the Christian "Kingdom of Heaven" after the end of the world. Like Christianity, Marxism plays on deep-set fears and hopes out of which it develops an urge to conversion. "The victory of the revolution is inevitable. Therefore, let those who can purge their class guilt join with the proletariat and escape the judgment." [64] Like the Christian believer, the Marxist devotee is exhilarated by being "in" on the secrets of social destiny.

Other Christian Parallels.   Other writers have noted still more parallels between Christian and Marxist concepts. The primitive society portrayed by Engels, for example, in *The Origins of the Family* parallels

---

[61] See, for example, the work of Waldemar Gurian, Carl J. Friedrich, Nicholas Berdiaev, and Eric Voegelin.

[62] Quoted in Donald G. MacRae, "The Appeal of Communist Ideology," in A. Inkeles and K. Geiger, *Soviet Society* (Boston: Houghton-Mifflin, 1961), p. 106.

[63] *Ibid.*

[64] *Ibid.*, p. 107.

the role of the Garden of Eden in the Christian story. Like Eden it is peaceful, a happy place. But like Eden it is a beginning, not a perfection. The happiness of Eden is innocence, but the Heaven of spiritual perfection after sin and suffering is a better place. Primitive society is peaceful but poor, is innocent but undeveloped, whereas perfect material development—and with it the fulfillment of sociality—is found only in the Communist utopia which follows upon a period of class conflict and exploitation, of sin and suffering. The historical appearance of private property as the cause of social conflict parallels the Original Sin as the cause of human discord and unhappiness. Marx, like John the Baptist, is a prophet figure, telling of the coming of a Savior. Lenin is that Messiah, the Christ figure, who leads the proletariat to the Promised Land. But this is possible only after an Armageddon in which class antagonisms are at once simplified and intensified in the final showdown between the forces of good and evil.

Parallels are seen not only between the two doctrines but also between the institutional orders which keep and teach the doctrines— between the Christian Church (especially its orthodox forms) and the Communist Party. In each case there is a body of believers in communion with one another and under hierarchical discipline. The sacred texts (Holy Scripture in the one case, writings of Marx in the other other) are in the keeping of theologians and Communist intellectuals who understand meanings hidden to the average faithful. Both Lenin and Stalin performed a kind of Papal function of ultimate infallible interpretation. Those who refuse to accept the faith are infidels (unreconstructable capitalists).

Nicholas Berdiaev in *The Origin of Russian Communism* attempts to show how the specific form of Christian culture in Russia gave rise to the specific form and institutionalization of Communist culture after 1917. Russian Christianity, he tells us, was characteristically apocalyptic and nihilist, always reaching out to eternity and transcendence, and Russians were always ready to suffer for their faith. This could be readily translated into revolutionary fervor which, through one great nihilistic act, would clear the ground for the final capture of transcendence—the classless society of love and freedom, and the establishment of perfect justice. The fusion of the political with the religious in traditional culture, he adds, also paved the way for their fusion under Communism. Traditional Russians always felt the need for an orthodox faith and both feared and hated heresy, while at the same time they defined the political community in terms of this faith. To be a Russian was to be a true believer, to hold the Orthodox Christian faith. In addition, the church hierarchy was a part of the political hierarchy, with the Czar as head of both temporal and ecclesiastical establishments. The Muscovite state, out of which modern Russia grew, was also shaped by the Messianic concept of the "Third Rome," in which the Russian national mission and the Christian mission of carrying the gospel were joined as one. This experience was specifically different from that of Western Europe, where political and ecclesiastical hierarchies were largely independent of one another and frequently set over against one another in a competitive and antagonistic relationship throughout the medieval period. (In an earlier chapter we have seen how this competition gave rise to notions of limited government, freedom, and popular control which formed part of the raw material of our modern secular Liberal Democratic political culture.) The Russian experience was one of Caesaro-Papist absolutism interspersed with brief periods of disorder and anarchy, a kind of proto-totalitarianism. This experience, as Berdiaev sees it, formed a natural root for Communist totalitarianism, which also insists on a single orthodox faith, which is at once political and pseudo-religious, in the keeping of a single authoritative and absolute hierarchy, with a Czar figure (until the death of Stalin in 1953) at the top. A recurrent popular fear of religious schism—of dark forces taking over Church authority—has been repeatedly reactivated by Communist authority, with the dark forces now personified by Western capitalism. In contrast with all this, it is interesting that the most successful Marxist parties in the West have been the revisionists whose doctrines dovetail with the liberal parliamentary tradition of Western culture and eschew absolutist and totalitarian recipes.

Liberty, Equality, and Poverty.   Scholars find in still other aspects of traditional Russian culture a natural root for Marxist-Leninist doctrine and practice. Donald MacRae argues that in areas of economic impoverishment where despotic government is also a tradition and individual liberty historically unknown, the relationship that Marxism-Leninism sets up between liberty and equality is both intelligible and acceptable. Equality and economic advance are seen as much more pressing problems than the problem of freedom, and there is a willingness to postpone freedom. Freedom actually may appear as a burden in peasant cultures (as Mannheim and Lane also have suggested—see above, pp. 84-85), for it assumes an attitude of self-reliance and the capacity for making manifold decisions which belong to the middle-class entrepreneur or yeoman farmer, but not to the dependent peasant, especially one whose religion teaches that he is a depraved creature. "After the revolution, after the dictatorship of the proletariat comes freedom, but a freedom that does not burden, for human nature will have been re-made to innocence, and human life remoulded to simplicity. Until then humanity must be re-educated by history and by the chief agent of history, the Communist Party." [65]

Traditional Socialism. Berdiaev tells us that the central Marxist concept of the good society as a socialist society found a sympathetic response from traditional Russia. The peasantry, he argues, never accepted either the vast aristocratic estates nor the institution of serfdom as legitimate, despite the antiquity of both institutions. The soil, they believed, had been given to the laboring man by God, from whom the aristocrats had plotted together to steal it. "A naive agrarian socialism was always an accepted principle among the Russian peasants." And there was a tradition that the Czar, the "little father," would one day save them from the toils of the nobility.[66] When this salvation was in fact promised them by Lenin, they were ready to accept him as a new embodiment of the "little father."

Native Russian "Dialectics." Berdiaev also maintains that the leading Marxist "belief," the idea of reality as dialectical, as consisting of combined opposites, also matches to an astonishing degree the characteristic psychology and behavior of traditional Russia. "The bringing together of principles which are antinomies and polar opposites is characteristically Russian. Russia and the Russian people can be characterized only by contradictions." As examples he tells us that the Russian people always have been both imperial-despotic and anarchic–freedom-loving people in their political attitudes and behavior; they are both nationalist and universalist at the same time.[67] The first of these antinomies has been remarked repeatedly in the social-psychological literature on the foundations of Russian Communism.

Dialectical Psychology. Anthropologist Margaret Mead, for example, in a study of 1951 carried out in collaboration with political scientists, historians, and psychiatrists, grounds Soviet concepts of authority in the persistence of certain traditional psychological traits. "Strict forms of control," she writes, "centralization of government and industry and political police who watched over a people adept at indirect forms of resistance did not need to be invented but had merely to be shaped to new purposes." [68] The root of these institutions she finds in the traditional

[65] *Ibid.*, p. 110.

[66] Nicholas Berdiaev, *The Origin of Russian Communism*, trans. R. M. French (London: G. Bles Centenary Press, 1937), p. 13.

[67] *Ibid.*, pp. 14, 15.

[68] Margaret Mead, *Soviet Attitudes Toward Authority: An Inter-Disciplinary Approach to Problems of Soviet Character* (New York: McGraw-Hill Book Company, 1951), p. 14.

psychological set of the Russian people, whom she describes as "prone to extreme swings in mood from exhilaration to depression, hating confinement and authority and yet feeling that a strong external authority was necessary to keep their own violent impulses in check." [69] This is just another way of talking about the "antinomies" described by Berdiaev. In traditional Russian personality, Mead tells us, the qualities of self-control, measurement, and calculation were underdeveloped, whereas endurance, unstinted commitment, and spontaneity were overdeveloped. The political result was at one and the same time a felt need for strong external control to compensate for the lack of inner discipline, and also a revulsion against external government, a love of wild and anarchic freedom. We are reminded of the inner conflicts of Lane's four undemocrats, and of their fear that society would pull itself apart if it were not for police discipline.

Broad psychological generalizations of this sort, with their equally broad political derivations, should be approached warily, as we learned in Chapter 7. In the studies discussed there, however, substantial empirical evidence was lacking for the statements made. Mead's research, however, rests in large part on a volume of empirical findings, which was subjected to a rigorous cross-disciplinary analysis. Mead and her colleagues used as their data published materials from the USSR, emigrant interviews, and the personal experiences of the research group in the Soviet Union. Their conclusions are the same as those of historians like Berdiaev and of contemporary journalists, working with still other methods. [70]

The Boyhood of Maxim Gorky.   Russians themselves, in interpreting their own psycho-political order, have produced similar judgments. One such work in particular is of importance because it took the form of an educational film produced by the Soviet government. (It could be argued that if the Russians believe such things about themselves and use them as the basis of public policies they must be true, apart from all other evidence.) This is a motion picture about the boyhood of the popular Russian writer Maxim Gorky, which is described by Erik Erikson in his *Childhood and Society*.[71] Professor Erikson writes that he was introduced to the film by Miss Mead, who was serving as seminar leader of the Rus-

---

[69] *Ibid.*, p. 26.

[70] See, e.g., Klaus Mehnert, *Soviet Man and His World*, M. Rosenbaum, trans. (New York: Frederick A. Praeger, 1962), p. 29. Mehnert tells an anecdote about a prerevolutionary holy man who returned home from a lengthy ascetic retreat, only to get drunk, rape his daughter, and burn down his house his first night home. He then disappeared once more. The well-known figure of Rasputin embodies the same antithetical qualities.

[71] Erik H. Erikson, *Childhood and Society* (New York: W. W. Norton & Company, Inc., 1950), Chapter 10.

sian group in a Columbia University Research Project in Contemporary Cultures, which he served as occasional consultant. It was the work of this seminar which produced *Soviet Attitudes Toward Authority*.

The film was first shown in Moscow in 1938 and was produced by Soyuztetfilm. In the picture Gorky's uncles, a crew of drunken, rapacious, and fratricidal beasts, represent the Russian peasantry. The extended family is governed by an alternately sadistic and masochistic old grandfather. The "good" side of traditional Russian life is depicted in the figures of the grandmother and a foundling Gypsy, an apprentice in the family business. They represent patient and loving endurance of the villainies perpetrated by father and sons. They give in and charitably suffer the blows rained on them by the rest. The picture of traditional life is completed with the contrasting figure of the revolutionary anarchist, depicted as a stranger in his own country, who rejects apathy and serfdom. He disappears from the scene in a group of shackled prisoners on their way to Siberia. The first part of the film, which shows young Gorky living out his childhood amidst these people, focuses on his temptations to identify now with one, now with another of the traditional figures—temptations which he painfully but sovereignly rejects. The rest of the picture is about the emergence of Gorky as the model of the "New Soviet Man," which we shall discuss shortly.

Political Derivations.   According to Mead, the sadistic-masochistic and psychological pattern described above, with its attendant oscillations between submission to despotic authority and anarchic freedom, has produced three other behavior patterns which are central for the understanding of contemporary Soviet experience. "Mir, large extended families, and religious and social rituals," she writes, "stressed confession and complete revelation of self to others and the merging of the individual in the group." [72] On such a foundation one could easily construct the discipline of the Communist cadre party and the practice of "self-criticism" as a device whereby those who resist the Party line can be brought to heel. A corollary to this is the tendency of the traditional Russian to see good and evil in all. Friends could act like enemies, but they could also be expected to repent and be restored to the group. This in turn leads to a lack of distinction between thought and deed and to a sense of diffused sinfulness as against individual sinfulness. No one could be expected to act responsibly in a consistent fashion, and all harbored the potentiality for antisocial acts. Responsibility could be meaningful only as a collective concept. Therefore, it mattered little who performed a particular antisocial act, for all had contemplated it. It is a short step

[72] Mead, *op. cit.*, p. 26.

to the proposition that it therefore matters little who is called to atone for the "sin." Any victim at all will do, so that the group may be purged of its wickedness.

9. Ideology as a Weapon against the Past

We have been accounting for continuities in Russian political culture—the continuation into the Communist era of centralized, authoritarian government employing arbitrary and repressive police force, and of group rather than individual orientation, with its consequences for the diffusion of social responsibility. Equally important are the attempts of the Communist leadership to employ their totalitarian authority to break with salient elements of the old culture by refashioning the psychic pattern we have just described. The felt need to do this flows from the recognized discrepancy between the undisciplined behavior of the traditional culture and the need of the modern industrial state for a rational, goal-oriented citizenry. This is reflected in the emphasis on restrained pragmatism in the Party's operational code and Stalin's inclusion of a work ethic in that code.

The "New Soviet Man" and the Work Ethic.   Since leaders not only set the moral tone of society but also direct its operations, the need to create a "new Soviet man" manifests itself first of all in an ideology of leadership—an image of the good leader, of the ideal Bolshevik personality. He is goal-oriented, in the sense that he calculates, measures the proportion between ends and means, and in the sense that he conforms his behavior to a self-consistent pattern. He is internally disciplined, he works hard. "The Left deviation," writes Mead, "represents uncontrolled, romantic, not properly calculated behavior; and the Right, spineless pessimism and a tendency to surrender easily before setbacks or obstacles." By contrast "the Bolshevik leader must remain indeflectable, calm, . . . wary." [73] He is also watchful, restless, and all-seeing, all-directing. Soviet training seeks to internalize in the Communist cadres a deep dissatisfaction with the status quo and a recognition of the "struggle between the new and the old." Each success in self-conquest and at one's job produces the desire to go farther. The object is to create a "self-promoting anxiety." [74] We are reminded of the anxious but determined striving and self-discipline of Walzer's Puritan "saints" and of Weber's concept of the "Protestant Ethic." Erikson interprets the film representation of young Gorky as demonstrating "the way stations of an emergent new Russian frame of mind, a Russian individualism." And he makes an explicit com-

[73] *Ibid.*, p. 64.
[74] *Ibid.*, pp. 72, 73.

parison between this development and the psychic revolution of Protestantism. "No Luther, no Calvin," Erikson writes, "has shown him new recesses of the mind; and no founding fathers and pioneers have opened up uncharted continents where he might overcome his inner and his outer serfdom. By himself, and in secret agreement with kindred minds, he must learn to protest, and to develop—in the very widest sense—a 'protestant' morality." [75] Erikson sees in the Communist elite's selection of names ("Stalin"—steel, "Molotov"—hammer) a symbol of the connection between the new mentality and the building of an industrial society. "The imagery of steel suggests incorruptible realism and enduring, disciplined struggle. . . . As it is forged, steel forges a new generation and a new elite . . . which underscores without cessation the incorruptibility of Bolshevik perception, the long range of its vision, its steel-like clarity of decision, and the machine-like firmness of action." [76]

Lenin, as the founder of the new order, embodied the central "Protestant" traits of the "new Soviet man." Berdiaev describes him as liking order and discipline in his private life, in contrast to the bohemianism of Martov and Trotsky, who lost out in the contest for power. He rejected anarchism and hated revolutionary romanticism. Lacking breadth of knowledge and intellectual culture, he subjected knowledge to the demands of action. As a successful political enterpreneur, he also resolved the problem of combining a determinist metaphysic (which implies, purely logically, human passivity) with an activist and voluntarist political ethic, like the English Calvinists before him. Leopold Haimson, in a study of the evolution of the Russian revolutionary mind which focuses on the concepts of "consciousness" (rational determination) and "spontaneity" (activist voluntarism), shows that of all the leaders of Russian Marxism it was only Lenin who found a way of combining the two concepts in a politically viable formula, and one in which the individuality of the leader is not swallowed up in an identification either with popular forces or with the laws of history. Pavel Akselrod's confidence in the spontaneous force of the Russian people to bring the revolution represents one pole in the theoretical choice posed to the Marxist leadership. Georg Plekhanov's reliance on outside forces to bring into being the rational order determined by the law of history (which he read as identical with his own concept of rational order) is the other. Lenin demanded instead that one swim against the tide, pit one's will against recalcitrant circumstance, and strive to conquer it, accepting, however, the outcome as the will of history. "The continuous conflict created in his personality by the clash between the will to master and the principle of reality was reflected in the image of a world in

[75] Erikson, *op. cit.*, p. 323.
[76] *Ibid.*, p. 354.

flux, and therefore a world which could be molded and shaped by man." [77] Lenin's view of historical necessity gave much more room to individual will as a shaping force than Plekhanov's or Akselrod's. And it was his counsel that triumphed and that made a successful revolution. "No mechanical objective law . . . could prevent the man of the new age from deciding his fate and mastering the world." [78]

We have been dealing with new elements in Russian political culture as represented by the ideology of the good leader defined as the "new Soviet man," and we have drawn parallels between this model and the Western European (or American) bearer of the "Protestant Ethic." Inasmuch as the latter personality model has been an integral figure of Liberal Democratic political culture, we might suppose that his emergence in Soviet Russia portends the liberalization of the political scene there. This is not likely to be the case, however, for the parallel is not complete. Traditional Russian modes surround and modify the image we have just drawn.

Work Ethic East and West: Differences.   One important difference between the new Soviet "Protestant" and the Western European has to do with the matter of self-reliance and independence of judgment. These qualities are of the essence of the Liberal work ethic, but they are quite lacking in the Soviet model, except for the charismatic leader at the top of the hierarchy of power. The "new Soviet man" as the typical cadre member of the Communist Party is expected indeed to be rationally goal-oriented, disciplined, moderate, and pragmatic, but not self-reliant. His discipline is that of the soldier, not the free citizen, and his reliance is totally on the authorities set above him in the Party. This is at least in part the result of a carryover from the traditional culture of the old fusion of individual with group and its attendant features. "An important element in contemporary Soviet practices designed to make . . . new types of men and women," writes Mead, "is the assumption that each individual carries within him a whole series of disallowed attitudes." [79]

To insure the steadfastness of his course, the continuance of rational behavior, the individual (every individual) is called upon to bare himself to the group, to confess his temptations and errors, and be corrected by the group. His interior resources for a *pure* self-discipline are thought to be inadequate. Everyone remains capable of complete betrayal and complete irrationality; hence the group must be vigilant, constantly overseeing its members' state of mind. This produces the device of "self-criticism" as an instrument of insuring discipline—a

---

[77] Leopold H. Haimson, *The Russian Marxists and the Origins of Bolshevism* (Cambridge, Mass.: Harvard University Press, 1955), p. 46.

[78] *Ibid.*, p. 218.

[79] Mead, *op. cit.*, p. 31.

weapon whereby the top leadership keep the middle echelon cadres and the rank and file of Party members in step with changes in the Party line. It plays a most important role in dealing with opposition forces as new dominant coalitions form and reform. An important motive of the "new Soviet man" is the avoidance of the shame which he is made to feel for slackness or other deviation from the standards set by the Party group to which he belongs. This is of particular psychological importance because the Party takes the place of the old multiple authorities—God, Church, and father of the family.

An important reinforcement of the individual's dependence on the Party organization derives from the continued authority of the idea of an absolute and all-encompassing Truth in the keeping of a visible public authority, an idea which received a mortal blow in the West as a result of the Protestant Reformation and its attendant political effects. In Russia the One Truth of Caesaro-Papist orthodoxy was not destroyed, as in the West, but simply replaced by another single and absolute Truth—that of Dialectical Materialism as interpreted by the top leadership of the Communist Party. One result of all this is that in Soviet theories of good character structure it is held that "the will should be developed without . . . any sense of the possibility of choice." [80] Choices are made at the top of the Party hierarchy, and the role of the "new Soviet man" down the ranks is to carry out those choices in a rational way.

The elitist and hierarchical conception of truth which predominates in the Soviet Union also accounts for the attitude of the Party toward the general public, "the masses." Unlike the Western Liberal Democratic doctrine of "the People" as the oracle of the general will, and hence the proper master of public policy, the Russian masses are viewed instead as a great, enthusiastic crowd producing the energy to execute the Party's will. They are seen as having a "passionate desire" to match the leaders' control, reserve, and dispassion. They are the embodiment of strength and endurance, the virtues of the grandmother figure in the film about Gorky's childhood. They possess zest, optimism, cheerfulness—but not self-reliance or the capacity to decide.[81]

Gayle Hollander, in a recent study of Soviet political indoctrination, has synthesized the literature on the subject and distilled a list of eleven qualities that define the ideal citizen of the USSR. They include a love of work, total politicization (i.e., absolute subordination of the individual's will and needs uncritically to the Party leadership), political and social activism, political literacy according to ideological guidelines,

---

[80] *Ibid.*, p. 78.

[81] *Ibid.*, p. 84. For a detailed study of political socialization in the Soviet Union, see Herschel and Edith Alt, *The New Soviet Man: His Upbringing and Character Development* (New York: Bookman Associates, 1964).

self-discipline, the display of Socialist solidarity, patriotism, collectivism rather than individualism in motivation, nonpolitical virtues (honesty, sobriety, modesty, courage, humility), and, lastly atheism—having no religious need.[82]

Conclusion. The Soviet regime thus works very hard at instilling "correct" ideological views among the Russian people. The program may be summed up as a "three-pronged effort: (1) political indoctrination, (2) positive coercion, and (3) negative coercion. Individuals are bombarded throughout their life cycle with a steady stream of messages meant to convince them of the legitimacy and moral rectitude of the regime's policies and to mobilize 'the masses' for the fulfillment of those policies. This is the Soviet version of overt, purposeful political socialization." [83]

10. Results of Ideological Indoctrination

Survey Data. We have seen that Marxist ideology in Russia both builds upon traditional Russian political culture and offers a challenge to it. What success have the Communists had in the revolutionary inculcation of the new ideological system? Government control of the communications system and the authoritarian institutions of the Soviet system make it difficult to get reliable data on feelings of legitimacy about the new order and the degree to which its values and beliefs have been internalized by the Russian people. A survey of refugees from the Soviet Union done in 1950 and 1951 by a group of Harvard scholars, though now twenty yeads old, contains some of the most reliable (and probably still valid) empirical material that we have on the subject.[84] Predictably, as refugees, many of the respondents said that they would keep none of the institutions of the Communist regime if they were given the opportunity to pick and choose. However, when quizzed obliquely about specific aspects of the Soviet system, it was found that they heartily approved certain of them. These included the program of public education, the socialized health services, and workers' benefits. Respondents were much less interested in state ownership and social equality by comparison with these things, but when asked specifically about the control of industry, all groups participating in the survey

[82] Gayle Hollander, *Soviet Political Indoctrination: Development in Mass Media and Propaganda Since Stalin* (New York: Frederick A. Praeger, 1972), pp. 8, 9.
[83] *Ibid.*, p. 5.
[84] Alex Inkeles and Raymond A. Bauer, *The Soviet Citizen* (Cambridge, Mass.: Harvard University Press, 1959). This study was based on 875 long interviews and three thousand questionnaires.

supported government control of transport and heavy industry. There was much less desire shown for government-owned light industry, and there were high percentages against the system of collective farms. Nevertheless, the data show overwhelming support for the basically socialist economy.

Turning from economics to the realm of personal freedoms, the respondents registered extreme disapproval of absolutist terror, together with support for guarantees of personal rights. However, they did not emerge from the survey as individualists, and, in fact, expressed strong dislike for the display of freewheeling individuality:

> Less than half the respondents felt that the government had no right to intervene in an assembly if the purpose of the assembly is to "attack" the Government. Only about a third believed people should be permitted to say things against the government. Sentiment in favor of civil liberties was weakest among the lower classes.[85]

They also came out against "American freedom." A fifty-nine-year-old professor of engineering, for example, said: "When I arrived in America, I thanked God that we did not have the demoralizing comic strips, the cheap vulgar literature that is available to children here." [86] And an engine mechanic of thirty-one was quoted as saying that "In America youth is allowed to attend all kinds of films which make it sexually premature." The respondents also expressed a strong negative reaction to American tolerance of dissident opinions. And the group was disturbed that the government did not do more to direct citizens' actions for their own good, that there were not more routine regulations. They had thus largely internalized the elitist and authoritarian assumptions of the regime, as well as its socialist features, probably because of the continuity of these assumptions with the principles of the traditional culture.

The Maintenance of Fervor.   The Harvard data indicate a basic habitual pattern of political and economic attitudes which legitimate the Communist system. They do not, however, show to what extent the Soviet leadership has been able to maintain conscious enthusiasm for the regime and for the myth of cooperative construction of a future Communist utopia which demands from the present generation the deferral of many values. Such evidence as we have suggests much less success at this level. Klaus Mehnert, for example, thinks that the Russian people have grown weary of the propaganda over the years and are now largely depoliticized.

[85] *Ibid.*, p. 247.
[86] *Ibid.*, p. 249.

The process of stripping the revolutionary anniversaries of their political significance is part of the general decline of interest in politics. When I was in the Soviet Union around 1930 every conversation sooner or later turned into a political discussion. Today that seldom happens unless a foreignor deliberately turns the conversation in that direction.[87]

Robert Tucker thinks that the average man is not very future-oriented and would prefer to have his values now. Malenkov, he writes, tried to give representation to this attitude, but Khrushchev, despite the fact that he increased the production of consumer goods, attempted to restore the future orientation.[88]

The Soviet Opportunist.   So far as the motivation of the Party cadres is concerned, the evidence is mixed. John Kosa thinks that the number of "true believers" is probably quite high because of the selection process of the Party:

> Like a huge suction pump, the party draws in all kinds of people but ejects the majority and keeps only the selected ones. It culls the incomers and subjects them to tests of loyalty and devotion. Those who fail are dropped; those who pass are formed, influenced, and strengthened in their belief till, in due time, they reach the degree of perfect identification.[89]

Jerzy Kosinski, however, has drawn a detailed portrait of the opportunist who uses the value-language of the ideology and its operational rules to further his own private ends of income, safety, and deference. A passage from one of his interviews deserves quotation:

> I saw that all the social, scientific, political and administrative institutions were open, first of all, to the likes of us, people with proper class origin, devoted to the Party and to the cause of the USSR. This became my signpost. I was uncompromising to myself and even more so to others. . . . I obeyed all orders I received. During vacations I harvested to "help the nation." I reported the hostile attitude of one of my schoolteachers who was dismissed as a consequence, "on behalf of the working class." I frequently criticized myself "for my own good."
>   . . . After graduation [from a Party school] I was delegated to work in the Komsomol. . . . I set up youth organizations and dissolved those whose work was not satisfactory. I was a lecturer, agitator and propagandist, and sometimes, when necessary, even a prosecutor. As I told you, I was uncompromising.

[87] Mehnert, op. cit., p. 224.
[88] Robert C. Tucker, The Soviet Political Mind: Stalinism and Post-Stalin Change, rev. ed. (New York: W. W. Norton & Company, Inc., 1971).
[89] John Kosa, Two Generations of Soviet Man (Chapel Hill: University of North Carolina Press, 1962), pp. 141–42. See also pp. 142–43.

I knew that when I spoke the audience had the reactions and the conclusions that I wanted them to have. I also saw how those whom I accused broke down though they still could have defended themselves or answered the questions put to them. I saw them try in vain to collect their thoughts and then I saw them panic.

. . . To be always attacking others, to bring to life the Party line, and at the same time not to come into conflict with that line is the most difficult game. I think that I have been able to maintain it.[90]

Robert Beck similarly suggests that a success ethic is a widespread motivation among Soviet Party elites. But he finds this motivation combined with patriotic sentiments, and both these motives reinforced by group criticism which induces shame for lax behavior and threatens ostracism.[91]

Even though opportunism and ideological cynicism may be widespread in the Soviet Union, it is important that both are clothed with an apparent orthodoxy. This is itself a testimony to the strength of the new political culture. As Gayle Hollander writes:

Even if an individual resists internalizing the Soviet Communist world view presented to him, he is coerced to behave in ways which demonstrate that he has accepted it. It is imperative to go through the motions of enthusiasm and loyalty, and to continually express boundless confidence in the regime. This is accomplished by intensive pressures to participate in mass demonstrations, to attend political meetings and rallies, or to vote en bloc with neighbors and colleagues. The assumption . . . is that the individual playing the role of good citizen will eventually come to think and feel like one.[92]

Problem Youth.   Certain segments of youth have posed a problem for those charged with ideological mobilization. One consists of the *jeunesse dorée*, the gilded youth of the elite families whose attitudes are characterized by "satiety and boredom":

A scandal reported by *Komsomolskaya Pravda* (August 15, 1956) involved the two sons of I. G. Kabanov, minister of foreign trade. The lads teamed up with a third youth to rob apartments and used the proceeds from the lootings to finance drunken orgies with three girls, whose fathers turned out to be a general, an aviation colonel, and a colonel in one of the police agencies.[93]

[90] Jerzy Kosinski, *The Future is Ours, Comrade* (Garden City, N.Y.: Doubleday, 1960), pp. 210ff. The author is an East European journalist.

[91] Robert Beck, "Soviet Education as Training for Life," in Robert T. Holt and John E. Turner, eds. *Soviet Union: Paradox and Change* (New York: Holt, Rinehart & Winston, Inc., 1962), pp. 150–51.

[92] Hollander, *op. cit.*, p. 5.

[93] Thomas Magner, "Soviet Youth," in Holt and Turner, *op. cit.*, p. 171.

This behavior by the new elite, hardly in keeping with the ideology of the "New Soviet Man," has disillusioned still others, as has the opportunism of those who exploit the ideology for reasons of personal achievement.

Ideological Oppositionists.   Small groups of ideological oppositionists are to be found among the politically conscious sections of the youth. T. F. Magner describes three such deviationist groups. One consists of Neo-Leninists, who emphasize egalitarianism and argue that the regime has forgotten the ultimate goals of the October Revolution. They want the power of the party bureaucracy and of the police reduced, and more economic and political democracy. They do not challenge the one-party system, however, nor the centralized economy. A second group are Liberal Socialists, who have lost faith in the utopian dream and are ready to settle for political democracy and a collectivist economy operated by democratically organized cooperatives. A third group are anti-Socialists who maintain limited contacts with foreign visitors and read foreign literature. They are convinced of the superiority of the Western democratic system and want political democracy and private property established in Russia. Most of these people are technologically oriented, however, and are not comfortable in involved ideological discussion. These are all very small groups and in no way pose a threat to the stability of the regime.[94]

Strategic Mistakes.   Allen Kassof, writing about the Soviet program for the political socialization of the youth, reports that the majority who are activists in youth organizations are mildly committed to the mobilization norms of the ideology. Too many true believers, Kassof argues, would make the program rigid, whereas moderate commitment permits a degree of flexibility necessary to its success. By giving youth a sense of partnership in the building of a Communist society it gives them an identification. Kassof finds excessive bureaucratization, however, and the exclusion of the rank and file from the making of decisions. Despite the presumptions of traditional Russian culture, he finds that there is resentment among the youth at their deprivation of the right of independent thinking. There is also resentment at the invasion of privacy, and a certain boredom and apathy created by the stifling of creative imagination in favor of routine. Also, the program is all seriousness and includes no specifically youth culture, which may account for certain deviant behavior in a bizarre direction.[95]

---

[94] *Ibid.*, pp. 179–80.
[95] Allen S. Kassof, *The Soviet Youth Program, Regimentation and Rebellion* (Cambridge, Mass.: Harvard University Press, 1965).

11. The End of Ideology?

Deradicalization.   The Twentieth Party Congress of 1956, and the events that followed from it, appear to represent a watershed in the evolution of Soviet Communism. The doctrine of peaceful coexistence came into prominence and the possibility of a parliamentary path to Socialism was officially recognized. Proposals were made for rapprochement with the "heretical" Social Democrats of Western Europe, an independent-minded national Communism was recognized as a legitimate regime in Yugoslavia, and the neutrality of the "Third World" was accepted as a fact. At home no new charismatic tyrant appeared at the summit of the Soviet hierarchy, and collective government became the normal pattern. Elements of due process were gradually introduced into the judicial system, and a new emphasis on consumer production was seen in the economy. The militant phase of revolutionary change seemed at an end; Russian Communism had become deradicalized.[96]

Do these developments imply a profound change in Russian political culture? Has an age of self-conscious revolutionary ideology come to an end? If it is true that Marxist Communism is a Liberal heresy, do these changes represent a new ecumenicism and perhaps a growing together of the two "faiths"? What precisely does "deradicalization" imply, and how can it be formulated as a general theoretical concept of use in the understanding of ideology and political culture?

The difficulty of giving clear and adequate answers to these questions is demonstrated in an essay by Robert C. Tucker on the deradicalization of Marxist movements in his recent book, *The Marxian Revolutionary Idea*. He suggests that we might identify the "radical mind" by three characteristics: (1) it denies and rejects absolutely the existing order of things; (2) it envisages a perfect alternative to this order, a right social order whose lineaments are sketched in a doctrinaire and forensic ideology; and (3) it is activist, demanding revolutionary politics. The revolutionary movement then develops as an "institutionalization of the radical doctrine, as the organized activity of a group dedicated to the realization of the vision of a new society." [97] Deradicalization, Professor Tucker suggests, involves the settling down of the movement and its adjustment to the order at whose overthrow it had connived. The movement becomes "reformist," loses revolutionary ardor, accommodates to the existing world. Organizationally this phase is characterized by the growth of large struc-

[96] Robert C. Tucker, *The Marxian Revolutionary Idea* (New York: W. W. Norton & Company, Inc., 1969), Chapter 6.
[97] *Ibid.*, pp. 184–85.

tures, a mass social constituency, and a recognized place in society. All these things happened to the Western European Social Democratic parties during the nineteenth century.

If we were to apply this model to an understanding of ideological dynamics in the Soviet Union, Professor Tucker tells us, we might be inclined to agree with Trotsky that Stalin brought about the beginning of deradicalization with the creation of vast bureaucratic structures and with the great purge of Old Bolsheviks in the 1930s. However, not all Stalinist behavior fits the model. Stalin wanted to move from a money economy to "product exchange," and he demanded that the Russians accept a program of austerity in order to achieve full Communism. Mao Tse-tung saw him as a radical, in fact, if Trotsky did not. And in the area of foreign policy, we find Stalin presiding over forcible communization after World War II.

Since Stalin's death the model seems to have a better fit, as evidenced by the rapprochement with non-Communist regimes abroad and the abandonment of a doctrinaire line for a pragmatic one in economic affairs, including experiments with market principles that smack very much of essentially capitalist practice. However, Tucker tells us that it cannot be said that the Soviet Union has entered upon the "end of ideology" in anything like the Western Liberal sense. He finds that there has been no diminution in ideological rhetoric in the Soviet Union, and that, if anything, its use has been intensified. Dedication to the final goals of the revolution has been reaffirmed, and *ideological* coexistence has been rejected. "Intensified verbal allegiance to ultimate ideological goals belongs to the pattern of deradicalization," he writes. Or, at least this is true in the Soviet Union. What, then, is the chief mark of deradicalization there? "Not the end of ideology but rather the growth of a stable discrepancy between ideological symbols and political deeds is the true mark of deradicalizing change in once-radical movements," Professor Tucker concludes.[98]

While the volume of ideological propaganda remains high, the role of many official ideologues has been changing. L. G. Churchward reports in a recent study of the Soviet intelligentsia that many who formerly were put to work to legitimate the regime through ideology making have now become social scientists whose work is the systematic study of government and Party administration. In short, the technical expert is replacing the word and symbol maker.[99] It is also encouraging that the continued focus of domestic attention on ideological themes has

[98] *Ibid.*, p. 214.
[99] L. G. Churchward, *The Soviet Intelligentsia, an Essay on the Social Structure and Roles of Soviet Intellectuals During the 1960s* (London: Routledge and Kegan Paul, 1973).

not prevented an epoch-making international political detente between the USA and the USSR. During his June 1973 visit to the United States, Party First Secretary Brezhnev declared the end of the "Cold War," surely a testimony to the "end of ideology" at a most significant level.

A Cyclical Pattern?   This analysis seems to interpret recent changes in Russian ideological behavior in terms of secular linear developments. In an earlier study Professor Tucker analyzes them rather in terms of a cyclical phenomenon described as a recurrence of a pattern established in the traditional political culture. In *The Soviet Political Mind* Tucker writes on the recent "thaw" as a parallel to the thaw of the nineteenth century which set in following the death of Nicholas I in 1855. Both events he subsumes under a generalized "dual image" pattern. The theme has also been developed by Harrison Salisbury in an essay of 1962 on "The New Men of the '60s" in which he compares trends among the post-Stalinist intelligentsia with changes in the 1860s.[100] Tucker describes the two periods of liberalization, a century apart, as representing a shift of emphasis from one to another of two principles of authority which alternate in ascendency in Russian political life. On the one hand there is the principle of *"vlast"* or *"gosudarstvo,"* which signifies the centralized and autocratic state system of all-encompassing and bureaucratized "official Russia." On the other there is the image of *"obshchestvo," "narod"*—the nation, the people, "popular Russia." The state is seen as an alien, conquering power, freely manipulating and organizing society; "popular Russia" is a passive party, that which is manipulated.

Change in the 1860s involved the contraction of "official Russia" in favor of autonomy for "popular Russia." This was signaled by the liberalization of the regime from above, evidenced in the abolition of serfdom, the establishment of local government councils, and other reforms. Tucker writes of the beginning of a "dialogue" between state and society, in which society was represented by the Liberal intelligentsia of the time. Tucker describes the birth of Slavophilism at the time as the emergence of an anti-totalitarian doctrine of cultural autonomy. The conception of the two Russias at war with one another became part of the revolutionary idea.

The final collapse of "official Russia" as a result of the Revolution of 1917 and the triumph of "popular Russia" was followed by the gradual resurgence of "official Russia," which reached its climax during the Stalinist period. This brought with it the withdrawal of popular life from the state and the development of an underground culture, which

[100] Harrison Salisbury, *A New Russia?* (New York: Harper & Row, 1962).

in turn produced scoldings about "apolitical" and "nonideological" attitudes. Then came the "thaw" and the beginnings of a new relaxation of official Russia. The explanation reminds us of the dialectical antinomies observed by Berdiaev and of the psychical oscillations in Mead's description of Soviet attitudes toward authority.

12. The Russian "New Left" and Other Dissidents: Pressures on the Ideological System

In a recent essay Lewis Feuer focuses attention on the current student vogue of the early writings of Marx, an event which may herald the beginning of important ideological changes in the Soviet Union.[101] The writings in question are the *Economic-Philosophical Manuscripts of 1844*, which predated Marx' collaboration with Engels and which reveal a very strong Idealist influence. In these manuscripts Marx appears as a metaphysical dualist, acknowledging the equal reality and autonomy of matter and spirit. Man is thus accorded a certain independence of the process of material change and is seen as an active agent in historical development.

Alienation.   The leading concept of the early manuscripts is "alienation." In the present state of the world man is alienated from his true self, which is a free, creative, communal spirit. He is dominated from without and exploited as though he were a thing. He is artificially sundered from his fellows in individualist society. This is particularly seen in his economic relationships, which are produced by a system of private property involving the division of labor. In revulsion against this state of things, Marx does not appeal to the determinisms of the dialectic for release, but rather "to the 'categorical imperative' to overthrow all those conditions in which man is an abased, enslaved, abandoned, contemptible being." [102] He espouses a voluntary community approach to the solution of the evils of alienation.

Feuer reads the "alienationist trend" as an effort to restore to Marxism ethical consciousness and an irreducible freedom for the individual from the vast demands of state and society made in the name of an inexorable dialectical determinism. The trend arose, Feuer notes,

> after an era of Stalinism in which contempt for ethical considerations had been carried to the last extreme. There was a revulsion too against

[101] Lewis Feuer, "Alienation: The Marxism of Contemporary Student Movements," in Milorad Drachkovitch, ed. *Marxist Ideology in the Contemporary World*, Hoover Institute Series (New York: Frederick A. Praeger, 1966). Copyright 1966 by the Board of Trustees of Stanford University. Quotations with permission.

[102] *Ibid.*, p. 40.

the historicism which Marx and Engels had used in their repression of the ethical consciousness. Also, post-war thinkers realized clearly that a socialist economic foundation was no sufficient basis for the superstructure of a free society; the concepts of bureaucratic collectivism, managerial control, the organized system, and mass society, were all ways of viewing new forms of human repression. And the common denominator of all the repressive features of social existence seemed to be man's alienation. . . . No longer was history a locomotive on predetermined dialectical rails; rather it consisted of man's own gropings to realize his essence. . . . An historical voluntarism arose to supersede the historical materialism of mass impersonal movements.[103]

Interest in the young Marx in the Soviet Union was first evidenced in philosophical literature in 1958, and on a visit of 1963 Feuer found that "alienation" was considered a most provocative and pregnant concept among young Soviet philosophers. The vogue has spread to Marxist circles all around the world. Feuer notes that Mario Savio made great use of the notion of "alienation" in the confrontations at Berkeley and that the president of the Japanese Zengakuren has identified the overcoming of alienation as the primary problem to which his following must address itself. The freedom-oriented young Marx thus speaks to the "New Left" in all political cultures, whether Liberal Democratic or Communist. His concept of "alienation" furnishes them with a way of comprehending the impersonal disciplines of bureaucratic industrial society which transcend the differences between East and West, between the Liberal and the Communist worlds. It also furnishes an ideological weapon against those disciplines that are seen as repressive and destructive of the human spirit.

Three and a half decades of Stalinist industrialization and mobilization for total war have thus produced a degree of revisionism in the intellectual strata of Soviet political culture, which points toward a certain relaxation of totalitarian control of Russian society. The ultimate effect of this new way of thinking on public policy, however, remains ambiguous. In the early sixties the new "Liberals" captured their own journals—*Novy Mir, Voprosy Literatury, Literaturnaya Gazeta*—although the "reactionaries" remained entrenched in their own. When in 1962 and 1963 Khrushchev openly denounced the Liberals, the editor of *Novy Mir* publicly announced a program of publication which included the works of men like Solzhenitsyn and Yevtushenko who had been critical of the regime. The literature of the sixties employed themes which focused on escape—running away from home, from school, from discipline.[104] At this writing, however, the newspapers in the West are

---

[103] *Ibid.*, pp. 37–38.
[104] Daniel Bell, "The End of Ideology in the Soviet Union?" in Drachkovitch, ed., *op. cit.*, pp. 76–112.

carrying stories of the intensified persecution of writers like Solzhenitsyn, including illegal searches and arbitrary beatings. And a wave of Jewish persecution also has received considerable publicity. In certain areas, therefore, "liberalization" appears at best sporadic and uneven.

Control of the Intelligentsia.   L. G. Churchward reports that persecution of intellectuals has occurred during the permissive sixties—the period of the "thaw"—broken by brief moments of relaxation. "There was never any abandonment of the struggle to maintain party hegemony," he writes.[105] The pressure has been relaxed somewhat, however, since the fall of Khrushchev. The Ideological Commission, a kind of Holy Office or Inquisition, was abolished in 1965. What this has meant, however, is largely an exchange of more formal for less formal procedures. Professional organizations and the press are employed to bring pressure to bear on dissident intellectuals. And broad-scale ideological campaigns are staged by the Party at such symbolic times as the jubilee of the Revolution and the centenary of Lenin's birth. Individuals who pit their consciences against the government line lose their jobs and Party membership. Churchward notes that such ousters are carried out by district committees, not by primary organizations, which indicates support for dissidents in their local groups.[106]

Symbolic of the continued concern for ideological purity on the Party's terms was the attack launched in the Soviet press in the fall of 1972 against three new plays. A reviewer for the Moscow *Pravda*, known as a theater watchdog, accused the playwright of an historical drama that dealt with the relations between Pushkin and Czar Nicholas I of posing too simple a conflict between the poet and the representative of political power, and for failing to underline the class basis of their conflict. It was obviously feared that contemporary parallels would be drawn. The attack was a surprise since the play was performed at the Vakhtangkov Theater, which caters to the literary tastes of the political establishment. The same reviewer accused two other authors of failing to give a sufficiently positive view of Soviet life today. Both dealt with career-mindedness, chicanery, and arrogance toward the little man by Soviet bureaucrats and scientists. One wonders whether this does not reveal a greater concern for the image of the elite than for ideological orthodoxy.[107]

Scientific Impatience with Ideology.   Russian scientists seem to have had greater success in their bid for autonomy than have the humanist

---

[105] Churchward, *op. cit.*, p. 139.
[106] *Ibid.*, pp. 141, 142.
[107] Hedrick Smith, *New York Times*, October 27, 1972.

literati. No longer are the formulas of dialectical materialism a guide (or a hobble) of Soviet science, as they were during the Stalinist days. S. L. Sobolev, a leading member of the Soviet Academy of Science, has publicly decried those who speak of idealist and materialist theories of science. And the English philosopher A. J. Ayer, after delivering a series of lectures at Moscow University in 1962, remarked that "the prestige of science is so great that it is now becoming much more a question of [the philosophers] having to adapt their philosophical principles to current scientific theory than the other way about." [108] The "dialectic of nature" has thus been abandoned in favor of a truly experimental method. The manifest results of a free science for the modernization of Russia, with its concomitant increments for national power and glory, are no doubt an important cause of this result.

Other developments also pose a problem for the continued authority of salient elements of the original ideological dogma. The very idea of an objective "law of social development," for example, has come into question. Not even the leeway for indeterminacy afforded by the pragmatic theory of exegesis which we described in detail earlier in the chapter seems capable of saving its fundamental outlines. For one thing, the theory of industrial society formulated by Max Weber, and more recently by Raymond Aron, shows quite definitely that Capitalism and Socialism are not successive social systems but rather two aspects of one process—the bureaucratization of society. Capitalism has not led to increased poverty and decline but has maintained itself by state action. No Marxist revolution has been successful in mature capitalist countries, but only in rural areas where modernization is just beginning, such as Russia and China. And in these areas it has been carried through by intellectuals, not by the working class.[109] Developments within the Communist world also challenge the assumption of unilinear development. Formulas like Khrushchev's "law of the equalization of development" do not give an adequate explanation of the present sharp antagonisms between the Soviet Union and Communist China.

The idea that "planning" is more economically rational than market mechanisms has always been a distinguishing feature of Marxist-Leninist thought, and, indeed, of all Socialist theory. Lately, however, rationality is being sought in the USSR with concepts which "more and more resemble the 'rationality' of 'bourgeois' economic thought." [110] An interest rate, formerly an instrument of "exploitation," is now commonly employed in the allocation of capital. Mathematical models and linear

---

[108] Quoted in Bell, *op. cit.*, p. 86.
[109] See Raymond Aron, *The Industrial Society: Three Essays on Ideology and Development* (New York: Simon & Schuster, 1967).
[110] Bell, *op. cit.*, p. 94.

programming, formerly seen as "bourgeois" and "formalistic," are now accepted. Consumer goods are now furnished according to the principle of supply and demand and profits have become a criterion of economic success. When L. Leontiev, a noted Soviet economist, recently criticized the "basic economic law" derived from Stalin's *Economic Problems of the USSR* he was warned by the Secretary of the Party Central Committee responsible for ideological work that his ideas "might cast doubt on the whole political economy of socialism." [111] In short, recent developments in Soviet economics point toward the emergence of a single worldwide economic theory as an analytical scheme which is quite independent of any ideological dogma.

All these pressures for change produced a certain new accent in the official program of the CPSU written by Khrushchev in 1960. (It was the first fundamental reworking of the program since 1919.) The program carried a promise that the second and higher stage of Communism, based on the principle "to each according to his need," would be achieved by the end of the present century. There was an express promise of judicial legality in administration, and the avoidance of outright violations of the rights of the person. We have thus a clear recognition that terror and direct coercion are no longer viable principles of order, and that persuasion has to be given a place. The program included a promise that certain state functions would be transferred by the century's end to "public organizations" such as "comrade courts." But no explicit commitment to the "withering away of the state" was made.[112] As Professor Bell has pointed out, the test of whether this change of emphasis within the ideology will contribute to its long-run strength and legitimacy is an empirical one. The Russian people have been given a promissory note.

13. The Future of Soviet Ideology

We have been observing certain "straws in the wind," from a variety of perspectives, which point to ideological change as the Russian Communist revolution matures and settles down. What is likely to be the final upshot of these changes? Can they be expected to bring ultimately a full "liberalization" of the doctrine and of political practice, and a genuine growing together of Communist with Liberal Democratic political culture? This is surely a theoretical possibility. The economic institutions of socialism have been demonstrated in the British Fabian and West European Social Democratic experience to be fully compatible with political Liberalism.

[111] *Ibid.*, p. 95.
[112] *Ibid.*, p. 98.

We must now try to answer this most salient question, which we originally raised at the beginning of the section on ideological change. We must also try to determine whether change is most likely to be cyclical or unilinear.

Limited Liberalization. Daniel Bell expects continued liberalization and decentralization as a managerial elite guided by rational economic and scientific norms improves its position within the Soviet system. The degree of control exercised by Party bureaucrats and the insistence on conformity to specific tenets of the creeds will continue to lessen, he believes, as the external mission is redefined in terms of coexistence and as domestic mobilization is relaxed as a counterpart of increased technical capacity developed in conjunction with a decentralized system of production. "As society becomes more differentiated and complex," he writes, "a new 'organic solidarity' begins to appear in which activities—primarily intellectual and artistic, and even to some extent economic—seek to detach themselves from the single political system and attain some degree of autonomy." [113]

In Bell's view, however, there are fixed parameters to these predicted changes. One is the claim to an "historic mission" to "realize communism," and the other is the legitimacy of the Communist Party as the "chosen instrument" to fulfill this mission. In other words, Bell does not expect a fundamental diminution in the importance of the ideology of the Party, which we have described above as having central importance in the life of the new regime from the beginning. He expects this to be the case, even though the practical "truths" of the technical expert play an increasingly larger role than the abstract "absolute truth" of the Party cadres in daily decision making. As the central institution of the system, the Party will remain the arena where the various factions of Soviet life coalesce to form a national will. "This does not mean that ideology, in the sense of a formulated creed or an articulated belief system, will disappear," he writes. "But it may signify 'the end of ideology' in the sense that the idea has been postulated: as the abatement of the *dynamism* of a creed and the reduction of the role of ideology as a 'weapon' against external and internal enemies." [114] This appears to be compatible with Tucker's judgment that deradicalization does not mean a basic alteration in political terms or concepts, and may even be compatible with an actual increase in the use of ideological rhetoric. The important difference will lie in the significance of this rhetoric in the shaping of behavior. Behavior will tend to evidence more autonomy and to display patterns of freedom and of Thermidorean accommodation that the rhetoric does not explain.

[113] *Ibid.*, p. 111.
[114] *Ibid.*, p. 112.

The Administered Society.   Allen Kassof, using the concept of the "administered society" to predict the Russian future, foresees a lesser degree of change. The "administered society" is one in which an entrenched elite lays claim to ultimate and exclusive scientific knowledge, and is impelled by a belief in the moral necessity of elite planning for welfare and progress. It is a society which remains totalitarian, in that the total coordination of human efforts by government action continues to be a goal. The major difference from the past would lie in the abandonment of gross methods of physical violence and psychological terror as methods of social control. But the population would remain subject to superorganization, so that existing rhetoric would have more significance for action than in the future predicted by Bell.[115]

In a major study of change in the Soviet Union, Holt and Turner predict a future which represents a kind of halfway house between that predicted by Kassof and that predicted by Bell. They point out that the Liberal Democratic movement of the turn of the century never sank deep roots in Russian culture. Russians always have and continue to take pride in "monolithic solidarity," and they do not expect the emergence of a loyal opposition within the one-party system. "The great investment in the programs of indoctrination," they write, "has paid off, for apparently most citizens, especially the younger people, accept the basic values of Soviet society." [116] They expect a continued abatement of the terror and the development of legal due process along with a certain decentralization of power, both of which they see as requisites of the smooth functioning of a maturing industrial society. Efficiency demands the devolution of discretionary authority on trained technical managers. It also recognizes that skilled technicians do not respond well to physical coercion. The growth of a professional class may, in addition, of itself produce a more critical and skeptical outlook on politics. In the view of Holt and Turner, however, the rhetoric of the ideology may serve as a brake on change.[117] Thus they foresee the possibility of an oscillation between decentralization and recentralization as a result of the natural competition between Party activists and the technical bureaucracy for control.

Conclusion.   The key question to be resolved in estimating the likelihood of a decisive liberalization of the Russian regime is the question of the Party's monopoly of social control. The problem was underlined recently in a very graphic way in an interview of Harrison Salisbury with Valery Chalidze, a Soviet physicist who has been active in an association

---

[115] Allen Kassof, "The Administered Society," *World Politics*, 16(4), July 1964: 558–75.

[116] Holt and Turner, *op. cit.*, p. 212.

[117] *Ibid.*, p. 226.

called the Committee for the Rights of Man. Mr. Chalidze was deprived of his Soviet citizenship while on a lecture trip to the United States in December 1972.[118]

Salisbury's and Chalidze's discussion centered on the contrast between the liberal words of the Soviet Constitution of 1936 which guarantees an array of individual rights and vests authority in society as a whole through representative organs, and the monopolistic position of the self-perpetuating Communist Party. Mr. Chalidze admitted that many violations of law had been corrected since Stalin's death. Especially important was the abolition of the "troika," a special secret police panel that sentenced people to prison without trial and for indefinite periods. Now defined sentences are imposed only by judges. The investigators of the KGB have also become polite and correct in the conduct of their office. So far as the centralization of political power is concerned, one-man rule has given way to collective leadership—a beginning of devolution of decision-making authority. For Mr. Chalidze, however, the crucial factor in the present situation is the absence of any juridical procedure whereby society can establish control over the government and the Party —in his view the sole guarantee of right and the sole means of preventing a new dictatorship.

> What I am talking about is the existence of a juridical procedure to control the supreme authority. Everything is arranged so that the Government controls society. At least the possibility of control should exist. At election time people elect deputies to the Supreme Soviet. But do they elect members of the Communist Party? I think not. The party itself selects its members. The party perpetuates itself. Yet this party controls all the activities of the Government. It rules in accordance with its own regulations.[119]

Chalidze also pointed to the symbolic fact that the First Secretary of the Party takes it upon himself to conduct the official business of government, in place of the Premier, and is recognized by foreign powers as Head of Government.

That men like Valery Chalidze have formed a human rights movement and have been attempting by peaceful and legal means to make the formal processes of the Soviet constitution a vital legal and political reality is of considerable importance. It represents an ideological development of the first magnitude—the triumph of the idea of individual and social right over the idea of an official truth. The movement is confined, however, to a narrow circle (interestingly enough made up of scholars

[118] Harrison Salisbury, "Struggling Now for Human Rights: A Talk with Valery Chalidze," *New York Times Magazine*, March 4, 1973.
[119] *Ibid.*

and scientists rather than humanist literati). The fact that the Party officials are able summarily to deprive Mr. Chalidze of his citizenship and to incarcerate General Grigorenko (another activist in the civil rights movement) in a mental hospital without a public outcry is a testimony to the continued power of officialdom. A workable guarantee of individual and social right depends on a wide popular concern for these things and upon the organization of independent centers of power in Soviet society to give that concern meaningful institutional form. It is difficult to envisage such a development at this point in Soviet history.

14. Soviet Nationalism

A special aspect of Soviet political culture requires separate treatment—the nationalist component. One might well suppose that nationalism would have no role at all in a universalist and class-based ideology. It is also true that in the *Communist Manifesto* Marx said that "national one-sidedness and narrow-mindedness become more and more impossible." [120] It is nevertheless the case that the national idea has played just as large a role in Russian Communist political culture as it has in the Liberal Democratic cultures of the West and in the world of Nazism and Fascism. Of all the concepts of modern political culture it is the most widely shared.

Soviet Patriotism.   Professor Frederick Barghoorn, in a full-length study of 1956, writes of Soviet Russian nationalism (which in Soviet sources is called "Soviet patriotism") as "*the* unifying symbol pattern" of the Russian political system. Nationalism, not Communism, is the great cement of the society. This is true despite the fact that the national idea is frequently wrapped up in internationalist language, a circumlocution required by the universalist character of Marxism. Thus, in the patriotic literature we have such statements as: "The unity of patriotism and internationalism of the Soviet people is manifested in the support, moral, political and material, which the workers of the USSR have rendered and continue to render to the international proletariat in its struggle for democracy and socialism." [121] That it remains nevertheless a national idea is clear from such other pronouncements as the following:

> Soviet patriotism constitutes the fusion of the progressive national traditions of the peoples with the common vital interests of all toilers of the

[120] Marx and Engels, *Communist Manifesto*, p. 18.
[121] Matyushkin, quoted in Frederick Barghoorn, *Soviet Russian Nationalism* (New York: Oxford University Press, 1956), pp. 9–10. Copyright 1956 by Oxford University Press. With permission.

USSR. This marvelous fusion was created by the Party of Bolsheviks. The Party of Lenin and Stalin is the inspirer and teacher of Soviet patriotism, the founder of the new patriotic traditions of the working people of the USSR.[122]

It is also clear in statements that speak of the "boundless love of the Soviet people for the Socialist motherland." [123]

In Russian political literature Soviet patriotism is sharply distinguished both from "bourgeois nationalism" and from "cosmopolitanism." The first is described simply as the ideology of the bourgeoisie designed to defend class interests as though they were the interests of the nation as a whole. "Cosmopolitanism" is a deceptive stance through which the bourgeoisie seek to imperialize the world. The Russians like to apply it especially to "the reactionary ideology of American imperialism." [124]

Nationalism and War.   The use of national symbols tends to be emphasized when the Party feels especially threatened, as during World War II. Films showing the exploits of Ivan the Terrible and Alexander Nevsky, hardly Marxist hero figures, for example, were widely disseminated to increase the national fervor of the Russian people in their struggle with German Nazism. A content analysis of the Soviet daily press showed that the use of national symbols in the news media diminished markedly after the war. Barghoorn thinks this was done in order to maintain Soviet leadership of the Communist movement abroad.[125]

In 1918 Russian Communist theoreticians explicitly repudiated nationalism in favor of a class ideology and the concept of the "class state." Lenin allowed a Russian national empire, put together by the Czars, to dissolve under the impact of demands for autonomy of the hundreds of ethnic groups that formed that empire. The larger polity was soon restored, however, on a superficially federal basis, as the Union of Soviet Socialist Republics, through the cooperative effort of local Communist parties, which seized power in the various regions, and the skillful politics of Lenin.[126] Indeed, calls for the defense of the "socialist fatherland" are to be found in the early literature of the revolution. There is evidence that the foreign intervention especially stirred Russian national loyalties, even though the national idea was definitely subordinated during this period.

Covert Russification.   According to Professor Barghoorn, Soviet patriotism is a somewhat covert label for Great Russian nationalism, which

---

[122] Matyushkin, in *ibid.*, p. 9.
[123] *Ibid.*
[124] *Ibid.*, p. 10.
[125] *Ibid.*, pp. 59–60.
[126] See Hans Kohn, *Nationalism in the Soviet Union* (New York: Columbia University Press, 1933).

implies a policy of Russification of the minor nationalities of the Soviet Union. A concealed Russianism, for example, can be detected in the following statement:

> Soviet patriotism by its very essence is incompatible with nationalism, which seeks to set the peoples of the USSR apart from one another, to separate the peoples of non-Russian nationalities from the Russian people and its culture, from the highest achievement of Russian and world culture, Leninism.[127]

The progress of Russification is especially noticeable from 1933 on. In that year the constituent republics were denied the right to award orders of distinction, and the Russian Association of Proletarian Writers together with its affiliated non-Russian national associations was supplanted by a new centralized Union of Soviet Writers. Whereas in 1925 Stalin had written that "the universal human culture toward which socialism is moving" was to be "proletarian in content, national in form," by 1938 he is speaking of the USSR as having a "proletarian" or "socialist" culture. In this period it is also asserted that national cultural forms are a temporary arrangement to facilitate the establishment of Soviet control over the eastern peoples of the Union. It was also predicted that some nationalities would be assimilated in building the new "universal proletarian culture," whose basic component was Russian.[128]

The new Constitution of 1936, though federal in form, produced a state which was unitary in practice. In 1938 the Great Russian language was made compulsory in non-Russian units of the system and gradually became the *lingua franca* for the USSR as a whole. With all this it was never asserted that the Soviet Union was a nation or a nation-state. The preferred formula was "Soviet people" under the leadership of the "Great Russian people." But the Russifying trend was nevertheless very evident. Witness, for example, the following toast by Stalin to the Red Army commanders in May 1945:

> I would like to propose a toast to our Soviet people, and in particular to the health of the Russian people.
> I drink first of all to the health of the Russian people because it is the leading nation of all the nations belonging to the Soviet Union.
> I propose a toast to the health of the Russian people because it earned in this war general recognition as the guiding force of the Soviet Union among all the peoples of our country.
> I propose a toast to the health of the Russian people not only because it is the leading people, but also because it has a clear mind, a firm character and patience.[129]

[127] Quoted in Barghoorn, *op. cit.*, p. 11.
[128] *Ibid.*, p. 19.
[129] Quoted in *ibid.*, p. 27.

In the first months after Stalin's death there was some diminution of the Great Russian theme and even of the theme of Soviet patriotism. "Internationalism" and "friendship of peoples" were the leading slogans. In June 1953 a leading Russifier was dismissed as First Secretary of the Ukrainian Party and replaced with the first native Ukrainian incumbent of the job. In the same month a call went out in the Latvian Party for the promotion of more native Latvian cadres. This was followed by an article in *Kommunist* emphasizing the concern of the Party for the development of the "economy, national culture, and statehood of all the Soviet Republics." Other writings stressed the "mutual enrichment of cultures in the Soviet Union" and the "further development of the 'spiritual individuality and national character' of all the socialist nations." [130] Such concessions as these to the continued force of regional nationalisms, however, have been combined with the continuing theme of Great Russian leadership. It has been shown that the Great Russians are careful to retain a monopoly of leading positions within the CPSU.

Recent Evidence. The most recent literature on the national theme has tended to play down both Great Russian leadership and the importance of national autonomy for the lesser cultures of the Soviet Union in favor of a purely internationalist language. An article of February 1969 carried in *Voprosy Filosofii*, for example, tells us that more and more elements of culture of the various nations are being amalgamated today, and that the "objective tendency toward the internationalization of all aspects of social life is making its way into one form or another, relying, as a material basis, on the internationalization of production." [131] The decreased economic unity of the Soviet Union, the article tells us, makes for "the increasing rapprochement of national cultures," in which "international elements are taking up more and more space." "Socialist realism has firmly established itself as a uniform method" and "the culture of the Soviet people is now no longer merely the sum of national cultures . . . [but] interpenetrating parts of a single whole." The same article presents us with the latest definition of "Soviet patriotism":

> Soviet patriotism is a concentration of national feelings that express pride in the progressive traditions of one's nation and love for one's native region. . . . The chief elements in Soviet patriotism are devotion to the socialist system and the unified Soviet homeland, and hence to general Soviet traditions that have evolved as the basis of common history, and the desire to strengthen the might of the Soviet state and its defense capability. These main features must not be obscured by a one-sided idealization of the past and of national features. In Soviet patriotism na-

[130] *Ibid.*, pp. 45, 46, 47.
[131] P. M. Rogachev and M. A. Sverdlin, in *Current Digest of the Soviet Press,* 21, June 11, 1969: 3–5.

tional feeling is subordinated to Soviet community consciousness, which by its nature is class-oriented.[132]

Whether this language simply provides a more complete disguise for Russian cultural domination than the earlier rhetoric, which spoke of Great Russian leadership, or whether it represents a true cultural amalgamation is not clear.

In the realm of international power politics the Soviets continue to use the concept of nationalism as a weapon against antagonists both Capitalist and Communist, while at the same time giving it a positive connotation in relation to friends and neutrals. One writer, for example, tells us that "Marxist-Leninists do not put an equal sign between national consciousness and nationalism. The growth in the national pride of the peoples of the socialist countries is a positive fact. . . . But in certain circumstances sentiments of national exclusiveness, a relapse into the old ideology, may gain the upper hand. . . . This is exactly what happened in China." "Bourgeois nationalism" is described as a "reactionary device" to split the Socialist world, and the nationalism of the Communist Chinese is described as "great power chauvinism." "It is nationalism that is now the common denominator of both right and left opportunism," we are told, but it "would be an obvious mistake to confuse . . . reactionary nationalism with the nationalism of the 'third world' countries, where it can really play a definitely positive role, insofar as it has an anti-imperialist content."[133]

It is clear from all this that the pragmatism of power, which has characterized the use of ideology in all other areas of Russian political culture, also dominates the manipulation of the concepts of nationalism by the Communist leadership. That these concepts should prove so useful is a testimony to their enormous psychological importance in modern political culture.

Bibliography

ARMSTRONG, JOHN A., *Ideology, Politics and Government in the Soviet Union*, Rev. ed. New York: Frederick A. Praeger, 1967.

AVINERI, SHLOMO, *The Social and Political Thought of Karl Marx*. London: Cambridge University Press, 1968.

BARGHOORN, FREDERICK C., *Soviet Russian Nationalism*. New York: Oxford University Press, 1956.

BERDIAEV, NICHOLAS, *The Origin of Russian Communism*, trans. R. M. French. London: G. Bles, Centenary Press, 1937.

[132] *Ibid.*

[133] E. Bagramov, in *Current Digest of the Soviet Press*, 21, April 24, 1969: 13–15.

BERLIN, ISAIAH, *Karl Marx: His Life and Environment.* New York: Oxford University Press, 1959.

BRZEZINSKI, ZBIGNIEW, *Ideology and Power in Soviet Politics,* rev. ed. New York: Frederick A. Praeger, 1967.

CURTIS, MICHAEL, ed., *Marxism.* New York: Atherton, 1970.

DRACHKOVITCH, MILORAD, ed., *Marxist Ideology in the Contemporary World: Its Appeals and Paradoxes.* New York: Frederick A. Praeger, 1966.

HOLT, ROBERT T., and JOHN E. TURNER, eds., *Soviet Union: Paradox and Change.* New York: Holt, Rinehart & Winston, 1963.

INKELES, ALEX, and RAYMOND R. BAUER, *The Soviet Citizen: Daily Life in a Totalitarian Society.* Cambridge, Mass.: Harvard University Press, 1959.

LEITES, NATHAN, *The Operational Code of the Politburo.* New York: McGraw-Hill Book Company, 1951.

LOWENTHAL, RICHARD, *World Communism: The Disintegration of a Secular Faith.* New York: Oxford University Press, 1964.

MEAD, MARGARET, *Soviet Attitudes Toward Authority: An Interdisciplinary Approach to Problems of Soviet Character.* New York: McGraw-Hill Book Company, 1951.

MEYER, ALFRED G., *Marxism: The Unity of Theory and Practice—A Critical Essay.* Cambridge, Mass.: Harvard University Press, 1959.

——————, "The Function of Ideology in the Soviet Political System," *Soviet Studies,* 17(3), January 1966: 273–85.

TUCKER, ROBERT C., ed., *The Marx-Engels Reader.* New York: W. W. Norton & Company, Inc., 1972.

——————, *The Marxian Revolutionary Idea.* New York: W. W. Norton & Company, Inc., 1969.

——————, *The Soviet Political Mind: Stalinism and Post-Stalin Change,* rev. ed. New York: W. W. Norton & Company, Inc., 1971.

9

Communist Modernity in China

We have seen in Chapter 8 how extensively a revolutionary ideology can be shaped by a society's special historical experience and by pragmatic considerations connected with the seizure and maintenance of power. Although of Western European origin, Marxism in Russia has become a vehicle for expressing distinctively Russian political beliefs, fears, and hopes. At the same time the new ideology has introduced new ideas which demand new forms of political and economic behavior. These comprise the industrialization norm and the rational discipline of the work ethic. Let us now see what kind of role Marxism has played in still another and in many ways different historical and cultural situation, China.

1. Special Aspects of the Chinese Revolution and of Chinese Marxism

An Agrarian Revolution. It has been remarked by one China scholar that Marx found Hegel standing on his head and put him on his feet, but that Mao Tse-tung has put Hegel back in a headstand.[1] The metaphor refers to the relationship between material and spiritual forces in social causation. Marx and Engels, in their original "gospel" (according to the

[1] Benjamin I. Schwartz.

336

"scientific," though not the "humanistic" reading), assumed the primacy of the material situation in the generation of revolutionary power. Where the dialectic had, through the processes of capitalist industrialization, created a proletariat, the groundwork had been laid for Communist revolution. We already have seen that this doctrine had to be considerably modified in the Soviet Union, where the proletariat was a relatively small class in a still largely agrarian society. Nevertheless it is true that the decisive revolutionary action was taken in the city of St. Petersburg and that working-class forces were instrumental in the Communist seizure of power. In China, by contrast, the revolution was fought almost wholly in the countryside, and its armies were manned not by industrial workers but by poor farmers. Marxism took hold in China as pure idea, preached by a class of fervent intellectuals to a rural population. It did not arise spontaneously from the matrix of capitalist economic organization in crisis.

The relationship between political and military action in the Communist conquest of power has been different in the Chinese experience both from the Russian pattern and from the original Marxian recipe. As the act of a newly created class coming into its own by the sudden displacement of an old ruling class, the classical Marxian image of the revolution was political. Political upheaval was simply the reflex of dialectical reorganization of the economy. Lenin stressed the political rather than the military character of revolution, and treated armed insurrection as only a "special form of the political struggle." The Civil War of 1917–1921 was not an element in his original strategy. In China, by contrast, the Communist seizure of power was not a strategic political act executed in a brief space of time, but rather a long and laborious military operation begun in the far reaches of the countryside and gradually carried into the urban areas. Mao has expressed the special role of military action in his version of the Communist revolution by saying that "experience . . . teaches us that the working class and the toiling masses cannot defeat the armed bourgeoisie and landlords except by the power of the gun . . . the whole world can be remolded only with the gun." [2] It is not the dialectic, inexorably changing the structure of society from economic base to political superstructure, that is the primary cause of change, but the sustained will of revolutionary Communists using with dogged determination the firepower they can command.

The phasing of political seizure and social transformation is also different in the Chinese case. The taking of power in the Russian October Revolution preceded social and economic change. In China the two proceeded *pari passu*. "The socio-political revolution develops in the

² Quoted in Robert C. Tucker, *The Marxian Revolutionary Idea* (New York: W. W. Norton & Company, Inc., 1969), p. 161.

liberated base areas, where the communist movement seeks to build not only military strongholds but also enclaves of a new society and polity . . . new organs of public authority . . . schools, newspapers, and other social institutions." [3]

Nationalist Emphasis.   Another distinctive aspect of the Chinese revolution, the preoccupation of its makers with displaying unique Chinese features in a universalist ideological system, derives from the identity of its first major opponents. The original enemy of the Chinese Communists was not a class but a national foe. Their first significant conquests of power were made against the Japanese, during the Second World War, and by the time of the Japanese surrender half the population of China was living in Communist-controlled areas. The Civil War of 1947 to 1949 was only the last act in the struggle for power. Some scholars, as a consequence, tend to view the phenomenon as primarily a nationalist revolution, and it is true that during the war mass appeal among the peasantry was stimulated by anti-Japanese slogans of "national salvation." Chalmers Johnson says the Chinese revolution is the "offspring of indigenous nationalism" and that its Communism is the "theoretical expression of . . . nationalism." [4] George Lichtheim, a Marxist historian, went so far as to say, "What we have here is the last of the great national-popular convulsions inaugurated in the France of 1793, revived in the Russia of 1917, grotesquely parodied in the Germany of 1933, and now for a change exported to Asia. . . . National Socialism does not acquire a different character merely because it chooses to style itself communism." [5]

Ideology Dichotomized.   It is perhaps its role as a national ideology which accounts for the primary difference between the formulation of Marxist doctrine in China and in the Soviet Union. This difference of formula is the sharp distinction the Chinese make between Marxism-Leninism as the "pure theory" of Communism and the thought of Mao Tse-tung as the "practical ideology." An authoritative statement of the dichotomy is found in an editorial in *Jenmin Jihpao* for August 3, 1964:

> The spirit of Marxism-Leninism, in its philosophical-ideological aspects is dialectical materialism, especially the law of the unity of opposites. In its political-ideological aspects, it is the theory of class struggle, especially the theory of proletarian revolution and proletarian dictatorship. Real Marxist-Leninists must use the law of the unity of opposites to resolve problems, must always uphold the proletarian revolution and the proletarian dictatorship. . . . The thought of Mao Tse-tung is one which, in an era moving toward the collapse of imperialism and the victory of

[3] *Ibid.*, p. 157.

[4] Quoted in *ibid.*, p. 160. Tucker thinks this is an overstatement of the case.

[5] George Lichtheim, "Marxism West and East," in Michael Curtis, ed., *Marxism* (New York: Atherton, 1970), p. 86.

socialism, in the great revolutionary struggle of the Chinese people, united the universal truths of Marxism-Leninism with the practice of revolution and construction in China and creatively developed Marxism-Leninism. Our proletarian revolutionary successors must be real Marxist-Leninists and thus must firmly and unflaggingly study the works of Mao Tse-tung, actively learn and actively use the thought of Mao Tse-tung.[6]

According to the Chinese rubric, the "pure theory" of Marxism-Leninism is fixed and frozen, no longer subject to change. It is the permanent *Weltanschauung* of all good Communists. The thought of Mao Tse-tung as the "practical ideology" is, on the other hand, fluid and dynamic. As the operative part of the doctrine, which determines particular policy decisions, it is also notably native Chinese.

This is entirely different from the Russian way of thinking about the ideology. In the Russian view, the exegesis of the entire doctrine is a dynamic, developing matter, and this is in the keeping of the party hierarchs of the day. A kind of "Papal infallibility" vests in the leadership of the party to declare the content of the Absolute Truth at any particular moment by seeing it in the interstices of particular constellations of fact. This way of looking at things, of course, vests a special power in the leaders of the Russian Party in Moscow, because the exegesis of the ideology serves as a weapon to control opposition forces, just as Papal power "in faith and morals" was used as a political weapon in the European Middle Ages against a variety of opponents, both secular and ecclesiastical. Russian leaders have from the beginning used the ideology in this way, both at home and abroad. The Chinese, by declaring the abstract philosophical doctrine fixed once and for all, thereby exempt themselves from control of their policies by the Russians acting in the capacity of sovereign interpreters of the direction of dialectical development. As Schurmann sums it up, "If theory now has become universal and unchanging, no new Stalin can arise. Without active power over theory, the Soviets no longer have any authority to impose their organizational norms on the international movement." [7]

The felt need for independence of Moscow developed only gradually among the Chinese Communists. In 1957 on the fortieth anniversary of the Bolshevik Revolution Mao urged adoption of a declaration describing the Socialist camp as "headed by the Soviet Union." In the years immediately subsequent to this the Chinese experienced increasing disillusionment as a result of the dwindling of Russian economic and military help and the Soviet refusal to help the Chinese develop nuclear

---

[6] Quoted in Franz Schurmann, *Ideology and Organization in Communist China* (Berkeley: University of California Press, 1966), pp. 26–27. Copyright 1966 by the Regents of the University of California. With permission.

[7] *Ibid.*, p. 36.

weapons. In 1959 Russia took a neutral position in the Chinese-Indian border dispute, an unheard of action, because bourgeois governments had always been deemed *ipso facto* the aggressor in such disputes. This resulted in a swelling chorus of Chinese denunciations of the Russians as revisionists, which in turn prompted the abrupt withdrawal of Russian engineers and technical experts from China. From then to the present, Russian-Chinese relations have steadily deteriorated, with frequent reports of military movements on the frontiers and of border clashes. As we have pointed out in the preceding chapter, such division in the Marxist ranks casts doubt on the plausibility of the whole doctrine, which contains no formula to account for such opposition within the Communist world. The Chinese resolve the matter by condemning the Russians as wayward heretics and by arrogating orthodoxy to themselves and their allies.

The Dictatorship of the Proletariat.   Trotsky, in asserting that Stalin had established a dictatorship by the Communist Party *over* the proletariat—rather than the dictatorship *of* the proletariat—was accusing Stalin of violating a leading canon of Marxist doctrine. Stalin never denied the authority of the doctrine; he simply read reality differently than Trotsky. The Chinese, however, have significantly modified the creed. During their long struggle for power of the 1930s and 1940s, against both the Japanese and domestic opponents, the Chinese Communists represented their objectives not as one-class rule but as a "joint dictatorship" of the whole people under proletarian leadership. This ties in logically with what we have said about the special circumstances of the Chinese revolution. It was also politically useful.

Since a proletarized urban working class was infinitesimally small in China, the proletarian character of the Chinese Communist Party could not be guaranteed by its objective class basis, but by the possession of a correct "proletarian attitude," and by its ability to develop those attitudes in its recruits. An "ideal" factor—the teaching of "the word"—was more important than the "material" substructure, the existence of a proletarian class. Correlatively, one could conclude that disciples could be found in any and every class, potentially in the entire nation. Since a major opponent of the Communists was a national enemy, the Japanese, the doctrine could serve to rally the whole nation to the Red banners in a national cause. It also emphasized the independence of the Chinese from Russian tutelage and the national uniqueness of the Chinese revolution.[8]

Time brought changes, however. After 1956 the doctrine was restored to the original concept of a unilateral "dictatorship of the pro-

[8] Benjamin I. Schwartz, *Communism and China: Ideology in Flux* (Cambridge, Mass.: Harvard University Press, 1968), p. 16.

letariat." This may have been partly a result of Khrushchev's having somewhat relaxed the Russian leading strings after Stalin's death. But perhaps the primary reason for change was a new domestic situation. The Japanese had long since been defeated and the Communist leadership was now faced with strong opposition within its own ranks. Mao had joined battle with the "revisionists" and it was useful to him to mount the attack against a "class enemy." [9] The restored doctrine was not Leninist, however, for it was turned against the Party itself. Not the teaching Party but Mao established the criteria of "correctness." And the dictatorship came to be wielded "by whatever group or individuals behaved in what Mao considered to be a proper proletarian way." [10]

The Idea of Contradictions.   Although Chinese Communism came into being and into ascendancy through no very plausible application of the Marxist-Leninist conception of dialectical development, the Chinese make extensive use of dialectical language in their use of the doctrine. They are especially fond of the notion of "contradictions" and analyze everything imaginable in terms of this concept. It is the procedural heart of the practical ideology. Contradictions are of two sorts: antagonistic ("between the enemy and ourselves") and nonantagonistic ("among the people"). Each kind is resolved by an appropriate "struggle." In the first case, struggle is to the death, and the "law of the unity of opposites" does not apply. It does apply, however, to nonantogonistic contradictions, which can be resolved peacefully in a manner allowing each of the conflicting elements to have an impress on the final product.[11] Contradictions are not understood as an unhappy aspect of life to be regretted and overcome, but rather as a very positive reality to be cherished. They are seen as the basic cause of all development.[12]

The idea of contradictions is used as the central concept for analyzing the condition of society at any particular time for the purpose of large public policy decisions, and it is used as a key notion in the development of procedural and organizational norms. As a general theory of social change, the theory of contradictions involves notions of both quantitative and qualitative change. The beginnings of change in the industrialization of society are seen as involving purely quantitative additions and subtractions, which leave the appearance that the society is still at rest. At a certain point, however, changes in quantity are converted into a change of quality (a notion found in the original

[9] *Ibid.*, p. 19.
[10] *Ibid.*, p. 22.
[11] Schurmann, *op. cit.*, p. 53.
[12] John W. Lewis, *Leadership in Communist China* (Ithaca, N. Y.: Cornell University Press, 1963), p. 48.

Marxist doctrinal corpus). "Industrialization . . . creates poverty, rural-urban imbalance, classes, strikes and thence a proletarian revolution. Conspicuous qualitative change takes place." [13] Within the movement which begins quantitatively and ends qualitatively, contradictions appear and are resolved by revolutionary action. Within any historical period there is understood to be one principal contradiction to be worked on, surrounded by numerous subsidiary contradictions. The problem of Communist leadership is to understand what the principal contradiction is and to work out a plan for its resolution, a "general line." For example, in the war with Japan the contradiction to be dealt with was the opposition of Japanese imperialism to Chinese survival. In 1952 the Chinese Communist Central Committee devised the general line of the united front to resolve it.[14]

Franz Schurmann presents the following quotation from a 1957 speech of Mao Tse-tung which illustrates both the social analytical and organizational uses of this concept:

> Under present conditions, the so-called contradictions among the people include contradictions within the working class, within the peasant class, within the intellectuals; contradictions between the working and peasant classes; contradictions of workers and peasants with the intellectuals; contradictions of the working class and other toiling people with the national bourgeois class; contradictions within the national bourgeois class, and so on. Our government truly is a government that represents the interests of the people; it is a government that serves the people. But there are certain contradictions between it and the popular masses. These contradictions include contradictions of state interest and collective interest with individual interest, the contradiction of democracy and centralism, the contradiction of leader and led, the contradiction of bureaucratism of some workers in state agencies with the masses. This is also a contradiction among the people. In general contradictions among the people are contradictions on a foundation of basic harmony of the people's interests.[15]

An example of the application of the concept of contradictions in a major policy decision is the Great Leap Forward of the late 1950s, when a kind of bootstraps effort was made to bring Chinese society in a brief space of time to the threshhold of a utopian Communist order. One policy that was employed to accomplish the Great Leap was called the "three-unification movement," which put party cadres, technicians, and workers together in single work teams. Prior to their combination as work teams these three groups in Chinese society were seen as constituting contradictory elements. Their unification, to the end of re-

[13] *Ibid.*, p. 49.
[14] *Ibid.*, pp. 49–50.
[15] Quoted in Schurmann, *op. cit.*, p. 75.

solving the contradictions by creating a unity of opposites, involved an exchange, or sharing of roles, in the united work team. Workers became technicians, technicians became workers, and both of these groups shared leadership positions with the party cadres.[16] A similar idea was at the base of the still more extraordinary effort of the 1960s known as the "Cultural Revolution," which we shall discuss more fully below.

In organizational practice, component units and principles are understood to be related to one another in terms of tension and contradiction. In carrying out the process of thought reform, a basic norm is to create a "juxtaposition of individual and group through struggle which sharpens contradictions to a point of polarization leading to a dialectical resolution." [17] In democratic centralism, a leading Marxist organizational scheme, the two parts of the system are seen as antagonistic opposites by the Chinese, with democracy representing impulses from below, centralism impulses from above.[18] The way in which the two are brought together as a "unity of opposites" will vary from problem to problem. Schurmann points out that during the Greap Leap Forward "this took the form of centralization of general policy impulses and decentralization of specific policy impulses." [19] Mao Tse-tung has referred to the system of democratic centralism as "the unity of freedom and discipline." [20] The concept also provides a rule for the patterning of discussion and decision making at the highest levels, such as within the Party's Politburo. It is expected that at the beginning there will be a variety of antagonistic opinions on the matter at hand, and that discussion will produce a polarization of opinion. At a certain point resolution is achieved by decision, after which the minority follows the majority. As in the Russian system, it is not legitimate for opposition groups or opinion factions to take on structured organizational form and to continue to oppose party policy after a decision has been taken.[21]

Sometimes the concept of contradictions is used to ferret out oppositionists in order to deal with them. Mao Tse-tung's "Hundred Flowers Speech" of 1957 was understood by some intellectuals as an invitation to renew the "impulses from below" as a legitimate and useful source of fresh and new ideas. When a variety of "Liberals" spoke up, however, criticizing regime practice in a number of areas, they found that instead of being met by a "Millian" tolerance, they were

16 *Ibid.*, pp. 75–76.
17 *Ibid.*, pp. 53–54.
18 *Ibid.*, p. 54.
19 *Ibid.*, p. 87.
20 *Ibid.*
21 *Ibid.*, p. 55.

faced with summary repression. Mao then made his purpose in inviting the blossoming of a hundred flowers clear: it was in order to facilitate the growth of the hidden weeds so that they could be rooted out:

> You may ban the expression of wrong ideas, but the ideas will still be there. On the other hand, correct ideas, if pampered in hot-houses without being exposed to the elements or immunized against disease, will not win out against wrong ones. That is why it is only by employing methods of discussion, criticism, and reasoning that we can really foster correct ideas, overcome wrong ideas and really settle issues. . . . When the majority of the people have clear-cut criteria . . . [they] can be applied to people's words and actions to determine whether they are fragrant flowers or poisonous weeds. These are political criteria.[22]

The idea of contradictions as a most general ideological principle expressing the relationship between the Communist and Capitalist worlds and the dynamic of that relationship were graphically spelled out by Mao in the Hundred Flowers speech:

> The question of whether socialism or capitalism will win is still not really settled. Marxists are still a minority of the entire population as well as of the intellectuals. Marxism therefore must still develop through struggle. Marxism can only develop through struggle. . . . What is correct always develops in the course of struggle with what is wrong. The true, the good, and the beautiful always exist in comparison with the false, the evil and the ugly, and grow in struggle with the latter. As mankind in general rejects an untruth and accepts a truth, a new truth will begin struggling with new erroneous ideas. Such struggle will never end. This is the law of development of truth, and it is certainly also the law of development of Marxism.[23]

Struggle.   In contrast to original Marxism and also to Russian versions of the doctrine, the historical struggle of the dialectic never ends in the Maoist Chinese reading. Clashing antinomies are never resolved in a final period of perfect harmony but are everlastingly there to challenge the resourcefulness and strength of will of a committed leadership.

---

[22] Mao Tse-tung, "100 Flowers Speech," Feb. 27, 1957, in Alan P. Grimes and Robert H. Horwitz, *Modern Political Ideologies* (New York: Oxford University Press, 1959), pp. 307–9. Stuart Schram has a different interpretation. He writes that when Mao delivered the "Hundred Flowers" speech he thought that the majority of the population had been convinced of socialist superiority and that an ideological consensus had been established. He was ready to give up a cultural and doctrinal emphasis for a technical one. The flood of criticism that ensued following the "Hundred Flowers" speech, however, disillusioned him on this score and sent him back to cultural and ideological politics. See "The Party in Chinese Communist Ideology," in John W. Lewis, ed., *Party Leadership and Revolutionary Power in China* (New York: Cambridge University Press, 1970). Copyright 1970 by Cambridge University Press. Quotations with permission.

[23] *Ibid.*, p. 307.

Like the emphasis on contradiction, we can attribute this idea to re-action against traditional Confucian doctrine. More importantly, how-ever, it plays a significant motivational role in the economy of Mao's thought. For thousands of years the Chinese peasantry had been taught to submit and to "eat bitterness"—to bottle up hostility and anger, never to display it. As a consequence, when the Communists set about making their revolution they found that a sense of injustice was inadequate motivation for the peasant. He had to be taught to "speak his bitterness" and display his aggression if change was to be accomplished. He had, therefore, to be saturated with the idea of everlasting struggle, especially since China, as a rural society, had so far to go in creating a modern industrial state as the ultimate vehicle of the good life.[24] The accent on struggle can also be attributed to the long Chinese experience of foreign exploitation. John Israel writes that "nineteenth-centry China's brutal experience in the international jungle forced many of her most perceptive minds to the conclusion that human affairs were governed not by the ancient principles of harmony and reconciliation but by a relentless contest for supremacy." [25]

It is interesting that the Chinese Communist espousal of struggle as never-ending establishes a link between the extreme right and the extreme left. In Nazism, it will be recalled, the emphasis was on struggle conceived as a never-ending competition for political power. Liberalism too, at the center of the ideological spectrum, embodies in many of its forms a version of the same idea, albeit one that is framed more in terms of developmental change than as naked "struggle," and one which emphasizes the peaceful character of evolutionary process, or "progrcss." (To be sure, some Liberal doctrines—e.g., that of Herbert Spencer—in-clude rawer language, such as the idea of nature being "red in tooth and claw.") All three ideologies keep the process of change open-ended. This expresses a crucial aspect of their common modernity and an emphatic difference with the static conceptions of traditional society. A related concept of the three cultures is that the process of develop-ment or struggle does not discover but rather *creates* truth and reality, another form of open-endedness which is also markedly different from the traditional view of truth and reality as divinely ordained.

Mass Line. One especially important application of the idea of non-antagonistic contradictions is the concept of the "mass line," an organiza-tional scheme for relating the leadership of party cadres to the popula-

---

[24] Richard Solomon, *Mao's Revolution and the Chinese Political Culture* (Berkeley: University of California Press, 1971).

[25] "Continuities and Discontinuities in the Ideology of the Great Proletarian Revolution," in Chalmers Johnson, ed., *Ideology and Politics in Contemporary China* (Seattle: University of Washington Press, 1973), p. 11.

tion in general and for mobilizing the energies of the population behind the revolution.[26] The first step in the development of the "mass line" is for the cadres to study the state of mind, the "scattered and unsystematic views" of the workers and peasants, in order to identify problems to be worked on and to discover areas of party strength and weakness. The findings are then formulated in information reports and sent up the line from the field level to the highest party headquarters for the area involved. General directives are drawn up on the basis of these reports and sent back down the line. They are used to indoctrinate the masses "until the masses embrace the ideas as their own, stand up for them and tranlate them into action by way of testing their correctness." [27] The resolutions involved in the process are treated as temporary, and the cycle is therefore repeated ad infinitum. One can see that the process employs both aspects of democratic centralism—flexibility and participation on the one hand, rigid centralized control on the other. Lewis reports that the system, by incorporating the masses into the leadership process, allows the overt exercise of party power to be minimized. This is important because of the salience of the Marxist idea that the working masses embody the highest social power. "The party leads in everything because the working class masses 'lead' China." [28] But is it the party or Mao, above the party, who leads the working masses?

The "Mass Line" concept also embodies Mao's view of the close linkage that should exist between thought and practice, the radical interdependence of the two. It is a warning against intellectual formalism, a traditional target of reformers in a society that has always given a leading political role to the scholar and thinker.[29] It also embodies Mao's personal disdain for academic intellectuals who sought to thwart him both early (the prerevolutionary intelligentsia) and late (Communist intellectuals surrounding him).[30]

2. Maoism

While Marxist practice in Russia featured the role of the charismatic leader in the persons of both Lenin and Stalin, and while this role was to an extent recognized in doctrine as well, the emphasis in Russian doctrine has always been on the Party as the instrument of revolution

[26] The following discussion summarizes the description of the concept to be found in Lewis, *Leadership in Communist China*, pp. 70–76.

[27] Mao Tse-tung, "Methods of Leadership," quoted in *ibid.*, p. 72.

[28] *Ibid.*, p. 75.

[29] See Solomon, *op. cit.*, p. 174. See also Joseph R. Levenson, *Confucian China and Its Modern Fate*, 3 vols. (Berkeley: University of California Press, 1968), I.

[30] Solomon, *op. cit.*, p. 173.

and of proletarian government, not on the person of the leader. In China, by contrast, it is the person of Mao Tse-tung that has been dominant. Benjamin Schwartz has stated the matter most succinctly in writing that "in China it is . . . reiterated *ad nauseam* that the Chinese Communist Party is wholly dependent for whatever proletarian charisma it may have on the leader and his thought. What is more, the qualities of the proletarian dictatorship which find their fountainhead in Mao Tse-tung may be shared by groups, institutions and individuals which lie outside the Party. Indeed, the Party as such, when considered apart from Mao Tse-tung and his thought, may wholly degenerate and become another 'partial interest' in the Rousseauist sense." [31]

Personal Charisma. As we have seen earlier, Communist Chinese practical ideology, the procedural norms whereby policy is made from day to day, in contrast with the fixed general *Weltanschauung* inherited from Marx and Lenin (which is used to generate enthusiasm in the masses), is identified as the "Thought of Mao Tse-tung." Mao is seen as the embodiment of "proletarian virtue," which is the ethos of the proletariat, conceived as a quasi-mystical and transcendent historic force, a god substitute. It is specifically Mao's dream or vision of a world Communist movement focused on Peking that is the central ingredient in Chinese Communist ideology.[32]

Background Factors. Stuart Schram has explained this emphasis of Communist Chinese doctrine in terms of the special circumstances of the Chinese Revolution. He has pointed out that during the years 1921 to 1941, when the Chinese Communist movement was taking shape and winning its first victories, its leaders did not operate within the context of an autonomous and strong Party organization, using methods which were primarily political. The Party during these years was rather an aspect of, or more precisely, as Schram has put it, existed in a symbiotic relationship with the Communist army which was the chief instrument of the revolution. Armed struggle came to be thought of as the principal form of class struggle, and to it was subordinated the development of the Party. Schram quotes Mao as writing in 1939 that "apart from armed struggle, apart from guerrilla warfare, it is impossible to understand our political line and, consequently, to understand our Party-building. . . . We know that in China there would be no place for the proletariat, no place for the people, no place for the Communist Party, and no victory for the revolution without armed struggle." This was

[31] Benjamin I. Schwartz, "The Reign of Virtue," in Lewis, ed., *Party Leadership and Revolutionary Power in China*, p. 164.
[32] *Ibid.*, p. 165.

the pattern of things for eighteen long years.[33] Within this context a
Party line did, indeed, evolve, but because there was "no visible Party,
the ultimate consequence was to define fidelity to the Party as the obedience to the author of the correct ideology—in other words, to the
leader."[34]

This view of things was, to begin with, Mao's own personal way
of understanding the relationships between Party doctrine and leadership. He carried it so far that in his vision of the utopia, the period of
the Great Harmony, the Party itself would wither away along with all
the coercive instruments of state machinery; whereas in the Leninist
view the Party would always exist as a prime teaching agency and as
an agency of social organization.[35] Schram points out that other leaders,
such as Liu Shao-ch'i, did not agree with Mao and made an effort to
propagate a more traditional theory of the Party. In 1938, for example,
we have Liu writing "every Party member, whatever his capacities, his
activities and his influence, is merely one of several hundred thousand
Party members, he is merely one element of the contradictory structure
which constitutes the Leninist Party. . . . Lenin and Stalin placed themselves within the Party in order to lead the Party and urge it forward,
they both played their role as a single Party member within the Party."[36]
Liu's view, of course, failed to predominate.

The Cultural Revolution.   The most characteristic emphasis of Maoism
in practice has been the Cultural Revolution. According to Stuart Schram,
this is intimately tied in with Mao's attitude toward the Party that we
have discussed above. It is also related to a reversal of the Leninist
view of the relationship between organization and spontaneous mass
action, between the working class and the peasantry, between the technical knowledge of managerial elite and the ingenuity of the rank and
file, and between material and moral factors.[37]

The Leninist approach both to the conquest of power and to the
building of Socialism was preeminently elitist and technocratic. It was
the proletarian consciousness of the intelligentsia that Lenin relied on
to make the revolution, and the technical knowledge of managers and
engineers on which both he and Stalin relied to industrialize Russia.
Beginning in 1955 we find Mao moving away from these premises to
a very different reliance on the spontaneous energy of the rural masses
to effect revolutionary change. The first policy area in which the new
approach showed up clearly was in the program to establish communes

[33] Stuart Schram, "The Party in Chinese Communist Ideology," in *ibid.*, p. 172.
[34] *Ibid.*
[35] *Ibid.*, pp. 180–82.
[36] *Ibid.*, pp. 175–76.
[37] *Ibid.*, p. 183.

prior to the achievement of mechanization. Mao's rivalry with the Party is shown in his charge during this period that local cadres had thrown in with the forces of capitalism to prevent the poor peasants from forming into cooperatives. He did not at this point, however, deny the need for cadre scientific and technical specialists.[38]

It was his disillusionment with the outcome of the "Hundred Flowers" policy in 1957 that led Mao to a renewed emphasis on the revolutionary role of the poor peasant and precipitated his active rejection of the technical elites along with a renewed minimization of the role of the Party cadres because of their embodiment of the technical roles and skills.[39] The "Great Leap Forward" of the following year was to be achieved primarily by the energy and enthusiasm of the untutored rural poor rather than by the skills of the managerial elite. Mao described them as "poor and blank," and of the "blankness" he made a virtue, "a symbol of the moral purity of the Chinese people, who are not afflicted with the maladies of materialism and individualism that have perverted not only the West but the Soviet Union." [40] The professionals of public administration and of middle management in industry were dismissed in large numbers. Whole structures of administration in both areas were dismantled. The "pure ideology" was intensively propagated, replete with utopian announcements about the imminent coming of pure Communism. "Organizationally," writes Franz Schurmann, "the Great Leap Forward can be seen as an attempt to eliminate the middle and to join top and bottom directly; leaders and masses were to be in intimate relationship, bypassing the professionals who earlier stood between them." [41]

After a few years' lull during which the Party technical cadres returned to ascendance, the Cultural Revolution broke out in full force in the mid-1960s, instigated and led by Mao himself against the Party organization and against the managers, who were attacked as "representatives of the bourgeoisie who have sneaked into the Party, the government, the army and various cultural circles," and as "a bunch of counter-revolutionary revisionists." [42] Mao called on the poor peasants, particularly the youth and the young students in the schools of China— who were soon organized as battalions of Red Guards—to smash the Party and all its works and build a new Communist order. "Put destruction first, and in the process you have construction," said the May 16th directive of 1966. In a student poster the Guards are urged "to turn the old world upside down, smash it to pieces, pulverize it, and create

---

[38] *Ibid.*, p. 184.
[39] *Ibid.*, pp. 189, 190.
[40] *Ibid.*, p. 190.
[41] Schurmann, *op. cit.*, p. 71.
[42] Schram, *op. cit.*, p. 194.

chaos—the greater confusion the better. . . . We are bent on creating a tremendous proletarian uproar, and hewing out a proletarian new world!" [43]

Ideology and Technology.   Though the ultimate technical impact of both the Great Leap Forward and of the Cultural Revolution was regressive, there was actually a concept of technical efficiency intertwined with the egalitarian ideological themes of the two events. It was assumed that the simplicity and the fresh approach of the masses, when placed in positions requiring technical skill, would elicit a native genius for inventiveness, that the poor peasant would be capable of feats of technical innovation. According to Marx, after all, the masses are the creators of history. There was also pride in national genius at work in the judgment. Furthermore, tradition was on the side of the experiment. We find the following editorial in an edition of the *Workers' Daily* for 1958:

> The forefathers of the Chinese working people were known for their creativeness. Inasmuch as they could invent gunpowder, the compass, etc., can there be any doubt that the liberated working people of China today, led by the Communist Party, enjoying the advantage of the Socialist system and becoming masters of the country will certainly invent new technology unknown to the world? [44]

Cultural Conflict.   Mao's chief objective, however, in launching both the Great Leap Forward and the Cultural Revolution, was not economic but cultural and political. It was to teach his people to overcome their age-old dependency on and deference to elite authority by compelling them to mass political participation. The revolution against the old regime had in itself been a lesson in independence. But in the creation of the new regime bureaucratic structures began to reappear, presided over by an elite brought up in the old ways. Mao feared that they would soon restore the old dependency pattern; old habits die hard. The new enemy was not the traditional Marxist target—a ruling class. It was rather a ruling culture. Cultural conflict had to be substituted for class conflict as the leading mode of "struggle" against fated "contradictions." [45]

It was not Mao's intention, however, to introduce western individualism into Chinese culture. "Mao's resolution of [the] 'contradiction' between his own valuation of self-reliance and the legacy of a culture which stressed dependence on authority has been to stress the autonomy of the group—to have the individual find self-realization in a mutually

[43] Quoted in *ibid.*, pp. 194–95.
[44] Rensselaer W. Lee III, "The Politics of Technology in Communist China," in Johnson, *op. cit.*, pp. 311, 314.
[45] Solomon, *op. cit.*, 250, 251.

supportive community of equals, rather than through submissive reliance on hierarchical authority." [46] Hence the communes policy of the "Great Leap." These were to be the units of society within which the Chinese peasant would become a "new man." In these self-contained decentralized industrial and agricultural units the social distinctions between industrial and agricultural worker would be diminished, as well as the difference between the mentality of the city and of the farm. They would also serve as "retraining centers" to which bureaucrats of the central administration and Party cadres could be sent to engage directly in production activities for extended periods of the year. Thus the gulf between mental and physical labor and its implicit hierarchical relationship was to be overcome, as well as the "contradiction" between society and the state. [47]

Resistance to the commune movement was intense, however, and the project proved to be in large part abortive. The departure from traditional Chinese psychological patterns, perhaps from fundamental human inclinations, proved too great. Richard Solomon writes that "the human relationships which integrate a society were seriously weakened, and some of the most basic motives for work and innovation—personal responsibility and remuneration according to effort—were eliminated." [48] There were also serious errors made in organizational judgment, especially in the scale of the communes. They were simply too big to be either economically or psychologically viable. [49]

Significance of the Cultural Revolution.   Benjamin Schwartz, in interpreting the significance of the Cultural Revolution, sees it as an assertion of the predominance of the social-ethical perspective over the technocratic one. "The aged Mao is bent on achieving the reign of virtue as he understands virtue and remains unprepared to accept any progress of the 'arts and sciences' which is not based on virtue." [50] This does not mean that he is against modernization, but rather that he sees virtue as the necessary and ultimate source of energy for the accomplishment of modernization. "Maoist virtue," writes Schwartz, "is to play the role of a kind of collectivistic Protestant Ethic. There is, however, no reason to believe that this ethic was regarded either then or now as nothing but a means to modernization, any more than Weber's Calvinists regarded their own ethic as simply a means to economic ends." [51] Its essence is to be the perfectly social man, who has no interests which

[46] *Ibid.,* p. 254.
[47] *Ibid.,* p. 341.
[48] *Ibid.,* p. 340.
[49] *Ibid.,* p. 371.
[50] Schwartz, in Lewis, ed., *op. cit.,* p. 165.
[51] *Ibid.*

are different from those of the general interests of society. The ideal proletarian is neither worker nor farmer, neither leader nor follower, nor has he any other specialized identity; he is simply man as the most social of all animals. At this writing, however, the revolutionizing of Chinese society in this direction has once again slowed down. Maoism has at least temporarily given way to another authority—not of the Party but of the Generals.

An important aspect of the politics of cultural revolution in China has been the process of thought reform, the process whereby "correct thinking"—the new ideological set of Chinese Communism—is produced within the individual. Mass movements with meetings and cultural events of all kinds and a barrage of propaganda through all available media are used to accomplish reform at the grass-roots level. An especially intensive regimen employing small-group devices is used to indoctrinate the Party cadres, however. Because of the power which derives from their expertise, as we have seen above, the correctness of their ideological position is viewed as particularly important. Furthermore, because it is assumed that technical expertise of itself militates for individualist selfishness and against the social virtues, the experts are subject to close scrutiny. Franz Schurmann describes the process of thought reform of a party candidate as follows:

> First, the Party collects as complete a dossier as possible on his background. If he measures up, he becomes a candidate member. Then, in Party small group sessions, he must recite, day after day, every detail of his personal life, both public and private. His statements are checked against the dossier. As the recital goes on, the group begins to criticize him intensely. This or that deed of his life, or fact of his background, is analyzed in great detail and criticized with vehement hostility. All the while, the individual is forced to use the categories and language of the ideology to analyze himself. Criticisms from the group are stated in similar ways. When he has completed his recital, he has made public every shred of what was earlier private. Moreover, he faces a hostile group that attacks every fault of his. This is the point of juxtaposition of opposites, when the contradictions have become more acute. At this time, the attitude of the group changes, and they begin to "help" him develop a correct standpoint. All this, one must add, does not only take place in Party small group sessions. The candidate member must go forth and prove himself through correct actions. If he finally arrives at a point of correct behavior, the group will then recommend that he be formally taken into the Party.[52]

Procedures similar to these, though without the "happy ending," are also used at the grass-roots level in order to eradicate from the peasant mind the idea of the landlord class and its superiority. At the "criticism"

[52] Schurmann, *op. cit.*, pp. 47–48.

sessions in these cases landlords, in the presence of the peasantry, are made to recant their "class sins" and adopt a new standpoint.[53] Schurmann reports that one result of widespread practices of thought reform is that refugees from Communist China interviewed in Hong Kong, whether they are members of the intelligentsia or not, are extremely articulate and demonstrate a passion for analyzing everything.[54]

3. The Functions of Secular Ideology in China

An Historical Parallel.   We have seen that in western political culture modern ideologies as they developed acted as surrogates for transcendental religion, and their specific forms even borrowed from the categories of Judaeo-Christianity (albeit in a distorted fashion). They came to fulfill the functions, especially that of legitimation, that had formerly been the province of religion; and there was an historical connection between the two. But what can we say of the role of Marxism in China, where its political and cultural development was altogether separate and different from that of the West and even of neighboring Russia, where it was literally a foreign import?

Traditional Chinese political culture had been cemented together not so much by transcendent religious creeds as by a semisecular ethical code, Confucianism. This was transmitted, however, at least to the intelligentsia, in numerous variations through a variety of writings that were the equivalent of Holy Writ. The "power of the word"—express ethical teaching—was a prominent theme in Confucian political culture. Richard Solomon tells us that "in their perceptions of political authority, Chinese reveal an intuitive assumption that a leader asserts his power through an 'ism' (*chu-i*), and seeks signs of submission on the part of subordinates through their willingness to 'study' his words." [55] Thus the happenstance of an historical similarity between the traditional modes of legitimating political authority both East and West may account for their similar capacity for secular transformations of these modes.

Why Do Political Cultural Revolutions Occur?   Reflecting on the functions of Marxism in modern China also helps us to understand why revolutions occur in any political culture. Ideas are carried by an intelligentsia. To be the spokesman of an established culture an intel-

---

[53] See Mu Fu-sheng, *The Wilting of the Hundred Flowers: The Chinese Intelligentsia Under Mao* (New York: Frederick A. Praeger, 1962), Chapter VI; Robert J. Lifton, *Thought Reform and the Psychology of Totalism: A Study of "Brainwashing" in China* (New York: W. W. Norton & Company, Inc., 1961).

[54] Schurmann, *op. cit.*, p. 48.

[55] Richard H. Solomon, "From Commitment to Cant: The Evolving Functions of Ideology in the Revolutionary Process," in Johnson, *op. cit.*, p. 51.

ligentsia must find satisfactions in the established order. The intelligentsia must at least be employed. One origin of the demand for ideological change in Confucian China was the abolition of the examination for civil servants in 1905. In that year a whole generation of scholars, bred in the "stern treatment school" of Confucian culture, suddenly found that their classical education no longer guaranteed them a career. The shattering of their career expectations produced in some an identity crisis that the espousal of revolutionary Marxism resolved. They could find meaning and a place in the world again by destroying the old order.[56]

Solidarity and Communication.   With old identities shattered and all the metaphysical certainties that gave meaning and purpose to life taken away by the discrediting of tradition, Marxism fulfilled yet another function in Chinese life; it provided an emotional rallying point—a principle of solidarity—and also a mode of meaningful communication, a "stylized set of concepts for interpreting and describing the world." [57] Most importantly it provided an instrument by which the revolutionary elite could move men to action. For Marxism, perhaps more than any other modern ideology, is action-oriented; it understands ideas as arising out of action and leading to action.[58] It was Marx who wrote that in the past philosophers had interpreted the world, but the point was to change it.

Ideology and Specific Goals.   In our study of Russian Communism we saw that the abstractions of an ideology may give meaning to what is done, but they cannot in any strict sense be said to specify particular policy goals in advance of action. The canons of the Soviet operational code are directed to the acquisition and maintenance of power and have little to do with achieving the final goals of the Communist utopia. In China, as our discussion of Maoism has implied, we have a rather different pattern. Power might have been the principal goal value of the years before 1949, but during the construction of the new society the Communist regime could begin to seek the "goals for which the original revolutionary struggle had been undertaken." [59] This was certainly the case during the Cultural Revolution, though since 1971 measures taken to diminish the importance of Mao's thought may show that a relationship between ideology and action more on the Soviet pattern may be developing.[60]

[56] *Ibid.,* pp. 53–59.
[57] *Ibid.,* pp. 60, 67.
[58] *Ibid.,* p. 66.
[59] *Ibid.,* p. 72.
[60] *Ibid.,* p. 76.

4. The Social and Historical Background of Chinese Communism

How shall we account for the special aspects of Chinese Marxism —the centrality of the concept of "contradictions," Maoist authoritarianism, the emphasis on moral virtue as the primary goal of the revolution, and the great emphasis on thought reform? As in the case of Russian Communism, we shall observe the paradoxical truth that, engaged in total revolution as the Chinese Communists are, their peculiar way of carrying it out is fashioned by the characteristic features of traditional Chinese political culture. As with the Russians, some aspects of the new way are simply embodiments of old norms; others are a revolutionary response to the specific character of the old.

We have seen in other chapters that many aspects of modern ideology are closely tied in with centrality of industrialization for modern society, and that ideology is shaped in particular ways by the specific kind of industrializing experience in a given area. This is also true in the case of China. We have already anticipated these conclusions in earlier paragraphs.

The Center of the World.   When British merchants first approached the Imperial Chinese authorities toward the end of the eighteenth century to secure a commercial treaty guaranteeing trading rights, they were treated as members of a small barbarian nation approaching the ruler of the "Celestial Kingdom" to beg a humble favor. Gifts brought to Peking by British emissaries were treated as tribute accorded to the natural suzerain of the world. Father Matteo Ricci, an Italian Jesuit who was one of the first Europeans to live for an extensive period at the Chinese Court, has stated this central tenet of traditional Chinese ideology for us as follows:

> Today we usually call this country Ciumquo or Ciumhoa, the first [suffixed] word signifying "kingdom," and the second "garden." When put together the words are translated, "To be at the center." . . . He whose authority extends over this immense kingdom is called Lord of the Universe, because the Chinese are of the opinion that the extent of their vast dominion is to all intents and purposes coterminous with the borders of the universe.[61]

Along with the dream of political supremacy went an equally grandiose conception of Chinese culture. Father Ricci writes that "they . . . dis-

[61] Quoted in Robert S. Elegant, *The Center of the World: Communism and the Mind of China*, rev. ed. (New York: Funk & Wagnalls, 1964), p. 34.

dain to learn anything from the books of outsiders because they believe
that all true science and knowledge belongs to them alone. . . . Even
the written characters by which they express the word 'foreigner' are
those that are applied to beasts, and scarcely ever do they give them a
title more honorable than they would assign to their demons." [62] They
also believed that their superiority was sustained by their moral virtue.
An accompaniment of all this was a requirement that European ambas-
sadors kowtow (prostrate themselves in obeisance) before the Emperor.
So far as commerce was concerned, while the Chinese were prepared
to welcome it, they did so only on restrictive terms which proved economically impracticable.[63]

Europeans were quick to measure the disproportion between these
Chinese pretensions and their actual physical power. It was the West
that had discovered the power of the machine and for the time being
had a monopoly of that power. It was prepared to use this power to
force the Chinese to yield to commercial demands, ultimately on terms
just as unequal as those offered by the Chinese, but with the relationship inverted. An English plenipotentiary of 1858 predicted that the
West could "achieve victories in the contest in which it will have to
engage only by proving that physical knowledge and mechanical skill
applied to the arts of production are more than a match for the most
perservering efforts of unscientific industry." [64]

Exterritoriality and Industrialization.   The upshot of the contest was
the progressive concession of exterritorial rights to western powers as
the sequel of a number of minor wars waged unsuccessfully with these
powers. Political autonomy was to be the guarantee of economic security
for the western traders and industrialists. The British were the first to
win such rights in 1843. Then in 1844 the United States and France
signed treaties granting similar privileges to their nationals, and in the
years immediately following the Belgians, Norwegians, Swedes, and
Russians acquired similar concessions. A treaty of 1860 confirmed what
had been acquired. Robert Elegant has summed them up as follows:

> Fifteen "treaty ports," some of them lying far inland, were open to resi-
> dence by foreigners, whose extraterritorial privileges made the cities in
> effect enclaves on Chinese soil ruled by foreigners. The Chinese paid the
> first of the indemnities that were to become a regular consequence of
> defeats by the West. Control of the Chinese Customs and a number of
> inland waterways passed to foreigners. Britain secured cession of Kow-
> loon, opposite Hong Kong Island on the mainland of China.[65]

[62] *Ibid.*
[63] *Ibid.*, p. 73.
[64] Quoted in *ibid.*, p. 74.
[65] *Ibid.*, p. 77.

During the rest of the century the western powers proceeded to seize various peripheral parts of the Chinese Empire outright.

This was the political context of the beginnings of Chinese industrialization and modernization. It was to breed on the one hand an extreme hatred of the foreigner and all his works, and on the other an extraordinary admiration of the foreigner's machine. It was a determination, in a slowly forming revolutionary elite, to reform in a comprehensive way those things in traditional Chinese culture that stood in the way of building a political and economic structure that would put that machine at the disposal of the Chinese and enable them to drive the foreigner out. Robert North has shown that it was precisely in those parts of China where western influence penetrated first and most extensively that men emerged who were to become the leaders of the Communist revolution.[66]

Yang and Yin and Marxian Dialectics.   We have seen that the passion for conflict and struggle bred by hatred of the foreigner and of things in traditional Chinese culture that have made China vulnerable to foreign imperialism has been conducive to the acceptability in the new Chinese political culture of the Marxian idea of dialectical tension. Does it also find a root in the traditional Chinese concepts of *Yin* and *Yang?* The best scholarship finds only a limited parallel between the two. For the ideas of *Yin* and *Yang,* although they work in opposition to one another, also complete one another. They both survive in the final state of things. Their interaction is not really one of struggle and conflict, but of reconciliation and fulfillment. If these ancient Chinese concepts have an embodiment in contemporary Chinese political culture it is in the Maoist notion of *non*antagonistic social contradictions (see p. 341), a concept that has no Soviet parallel.[67]

Patriarchal Ethics.   A principal target of the Communist Chinese cultural revolution has been the traditional Confucian moral code, which gives preeminence to family loyalties in the hierarchy of human allegiance. The Code of Li prescribes a system of obligation for the traditional Chinese which establishes five relationships: "(1) between ruler and subject; (2) between father and son; (3) between husband and wife; (4) between the older and the younger brother; and (5) between friend and friend." [68] The first relationship is understood to depend on the fifth, the tie of friendship, but this is seen as dependent on the duti-

---

[66] Robert North, *Kuomintang and Chinese Communist Elites* (Stanford: Stanford University Press, 1952), p. 46. See also Amaury de Riencourt, *The Soul of China* (London: Jonathan Cape, 1959), pp. 153–57.

[67] Israel in Johnson, *op. cit.,* p. 13.

[68] F. C. S. Northrup, *The Meeting of East and West* (New York: The Macmillan Company, 1953), p. 326.

fulness of men to their parents. Filial duty is thus prior to and the foundation of all wider social obligation.[69] Traditional Chinese society was therefore preeminently patriarchal, with all the nepotistic practice and parochial outlook entailed by that mode of organization. Family always came first, before polity.[70] It is easy to see that the impersonality of obligation to abstract law and the principle of geographical rather than patriarchal organization that are cornerstones of modern polity are radically incompatible with such a system of personal and familial allegiance. The Chinese tradition resembles the system of feudal morality, based on aristocratic families, that was destroyed in the West by the English and French Revolutions that produced the modern territorial state. The Chinese Nationalists of Chiang Kai-shek made no large effort to cope with this problem. But the Communists have waged all-out war against the Confucian ethic in their continuing cultural revolution, especially as it is waged by the procedures of thought reform.

In the greater importance of ethical over political regulation in traditional Chinese culture we find an important root for the Maoist stress on cultural conflict rather than on class conflict. As Mu Fu Sheng has written, "Since the Government played a much smaller part in the life of the people than the family, the adjustment which the Chinese people had to make in the modern world was not so much a change of the form of government as the increased importance of politics in people's life, not so much a change of law as the abandonment of *li* and the acceptance of public duty, not so much a revolution as the founding of a nation." [71]

A paradoxical counterpoint to all this is the fact that in destroying the authority of the family in order to build a modern state, the Communist Chinese have continued to be influenced by the concepts of family life in their political thinking and practice. In fact, it could be argued that they conceive of Chinese polity as a large closed family, and that the total submission now demanded of the individual to the state parallels the total submission of the traditional Chinese to his family. The total communal commitment required of the new citizen and the horror manifest at "Western industrialism" is one sign of the continuing authority of traditional "tribal" thinking in Chinese political culture. The father role played by Mao is another aspect of this ideological set.

Empiricism and Aesthetics.   Another characteristic aspect of traditional Chinese culture that militates against the building of a modern industrial society is its characteristic way of conceiving reality. F. S. C. Northrup

[69] *Ibid.*, p. 327.
[70] See also Mu Fu-sheng, *op. cit.*, pp. 51, 53, 60, 62, 64, 92.
[71] *Ibid.*, p. 60.

has called this "the immediately experienced aesthetic continuum," which he contrasts with the abstract conceptual modes typical of Western thought. This hyper-empirical aesthetic way of thinking is revealed in the ideographic symbolism of traditional Chinese language, in which each character has "its own independent, purely denotative, immediately experienced referent." [72] Thus the symbol for man 人 looks like a pair of legs, and that for house 介 resembles a primitive hut.[73] But abstract generalizing concepts are necessary tools of science, for without them one can develop no method of expressing the uniformities of nature, which is a precondition of prediction, a capability which doing science presupposes. It is also a precondition of everything that is meant by "rationality" and "rationalization" in the conduct of modern society. Northrup gives us a quaint example of the result of this way of thinking for Chinese behavior:

> The hold which this conception of man and the nature of things as in-determinate and indefinite has upon even such a concrete mind as that of the Chinese, showed itself in even so westernized an Oriental city as Hong Kong, when in 1920 one talked with even the most lowly of coolies. Again and again, when one asked them if they could do such and such a specific thing, the Cantonese word "wock-jeh" was given in reply. The dock might be five minutes away, and the boat which one wanted to catch might be leaving fifteen minutes later. Nevertheless, if one asked the ricksha boy whether he could get one there in time, the reply would be "wock-jeh" . . . "Perhaps." What he was saying was that the nature, not merely of human affairs but of all things, is in part indeterminate, and that consequently a wise man, an informed man, will never absolutely commit himself.[74]

Perhaps in the Communist desire to overcome this traditional way of understanding the world and to instill western habits of conceptual rationality we have an explanation of the extraordinary emphasis on analytical thinking manifest in the behavior of the refugees to which we referred above.

The extraordinary effort at ideological transformation represented by Chinese practices of "thought reform" have been encouraged by a traditional Chinese belief in the educability of man. With this has been combined "an extreme emphasis on the force of human will over nature and technology." In traditional writings of the nineteenth and the twentieth centuries we find "the belief that all reforms begin with the right state of mind." [75] The pattern of the life of Mao Tse-tung and his symbolic swim upstream in the Yangtze river at the inception of the Great

[72] Northrup, op. cit., p. 318.
[73] Ibid., p. 316.
[74] Ibid., p. 344.
[75] Israel in Johnson, op. cit., pp. 7, 9.

Proletarian Cultural Revolution are significant testimony to the continued currency of these traditional ideas and to the degree to which they have served as an inspiration to an all-out revolution against other elements of the cultural tradition.

Traditional Authoritarianism.   It is obvious that the discipline of authoritarian government is a more efficient instrument of cultural revolution and thought reform than Liberal Democracy, which in its developed form seems to presuppose settled political and cultural values, or at the most very gradual change. The logic of the problem therefore makes for authoritarianism and for the centralization of authority in the Chinese Communist system. Authoritarianism, however, also has a root in the traditional culture, something which has made it relatively easy for the Communists, and especially Mao, to legitimate their sway. C. P. Fitzgerald has pointed out that the traditional Chinese proverb that "Those who do not occupy the seats of authority should not concern themselves with the government" embodies a characteristic authoritarian view, the theory upon which the Confucian Empire was governed.

> The chün-tzu, the "aristocratic man," or as some translators have put it, the "superior man," reserved to himself the functions of administration and the full exercise of political power. As servant of his prince, who in turn ruled by virtue of the Mandate of Heaven, the superior man was educated and trained to govern.[76]

The tradition was frankly autocratic, and the new regime can therefore simply exploit a pattern already established. "You are autocratic [say the critics]. My dear gentlemen, you speak truth; we are indeed," says Mao Tse-tung.[77] In addition to these things, the natural necessities of the geographical situation also made for authoritarian patterns in traditional China, as Walt Rostow has pointed out. The recurrent tasks of flood control and irrigation required massive mobilization of manpower resources. "As a consequence, Chinese society developed within an implacable control mechanism founded upon the proposition that the individual had to be forced to do what was necessary for his society and thus for himself."[78] Once in being, this mechanism could be used by the despotic central government for purposes other than the fundamental necessities we have mentioned. Oddly enough, autocratic centralism in special areas of public jurisdiction went hand in hand with the patriarchal decentralization we have earlier described. Perhaps it was the very focus of

---

[76] C. P. Fitzgerald, *The Birth of Communist China* (New York: Frederick A. Praeger, 1964), p. 142.

[77] *Ibid.*

[78] Walt Rostow *et al.*, *The Prospects for Communist China* (New York: John Wiley & Sons, Inc., 1954), p. 104.

participatory responsibility at the family and local level that militated against efforts to establish popular controls over the central Imperial authority.

Added to the predisposition to authoritarianism inherited from the traditional political culture is the fact that the peace and order of Chinese life had been disrupted by forty years of civil and international struggle, a Hobbesian "war of all against all," which would eventuate in a longing for order at virtually any price.[79]

Another aspect of the tradition which continues to play a large role in Communist political culture is the authority of the scholar and of scholarly doctrine. It is significant that a large number of the top elite, especially the older people, were scholars in traditional China. Mao himself was a schoolteacher. As the mandarins and scholars in traditional China presided over the exegesis and inculcation throughout society of the extremely detailed Confucian ethic, so the new Communist mandarins preside over the exegesis of the doctrines of Marx and Engels and over the indoctrination of the entire population, from cadres to peasants in the field. For the average man the doctrine has been distilled as a collection of maxims, the "Little Red Book" of Mao Tse-tung, which is very similar in style and even in content to the sayings of Confucius. Like the sayings of Confucius in times past, one can hear the maxims of the "Little Red Book" chanted today by Chinese schoolboys in rote chorus.

Despite all these considerations, it is a paradox that the Chinese Communist revolution should develop authoritarianism as a characteristic and apparently irreducible feature. For as we have seen, an ultimate objective of Mao Tse-tung has been to eradicate the dependency psychology on which the old authoritarianism was grounded. The paradox is made intelligible by an understanding of the full psychological syndrome associated with the old authority pattern.

In inculcating filial piety Confucianism also taught a concept of authority that moved from the absolute authority of the father down— never from the family community up. With this was nurtured an anxiety in the face of authority that entailed the stifling of emotions to avoid rebellious conflict and the retribution that followed. Associated with patriarchal hierarchy was an idealization of tranquillity that embraced peer relationships as well as those of father and son. Aggressive emotions could not legitimately be expressed in any direction. And the child was taught that to achieve the exquisite control of his emotions required for this degree of social harmony he had to be absolutely dependent on authority. The education of the Chinese child produced in adulthood a

---

[79] Mu Fu-sheng, *op cit.*, p. 130.

recognition of the value of strict authority patterns and of the need of an external power to discipline dangerous emotions. With the withdrawal of authority was paired a terrifying picture of social chaos and anarchic disorder—*luan*.[80] Thus the only solution to any conflict was considered to involve the building up of authority. The result of all this was a psychological polarization of harmony and conflict, of the individual and of the group.[81] Harmony was either entire or absent; the notion of limited conflict had no status. And, just as in traditional Russian culture, the individual could not be trusted to be self-disciplined in his relations with the group. He was at any moment capable of perfect subordination to the good of the family's peace or of perfect treason against it. An ambivalence to authority resulted—a felt need for a strong external authority, paired with a feeling of anxiety at its near approach. This complicated patriarchal pattern was sanctioned in the conduct of the classroom and also by the authoritative classic texts. The growing child learned to develop an interpretation of political leadership on the basis of an analogy with these family patterns. He also learned willingly to accept the intrusion "of public power into all areas of social activity." [82]

In his own life experience Mao Tse-tung, like Maxim Gorky in the Soviet film, has rejected the entire complex of traditional dependency attitudes we have described. But he has been willing and able to reject only *some* of them for his people. Important elements of the dependency syndrome remain intact and perhaps have even increased power today.

In the first phase of the revolution it was Mao's purpose to encourage a spirit of struggle and aggressiveness to offset the traditional norms of harmony and acquiescence in order to get the revolutionary regime in power. Politics became an "emotional storm," and it was necessary to make people politically conscious by "mobilizing *feelings* which the old society said it was impermissible to express." Anxiety in the face of authority had to be overcome by transforming it into social anger directed, by the slogans of the ideology, against all the institutions of the old regime.[83] Later, to maintain political consciousness and independence of authority, it was necessary to stimulate new criticism and

---

[80] Solomon, *Mao's Revolution*, pp. 50–77.

[81] *Ibid.*, pp. 80, 81.

[82] *Ibid.*, pp. 78, 91, 138. Richard Solomon has described the pattern of traditional attitudes at length in his book, *Mao's Revolution and the Chinese Political Culture*, drawing on extensive interviews with three generations of adult Chinese which were designed to explore the phenomenon of Chinese political socialization. Open-ended questions, an attitude survey, and two psychological "projective" tests were employed in the research, which parallels the work on American political culture we described in Chapter 3 and on Soviet political culture presented in Chapter 8 (e.g. the work of Bauer and Inkeles). The subjects used were ninety-one emigrés from the mainland in Taiwan and Hong Kong.

[83] *Ibid.*, pp. 169, 194–95.

anger, this time directed against the intellectuals and bureaucrats of the revolution itself, in the Great Leap and in the Cultural Revolution. It was Mao's ultimate intention to "substitute controlled political conflict between the Party's operative cadres and those they lead, as well as between different social and economic groups, for the traditional ideal of 'the great unity' in which social conflict was denied legitimate expression." [84] The pattern described in these words by Richard Solomon looks remarkably like the clash of interest group politics that is characteristic of and authoritative for established Liberal democratic political culture today, the pattern of limited cleavage within overarching consensus.

Mao's ultimate intention, however, runs headlong into a recalcitrant fact of the Chinese mind. The traditions of the society have simply not prepared the masses of the people to play a responsible critical role in the participatory politics of a modern state.[85] Mao has to cope wtih the problem of disorder that such an invitation to limited conflict implies. But his way of doing this vitiates his prescription for equal freedom. He has scrupulously avoided the cultivation of a spirit of individual *self*-reliance, on the model of the Protestant Reformation and the ensuing Liberal revolution. This, he believes, could only be an invitation to anarchy. He has sought rather to substitute for reliance on hierarchical authority the absolute dependence of the individual on the group—a collectivist, not an individualist spirit. No collectivity ever speaks its "general will" through the mystical whole, however, only through some group or individual. Mao has tried to insure that he alone will be this spokesman of the "general will." But this has produced for China the problem of Rousseau's ideal democratic order. In diluting the authority of the head of the traditional family, has Mao fostered the end of political submissiveness or merely substituted a political totalitarianism for it?

Revolution and Virtue: Continuity and Change.   Lastly, the periodically renewed cultural revolution gives testimony to the continued authority of the idea of virtue as sovereign over all else in life, including the machine, which promises both freedom and power. Benjamin Schwartz has very lucidly summed up the role of this continuing aspect of traditional culture:

> When one examines the idiom of the Cultural Revolution one somehow feels that the untroubled image of Mao as the fountainhead of all morality, standing high above all laws and institutions, may owe more to certain Chinese cultural perspectives than to any Western source of inspiration. One feels this also in the tremendous emphasis on the power

[84] *Ibid.*, p. 516.
[85] *Ibid.*, p. 517.

of example attributed to such paragons as Lei Feng and Men Ho, who may, to be sure, be men of the people but who are nevertheless capable of heroic acts of ethical self-transcendence. Again, they are capable of these acts only because they draw inspiration from the sage-ruler himself.[86]

Thus as China moves under the auspices of a Communist elite into the world of the modern industrial state, and as she creates a modern political culture as its ideological counterpart and foundation, she carries along important elements of the old way into the structure of the new. Ideological change is an organic growth.

The supremacy of virtue in the modern context, however, has produced a new reality. The ideal of virtue traditionally acted as a limitation on royal authority. "The very insistence by Confucianists . . . that imperial virtue had something to do with what happened in history, and could be impugned by it, kept the emperor inside the arena of power (while it gave the arena walls)." [87] Today, however, when the thought of Mao Tse-tung is itself the criterion of virtue, the result is not a limitation of "Imperial" authority but its totalitarian absolutization.

Conclusion.   The Chinese experience has revealed, in a much more graphic way than the Russian, an implicit tension between the scientific-analytic elements in Marxism (the intractability of objective conditions, both material and psychological) and the revolutionary-activist element (the creative capacity of forceful will pitted against objective reality). The first produces caution and a spirit of compromise in policy making. The second eventuates in utopian activism. Communists themselves identify the first emphasis, when it appears in exaggerated form, with "right deviationism," a tendency to allow old, "bourgeois" habits and institutions to reassert themselves. The opposite emphasis is called "left deviationism" when carried to an extreme. Lenin attempted to steer a course midway between the two tendencies, as did his successor Stalin.[88] While their successors from Khrushchev to Brezhnev appear to lean more to the "right" side of the spectrum, it is noteworthy that Khrushchev promised that the culmination of the utopian order was just around the corner. Until this day the regime continues to place great stress on ideological orthodoxy and fervor.

The Chinese pattern seems to represent an oscillation between the two extremes rather than a midcourse between them. The Great Leap and the Cultural Revolution both embodied extraordinary efforts of

---

[86] Schwartz in Lewis, *op. cit.*, p. 167.

[87] Joseph R. Levenson, *Confucian China and Its Modern Fate*, 3 vols. (Berkeley: University of California Press, 1968), II, 71.

[88] See Leopold Haimson, *The Russian Marxists and the Origins of Bolshevism* (Cambridge, Mass.: Harvard University Press, 1955).

utopian activism, the celebration of the supremacy of will over the given-ness of things. But they were great failures because they ignored the "complexity and intractability of the real world." [89]

With the disappearance of Lin Piao, China seems to be in for a period of hard-nosed pragmatism. At home the Cultural Revolution has ceased. Abroad there have been decisive moves toward a detente with the West. The growing military threat to China posed by the USSR was probably a chief catalyst in precipitating movement toward the right on both fronts. Experts are needed to shore up the national defenses. And abroad it proved impossible in the face of great diversity to make convincing the idea that Peking had become the sole center of Marxist truth. Since 1969 the regime is better described as one based on a "nationalist" model than on a "revolutionary" one.[90]

It is an interesting irony that the effort to propagate the thought of Mao Tse-tung as the oracle of orthodoxy abroad—in order to foment foreign revolutions—should have had its greatest success not in the Third World, to which it was chiefly directed, but in the technically advanced capitalist countries of the western world.[91] This reveals the similarity between the ideals of freedom and equality in western Liberal culture and those of the Communist final phase. It also points to an implicit tension in Liberal culture between norms of technical efficiency and humanistic norms, which is like the tension in Marxist culture. The present detente seems to represent at least the momentary triumph of technical values in both cultures. This hopefully brings with it, however, the truly humanistic objective of world peace.

Bibliography

CHEN, THEODORE H. E., *Thought Reform of the Chinese Intellectuals.* Hong Kong: Hong Kong University Press, 1960.

COHEN, ARTHUR A., *The Communism of Mao Tse-tung.* Chicago: University of Chicago Press, 1964.

ELEGANT, ROBERT S., *The Center of the World: Communism and the Mind of China.* Garden City. N.Y.: Doubleday & Company, Inc., 1964.

JOHNSON, CHALMERS, ed., *Ideology and Politics in Contemporary China.* Seattle: University of Washington Press, 1973.

LEVENSON, JOSEPH, *Confucian China and its Modern Fate.* 3 vols. Berkeley: University of California Press, 1968.

LEWIS, JOHN W., *Leadership in Communist China.* Ithaca, N.Y.: Cornell University Press, 1963.

[89] Philip L. Bridgham, "The International Impact of Maoist Ideology," in Johnson, *op. cit.,* p. 350.

[90] *Ibid.,* pp. 341, 344.

[91] *Ibid.,* p. 339.

—————————, ed., *Major Doctrines of Communist China*. New York: W. W. Norton & Company, Inc., 1964.

—————————, ed., *Party Leadership and Revolutionary Power in China*. New York: Cambridge University Press, 1970.

LIFTON, ROBERT JAY, *Revolutionary Immortality: Mai Tse-tung and the Chinese Cultural Revolution*. New York: Random House, 1968.

—————————, *Thought Reform and the Psychology of Totalism: A Study of "Brainwashing" in China*. New York: W. W. Norton & Company, Inc., 1961.

NORTHRUP, F. S. C., *The Meeting of East and West: An Inquiry Concerning World Understanding*. New York: The Macmillan Company, 1953.

SCHRAM, STUART R., ed., *The Political Thought of Mao Tse-tung*. New York: Frederick A. Praeger, 1963.

SCHURMANN, HERBERT FRANZ, *Ideology and Organization in Communist China*. Berkeley: University of California Press, 1966.

SOLOMON, RICHARD H., *Mao's Revolution and the Chinese Political Culture*. Berkeley: University of California Press, 1971.

10

Conclusion

We have described the beliefs, values, and emotional attitudes—the ideologies—that produce, support, and are produced by the structures and processes of political modernity. In doing this we have avoided discussing any ideology in vacuo, as a self-consistent and autonomous thought structure with an integrity and life of its own. At every point we have dealt with political ideas as they actually operate in political life. For this reason we have not organized our chapters according to the catalog of the "isms," but rather according to country and political system. For a most important feature of ideology is its radical dependence on the special aspects of the experience of a particular polity, both for its form and for the role it plays. To demonstrate this we have shown the shaping influence of unique historical experience and of characteristic social, psychological, and cultural patterns on the generation, reception, and use made of ideas. In doing so we have not denied causal importance to ideology but have tried to distinguish those respects in which it has been a result from those respects in which it has been a forming, maintaining, or transforming factor in a political system. To be as comprehensive as possible we have employed the findings of a variety of social science disciplines in the presentation of relevant data, especially history, sociology, and psychology, along with both traditional and behavioral political science.

Our empirical scrutiny of political culture required in many cases a rather sharp distinction between leader and follower ideology—the political culture of elites and the political culture of masses—for ideas play different roles in the behavior of each. Leaders need ideas which not only explain the world but which also allow them to win and hold political power. Followers need to have the world of political action, in which their role is more passive, both explained and made legitimate. This has led to discriminations that usually are lost in analyses of ideologies as abstract systems of philosophy.

1. The Common Currency of Modernity

Abundance as Goal Value.   Our survey has revealed a broad area of common elements among the major forms of modern political culture. One is a paramount concern with material abundance as a leading goal value of the political system. Liberal culture was the first to articulate this value clearly and to develop institutions designed to produce its systematic realization. Communist regimes, born much later, after Liberalism had shown the possibility of overcoming scarcity, have revealed an even greater utopianism in their expectations, and a passion for accelerating the pace to economic superabundance. The need for acceleration has been acutely experienced by Communist regimes because they typically have rooted in areas much poorer than those where Liberalism was born and flourishes, and therefore have a greater distance to cover. Fascists also have made material abundance a priority goal, although their methods have differed from those of Liberals and Communists. While Liberals and Communists have concentrated on economic development and the rationalization of production at home (though they are not averse to waging war in special cases), Fascist and quasi-Fascist regimes have relied on war and conquest to acquire "living room." American Conservatism, the variety of Conservatism on which we have focused in this book, as a revival of Classical Liberalism, also keeps a watchful eye on the national growth rate. Although its more extreme wing is readier than Established Liberalism to rattle the saber, war has no more ultimate legitimacy for Conservatives than for Liberals or Communists, and the threat to use it is made in the name of defending values already acquired. Fascism legitimates a frankly aggressive war. (European Conservatism— for example in Spain—is not really a part of modernity, and instead of striving for generalized abundance contents itself with securing the property of the traditional elite and the traditional cultural values which surround that property.) Development ideology by its very name indicates its concern for economic growth. It can safely be said that every contemporary conflict, both domestic and international, so far as it is not a function of nationalism (the question of identity), is in some way tied in with our modern preoccupation with abundance.

Beliefs. We have emphasized throughout this book the importance of a work ethic as a central "belief" in political cultures that seek abundance through industrialization and the rationalization of production. An aspect of Liberal culture before Liberalism, its inculcation has been a self-conscious goal both in Communist and Third World polities in which new elites are seeking to revolutionize cultures which are still almost fully traditional. American Conservatism, again because of its affinity to an early version of Liberalism, also enshrines the value of work. It is not central either to Fascism or to European Conservatism, however, nor are the rational modes of thought and behavior which are aspects of the work ethic in Liberal and Communist culture. Hitler and Göring, as authoritative Nazis, were actually lazy and displayed decidedly nonrational, highly intuitive work patterns. Hitler hated and despised the rationality of bureaucratic order, and throughout his regime carried on a running battle with the bureaucrats of his own system.

The story is more complicated than this, however, for we have seen that at a certain stage of development both Liberal and Communist regimes engender a Left critique of hard work and scientific rationality. The hard and systematic efforts required to produce abundance run head on into other goal values of both Liberal and Communist regimes—the values of individual freedom and self-determination, and the value of human equality as well, for rational industrial order requires command hierarchy and highly structured individual role playing. Rationalized work also seems to militate against fraternity, or community, another common value of both Liberal and Communist cultures. What the final resolution of this logical conflict will be is hardly clear at this writing.

The metaphysics of modernity are the same wherever a modern political culture is found. Traditional gods and the mysteries associated with them, at least so far as elites are concerned, have no authority and give no legitimacy to political, social, or economic order. Liberalism is notably rationalist in its world view. In those places, like France and Italy, where it operated in the first instance as a revolutionary utopianism, it has been frankly agnostic and anticlerical. In those places, such as England and the United States, where its development has been evolutionary rather than revolutionary, it has fit best with those forms of religion (varieties of Protestantism) which are more concerned with the here than with the hereafter, and which exhort their adherents to "work for the night is coming" and to display holiness through hard work and middle-class respectability. Communism in all its forms is antireligious, and Fascist leaders at least privately have mocked traditional religion.

Mystery, awe, and charisma in these systems have notably been transferred from gods and priests to party leaders and to the mystical "class" or "people." Thus ideology has functioned in the place of holy writ to define the nature of the real, of the holy, and of human obligation.

Cultures controlled by the nation-building ethos appear to present a contrast with these ideological systems, for in many of them traditional religion—here Islam, there Buddhism, there Hinduism—is still cultivated by the ruling elites and its blessings invoked by them on its work. Appearances here are deceptive, however, for in most of these cases the elites are skeptics and simply make self-conscious use of the divine mysteries to give legitimacy to their regime. Where the norms of traditional religion run counter to their modernizing goals, they reject them and attempt systematically to expunge them from precept and practice. Conservatives in these regimes give a more independent value to the old religion and its prescriptions. Among Conservatives in some cultures, however, as in the United States, religion and nationalism tend to fuse, with the former figuring largely as an emotional aura and legitimating device for the latter (e.g., the struggle against "godless Communism" as a foreign conspiracy). The terrestrial and naturalistic character of the metaphysics of modernity are both attested by the fact that the subject of this book is not religion but secular ideology as the typical belief system of the modern state.

A leading belief that is shared throughout modern political culture, one which distinguishes it sharply from traditional culture, is the centrality of change. Modern political culture is dynamic. The world is not conceived as a static order, to be modeled once and for all on an eternal pattern of goodness. It is in process of development, and its ultimate goals are carried within it. They do not exist in heaven, but in the flux itself. Here is one ground of the "this-worldly" orientation of modern ideologies. The "good" is something to be sought in the process of living life, not by contemplative withdrawal from life; hence it is also a basis of the populist, participatory themes of modern political culture.

National Consciousness and Nationalism.   Another common element of ideological modernity is the concept of "nation," both as belief and as goal value. Its authority probably derives from a variety of nonrational needs in the context of skepticism about transcendence and the decay of public religion. Men seem to need to belong to a group to be happy and to honor an authority beyond that of their own minds and wills—at least most men do. (Again, here we have a difference between elites and followers.) In other words, they need group membership to establish their identity. Men seem to experience this need more acutely in times of rapid change than at others. Where Liberalism has evolved most naturally and gradually, the "nation" has played the smallest role and the autonomous individual has come most fully into his own. Where Liberal movements have had to revolutionize the old order, however, the national appeal has been prominent, highy emotional, and often strident, as in eighteenth-century France or nineteenth-century Italy. Where Liberal regimes have gotten into trouble and failed to realize their goals, especially the economic ones, the nation has served as a psychological support and has often acquired a primacy of value. We can see this in the emotional nationalism of American Conservatives, and in a much more extreme form in the aggressive nationalism of Germans and Italians, when Nazism and Fascism succeeded to the failed Liberalism of the interwar period.

In the Communist world, ironically, nationalism has stolen the thunder of "class" as the leading concept of community. Perhaps this is because classlessness has never become a tangible reality in Communist regimes, running counter as it does to the demands of rational industrialization, and also, perhaps, to the basic inclinations and differential capacities of human nature. Perhaps it is because it is easier to identify with people who look like you do and talk like you do than with a purely abstract notion with no clear empirical reference. In any case, it is certainly true that in both the Soviet Union and in China, ethnic and linguistic nationalisms have been vital psychological cements, especially in time of rapid change and of international conflict.

Conceptions of Authority. We have shown that in addition to being a principle of identity and of community, the nation is also a fount of authority in a man-centered world. "All authority proceeds from the nation," declared the revolutionary Declaration of the Rights of Man and of the Citizen, and its words have been echoed in every kind of modern ideological system from then until now. As conception of authority, the idea of the nation is at its vaguest and can be used to clothe any number of kinds of very different institutions of political administration, from an American Congress to a republican dictator like a DeGaulle, to a totalitarian "Führer" to a charismatic prophet like Mao Tse-tung, or a collective leadership like the Soviet Presidium (though the symbols in these two cases are veiled in international language) to the charismatic leadership (new-style) of the Islamic holy man calling for "Jehad." The term is infinitely malleable and always authoritative.

Allied with the idea of the nation as a leading modern conception of authority is the concept of the "people," meaning, in some sense, all the individuals in the polity as a collectivity. Whether the regime is Liberal, Communist, Fascist, or Third World, a modern government always must identify itself with the "people" and elicit as broad and active a support as possible from the serried or jumbled ranks of its silent or turbulent majorities. Elections, plebiscites, mass meetings of all kinds are crucial in all modern polities, since God and aristocratic virtue have lost their appeal as political authority. Again, as with nation, we have here a flexible concept which elites manipulate in a variety of ways to legitimate their acts. But they are always constrained to manipulate it, which means that the scope of modern politics, in terms of the number of individuals and groups who must be taken into account in elite planning, has become infinitely more vast than ever before in history. As a result, the problem of the construction and maintenance of a system of ordered power has become infinitely more complex than ever before. This alone, aside from the complexities of government deriving from the complexity of the modern economy, can account for the widespread instability and extensive conflict of modern politics.

2. The Salient Differences

The basic differences among modern political cultures are most succinctly stated in terms of the dichotomy of Established Liberalism and Revolutionary Collectivism. (Predominantly conservative—i.e., traditional—cultures are also numerous in the world, but we have not discussed them in this book.) I use the expression "Established Liberalism" rather than "Liberalism" because the beginnings of Liberal political culture in some countries are manifestly revolutionary and even Collectivist in character, paradoxical as that may seem. The Jacobin phase of the French Revolutionary, for example, which carried many essential ideas of Liberal Democratic modernity, was manifestly so in the methods employed to establish the system of modernity in France. And we have seen in the beginnings of the revolution of modernity in England, among the Puritan dissenters, clear marks of a totalitarian mentality. The American "New Left," which invokes imperfectly realized values of the Liberal revolution, also displays Collectivist features in some of its exponents. We must not forget that the label "Liberal" came into use only after the Liberal revolution had settled down, in the mid-nineteenth century.

Revolutionary Transformation.   This suggests that the basic differences in modern political culture may be understood as differences between the norms of a revolutionary regime attempting to transform social reality according to a grand design of perfection and one which accepts present reality as basically sound. Collectivism manifests itself, therefore, primarily in transformist procedural norms—especially the idea of thought reform to the end of propagating new ideas—a new set of values, beliefs, and attitudes to replace the old. The procedures range from rather old-fashioned methods of propaganda using the mass media employed by Dr. Goebbels to self-criticism in small groups among the Chinese Communists. The ultimate aim is the transformation of character, the creation of the Nazi "Superman" or the "New Soviet Man." (The secularization of conceptions of spiritual perfection and salvation seems to be what is involved here.) Collectivism also manifests itself in mobilization norms, for the entire population must be self-consciously organized for the purposes of indoctrination and for the realization of the industrial and military goals of the regime. This results in the proliferation of official organizations embracing all areas of living—labor unions, sports clubs, singing clubs, mothers' clubs, and a host of other cultural associations.

Revolutionary Collectivism also manifests itself in norms which demand obedience from the individual to the group leadership, in the name of the class or in the name of the people. Individual right—the central value of the Established Liberal order—is meaningless, though (as in Communism) the future utopia may be described as one of free-wheeling individualism. Along with this goes the suspension of traditional norms of ethical behavior against things like lying, murder, and violence of all kinds, a suspension justified by the notion that any means may be used against omnipresent and perfidious enemies if the group is to reach the promised land of the utopia. Due process becomes a meaningless idea and terror and arbitrary behavior are legitimated by revolutionary necessity.

Conflict and Harmony. Although all modern cultures understand the world as dynamic process rather than as static order, Established Liberal and Revolutionary Collectivist cultures differ in the way they conceive the process. For the Established Liberal it is peaceful and harmonious. Change itself is ordered. All basic conflicts have been settled in the Liberal cooperative commonwealth. For the Revolutionary Collectivist, on both the left and right, the process is rather one of fundamental conflict and struggle. And the metaphors of revolutionary ideologies are those of the battlefield. Conflictual concepts are also found in marginal subcultures within the Liberal order—among the New Left and the Far Right—whose members are angry men, unhappy with the status quo. Natural counterparts of the conflictual mentality are the interpretation of opposition as conspiracy and the elevation of the concept of conspiracy to the position of a mystical principle of evil. Again, the conspiracy syndrome is found on both right and left, wherever men are angry and anxious about the future. Only the happy Liberal can read opposition as a form of cooperation, à la J. S. Mill.

Absolute Truth as Myth and as Plan.   The ultimate legitimation of Collectivist measures seems to be the idea that the revolutionaries are in on a supreme truth. J. L. Talmon writes that the totalitarian approach is

> based upon the assumption of a sole and exclusive truth in politics. It may be called political Messianism in the sense that it postulates a pre-ordained, harmonious and perfect scheme of things, to which men are irresistibly driven, and at which they are bound to arrive. It recognizes ultimately only one plane of existence, the political. It widens the scope of politics to embrace the whole of human existence. . . . Its political ideas are not a set of pragmatic precepts. . . . They are an integral part of an all-embracing and coherent philosophy.[1]

This formula fits the Communist idea of historical truth, the truth of the classless society of superabundance, absolute individual freedom, and absolute sociality (harmonious, equalitarian community). It also fits the Nazi conception of truth as the raw truth of naked nature, truth as power (eternal elitist struggle). Established Liberal culture, in striking contrast, invokes no gnostic secret to justify its behavior. It hardly feels compelled to justification of any kind, for, as Boorstin has pointed out of Liberal America, we like to act as though we are already inhabiting the Promised Land: we are living the "Truth" and therefore do not have to talk about it. It is true that the manifestoes both from the dissident Left and Right within Established Liberal culture often, in their self-righteousness, imply that their authors are agents of a higher truth than the mundane hedonism of the Establishment. This is certainly the case of writers like Marcuse, on the Left. And on the extreme Right, the higher truth is not a new one but an old one, expressed in terms of the conception of a "Christian nation" fighting the devils of atheistic Communism. This is a paradoxical fact, since transcendence, as a public truth, is rejected all around.

Pragmatism: Liberal and Totalitarian.   This leads us to consider problematic points of contrast suggested by Talmon between Liberal and Collectivist culture in terms of pragmatism versus absolutism. He writes that the Liberal approach, in contrast to totalitarian absolutism, "assumes politics to be a matter of trial and error, and regards political systems as pragmatic contrivances of human ingenuity and spontaneity." [2] The data we have presented in this study indicate clearly that the elites of totalitarian regimes all engage in a *kind* of pragmatism and are prepared to amend the doctrine or general *Weltanschauung* to fit the needs of the moment. Both in the chapter on Nazism and in the one on

---

[1] J. L. Talmon, *The Origins of Totalitarian Democracy* (New York: W. W. Norton Co., Inc., 1970), p. 2.
[2] *Ibid.*, p. 1.

Russian Communism we have demonstrated that the political leadership in each case has always been guided by considerations of the security of its own power position above all else. But then, are not politicians in Liberal regimes also primarily motivated by their personal desire to get and stay in power? If we are to believe the game theorists, this is certainly the case.

What all this boils down to seems to be the following proposition: Elites the world around, as elites, are interested in the establishment and maintenance of their power and status and are ready to employ ideological concepts as instruments for this purpose. They are also ready to redefine and extend the ideology to suit their purposes. We are saying that the "interest" theory of ideology that we discussed in Chapter 1 best explains their behavior. The differences between Collectivist and Liberal culture, then, could be stated in terms of greater and lesser leeway for elites to engage in ideological manipulation. In Established Liberal cultures, values, especially those of individual freedom, are fixed as tradition and habit and thus set parameters within which elites must move. Elite pragmatism must operate within limits laid down by ideological and constitutional norms which are strong, and which, as Liberal norms, set constraints on the use of power—both as to its ends and the means to be employed. The elites themselves internalize these norms and are their most faithful guardians—as in the United States (McClosky). Collectivist regimes govern societies where traditional values and norms have lost authority and where new habits of thought have not taken form. There are, therefore, no parameters laid down to limit what elites may do (except for residual traditional habits, which are not Liberal). Both ends and means are wide open to the defining imagination and skill of the elites who run the system.

We must leave open the question as to whether Collectivist regimes —when they settle down, when new habits of thought about value and politics become fixed and stable in the population, and when society takes on a stable organizational form—will as a result approach the patterns of Established Liberalism. That the goal values of Communism are little different from those of historical Liberalism, and that Communism can be described as a Liberal heresy may be an indication that this will be the result. On the economic side, increasing government intervention in the economy in leading laissez-faire states like the United States, and the existence today of numerous regimes in which Socialism, both Marxist and other, has been successfully wedded to Liberal political values again make such a development within the Communist world seem a plausible future.

Historical Parameters.   On the other hand, we have seen that the great historical differences between the experience of the Western world and of the Russian and Chinese East may well prevent such a result. Liberal democracy in the West enshrines pluralism, constitutional power, and privacy. But not all these values are new in Liberal doctrine or practice. Constitutionalism, as we have shown, has important medieval roots, and may be the foundation stone of pluralism. The Protestant Reformation, signaling the success of heresy within the old order of transcendent truth, is surely a further cause of pluralism, a reality which began to take shape when the ridiculousness of competing public absolute truths became evident. And this was a special Western experience. Both in China and in Russia the modernizing elites came from societies in which the idea of a single absolute public truth had never been successfully challenged, despite disillusionment with transcendence; and we have seen that they have undertaken their work of modernization in the name of another absolutism, although in fact it cannot be shown that they have any kind of blueprint of perfection. In addition, they have built modernity up from a largely agricultural starting point, with all that implies for the mentality of the new modern men they are creating. To a large extent the "middle classes" of these regimes have been developed by the Collectivist regime itself, and shaped by that regime, whereas in the West it was a strong and independent-minded middle class which predated the Liberal revolution that carried out the transformations of modernity. Although there may be some growing together, it is doubtful that there will ever be a perfect identity.

Nevertheless, there is substantial similarity among all forms of modern politics and thought, as the first part of this chapter indicates. It is also displayed in the fact that a Raymond Aron could describe in detail a universal modern phenomenon called "The Industrial Society" whose unity in norms and behavior to a high degree transcends ideological differences between West and East.[3]

3. Crisis

The universalization of the industrial state, with its accompanying universalization of leading values and norms, does not, however, imply the "end of ideology" as forensic conceptual polemics in our time on a world scale. We have seen that both in the United States and in the Soviet Union the mature industrial state has produced ideological ferment of a significant kind. If the "interest theory" explains the ideological behavior of elites, both the social strain and cultural strain theories give a good account of followership behavior, and of the generation of

[3] Raymond Aron, *The Industrial Society: Three Essays on Ideology and Development* (New York: Simon and Schuster, 1967).

counter-elites. The modern, rationalized, and bureaucratic state has given rise to a number of severe strains at both levels—strains flowing from the constraints of disciplined role playing and strains arising out of a loss of meaning in an increasingly technical society. Ideological behavior not only gives catharsis and release from the strains of psychologically strenuous roles but also indicates an effort at a new mapping, the search for a new template to help modern man understand a world devoid of meaning. This was centrally involved in the beginning of the revolution of modernity in the face of medieval collapse. What is interesting is that the behavior of ideological protest against modernity that has occurred so far has not gone beyond ideas which have been present all along in the ideologies of modernity. We have seen that protest from the Left both within the United States and the Soviet Union is not made in the name of a new ideology, but in the name of forgotten or betrayed values of liberty and equality which have been within the culture for a very long while. On the Right the protest within the United States demands a return to an earlier reality, but one which was itself a product of the revolution of modernity. It is possible that the strains of rational bureaucratic life will give rise to new totalitarian reform presided over by some new elite in the name of a "genuine" utopia of peace, freedom, and equality. Anarchic disruption is another possibility. And it is likely that we shall also see new fascisms as well, offering another kind of substitute for rational, bureaucratic economic efficiency in the form of totalitarian efforts to create another kind of utopia, the world of free and equal supermen standing on the backs of a slave majority.

We also may find that the discovery of basic contradictions in the enterprise of building modernity according to any one of the formulas we have discussed in this book will lead to an entirely new ideological effort. If we have learned something by living through the contradictions of our present ideologies, perhaps the seeds of a new effort will deserve to be called philosophy.

Bibliography

BARBU, ZEVEDEI, *Democracy and Dictatorship.* London: Routledge & Kegan Paul, 1956.

BELL, DANIEL, and HENRY D. AIKEN, "Ideology: a Debate," *Commentary*, 37, October 1964: 69–76.

HARRIS, NIGEL, *Beliefs in Society: The Problem of Ideology.* London: C. A. Watts & Company, 1968.

JOHNSON, CHALMERS, *Revolutionary Change.* Boston: Little, Brown, 1966.

LERNER, DANIEL, *The Passing of Traditional Society: Modernizing the Middle East.* New York: The Free Press, 1958.

MACRAE, DUNCAN G., *Ideology and Society.* London: William Heineman, 1961.

MOORE, BARRINGTON, JR., *Social Origins of Dictatorship and Democracy: Lord and Peasant in the Making of the Modern World.* Boston: Beacon Press, 1966.

REJAI, MOSTAFA, ed., *Decline of Ideology?* Chicago: Aldine-Atherton, 1971.

TALMON, J. L., *The Origins of Totalitarian Democracy.* New York: Frederick A. Praeger, 1960.

Index